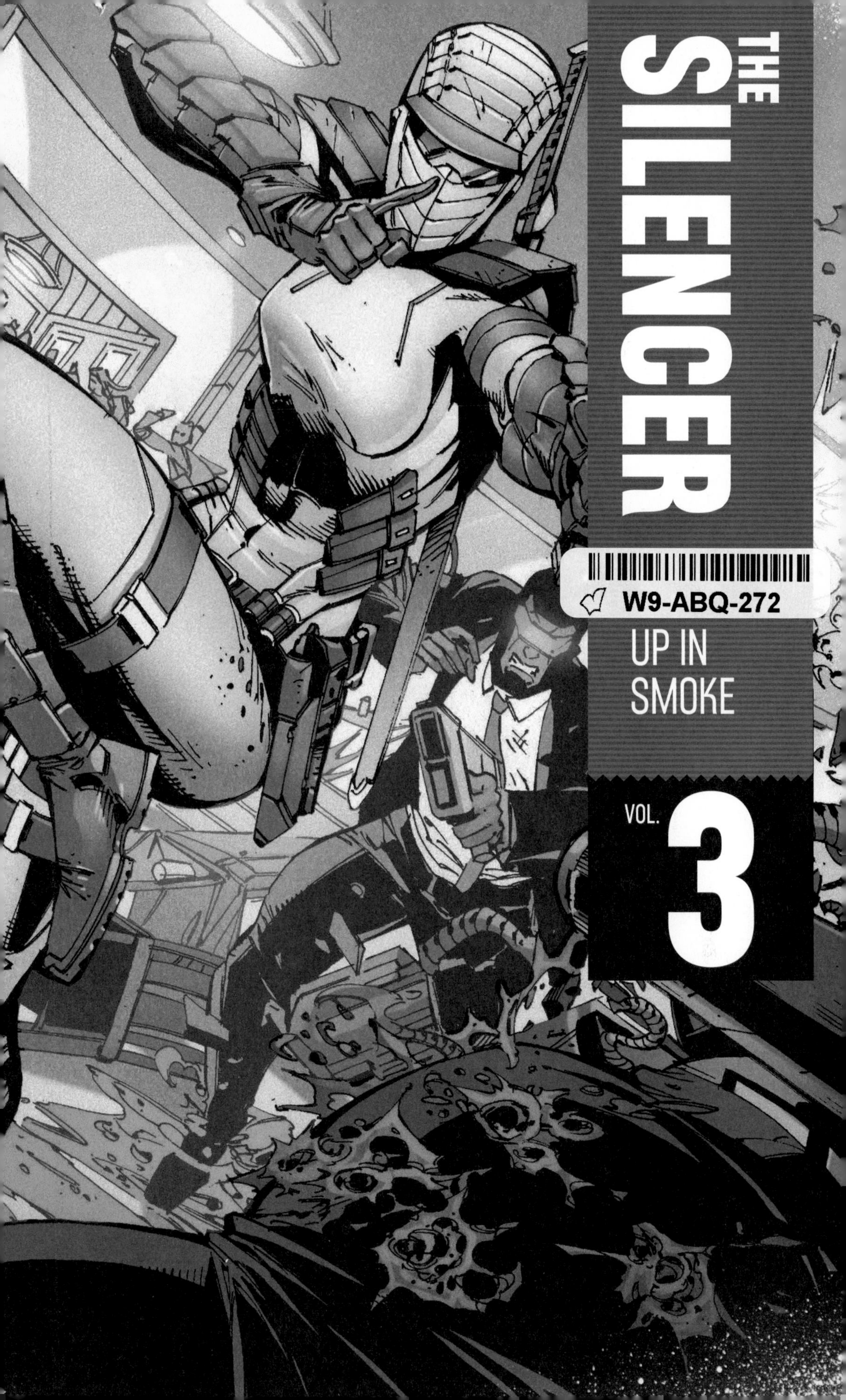
THE SILENCER
UP IN SMOKE
VOL. 3

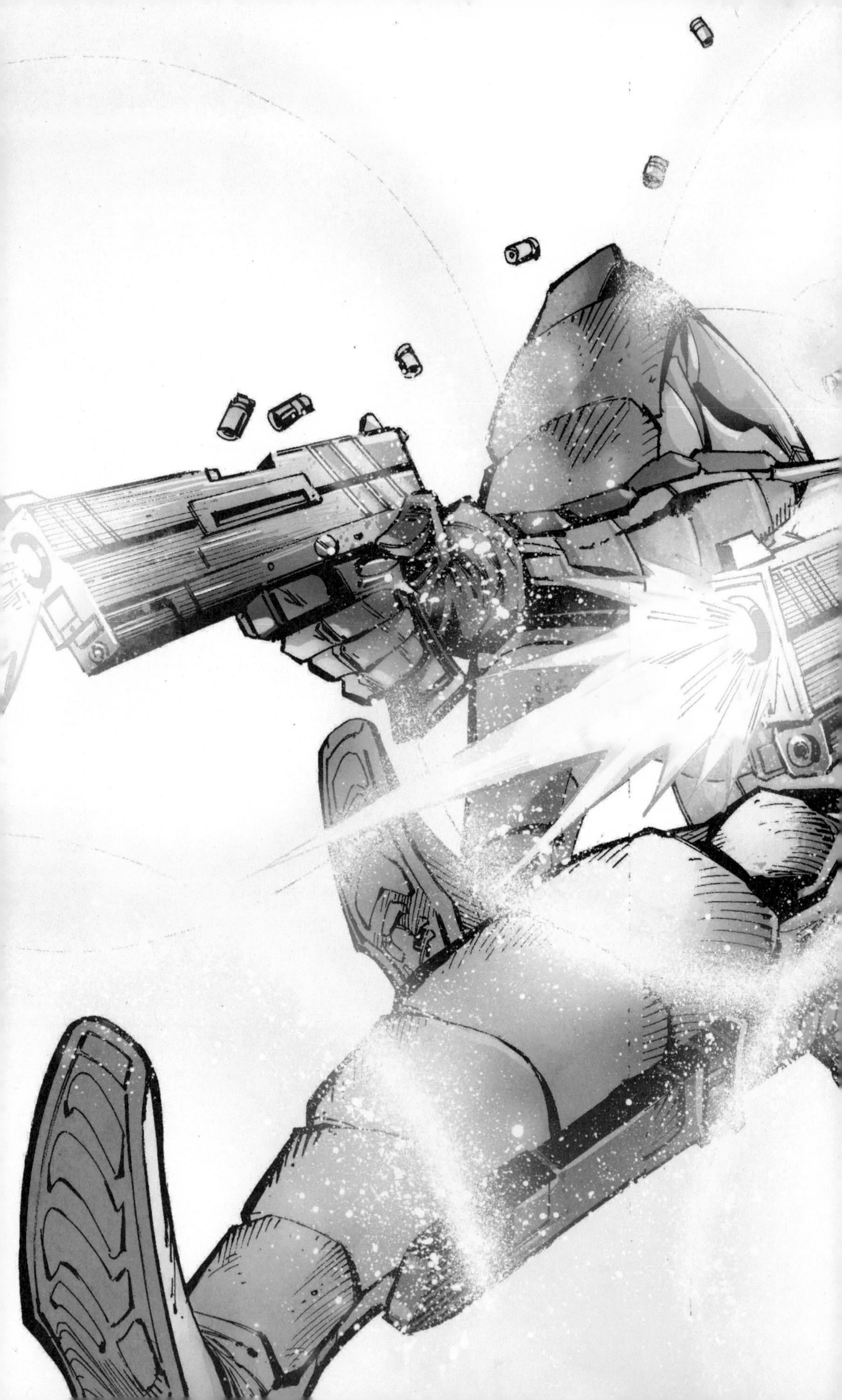

THE
SILENCER
UP IN SMOKE

penciller
V KEN MARION

inker
SANDU FLOREA

writer
DAN ABNETT

colorist
MIKE SPICER

letterer
TOM NAPOLITANO

collection cover artists
V KEN MARION, SANDU FLOREA
and ARIF PRIANTO

THE SILENCER created by **JOHN ROMITA JR.** and **DAN ABNETT**

VOL.

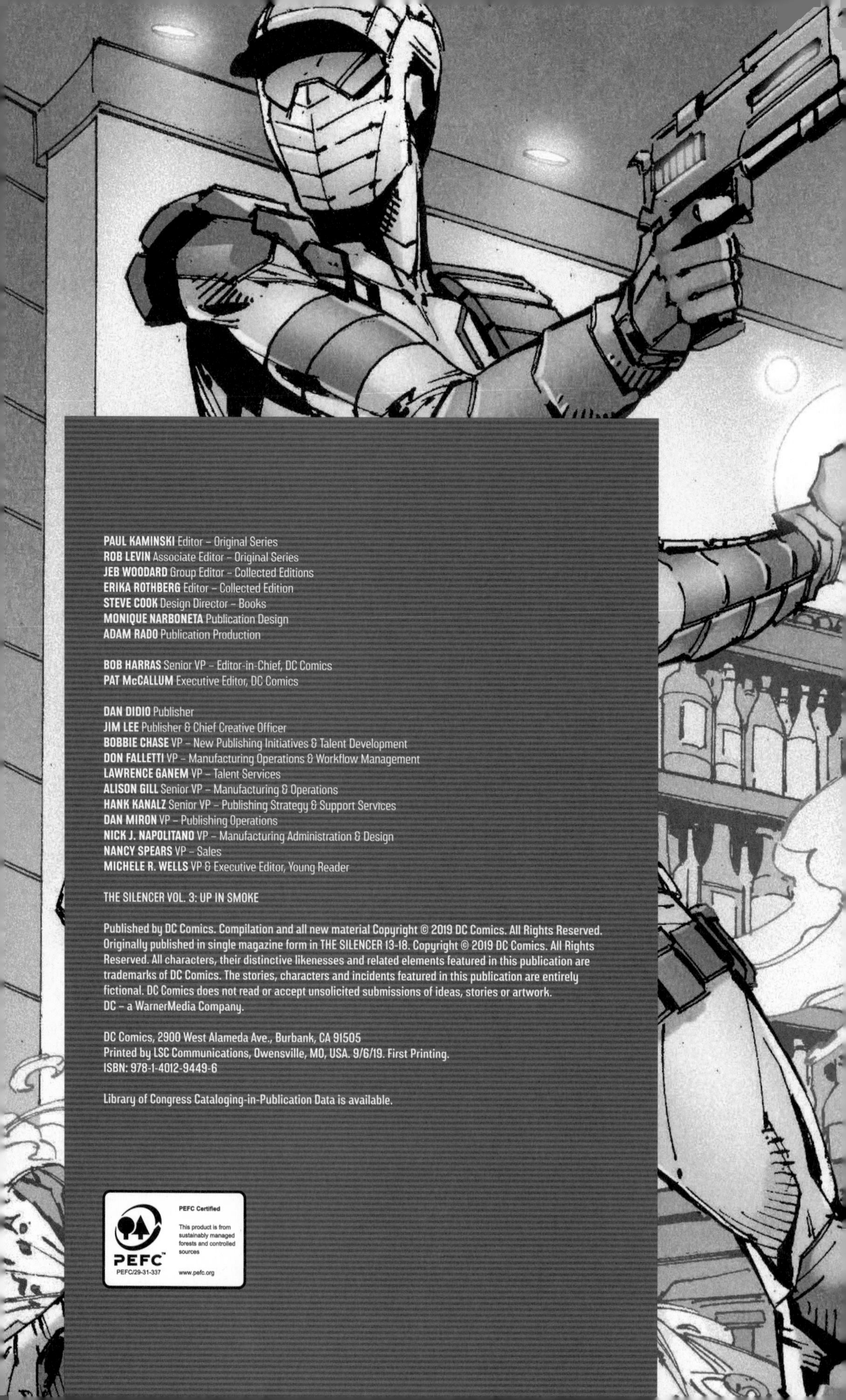

PAUL KAMINSKI Editor – Original Series
ROB LEVIN Associate Editor – Original Series
JEB WOODARD Group Editor – Collected Editions
ERIKA ROTHBERG Editor – Collected Edition
STEVE COOK Design Director – Books
MONIQUE NARBONETA Publication Design
ADAM RADO Publication Production

BOB HARRAS Senior VP – Editor-in-Chief, DC Comics
PAT McCALLUM Executive Editor, DC Comics

DAN DIDIO Publisher
JIM LEE Publisher & Chief Creative Officer
BOBBIE CHASE VP – New Publishing Initiatives & Talent Development
DON FALLETTI VP – Manufacturing Operations & Workflow Management
LAWRENCE GANEM VP – Talent Services
ALISON GILL Senior VP – Manufacturing & Operations
HANK KANALZ Senior VP – Publishing Strategy & Support Services
DAN MIRON VP – Publishing Operations
NICK J. NAPOLITANO VP – Manufacturing Administration & Design
NANCY SPEARS VP – Sales
MICHELE R. WELLS VP & Executive Editor, Young Reader

THE SILENCER VOL. 3: UP IN SMOKE

DC Comics, 2900 West Alameda Ave., Burbank, CA 91505
Printed by LSC Communications, Owensville, MO, USA. 9/6/19. First Printing.
ISBN: 978-1-4012-9449-6

Library of Congress Cataloging-in-Publication Data is available.

PEFC
PEFC/29-31-337
PEFC Certified
This product is from sustainably managed forests and controlled sources
www.pefc.org

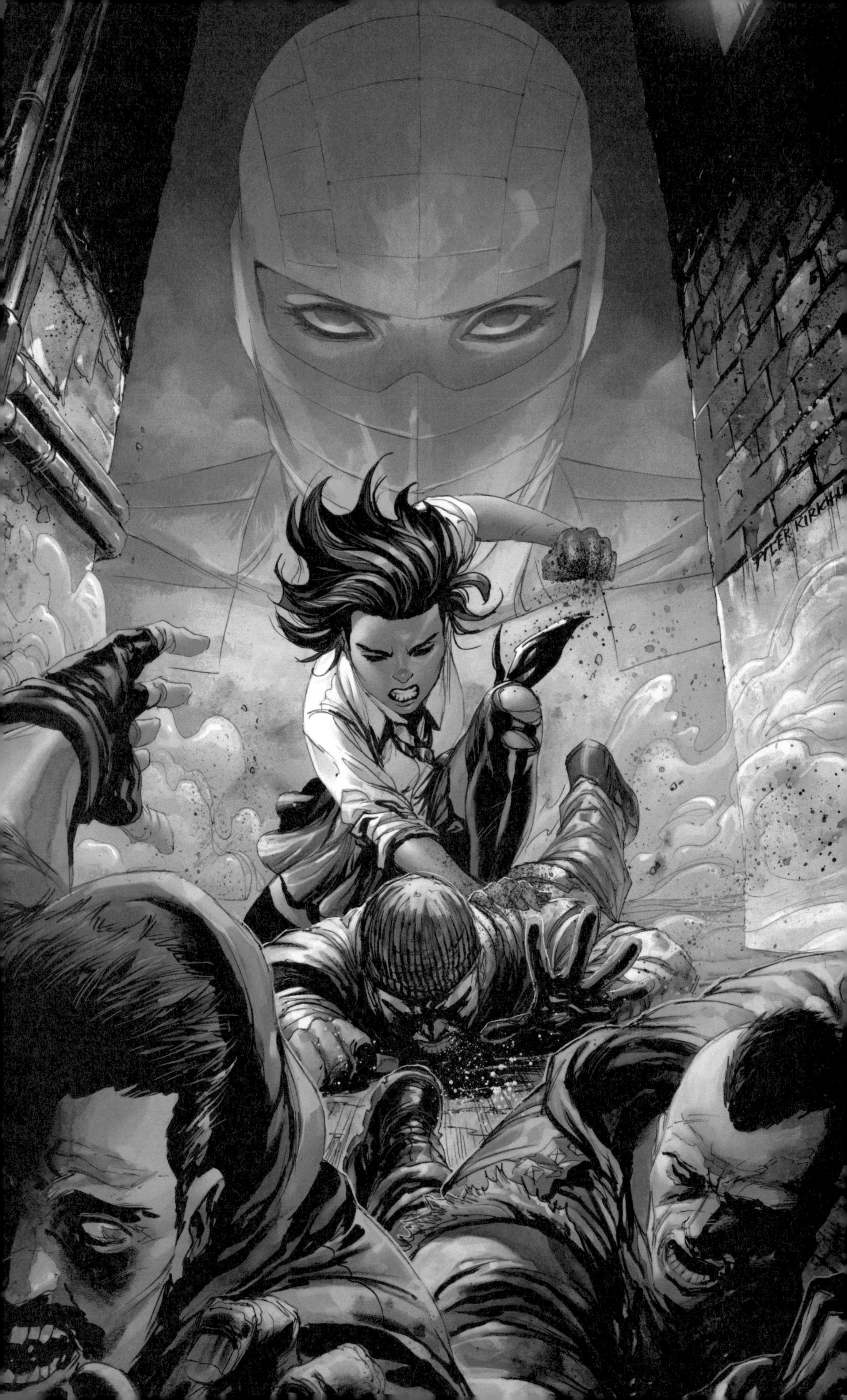
TYLER KIRKHA

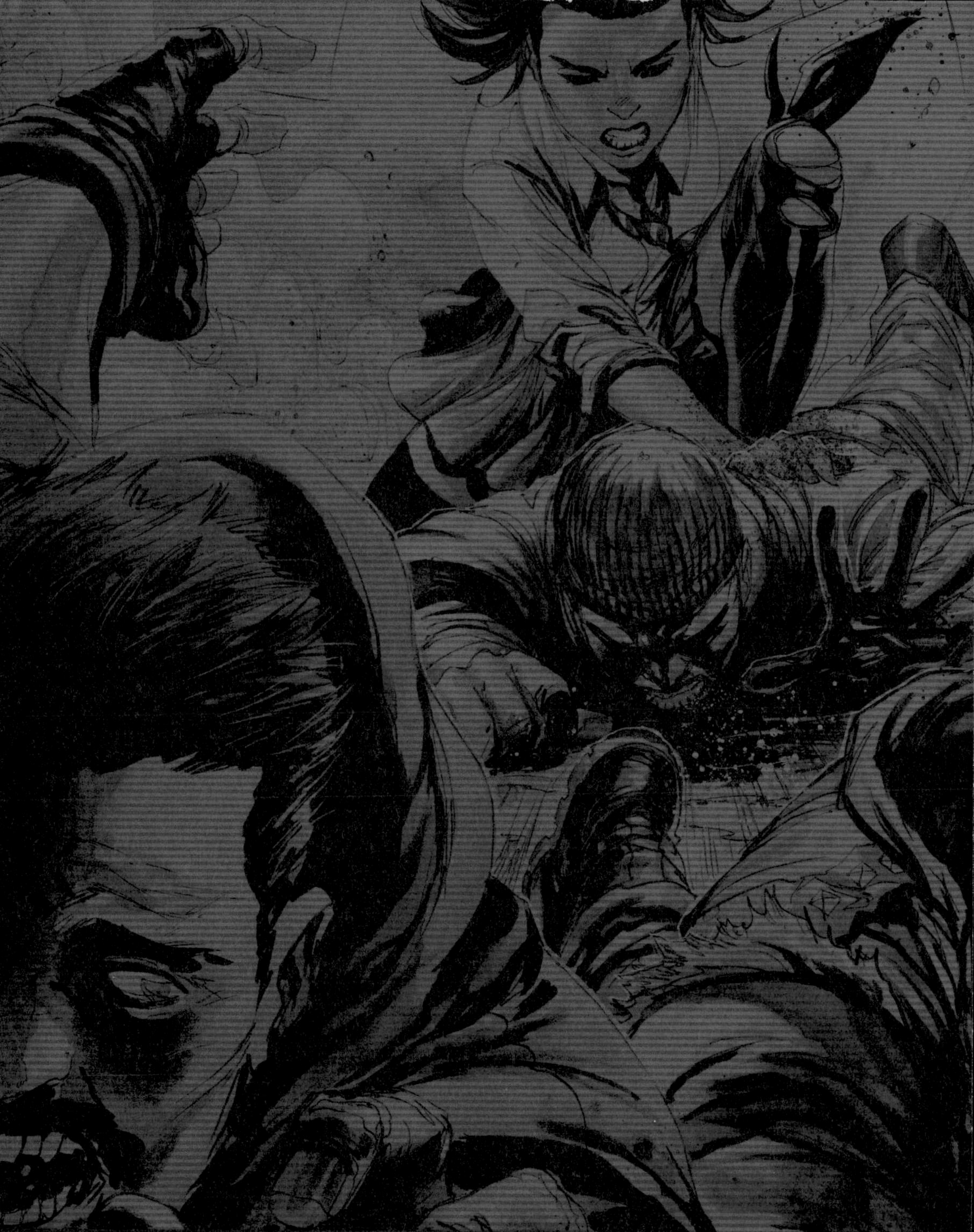

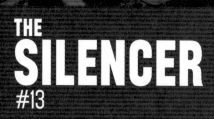

THE SILENCER
#13

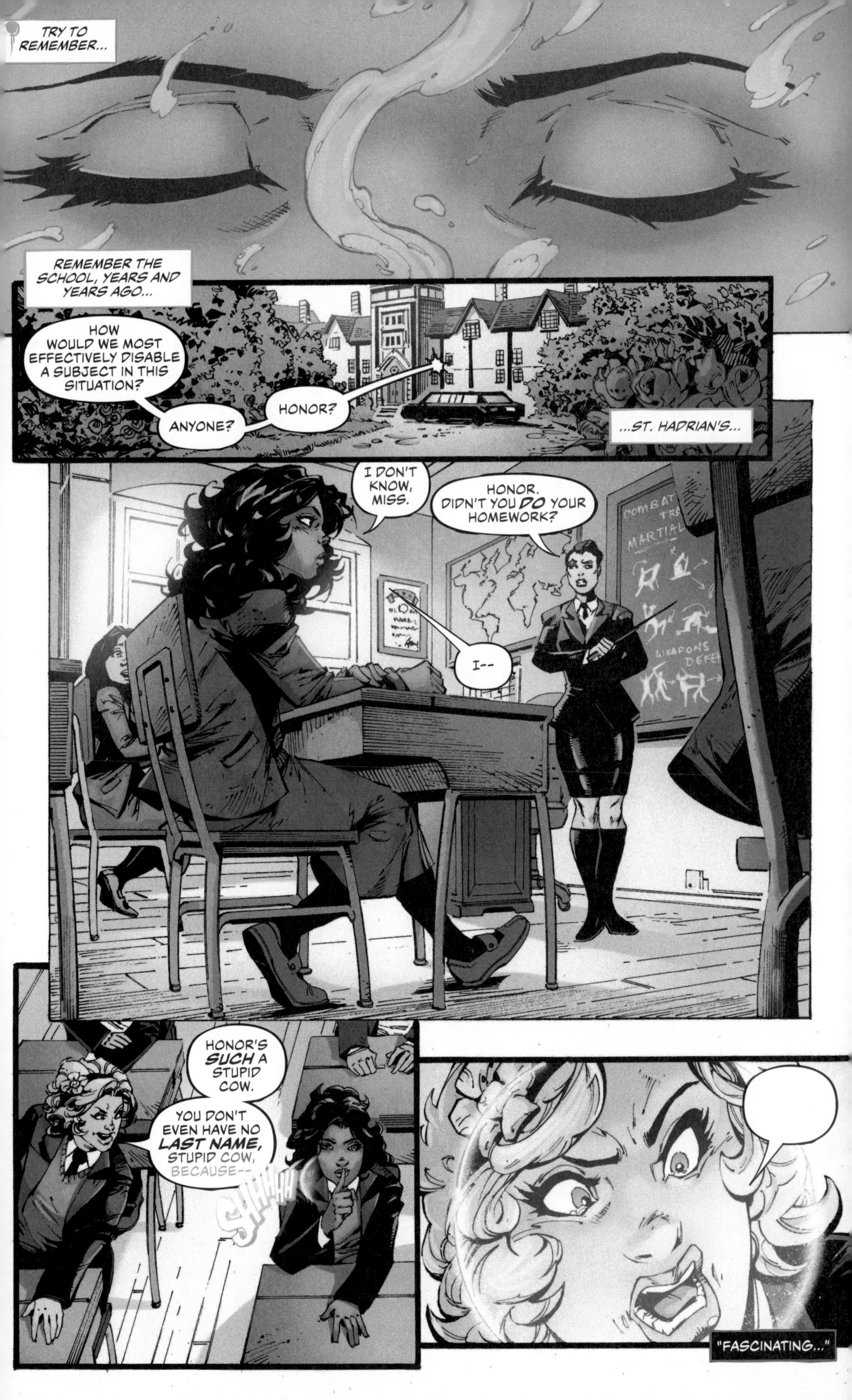
TRY TO REMEMBER...
REMEMBER THE SCHOOL, YEARS AND YEARS AGO...
HOW WOULD WE MOST EFFECTIVELY DISABLE A SUBJECT IN THIS SITUATION?
ANYONE?
HONOR?
...ST. HADRIAN'S...
I DON'T KNOW, MISS.
HONOR. DIDN'T YOU *DO* YOUR HOMEWORK?
I--
HONOR'S *SUCH* A STUPID COW.
YOU DON'T EVEN HAVE NO *LAST NAME*, STUPID COW, BECAUSE--
SHHHHH
"FASCINATING..."

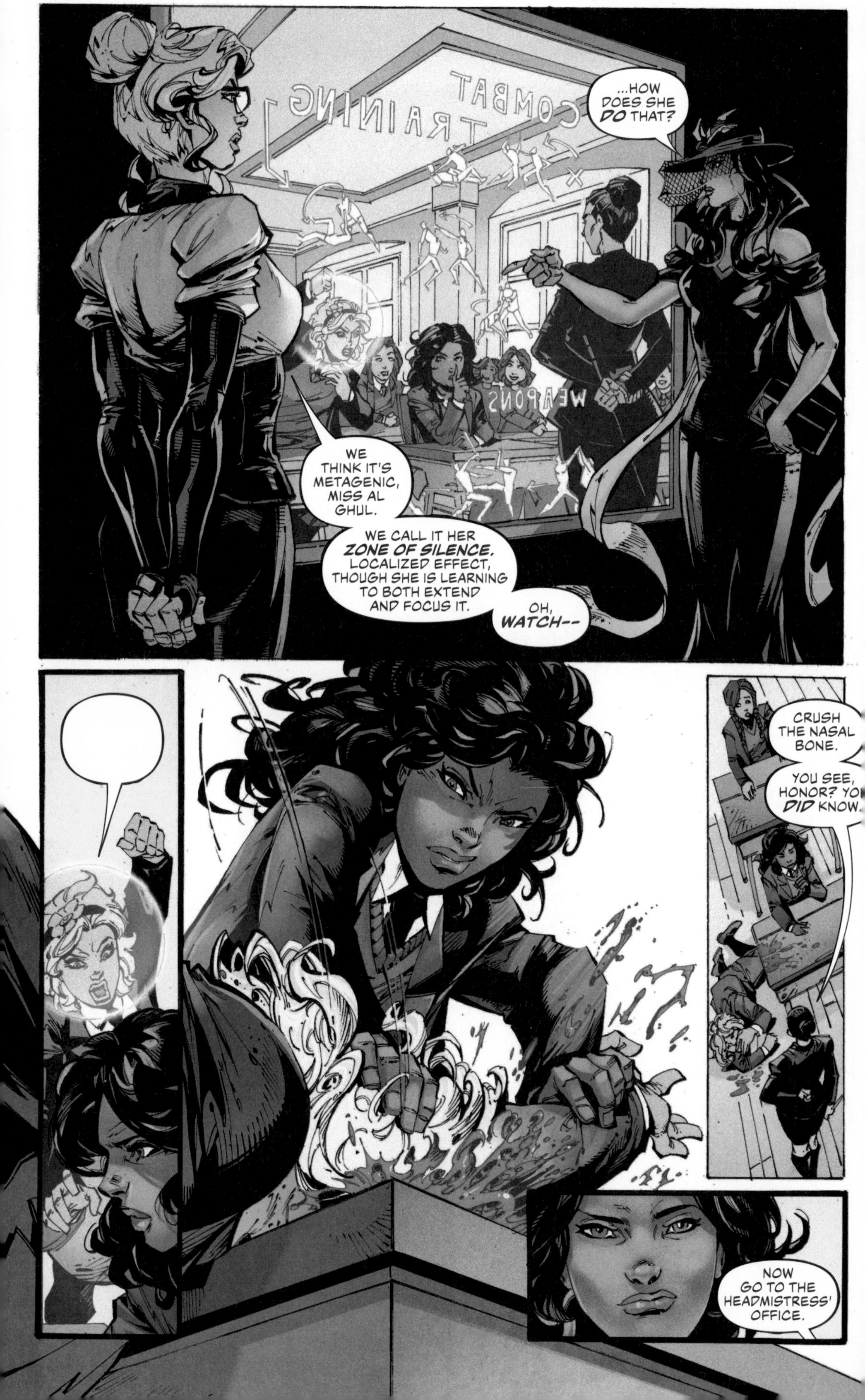
COMBAT TRAINING
...HOW DOES SHE DO THAT?
WEAPONS
WE THINK IT'S METAGENIC, MISS AL GHUL.
WE CALL IT HER ZONE OF SILENCE. LOCALIZED EFFECT, THOUGH SHE IS LEARNING TO BOTH EXTEND AND FOCUS IT.
OH, WATCH--
CRUSH THE NASAL BONE.
YOU SEE, HONOR? YO DID KNOW.
NOW GO TO THE HEADMISTRESS' OFFICE.

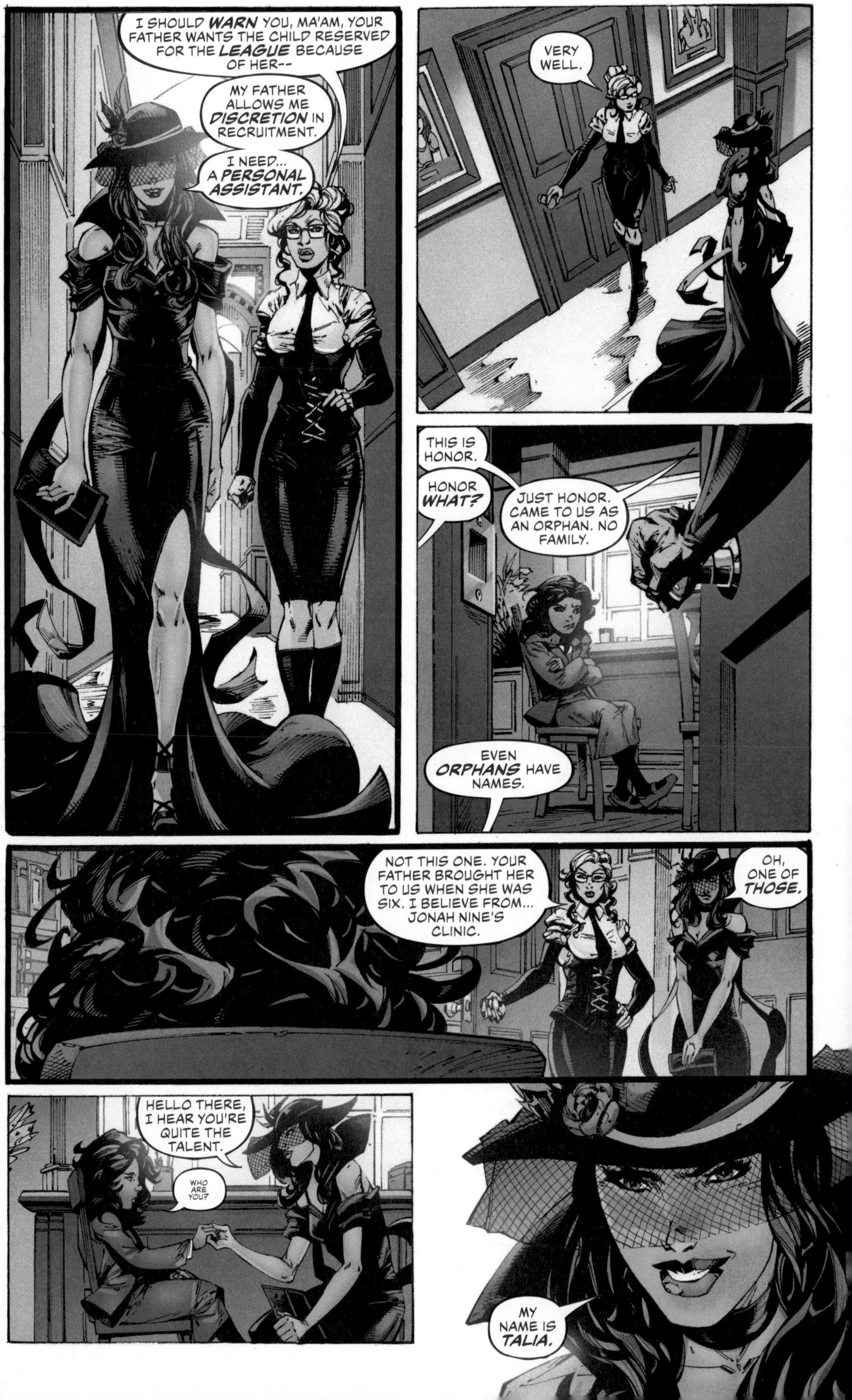
I SHOULD WARN YOU, MA'AM, YOUR FATHER WANTS THE CHILD RESERVED FOR THE LEAGUE BECAUSE OF HER--
MY FATHER ALLOWS ME DISCRETION IN RECRUITMENT.
I NEED... A PERSONAL ASSISTANT.
VERY WELL.
THIS IS HONOR.
HONOR WHAT?
JUST HONOR. CAME TO US AS AN ORPHAN. NO FAMILY.
EVEN ORPHANS HAVE NAMES.
NOT THIS ONE. YOUR FATHER BROUGHT HER TO US WHEN SHE WAS SIX. I BELIEVE FROM... JONAH NINE'S CLINIC.
OH, ONE OF THOSE.
HELLO THERE, I HEAR YOU'RE QUITE THE TALENT.
WHO ARE YOU?
MY NAME IS TALIA.

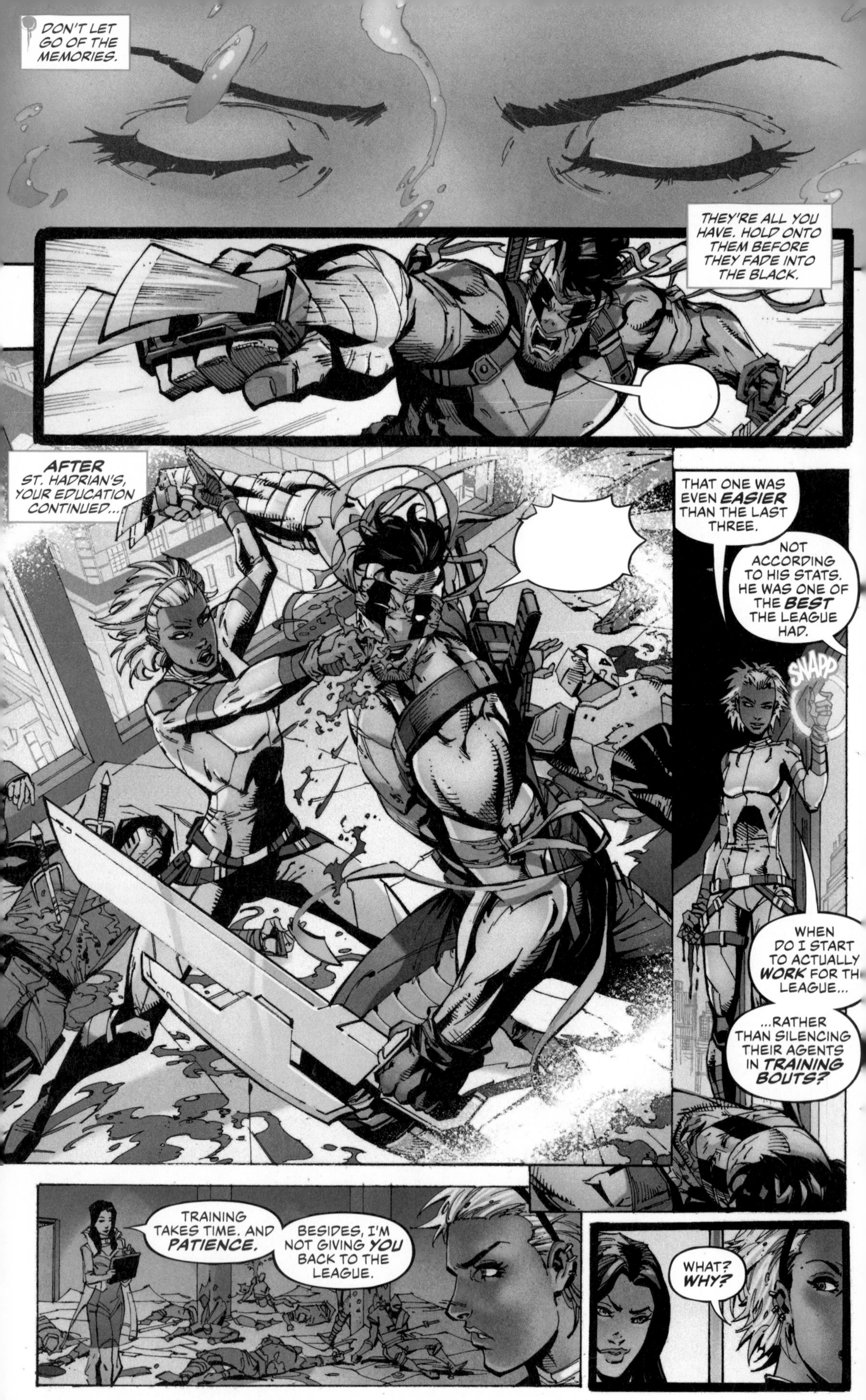
DON'T LET GO OF THE MEMORIES.
THEY'RE ALL YOU HAVE. HOLD ONTO THEM BEFORE THEY FADE INTO THE BLACK.
AFTER ST. HADRIAN'S, YOUR EDUCATION CONTINUED...
THAT ONE WAS EVEN EASIER THAN THE LAST THREE.
NOT ACCORDING TO HIS STATS. HE WAS ONE OF THE BEST THE LEAGUE HAD.
SNAPP
WHEN DO I START TO ACTUALLY WORK FOR TH LEAGUE...
...RATHER THAN SILENCING THEIR AGENTS IN TRAINING BOUTS?
TRAINING TAKES TIME. AND PATIENCE.
BESIDES, I'M NOT GIVING YOU BACK TO THE LEAGUE.
WHAT? WHY?

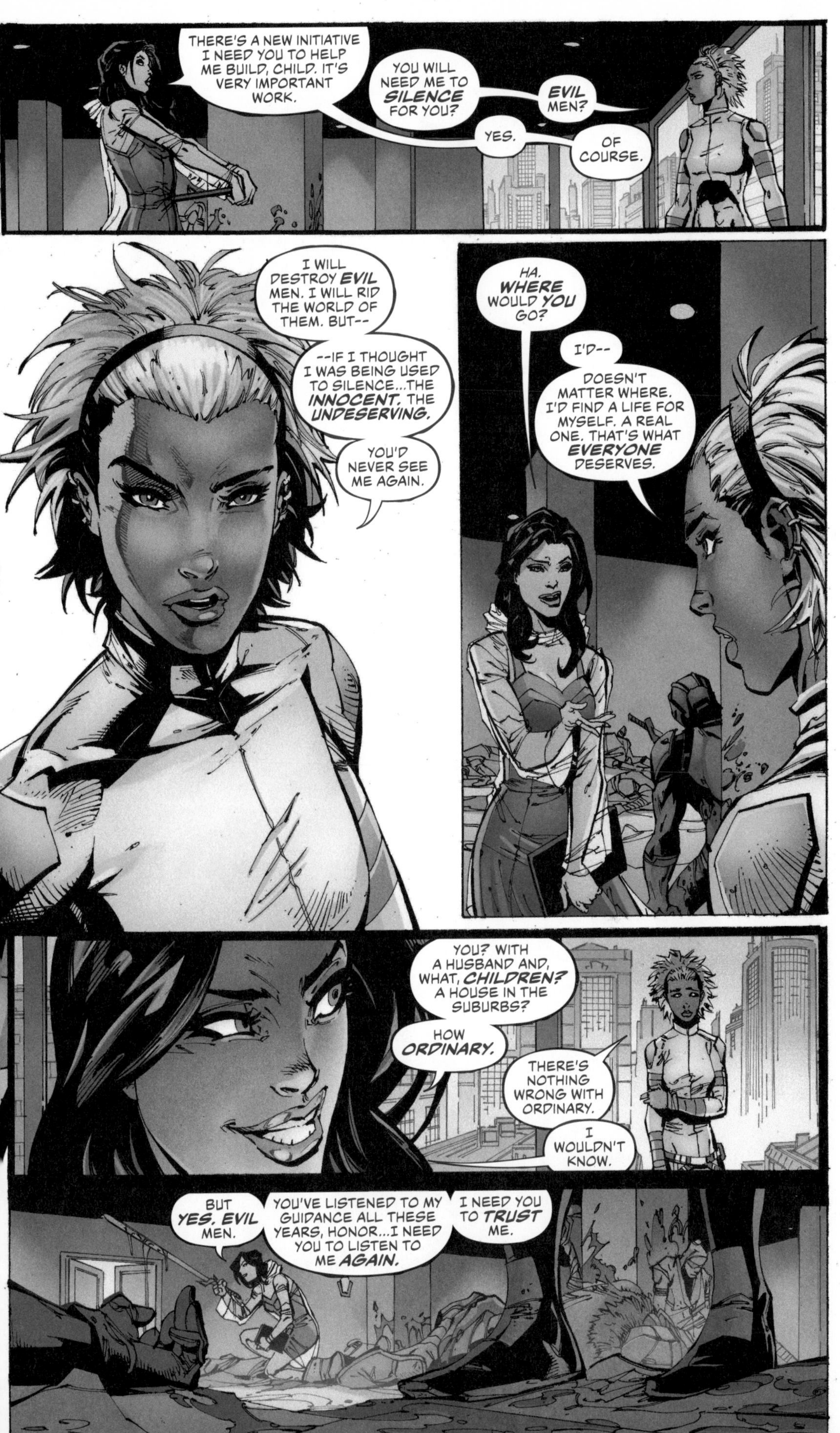
THERE'S A NEW INITIATIVE I NEED YOU TO HELP ME BUILD, CHILD. IT'S VERY IMPORTANT WORK.
YOU WILL NEED ME TO SILENCE FOR YOU?
EVIL MEN?
YES.
OF COURSE.
I WILL DESTROY EVIL MEN. I WILL RID THE WORLD OF THEM. BUT--
--IF I THOUGHT I WAS BEING USED TO SILENCE...THE INNOCENT. THE UNDESERVING.
YOU'D NEVER SEE ME AGAIN.
HA. WHERE WOULD YOU GO?
I'D--
DOESN'T MATTER WHERE. I'D FIND A LIFE FOR MYSELF. A REAL ONE. THAT'S WHAT EVERYONE DESERVES.
YOU? WITH A HUSBAND AND, WHAT, CHILDREN? A HOUSE IN THE SUBURBS?
HOW ORDINARY.
THERE'S NOTHING WRONG WITH ORDINARY.
I WOULDN'T KNOW.
BUT YES. EVIL MEN.
YOU'VE LISTENED TO MY GUIDANCE ALL THESE YEARS, HONOR...I NEED YOU TO LISTEN TO ME AGAIN.
I NEED YOU TO TRUST ME.

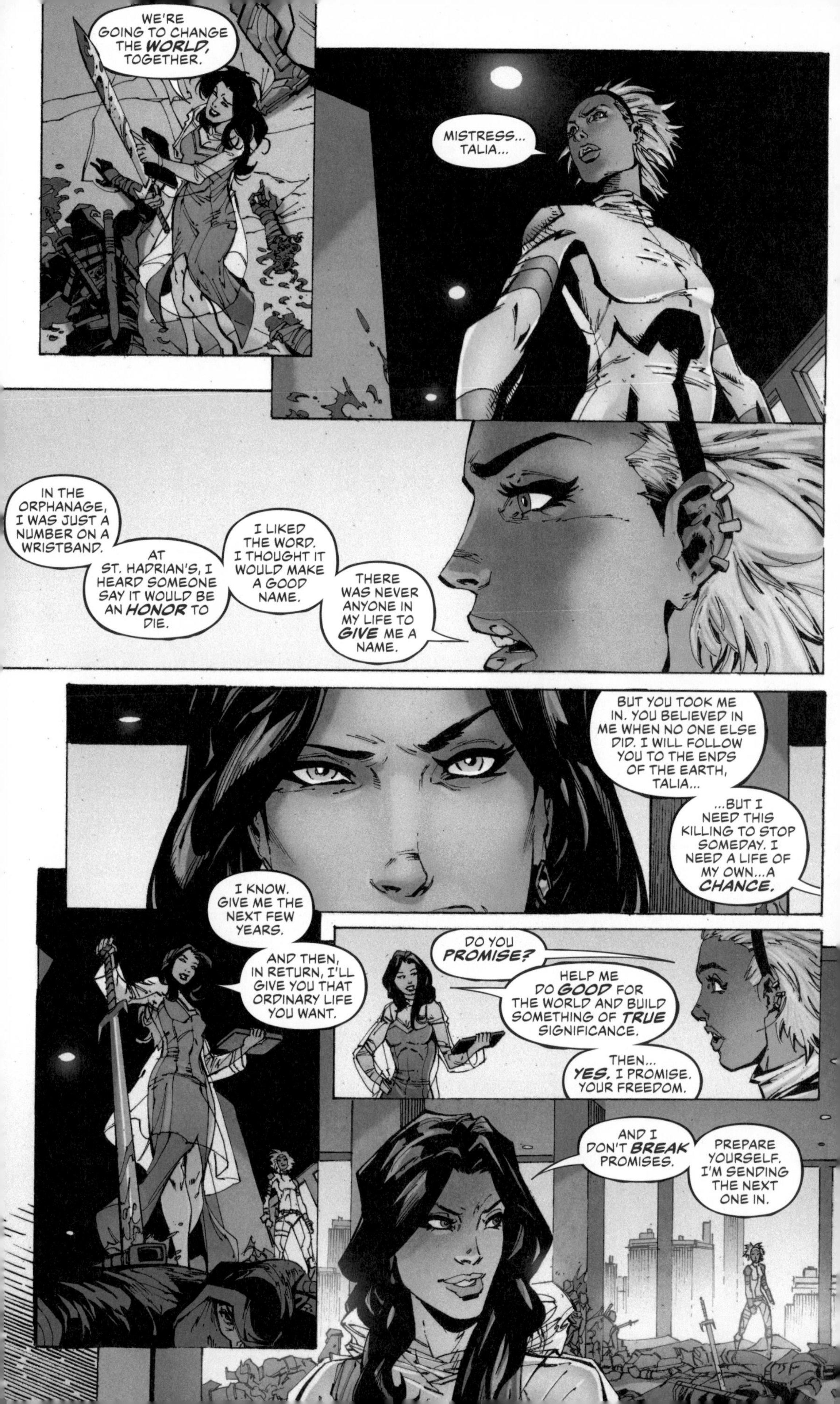

WE'RE GOING TO CHANGE THE WORLD, TOGETHER.
MISTRESS... TALIA...
IN THE ORPHANAGE, I WAS JUST A NUMBER ON A WRISTBAND.
AT ST. HADRIAN'S, I HEARD SOMEONE SAY IT WOULD BE AN HONOR TO DIE.
I LIKED THE WORD. I THOUGHT IT WOULD MAKE A GOOD NAME.
THERE WAS NEVER ANYONE IN MY LIFE TO GIVE ME A NAME.
BUT YOU TOOK ME IN. YOU BELIEVED IN ME WHEN NO ONE ELSE DID. I WILL FOLLOW YOU TO THE ENDS OF THE EARTH, TALIA...
...BUT I NEED THIS KILLING TO STOP SOMEDAY. I NEED A LIFE OF MY OWN...A CHANCE.
I KNOW. GIVE ME THE NEXT FEW YEARS.
AND THEN, IN RETURN, I'LL GIVE YOU THAT ORDINARY LIFE YOU WANT.
DO YOU PROMISE?
HELP ME DO GOOD FOR THE WORLD AND BUILD SOMETHING OF TRUE SIGNIFICANCE.
THEN... YES. I PROMISE. YOUR FREEDOM.
AND I DON'T BREAK PROMISES.
PREPARE YOURSELF. I'M SENDING THE NEXT ONE IN.

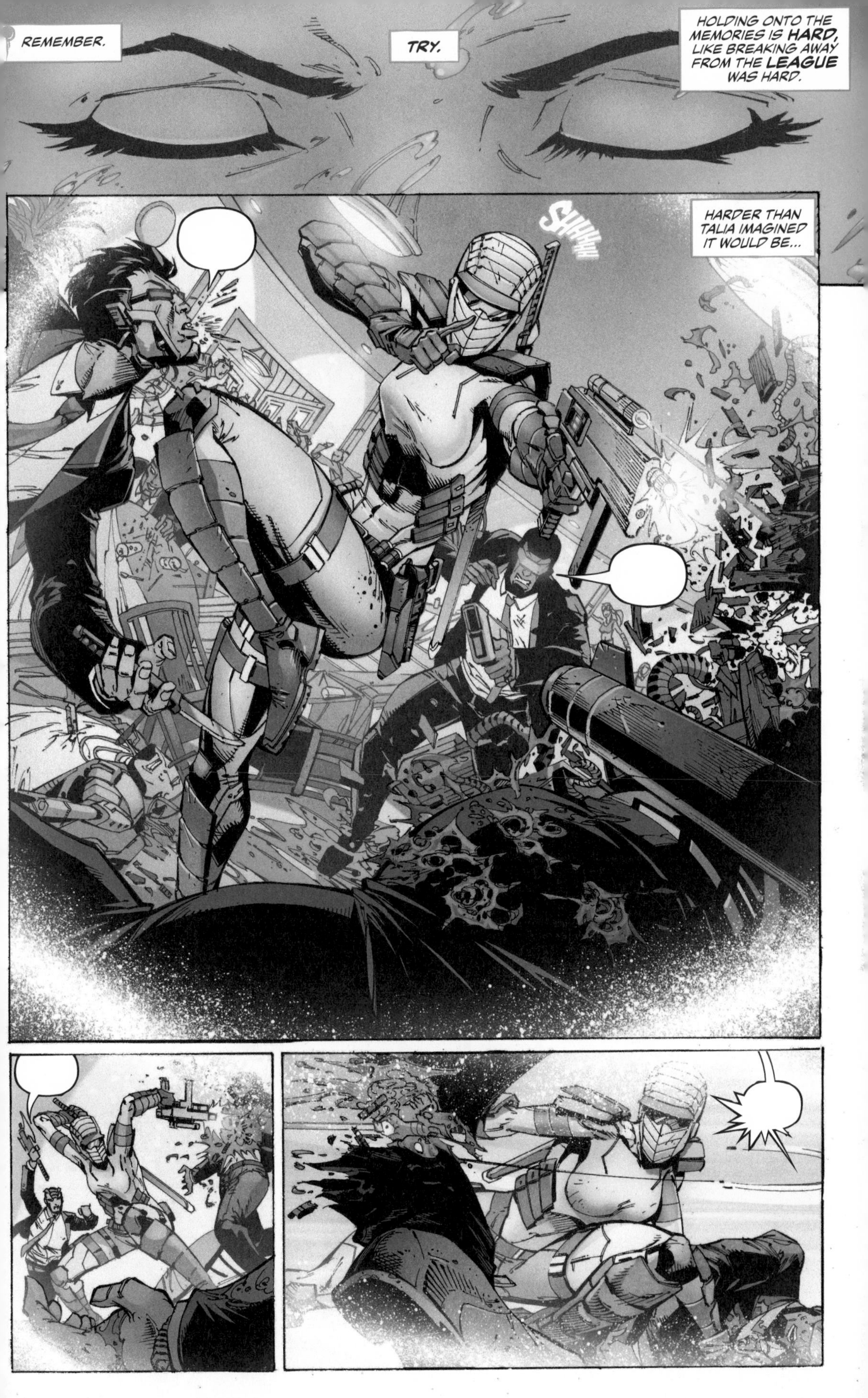

REMEMBER.
TRY.
HOLDING ONTO THE MEMORIES IS **HARD,** LIKE BREAKING AWAY FROM THE **LEAGUE** WAS HARD.
SHHHH
HARDER THAN TALIA IMAGINED IT WOULD BE...

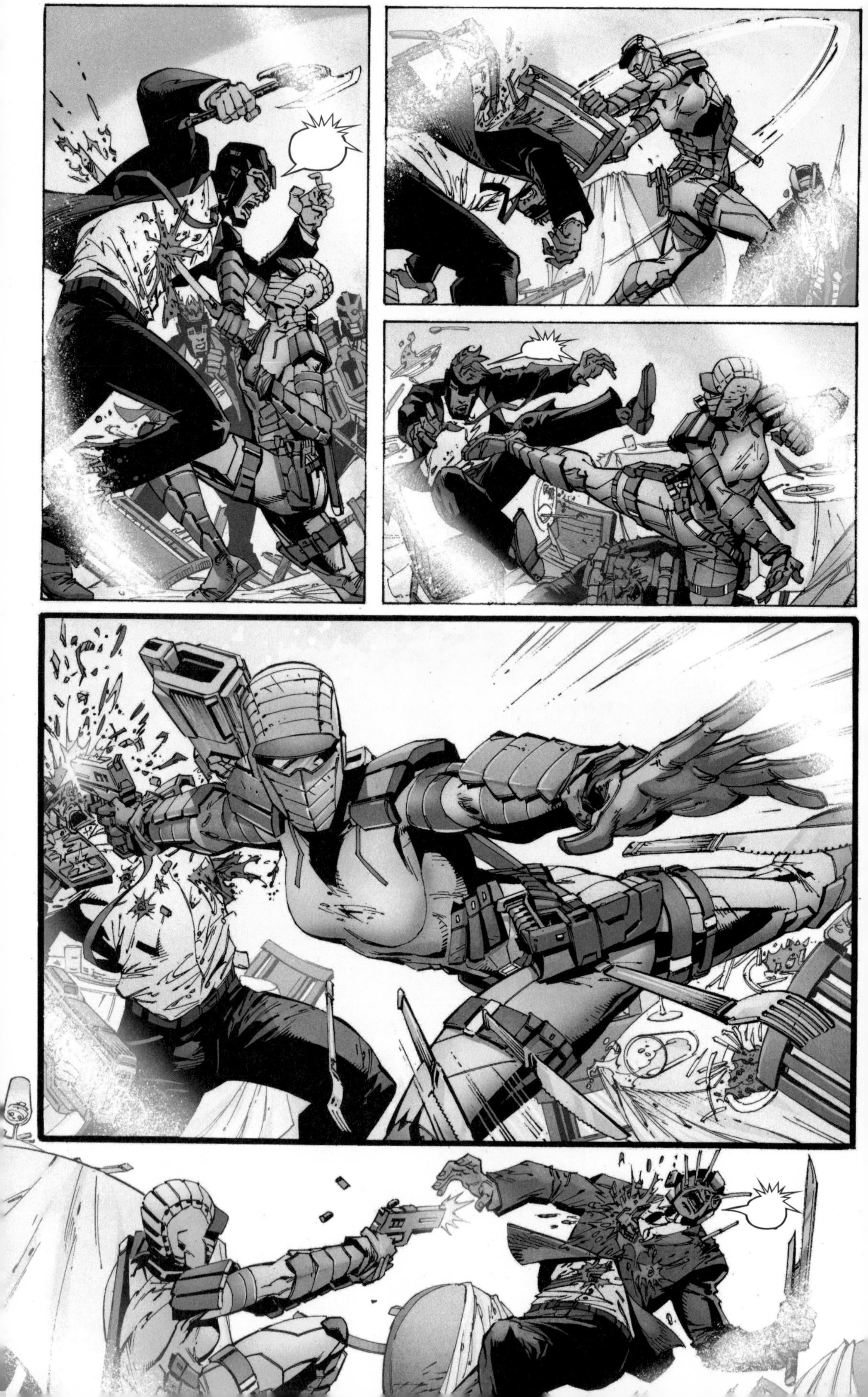

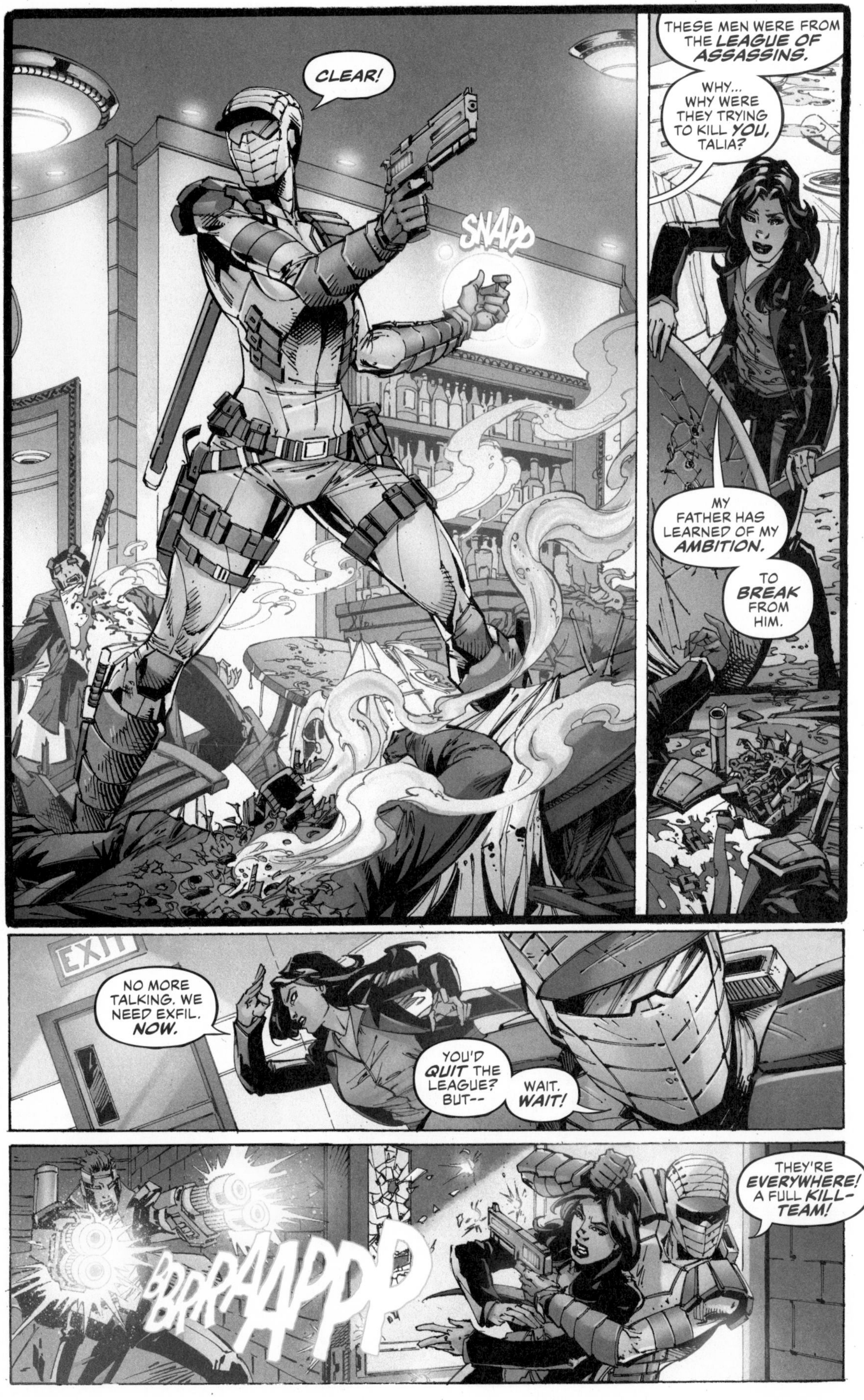
CLEAR!
SNAPP
THESE MEN WERE FROM THE LEAGUE OF ASSASSINS.
WHY... WHY WERE THEY TRYING TO KILL YOU, TALIA?
MY FATHER HAS LEARNED OF MY AMBITION.
TO BREAK FROM HIM.
NO MORE TALKING. WE NEED EXFIL. NOW.
YOU'D QUIT THE LEAGUE? BUT--
WAIT. WAIT!
THEY'RE EVERYWHERE! A FULL KILL-TEAM!
BBRRAAPPP

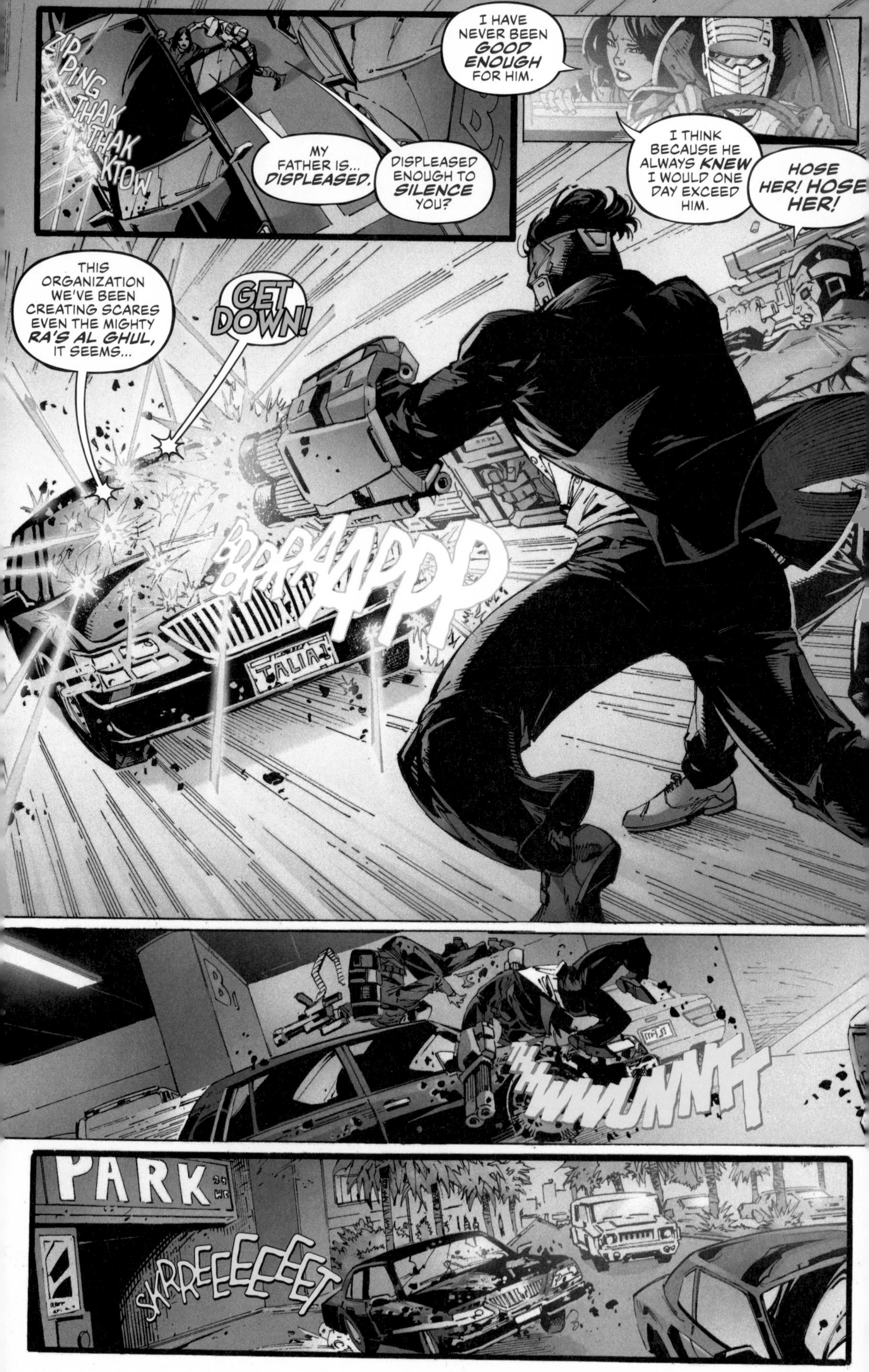
ZIP
PING
THAK
THAK
KTOW
MY FATHER IS... DISPLEASED.
DISPLEASED ENOUGH TO SILENCE YOU?
I HAVE NEVER BEEN GOOD ENOUGH FOR HIM.
I THINK BECAUSE HE ALWAYS KNEW I WOULD ONE DAY EXCEED HIM.
HOSE HER! HOSE HER!
THIS ORGANIZATION WE'VE BEEN CREATING SCARES EVEN THE MIGHTY RA'S AL GHUL, IT SEEMS...
GET DOWN!
BDDRRAAPPP
TALIA1
THHWWUNNK
PARK
SKRREEEEEEET

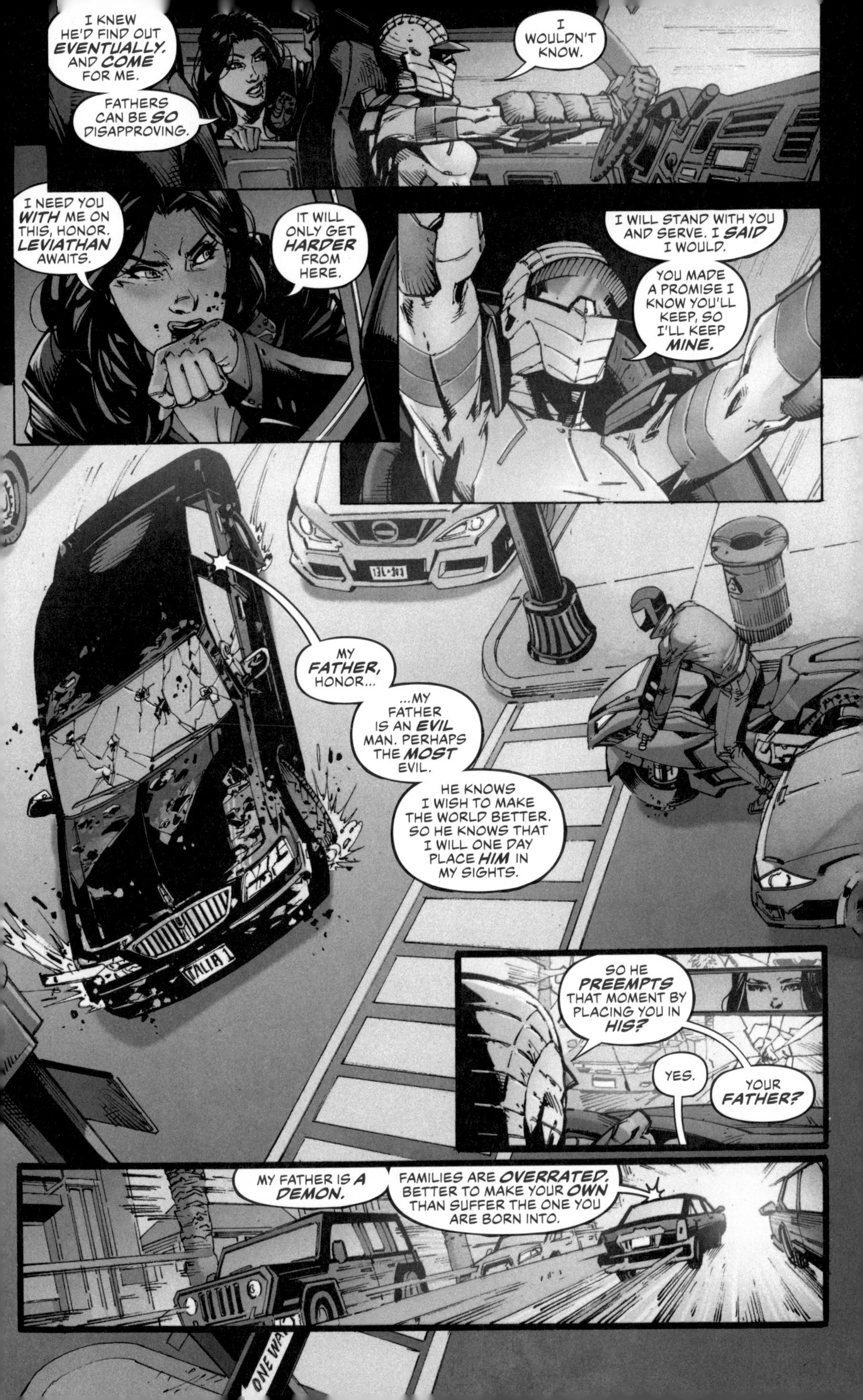
I KNEW HE'D FIND OUT EVENTUALLY. AND COME FOR ME.
FATHERS CAN BE SO DISAPPROVING.
I WOULDN'T KNOW.
I NEED YOU WITH ME ON THIS, HONOR. LEVIATHAN AWAITS.
IT WILL ONLY GET HARDER FROM HERE.
I WILL STAND WITH YOU AND SERVE. I SAID I WOULD.
YOU MADE A PROMISE I KNOW YOU'LL KEEP, SO I'LL KEEP MINE.
MY FATHER, HONOR...
...MY FATHER IS AN EVIL MAN. PERHAPS THE MOST EVIL.
HE KNOWS I WISH TO MAKE THE WORLD BETTER. SO HE KNOWS THAT I WILL ONE DAY PLACE HIM IN MY SIGHTS.
TALIA 1
SO HE PREEMPTS THAT MOMENT BY PLACING YOU IN HIS?
YES.
YOUR FATHER?
MY FATHER IS A DEMON.
FAMILIES ARE OVERRATED. BETTER TO MAKE YOUR OWN THAN SUFFER THE ONE YOU ARE BORN INTO.

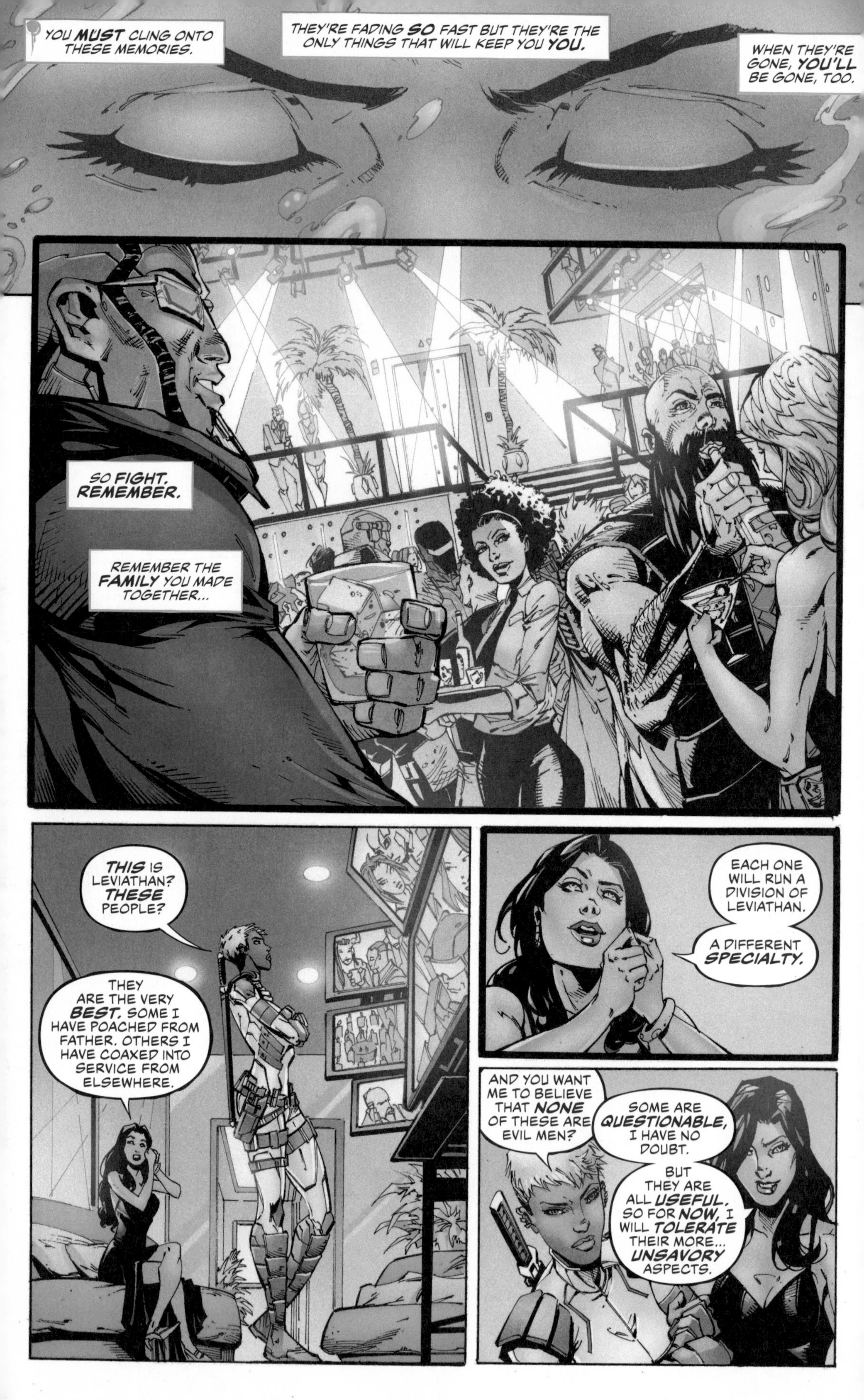

YOU MUST CLING ONTO THESE MEMORIES.
THEY'RE FADING SO FAST BUT THEY'RE THE ONLY THINGS THAT WILL KEEP YOU YOU.
WHEN THEY'RE GONE, YOU'LL BE GONE, TOO.
SO FIGHT. REMEMBER.
REMEMBER THE FAMILY YOU MADE TOGETHER...
THIS IS LEVIATHAN? THESE PEOPLE?
THEY ARE THE VERY BEST. SOME I HAVE POACHED FROM FATHER. OTHERS I HAVE COAXED INTO SERVICE FROM ELSEWHERE.
EACH ONE WILL RUN A DIVISION OF LEVIATHAN.
A DIFFERENT SPECIALTY.
AND YOU WANT ME TO BELIEVE THAT NONE OF THESE ARE EVIL MEN?
SOME ARE QUESTIONABLE, I HAVE NO DOUBT.
BUT THEY ARE ALL USEFUL. SO FOR NOW, I WILL TOLERATE THEIR MORE... UNSAVORY ASPECTS.

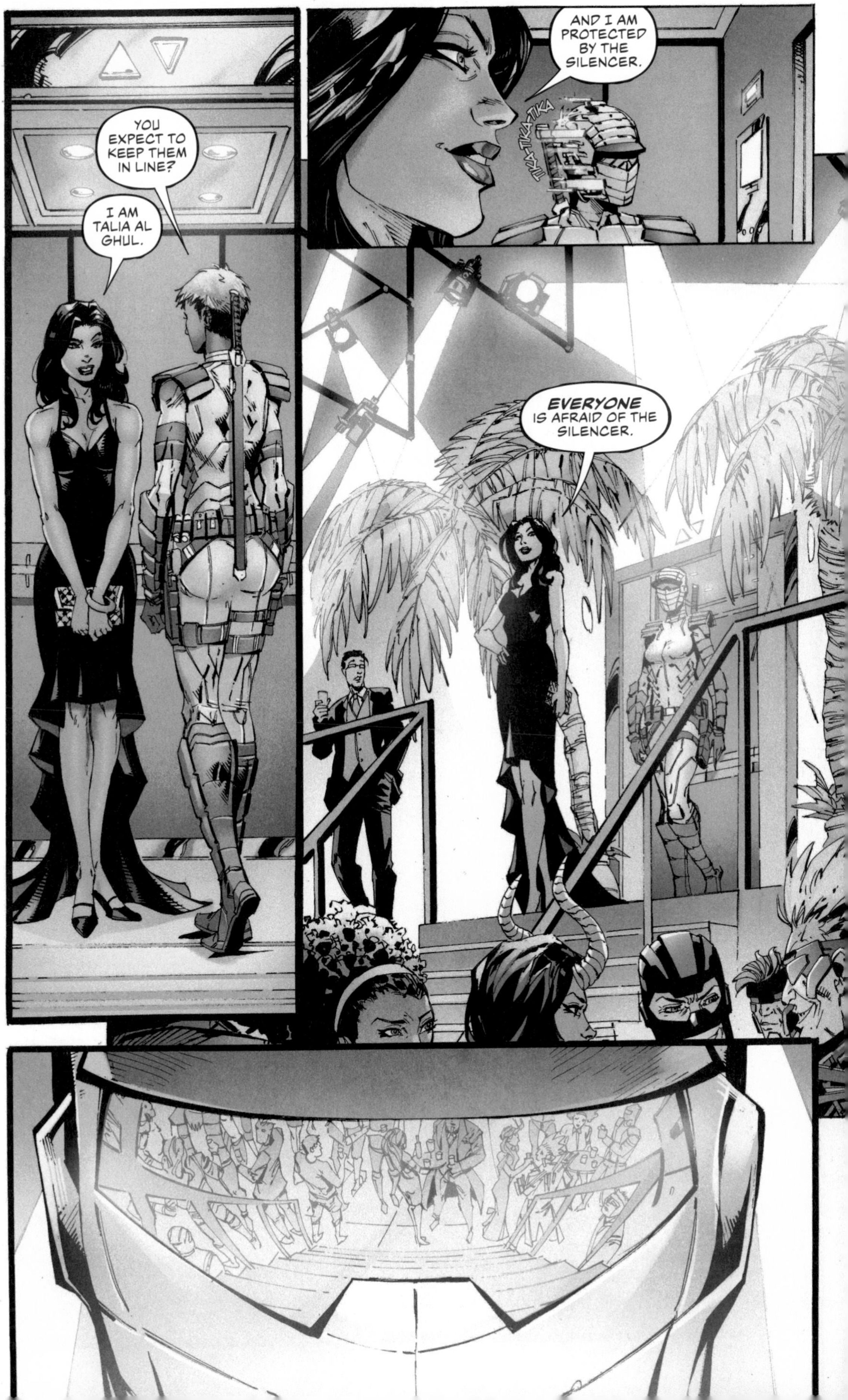
YOU EXPECT TO KEEP THEM IN LINE?
I AM TALIA AL GHUL.
AND I AM PROTECTED BY THE SILENCER.
TIKA-TIKA-TIKA
EVERYONE IS AFRAID OF THE SILENCER.

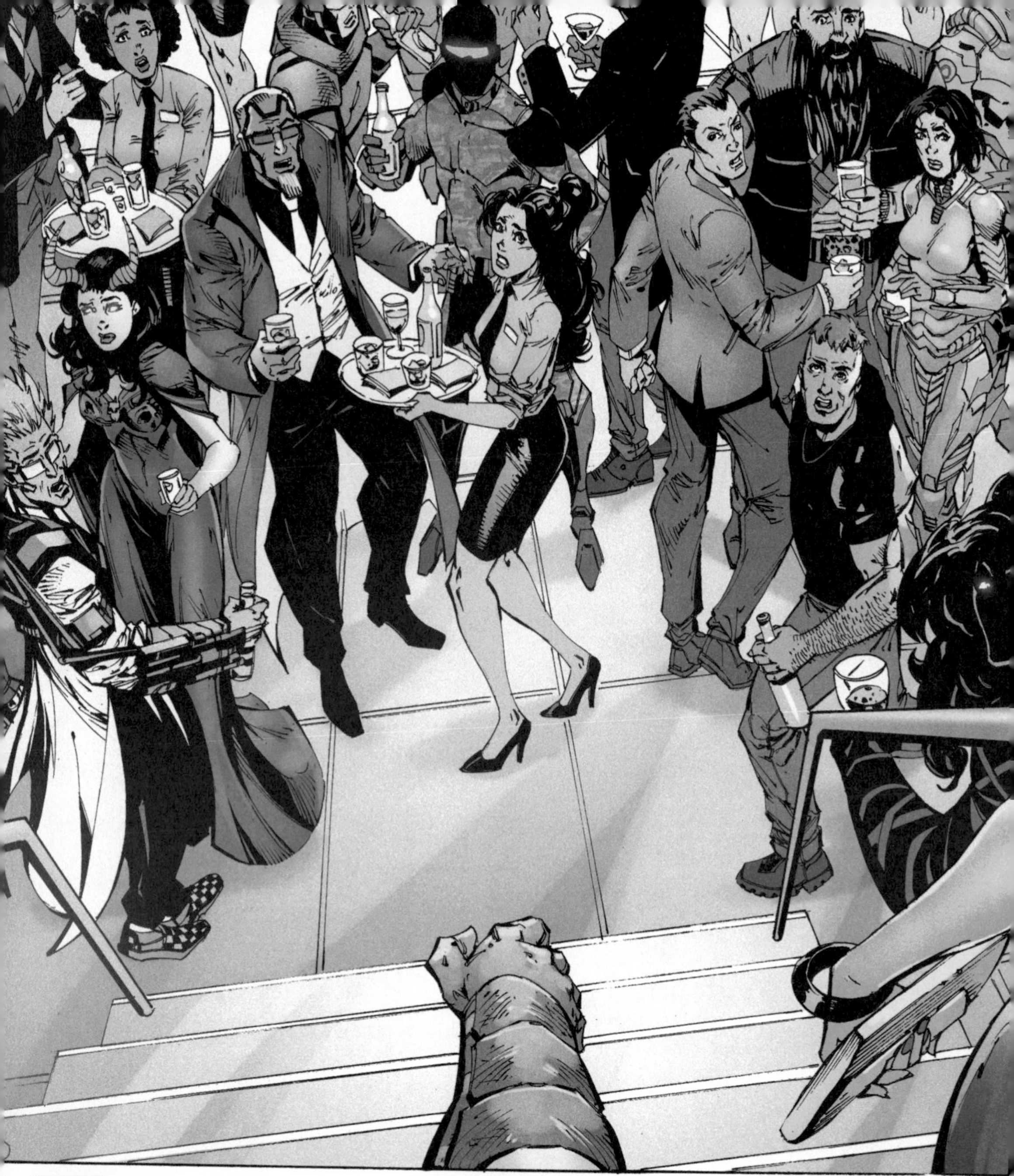

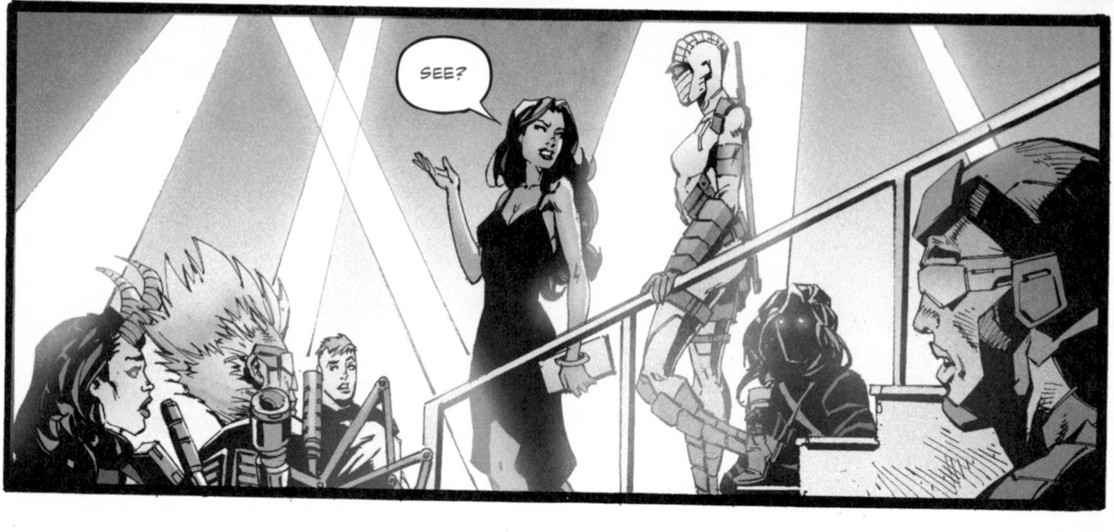
SEE?

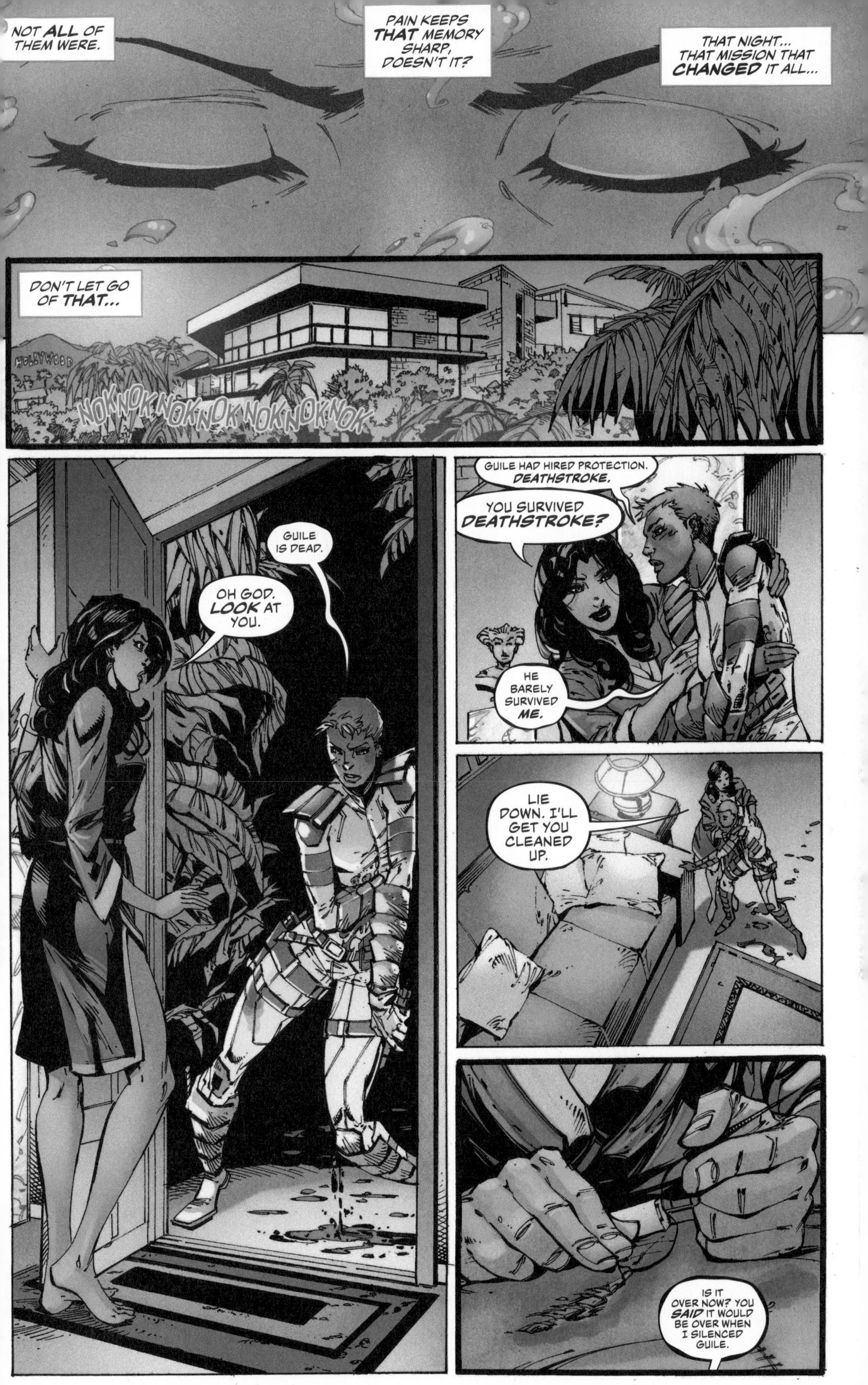
NOT ALL OF THEM WERE.
PAIN KEEPS THAT MEMORY SHARP, DOESN'T IT?
THAT NIGHT... THAT MISSION THAT CHANGED IT ALL...
DON'T LET GO OF THAT...
HOLLYWOOD
NOKNOKNOKNOKNOKNOKNOK
GUILE IS DEAD.
OH GOD. LOOK AT YOU.
GUILE HAD HIRED PROTECTION. DEATHSTROKE.
YOU SURVIVED DEATHSTROKE?
HE BARELY SURVIVED ME.
LIE DOWN. I'LL GET YOU CLEANED UP.
IS IT OVER NOW? YOU SAID IT WOULD BE OVER WHEN I SILENCED GUILE.

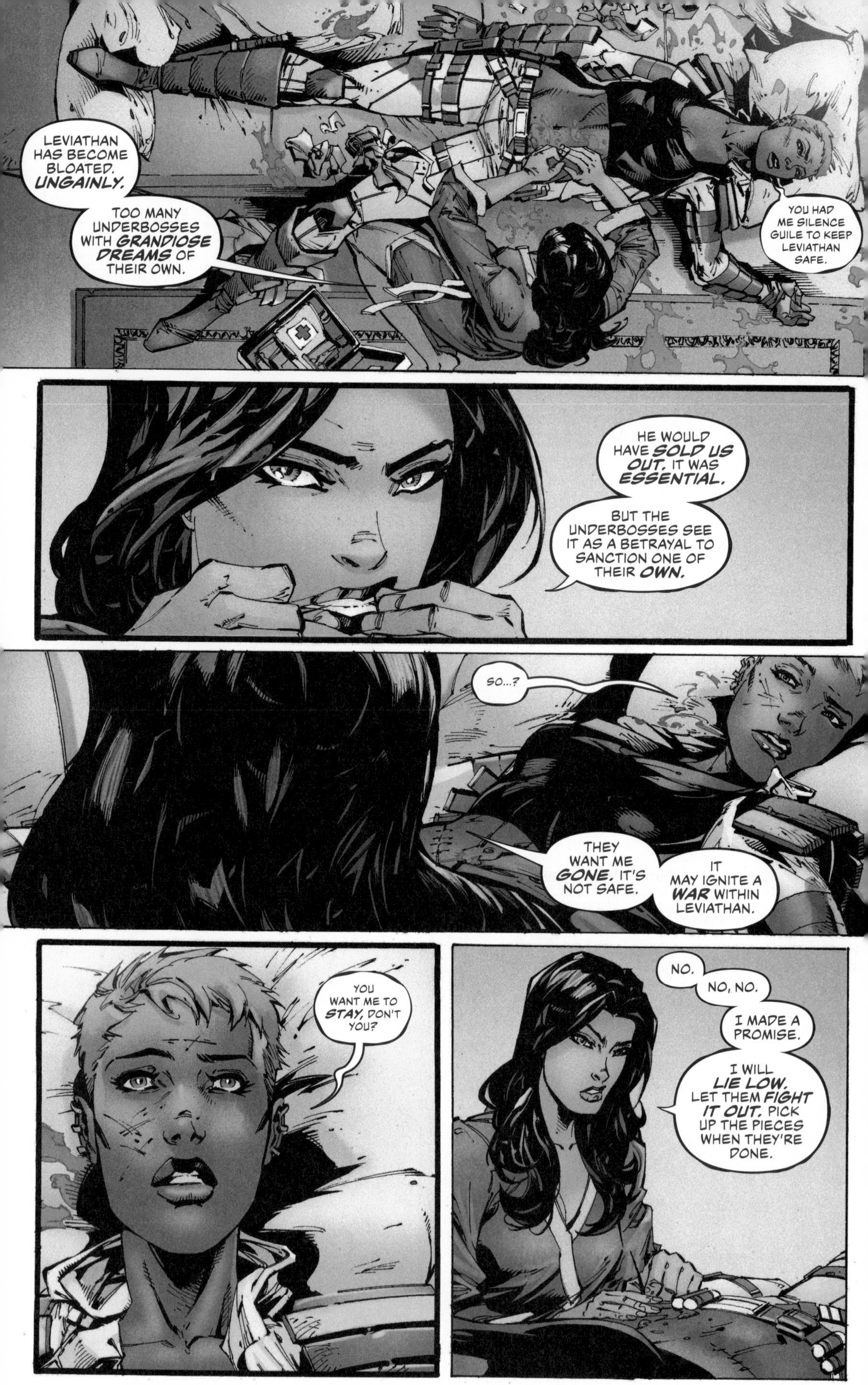
LEVIATHAN HAS BECOME BLOATED. UNGAINLY.
TOO MANY UNDERBOSSES WITH GRANDIOSE DREAMS OF THEIR OWN.
YOU HAD ME SILENCE GUILE TO KEEP LEVIATHAN SAFE.
HE WOULD HAVE SOLD US OUT. IT WAS ESSENTIAL.
BUT THE UNDERBOSSES SEE IT AS A BETRAYAL TO SANCTION ONE OF THEIR OWN.
SO...?
THEY WANT ME GONE. IT'S NOT SAFE.
IT MAY IGNITE A WAR WITHIN LEVIATHAN.
YOU WANT ME TO STAY, DON'T YOU?
NO.
NO, NO.
I MADE A PROMISE.
I WILL LIE LOW. LET THEM FIGHT IT OUT. PICK UP THE PIECES WHEN THEY'RE DONE.

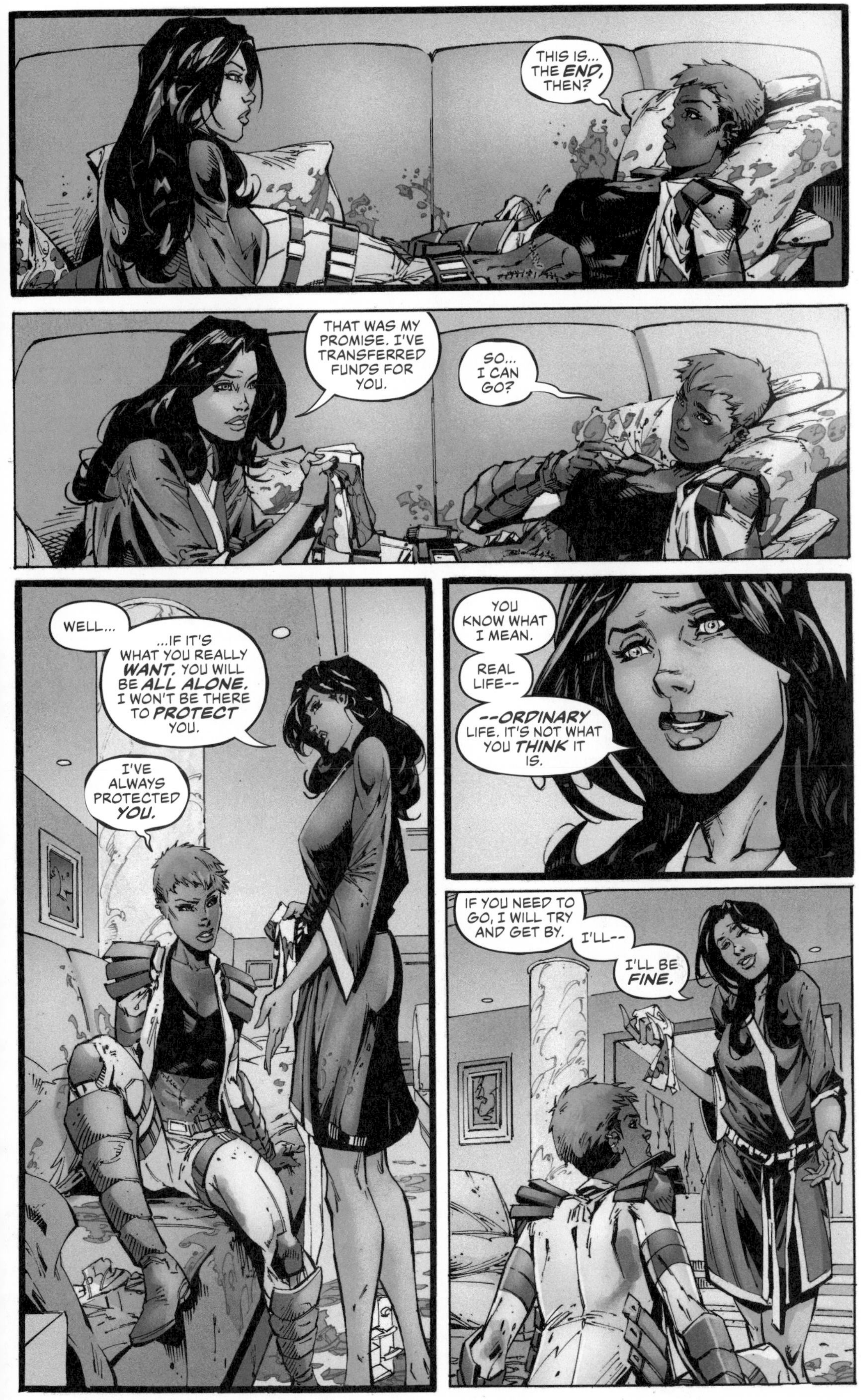
THIS IS... THE END, THEN?
THAT WAS MY PROMISE. I'VE TRANSFERRED FUNDS FOR YOU.
SO... I CAN GO?
WELL...
...IF IT'S WHAT YOU REALLY WANT. YOU WILL BE ALL ALONE. I WON'T BE THERE TO PROTECT YOU.
I'VE ALWAYS PROTECTED YOU.
YOU KNOW WHAT I MEAN.
REAL LIFE--
--ORDINARY LIFE. IT'S NOT WHAT YOU THINK IT IS.
IF YOU NEED TO GO, I WILL TRY AND GET BY.
I'LL--
I'LL BE FINE.

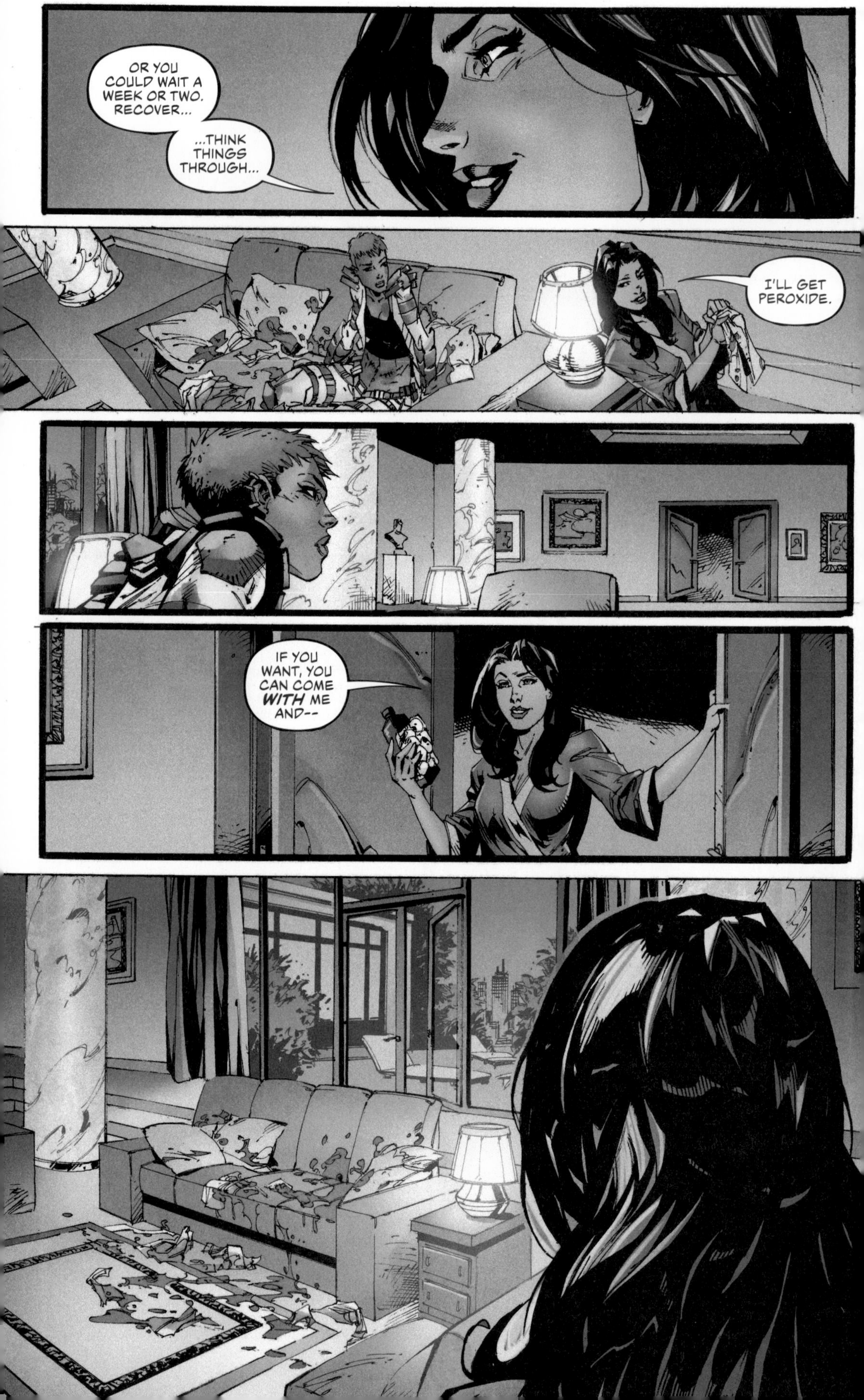
OR YOU COULD WAIT A WEEK OR TWO. RECOVER...
...THINK THINGS THROUGH...
I'LL GET PEROXIDE.
IF YOU WANT, YOU CAN COME WITH ME AND--

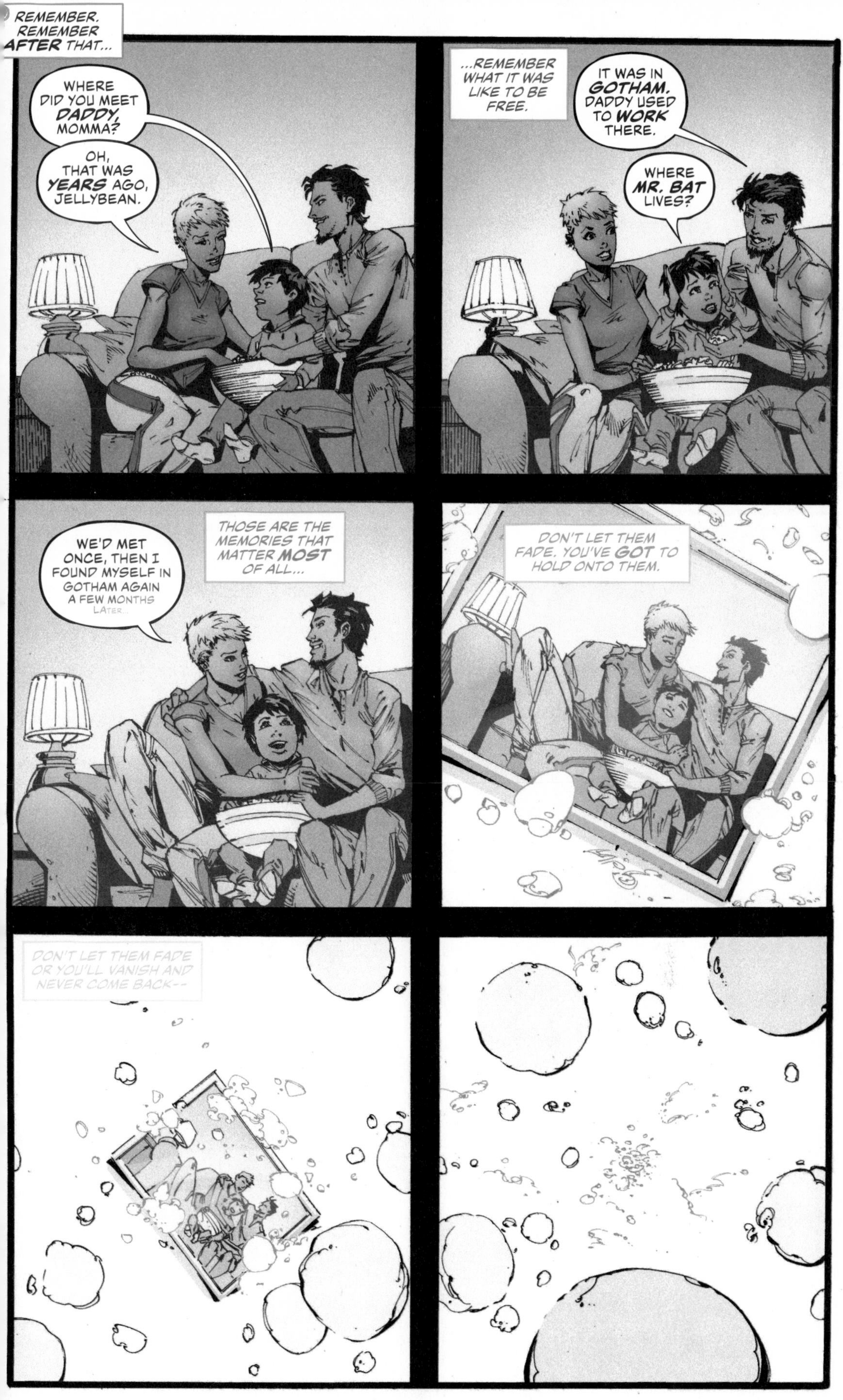
REMEMBER. REMEMBER AFTER THAT...
WHERE DID YOU MEET DADDY, MOMMA?
OH, THAT WAS YEARS AGO, JELLYBEAN.
...REMEMBER WHAT IT WAS LIKE TO BE FREE.
IT WAS IN GOTHAM. DADDY USED TO WORK THERE.
WHERE MR. BAT LIVES?
WE'D MET ONCE, THEN I FOUND MYSELF IN GOTHAM AGAIN A FEW MONTHS LATER...
THOSE ARE THE MEMORIES THAT MATTER MOST OF ALL...
DON'T LET THEM FADE. YOU'VE GOT TO HOLD ONTO THEM.
DON'T LET THEM FADE OR YOU'LL VANISH AND NEVER COME BACK--

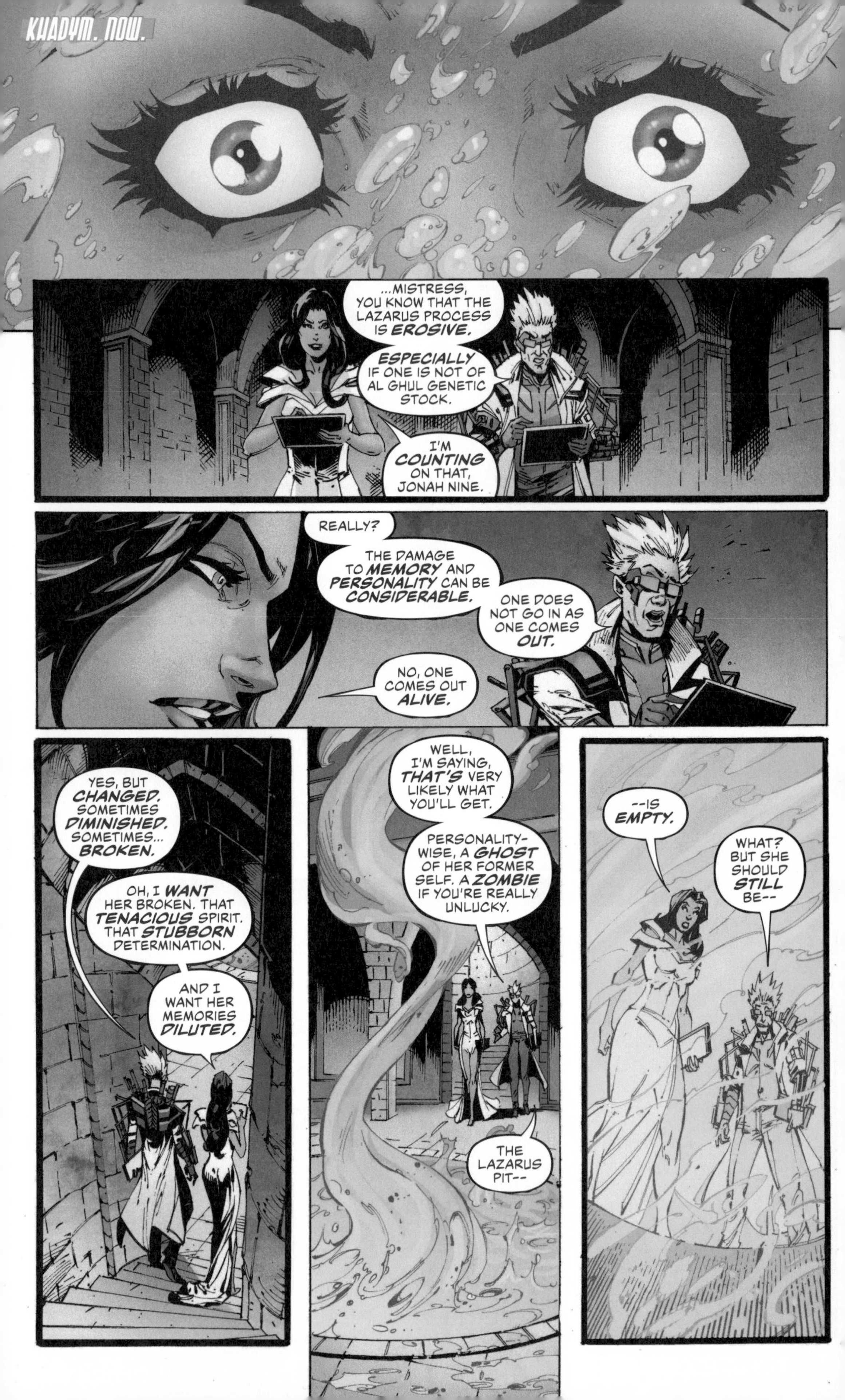

KHADYM. NOW.
...MISTRESS, YOU KNOW THAT THE LAZARUS PROCESS IS EROSIVE.
ESPECIALLY IF ONE IS NOT OF AL GHUL GENETIC STOCK.
I'M COUNTING ON THAT, JONAH NINE.
REALLY?
THE DAMAGE TO MEMORY AND PERSONALITY CAN BE CONSIDERABLE.
ONE DOES NOT GO IN AS ONE COMES OUT.
NO, ONE COMES OUT ALIVE.
YES, BUT CHANGED. SOMETIMES DIMINISHED. SOMETIMES... BROKEN.
OH, I WANT HER BROKEN. THAT TENACIOUS SPIRIT. THAT STUBBORN DETERMINATION.
AND I WANT HER MEMORIES DILUTED.
WELL, I'M SAYING, THAT'S VERY LIKELY WHAT YOU'LL GET.
PERSONALITY-WISE, A GHOST OF HER FORMER SELF. A ZOMBIE IF YOU'RE REALLY UNLUCKY.
THE LAZARUS PIT--
--IS EMPTY.
WHAT? BUT SHE SHOULD STILL BE--

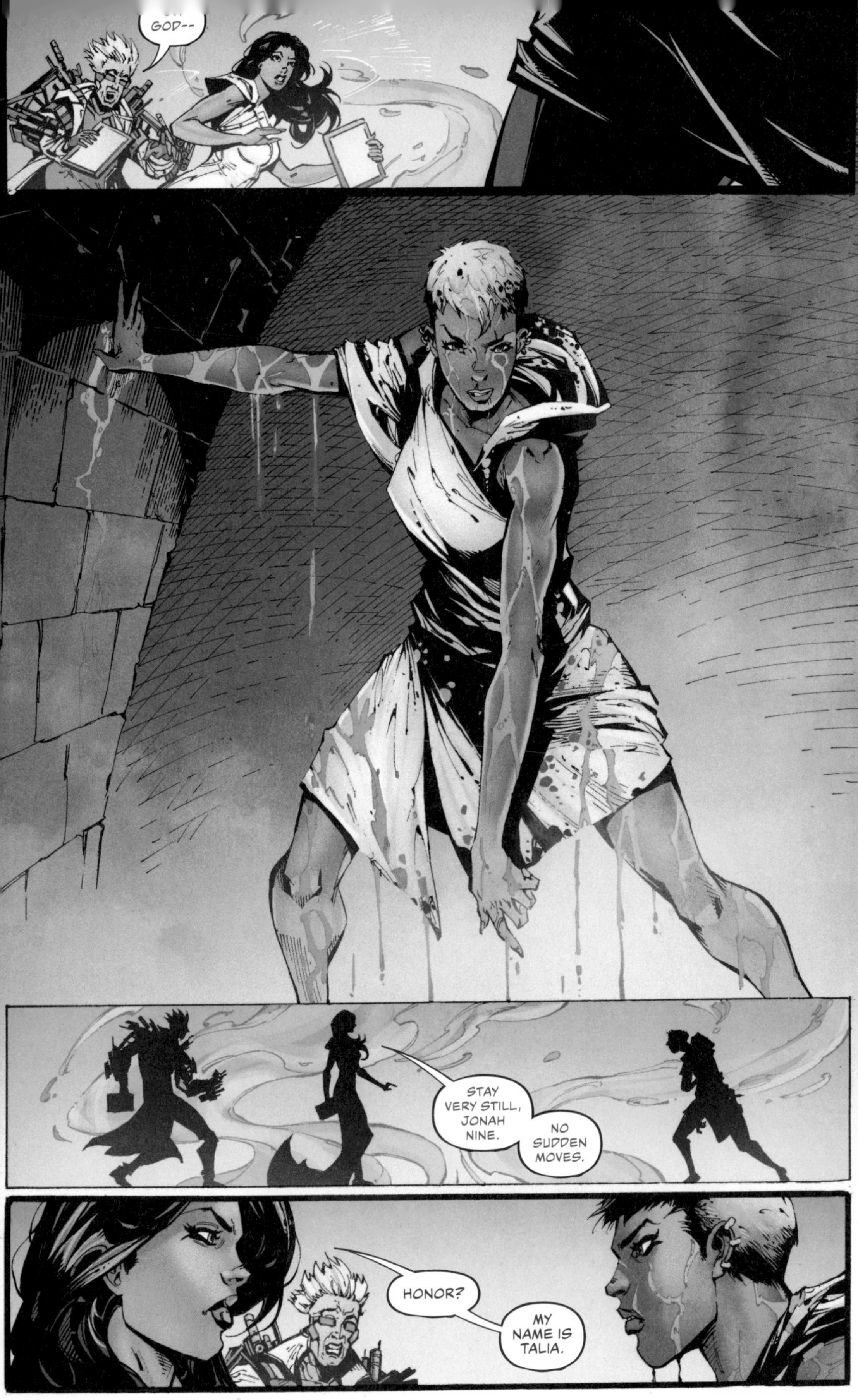
GOD--
STAY VERY STILL, JONAH NINE.
NO SUDDEN MOVES.
HONOR?
MY NAME IS TALIA.

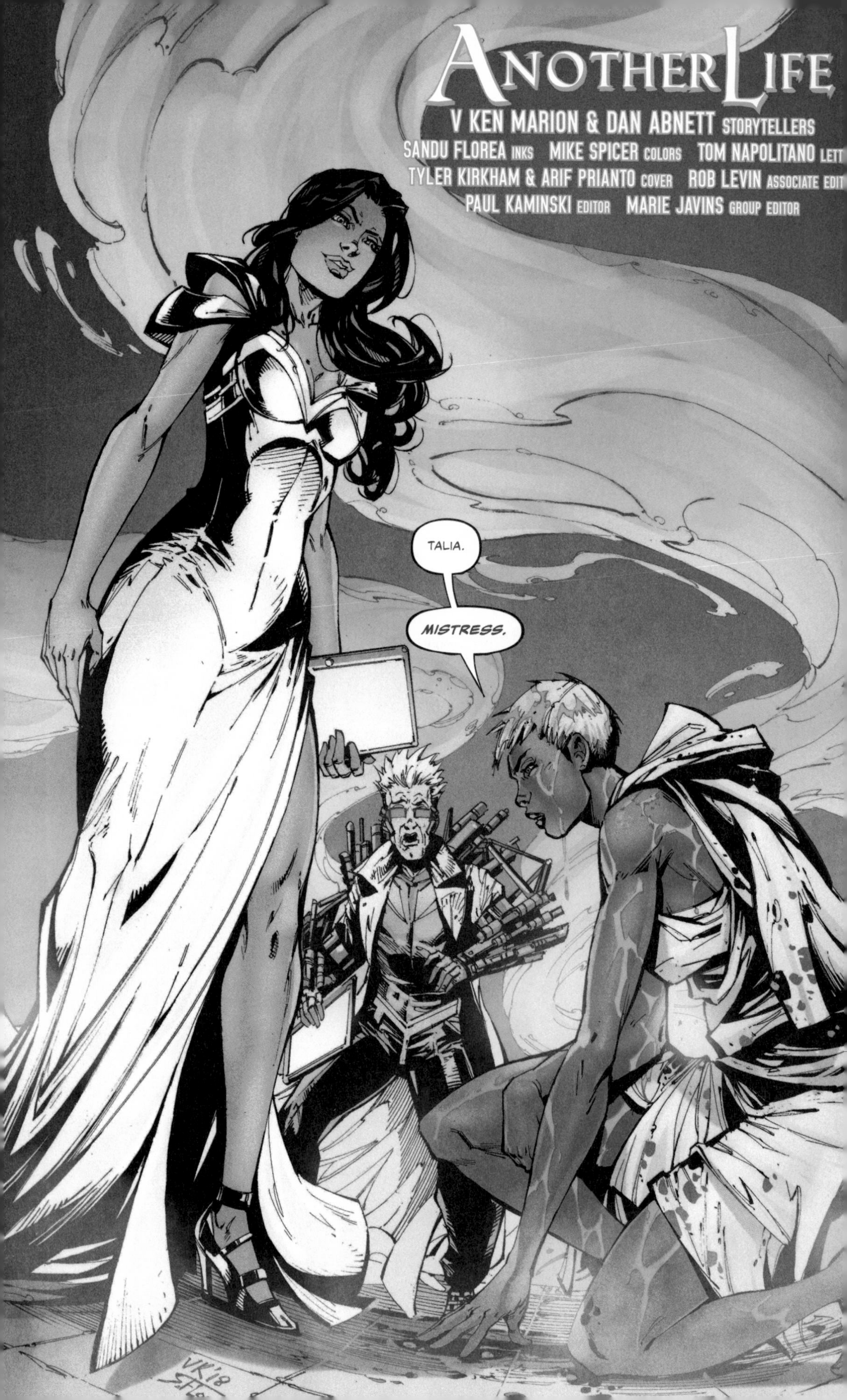
ANOTHER LIFE
V KEN MARION & DAN ABNETT STORYTELLERS
SANDU FLOREA INKS MIKE SPICER COLORS TOM NAPOLITANO LETT
TYLER KIRKHAM & ARIF PRIANTO COVER ROB LEVIN ASSOCIATE EDIT
PAUL KAMINSKI EDITOR MARIE JAVINS GROUP EDITOR
TALIA.
MISTRESS.

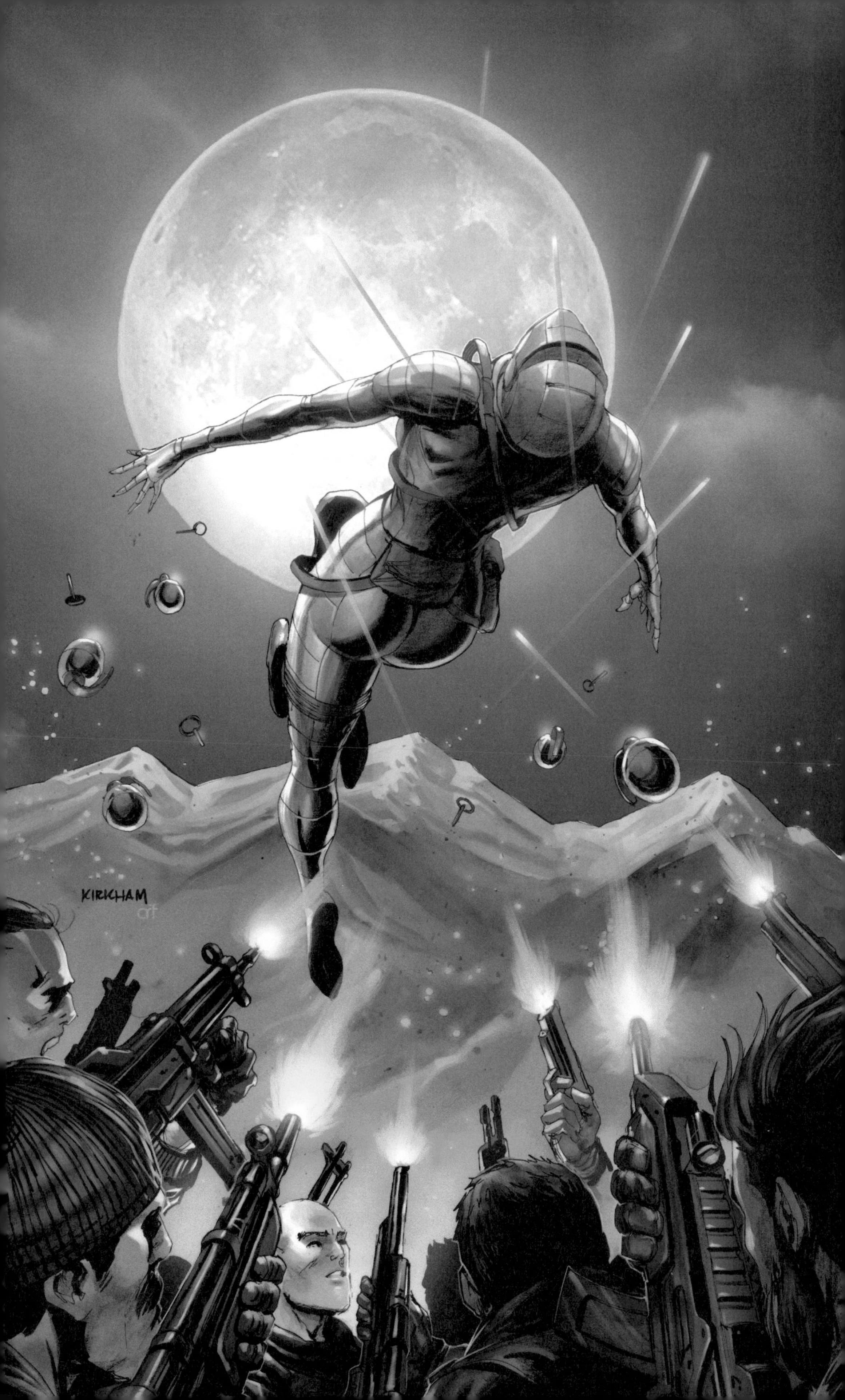
KIRKHAM
art

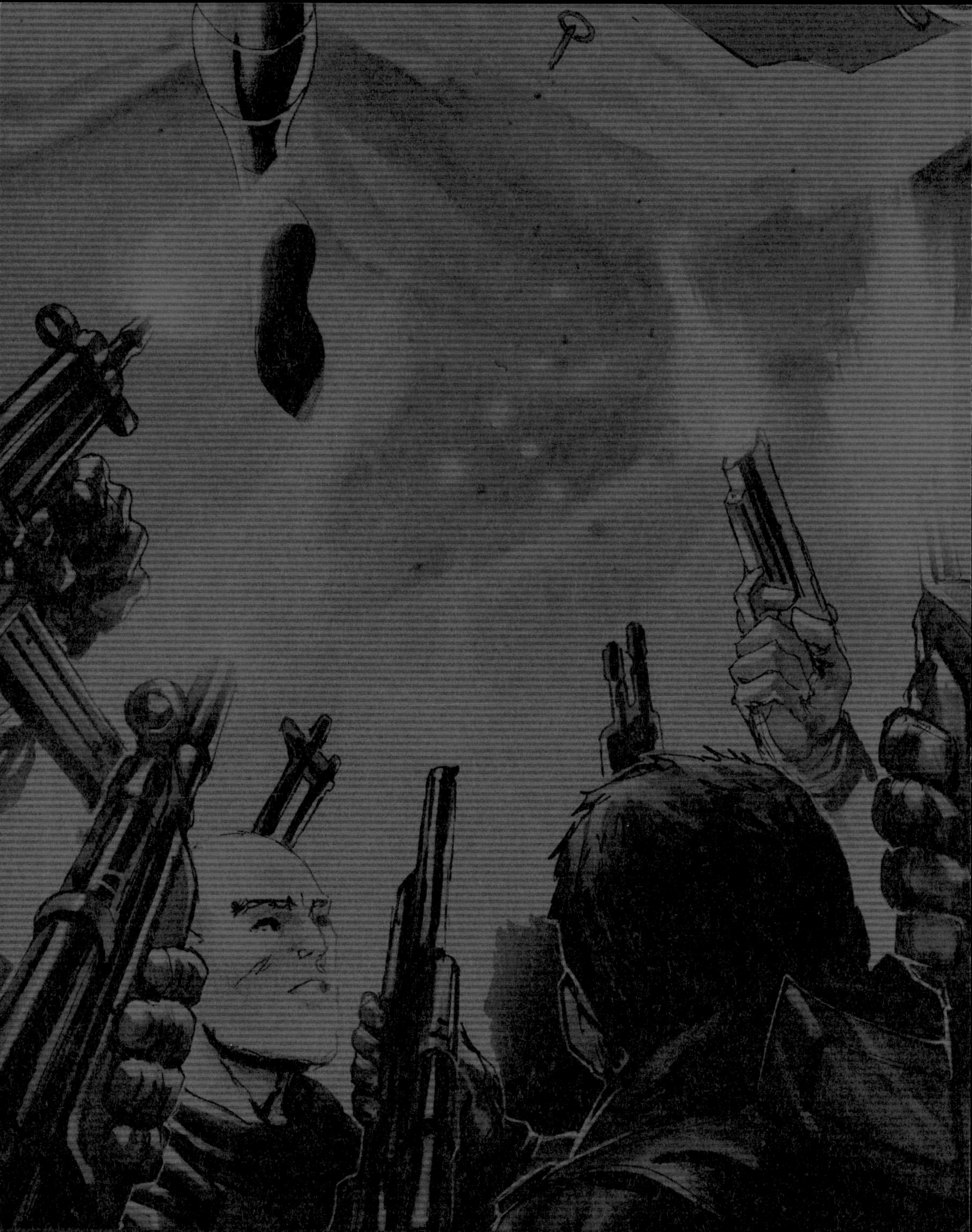

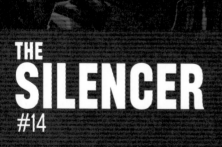

THE SILENCER
#14

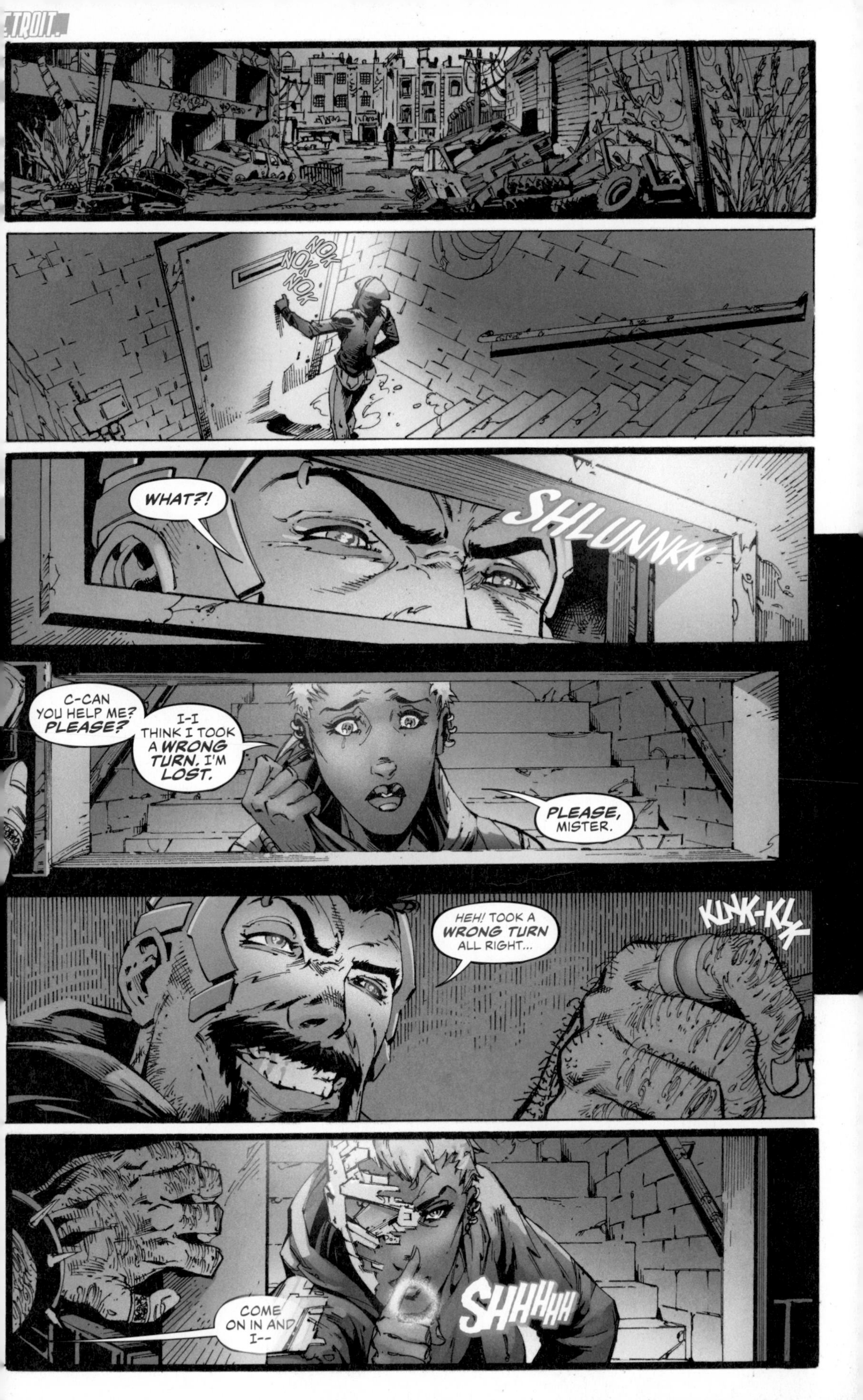

TROIT.
NOK NOK NOK
WHAT?!
SHLUNNKK
C-CAN YOU HELP ME? PLEASE?
I-I THINK I TOOK A WRONG TURN. I'M LOST.
PLEASE, MISTER.
HEH! TOOK A WRONG TURN ALL RIGHT...
KLNK-KLK
COME ON IN AND I--
SHHHHH

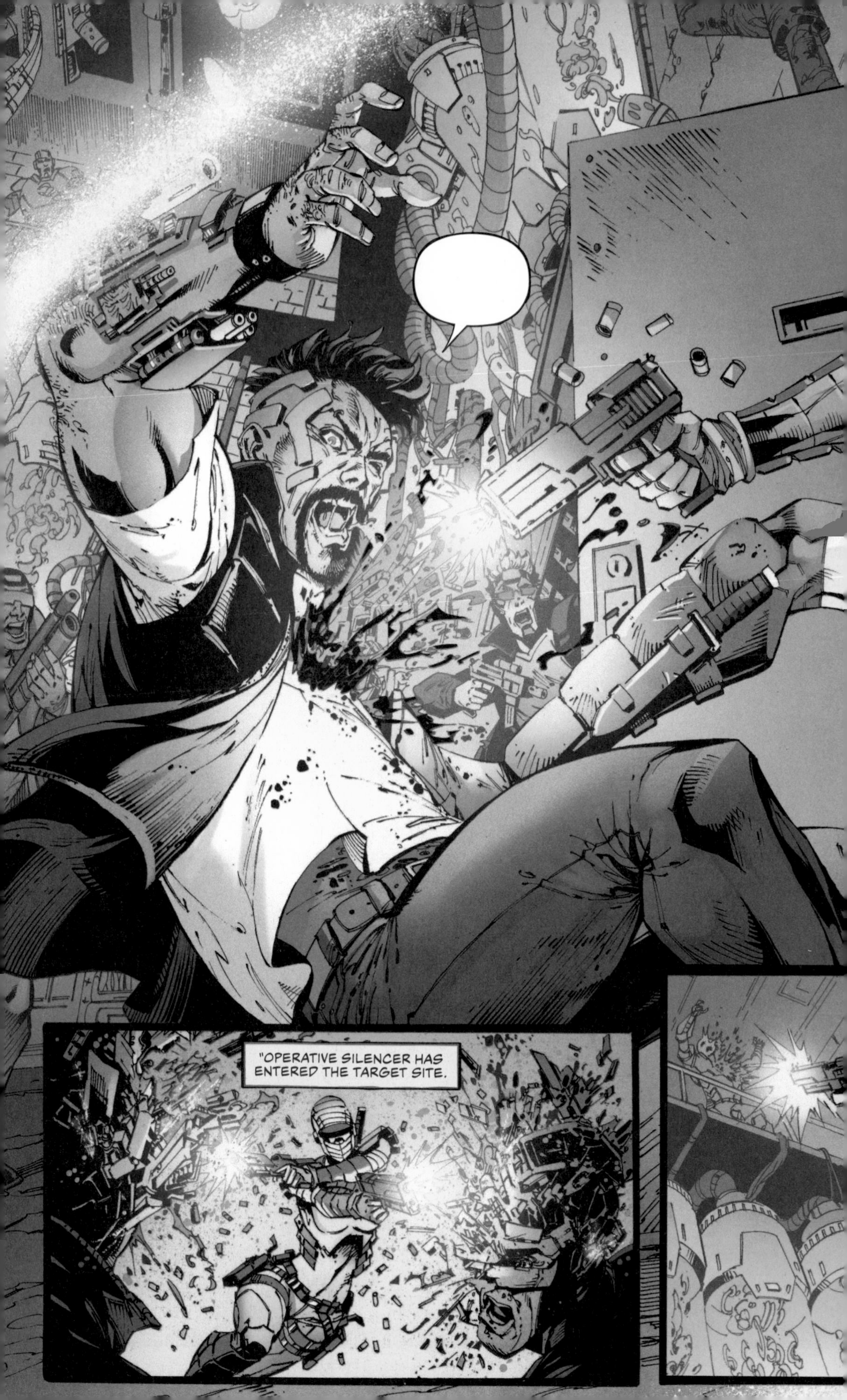
"OPERATIVE SILENCER HAS
ENTERED THE TARGET SITE.

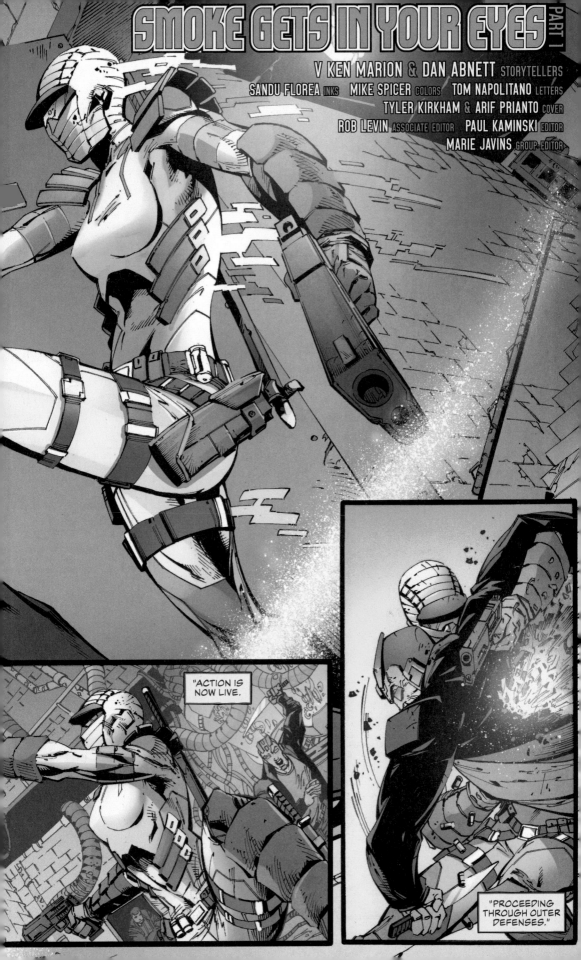

SMOKE GETS IN YOUR EYES PART 1

V KEN MARION & DAN ABNETT STORYTELLERS

SANDU FLOREA INKS   MIKE SPICER COLORS   TOM NAPOLITANO LETTERS

TYLER KIRKHAM & ARIF PRIANTO COVER

ROB LEVIN ASSOCIATE EDITOR   PAUL KAMINSKI EDITOR

MARIE JAVINS GROUP EDITOR

"ACTION IS NOW LIVE.

"PROCEEDING THROUGH OUTER DEFENSES."

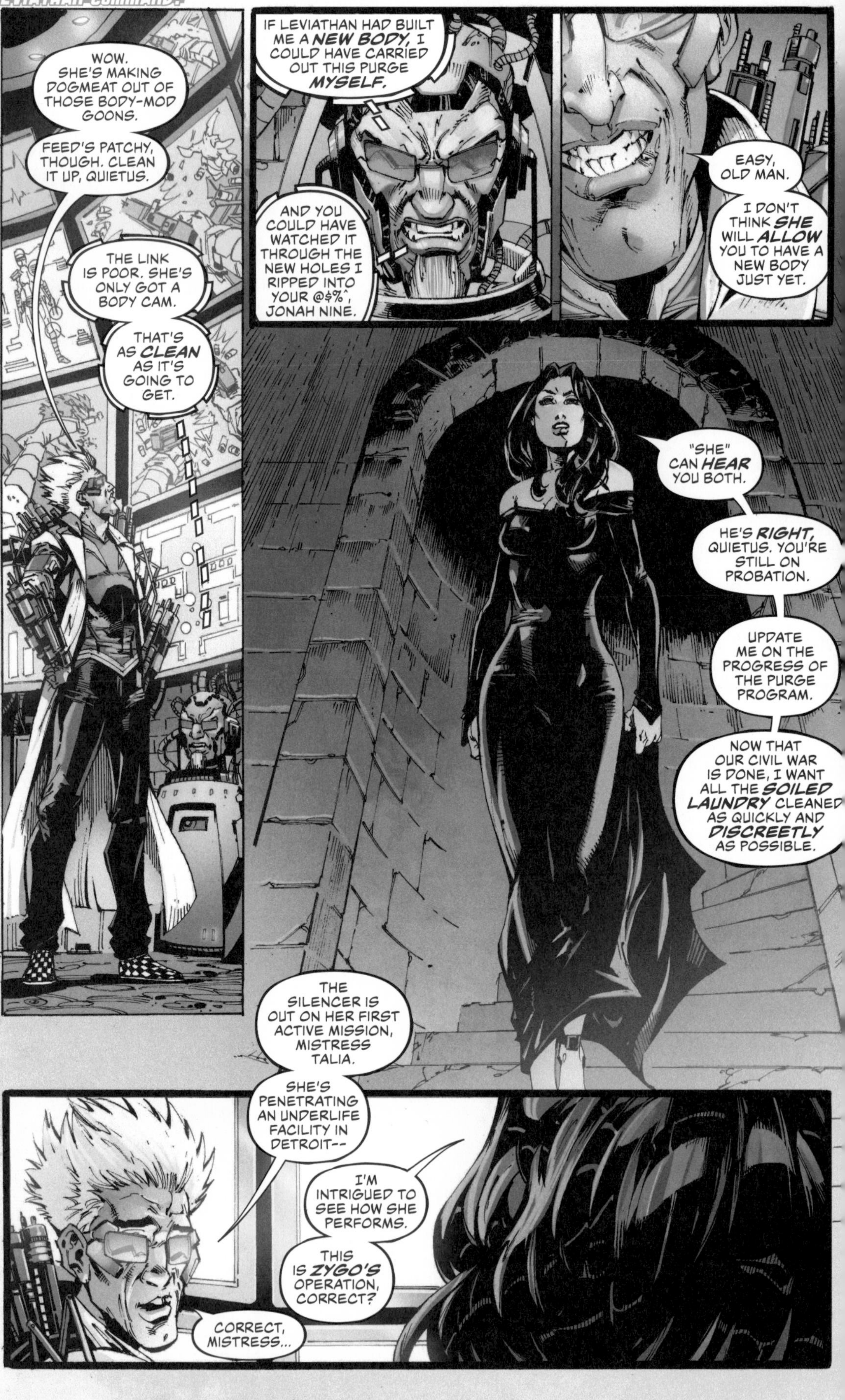
WOW. SHE'S MAKING DOGMEAT OUT OF THOSE BODY-MOD GOONS.
FEED'S PATCHY, THOUGH. CLEAN IT UP, QUIETUS.
THE LINK IS POOR. SHE'S ONLY GOT A BODY CAM.
THAT'S AS CLEAN AS IT'S GOING TO GET.
IF LEVIATHAN HAD BUILT ME A NEW BODY, I COULD HAVE CARRIED OUT THIS PURGE MYSELF.
AND YOU COULD HAVE WATCHED IT THROUGH THE NEW HOLES I RIPPED INTO YOUR @$%^, JONAH NINE.
EASY, OLD MAN.
I DON'T THINK SHE WILL ALLOW YOU TO HAVE A NEW BODY JUST YET.
"SHE" CAN HEAR YOU BOTH.
HE'S RIGHT, QUIETUS. YOU'RE STILL ON PROBATION.
UPDATE ME ON THE PROGRESS OF THE PURGE PROGRAM.
NOW THAT OUR CIVIL WAR IS DONE, I WANT ALL THE SOILED LAUNDRY CLEANED AS QUICKLY AND DISCREETLY AS POSSIBLE.
THE SILENCER IS OUT ON HER FIRST ACTIVE MISSION, MISTRESS TALIA.
SHE'S PENETRATING AN UNDERLIFE FACILITY IN DETROIT--
I'M INTRIGUED TO SEE HOW SHE PERFORMS.
THIS IS ZYGO'S OPERATION, CORRECT?
CORRECT, MISTRESS...

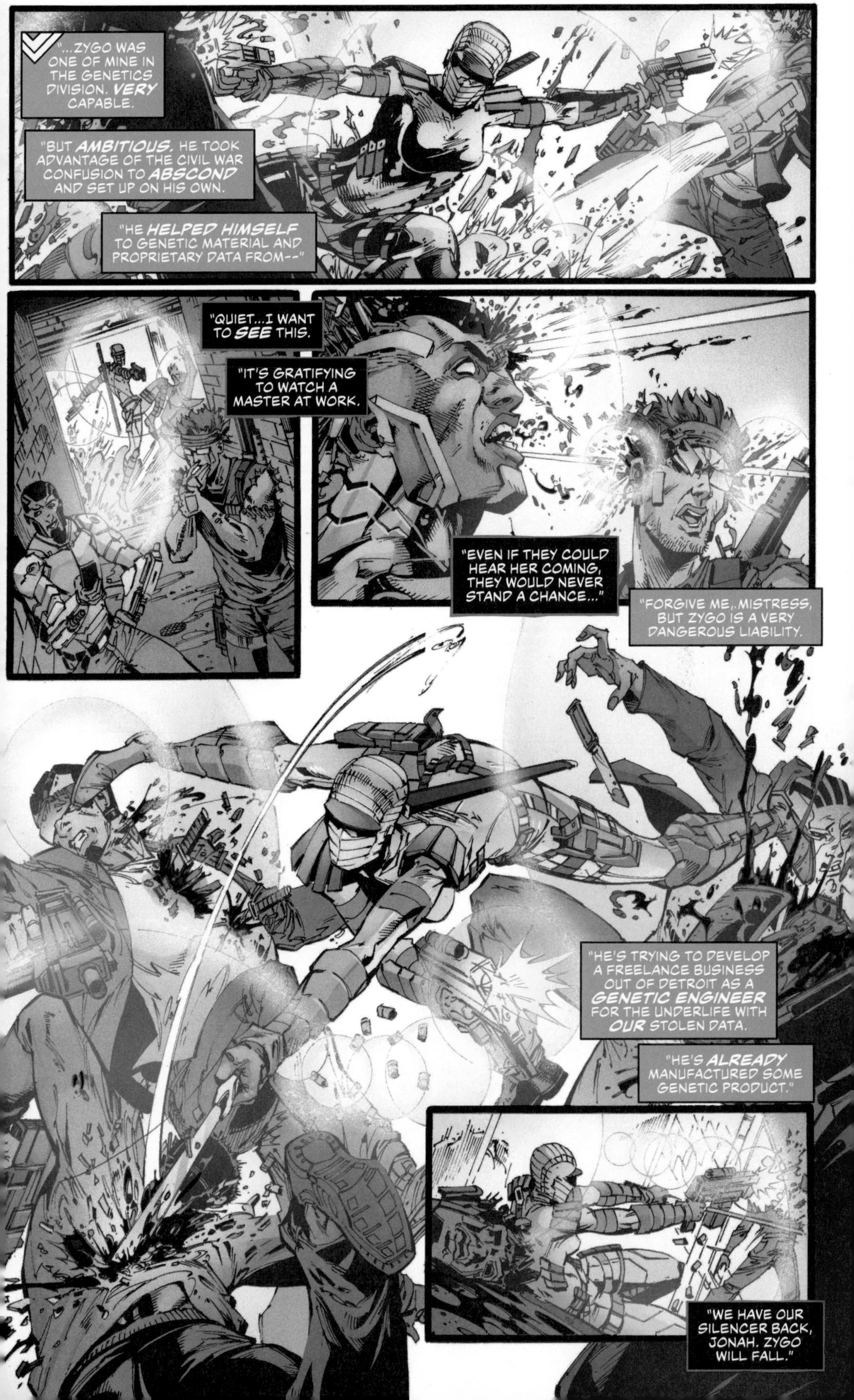
"...ZYGO WAS ONE OF MINE IN THE GENETICS DIVISION. VERY CAPABLE.
"BUT AMBITIOUS. HE TOOK ADVANTAGE OF THE CIVIL WAR CONFUSION TO ABSCOND AND SET UP ON HIS OWN.
"HE HELPED HIMSELF TO GENETIC MATERIAL AND PROPRIETARY DATA FROM--"
"QUIET...I WANT TO SEE THIS.
"IT'S GRATIFYING TO WATCH A MASTER AT WORK.
"EVEN IF THEY COULD HEAR HER COMING, THEY WOULD NEVER STAND A CHANCE..."
"FORGIVE ME, MISTRESS, BUT ZYGO IS A VERY DANGEROUS LIABILITY.
"HE'S TRYING TO DEVELOP A FREELANCE BUSINESS OUT OF DETROIT AS A GENETIC ENGINEER FOR THE UNDERLIFE WITH OUR STOLEN DATA.
"HE'S ALREADY MANUFACTURED SOME GENETIC PRODUCT."
"WE HAVE OUR SILENCER BACK, JONAH. ZYGO WILL FALL."

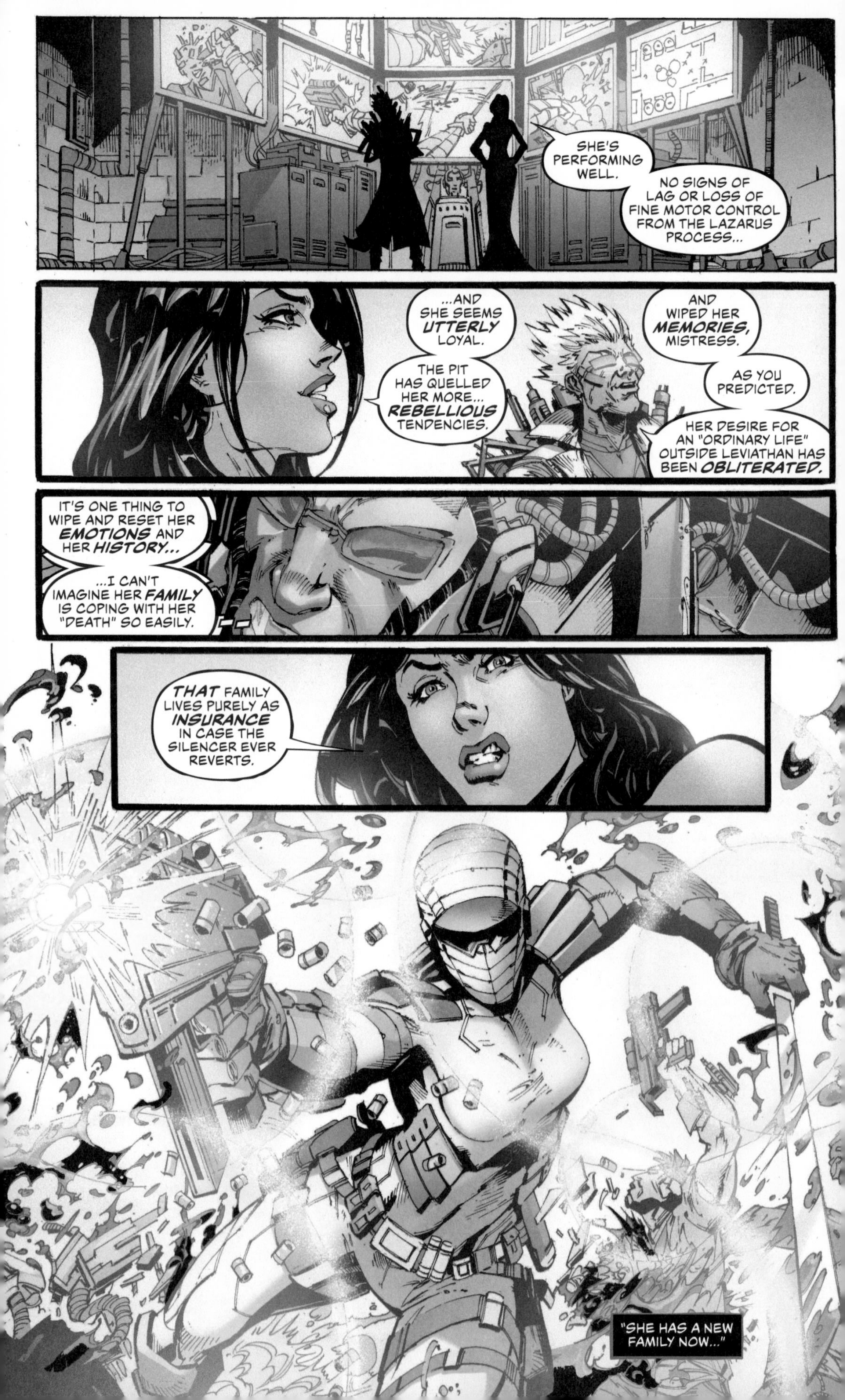

SHE'S PERFORMING WELL.
NO SIGNS OF LAG OR LOSS OF FINE MOTOR CONTROL FROM THE LAZARUS PROCESS...
...AND SHE SEEMS UTTERLY LOYAL.
THE PIT HAS QUELLED HER MORE... REBELLIOUS TENDENCIES.
AND WIPED HER MEMORIES, MISTRESS.
AS YOU PREDICTED.
HER DESIRE FOR AN "ORDINARY LIFE" OUTSIDE LEVIATHAN HAS BEEN OBLITERATED.
IT'S ONE THING TO WIPE AND RESET HER EMOTIONS AND HER HISTORY...
...I CAN'T IMAGINE HER FAMILY IS COPING WITH HER "DEATH" SO EASILY.
THAT FAMILY LIVES PURELY AS INSURANCE IN CASE THE SILENCER EVER REVERTS.
"SHE HAS A NEW FAMILY NOW..."

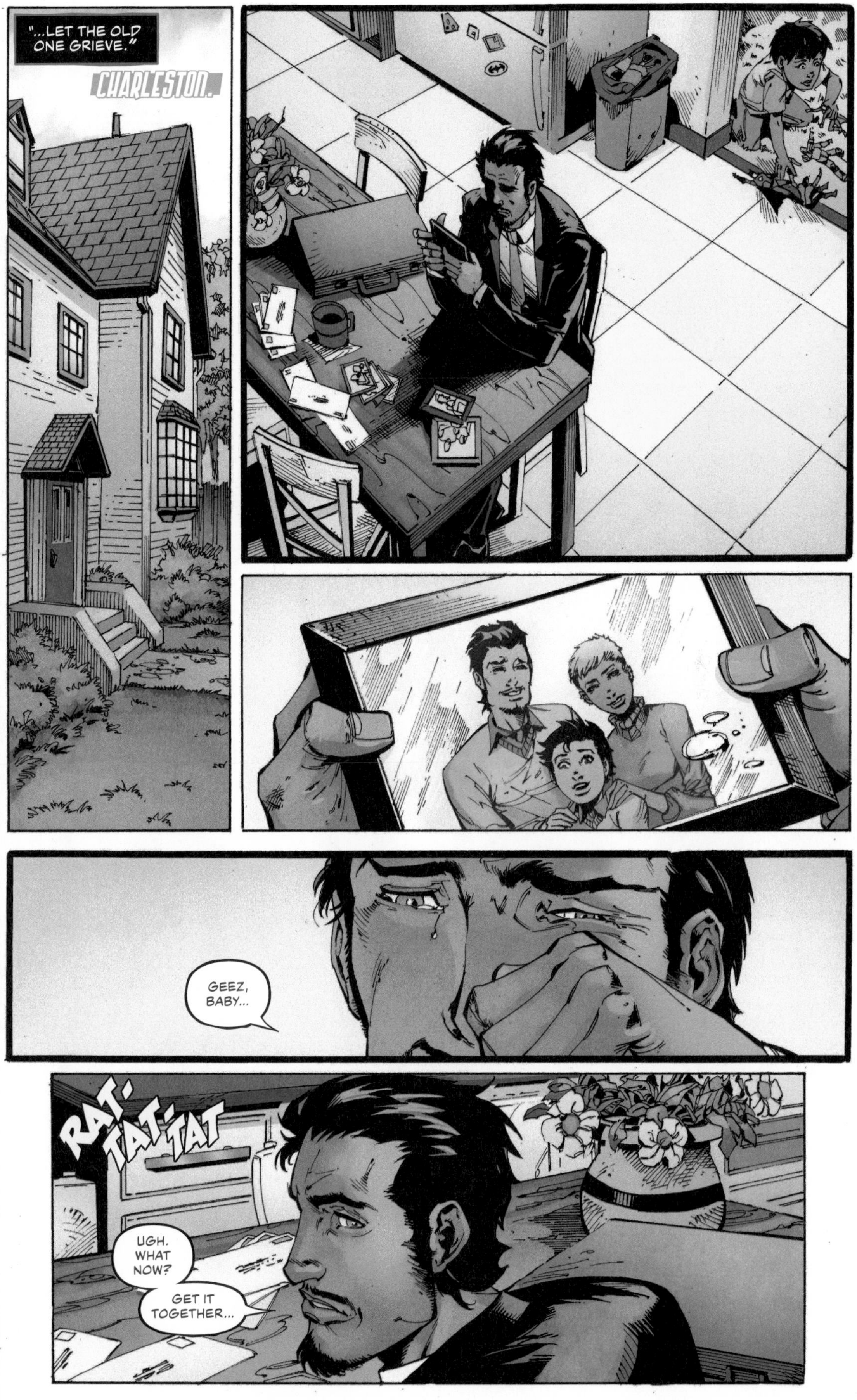
"...LET THE OLD ONE GRIEVE."
CHARLESTON.
GEEZ, BABY...
RAT-TAT-TAT
UGH. WHAT NOW?
GET IT TOGETHER...

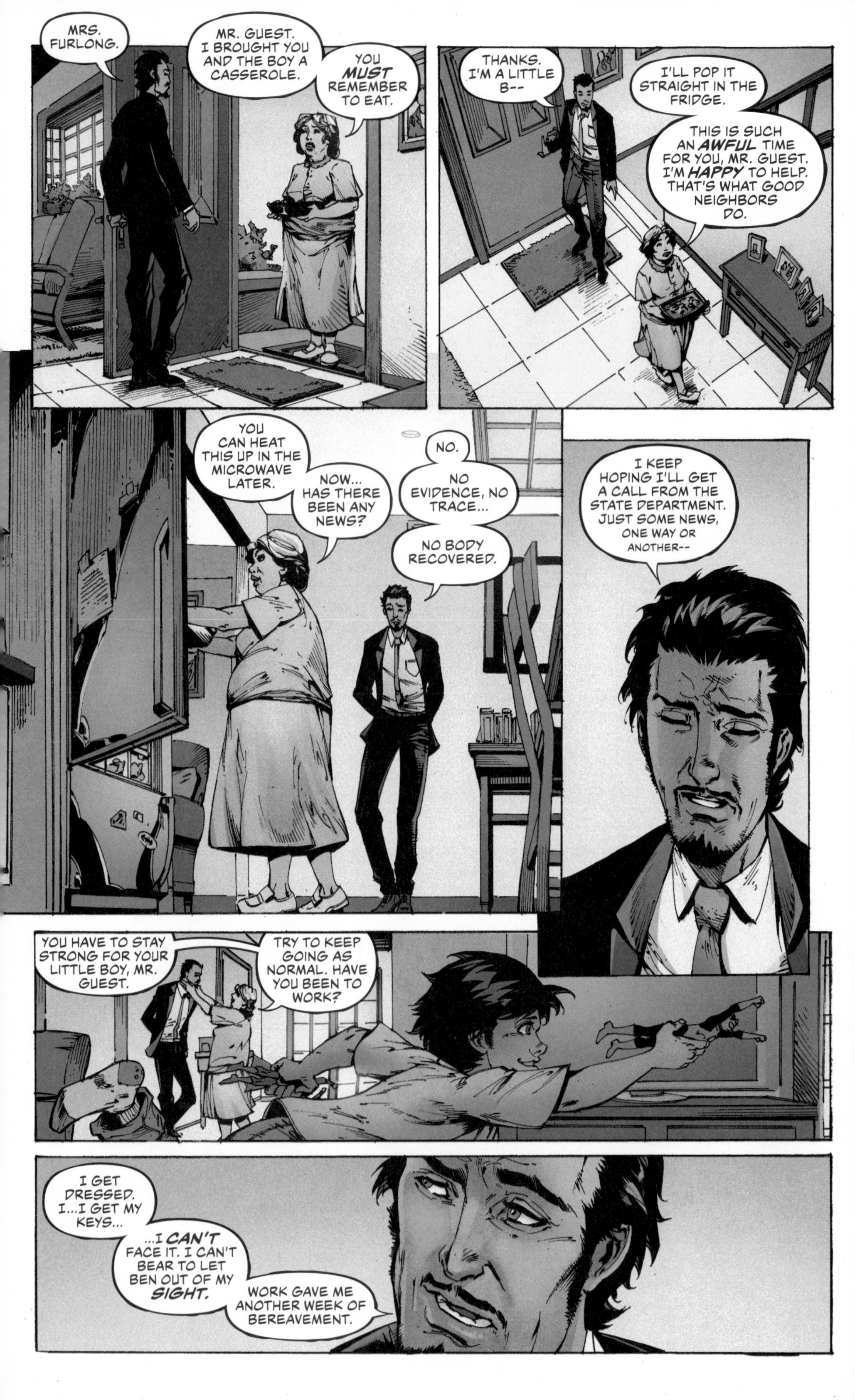
MRS. FURLONG.
MR. GUEST. I BROUGHT YOU AND THE BOY A CASSEROLE.
YOU MUST REMEMBER TO EAT.
THANKS. I'M A LITTLE B--
I'LL POP IT STRAIGHT IN THE FRIDGE.
THIS IS SUCH AN AWFUL TIME FOR YOU, MR. GUEST. I'M HAPPY TO HELP. THAT'S WHAT GOOD NEIGHBORS DO.
YOU CAN HEAT THIS UP IN THE MICROWAVE LATER.
NOW... HAS THERE BEEN ANY NEWS?
NO.
NO EVIDENCE, NO TRACE...
NO BODY RECOVERED.
I KEEP HOPING I'LL GET A CALL FROM THE STATE DEPARTMENT. JUST SOME NEWS, ONE WAY OR ANOTHER--
YOU HAVE TO STAY STRONG FOR YOUR LITTLE BOY, MR. GUEST.
TRY TO KEEP GOING AS NORMAL. HAVE YOU BEEN TO WORK?
I GET DRESSED. I...I GET MY KEYS...
...I CAN'T FACE IT. I CAN'T BEAR TO LET BEN OUT OF MY SIGHT.
WORK GAVE ME ANOTHER WEEK OF BEREAVEMENT.

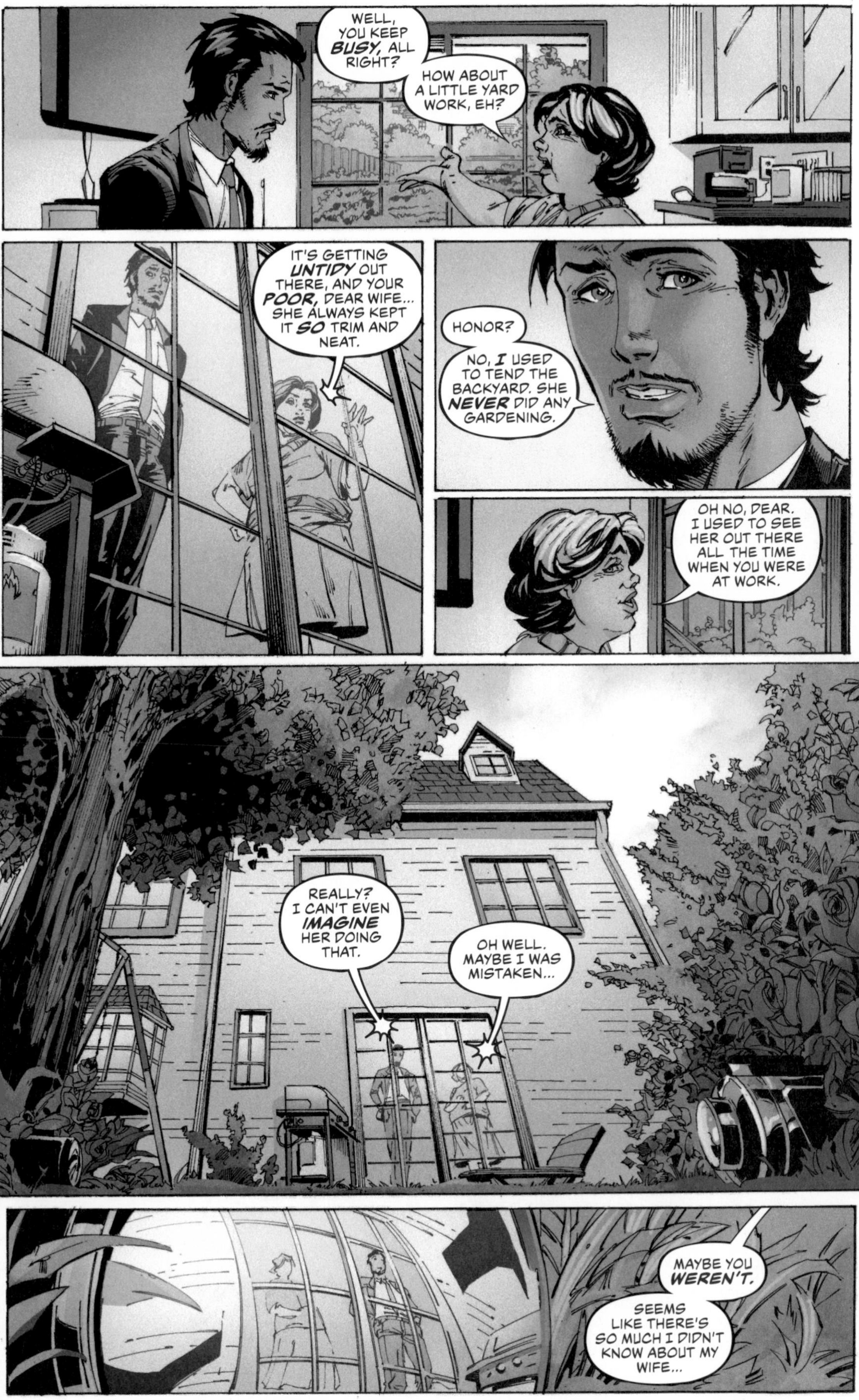
WELL, YOU KEEP BUSY, ALL RIGHT?
HOW ABOUT A LITTLE YARD WORK, EH?
IT'S GETTING UNTIDY OUT THERE, AND YOUR POOR, DEAR WIFE... SHE ALWAYS KEPT IT SO TRIM AND NEAT.
HONOR?
NO, I USED TO TEND THE BACKYARD. SHE NEVER DID ANY GARDENING.
OH NO, DEAR. I USED TO SEE HER OUT THERE ALL THE TIME WHEN YOU WERE AT WORK.
REALLY? I CAN'T EVEN IMAGINE HER DOING THAT.
OH WELL. MAYBE I WAS MISTAKEN...
MAYBE YOU WEREN'T.
SEEMS LIKE THERE'S SO MUCH I DIDN'T KNOW ABOUT MY WIFE...

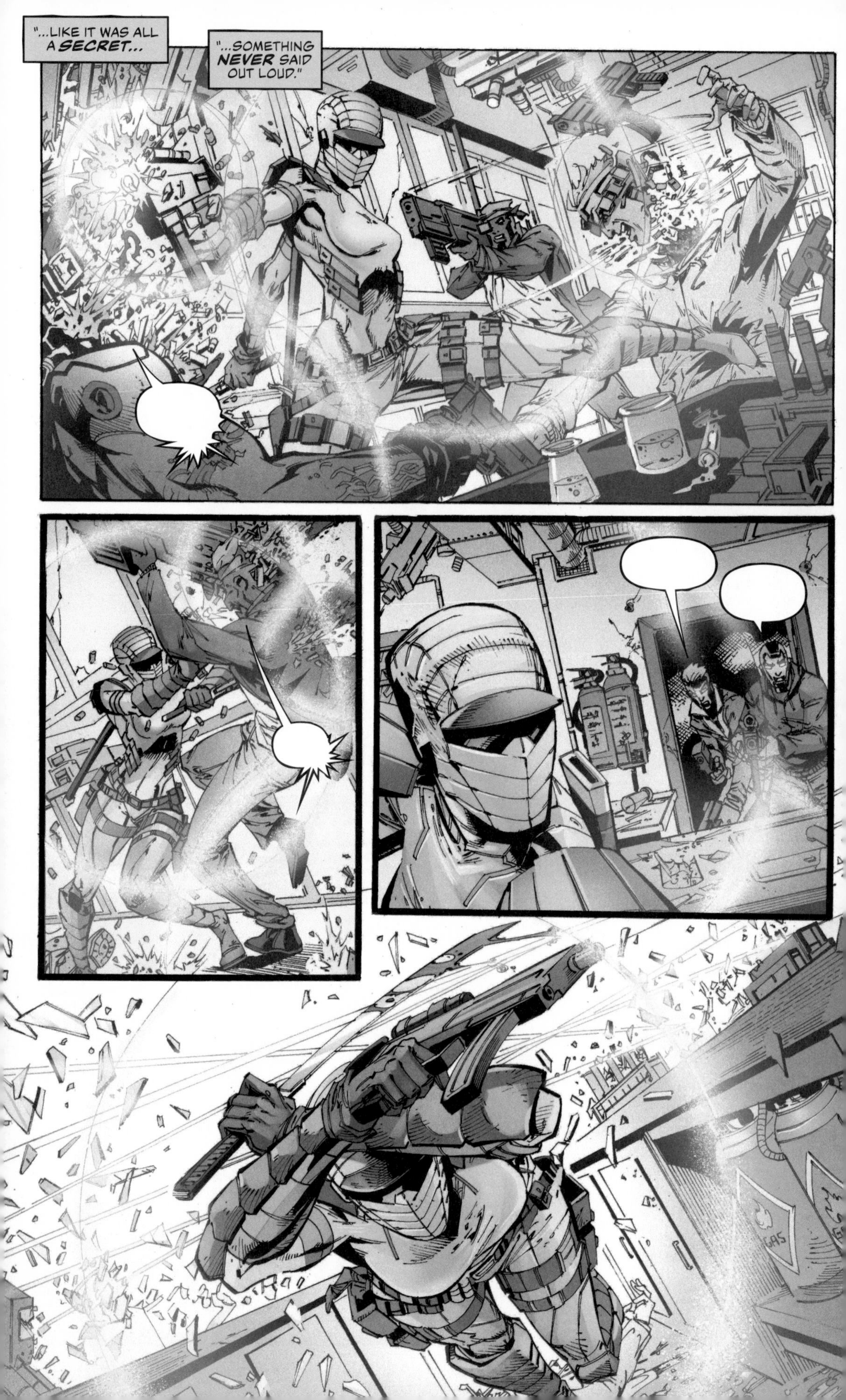
"...LIKE IT WAS ALL A SECRET...
"...SOMETHING NEVER SAID OUT LOUD."

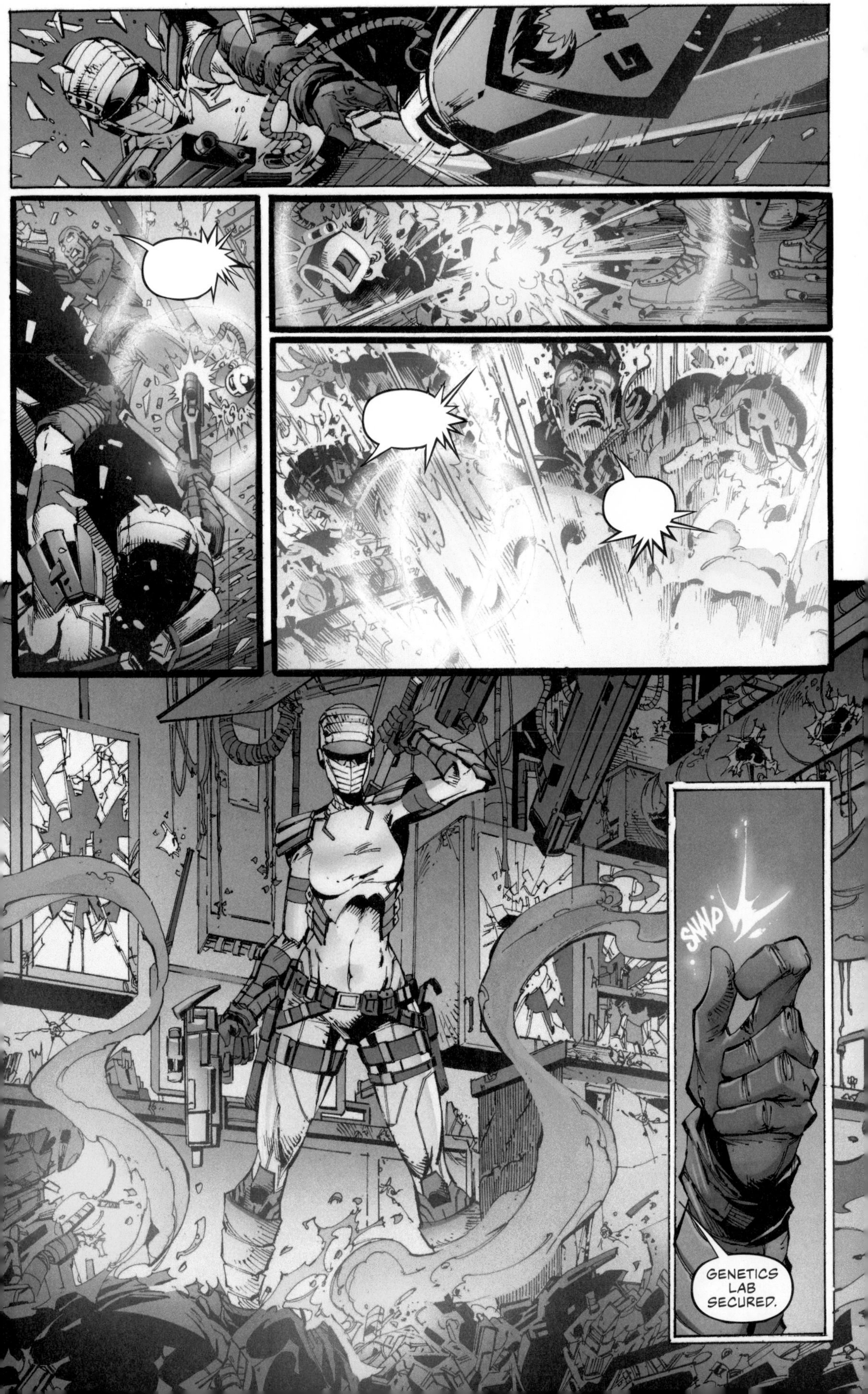
SNAP
GENETICS LAB SECURED.

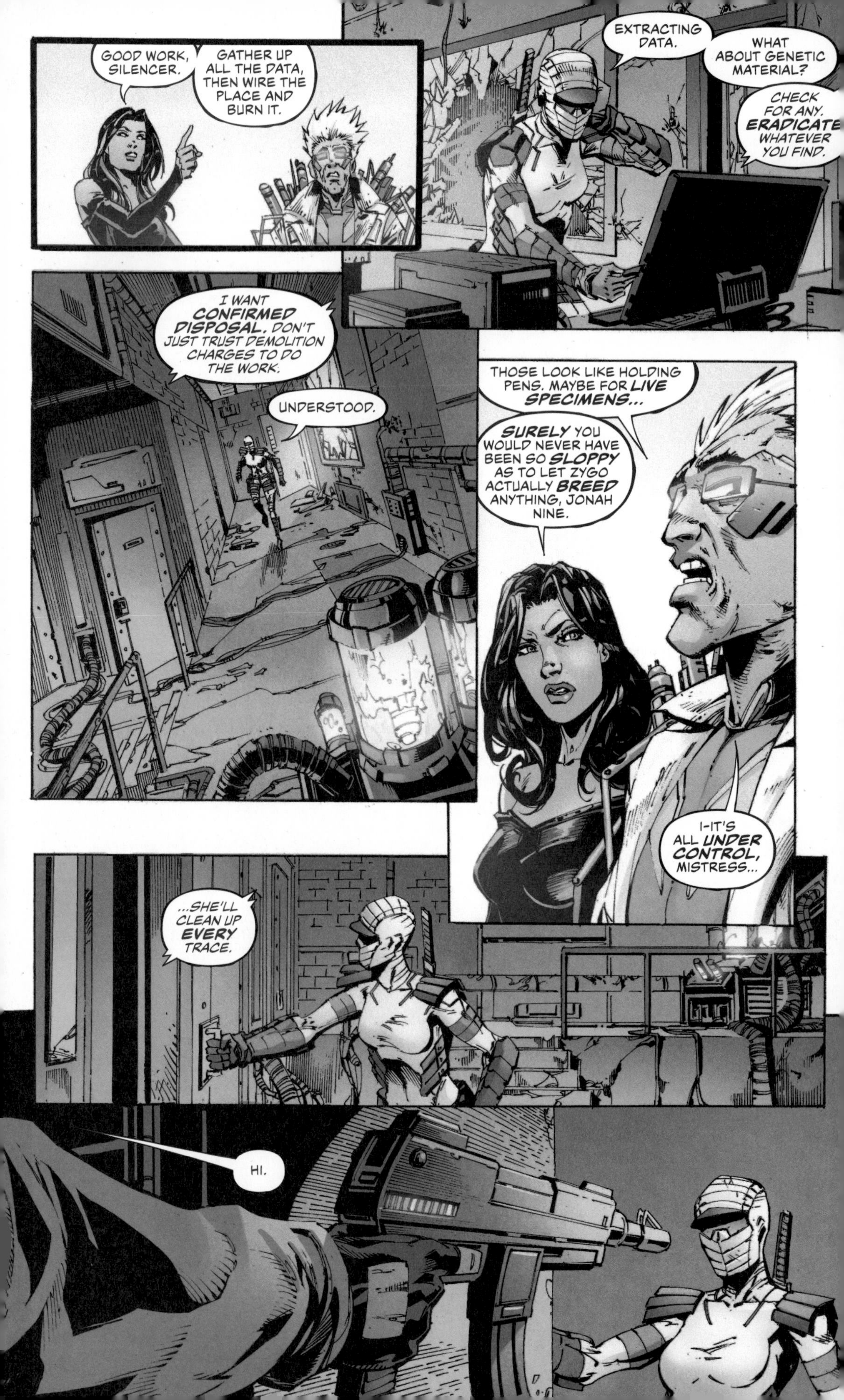
GOOD WORK, SILENCER.
GATHER UP ALL THE DATA, THEN WIRE THE PLACE AND BURN IT.
EXTRACTING DATA.
WHAT ABOUT GENETIC MATERIAL?
CHECK FOR ANY. ERADICATE WHATEVER YOU FIND.
I WANT CONFIRMED DISPOSAL. DON'T JUST TRUST DEMOLITION CHARGES TO DO THE WORK.
UNDERSTOOD.
THOSE LOOK LIKE HOLDING PENS. MAYBE FOR LIVE SPECIMENS...
SURELY YOU WOULD NEVER HAVE BEEN SO SLOPPY AS TO LET ZYGO ACTUALLY BREED ANYTHING, JONAH NINE.
I-IT'S ALL UNDER CONTROL, MISTRESS...
...SHE'LL CLEAN UP EVERY TRACE.
HI.

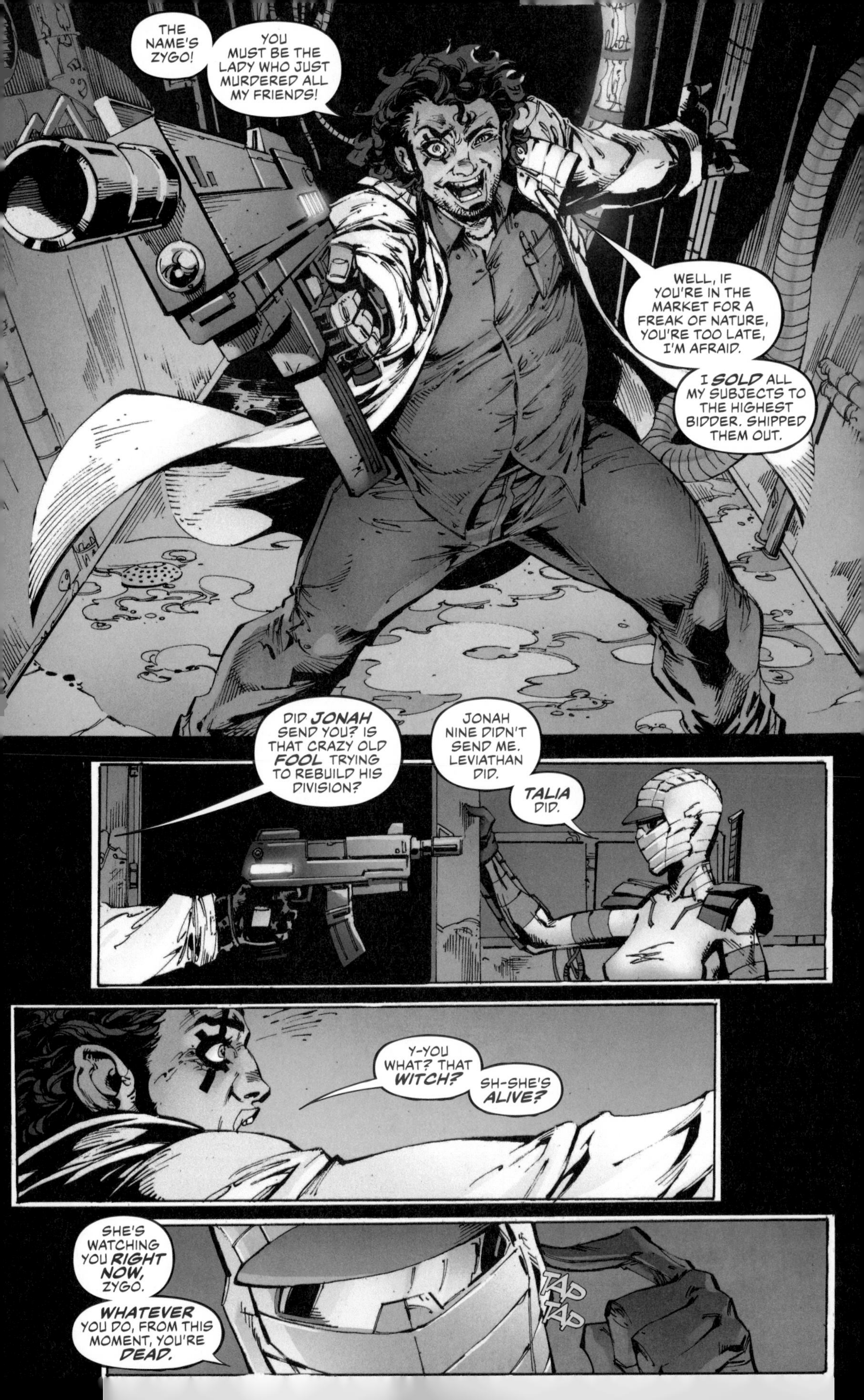
THE NAME'S ZYGO!
YOU MUST BE THE LADY WHO JUST MURDERED ALL MY FRIENDS!
WELL, IF YOU'RE IN THE MARKET FOR A FREAK OF NATURE, YOU'RE TOO LATE, I'M AFRAID.
I SOLD ALL MY SUBJECTS TO THE HIGHEST BIDDER. SHIPPED THEM OUT.
DID JONAH SEND YOU? IS THAT CRAZY OLD FOOL TRYING TO REBUILD HIS DIVISION?
JONAH NINE DIDN'T SEND ME. LEVIATHAN DID.
TALIA DID.
Y-YOU WHAT? THAT WITCH?
SH-SHE'S ALIVE?
SHE'S WATCHING YOU RIGHT NOW, ZYGO.
WHATEVER YOU DO, FROM THIS MOMENT, YOU'RE DEAD.
TAP TAP

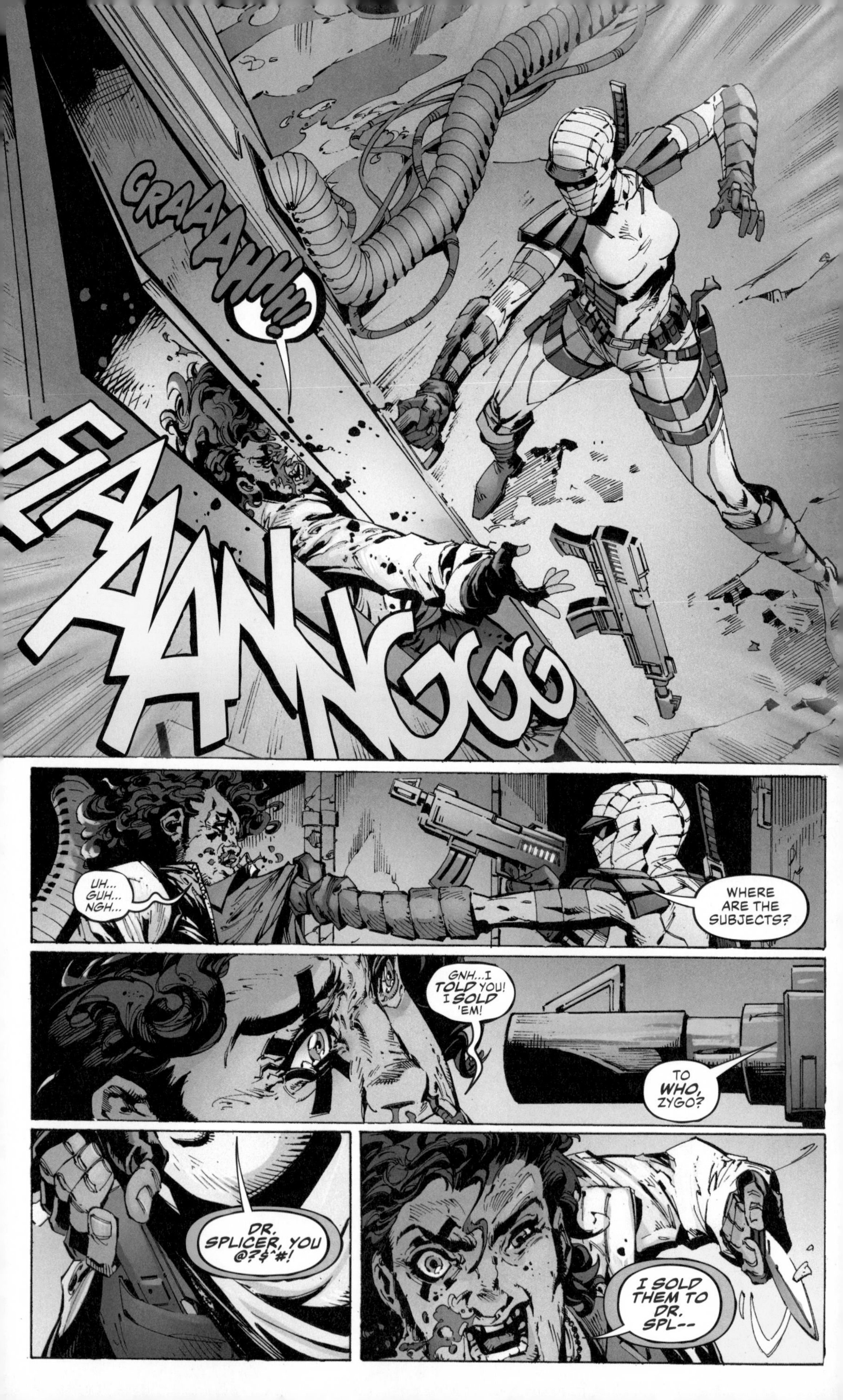
GRAAAHHH!
FFAANNGGG
UH... GUH... NGH...
WHERE ARE THE SUBJECTS?
GNH...I TOLD YOU! I SOLD 'EM!
TO WHO, ZYGO?
DR. SPLICER, YOU @?$^#!
I SOLD THEM TO DR. SPL--

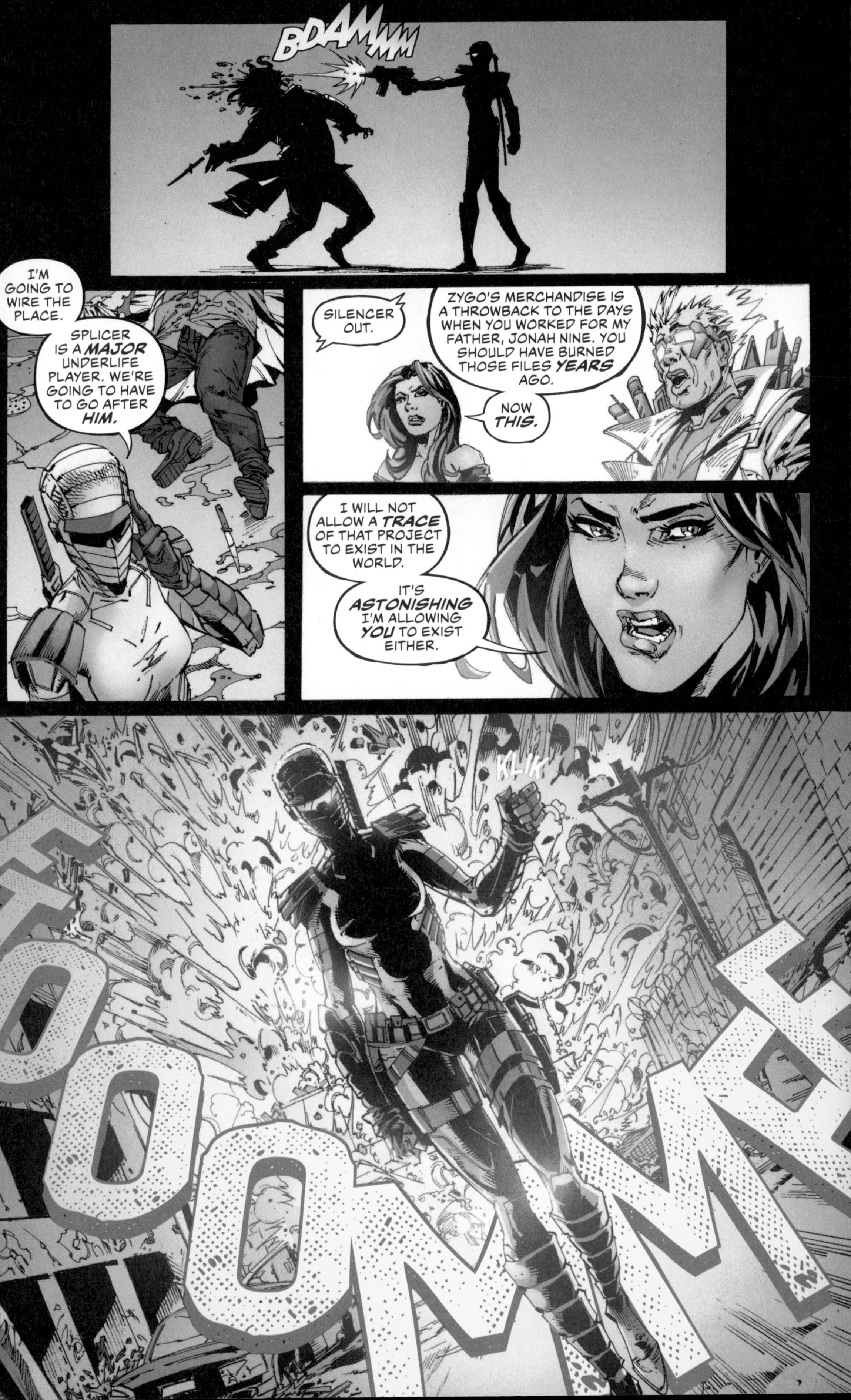
BDAMMM
I'M GOING TO WIRE THE PLACE.
SPLICER IS A MAJOR UNDERLIFE PLAYER. WE'RE GOING TO HAVE TO GO AFTER HIM.
SILENCER OUT.
ZYGO'S MERCHANDISE IS A THROWBACK TO THE DAYS WHEN YOU WORKED FOR MY FATHER, JONAH NINE. YOU SHOULD HAVE BURNED THOSE FILES YEARS AGO.
NOW THIS.
I WILL NOT ALLOW A TRACE OF THAT PROJECT TO EXIST IN THE WORLD.
IT'S ASTONISHING I'M ALLOWING YOU TO EXIST EITHER.
KLIK

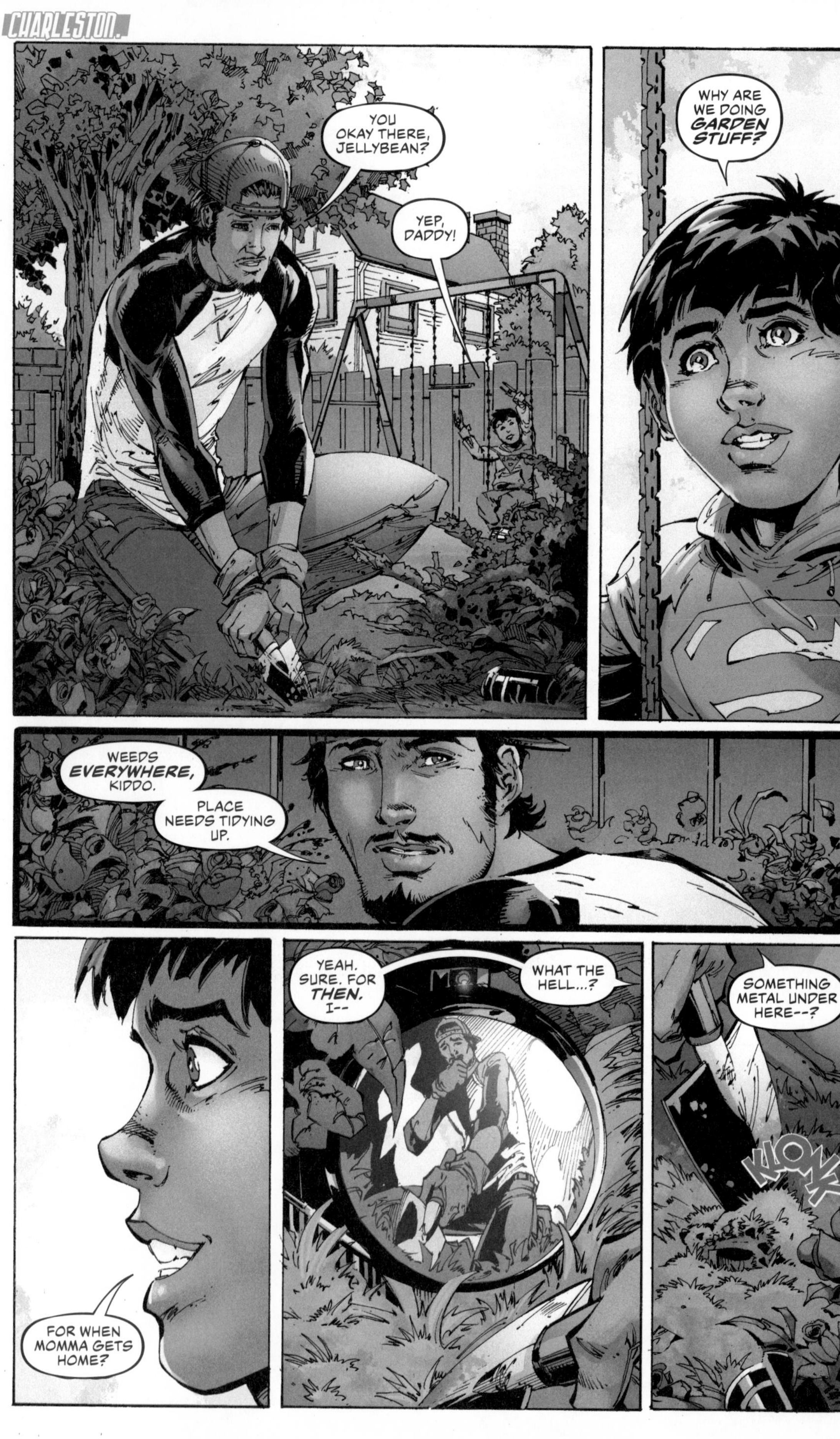
CHARLESTON.
YOU OKAY THERE, JELLYBEAN?
YEP, DADDY!
WHY ARE WE DOING GARDEN STUFF?
WEEDS EVERYWHERE, KIDDO.
PLACE NEEDS TIDYING UP.
FOR WHEN MOMMA GETS HOME?
YEAH. SURE. FOR THEN. I--
WHAT THE HELL...?
SOMETHING METAL UNDER HERE--?
KLONK

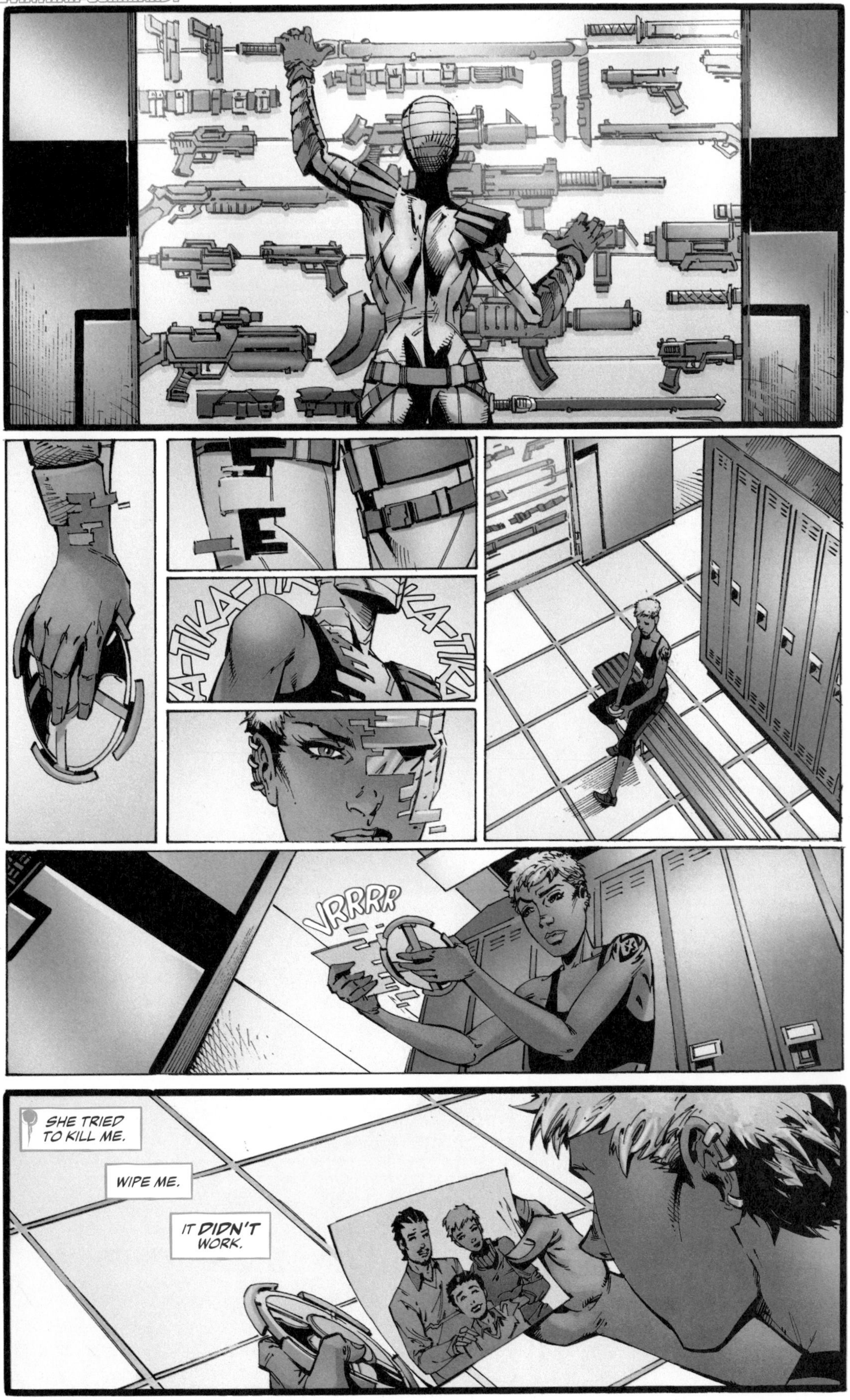
KA-TIKA
VRRRR
SHE TRIED TO KILL ME.
WIPE ME.
IT DIDN'T WORK.

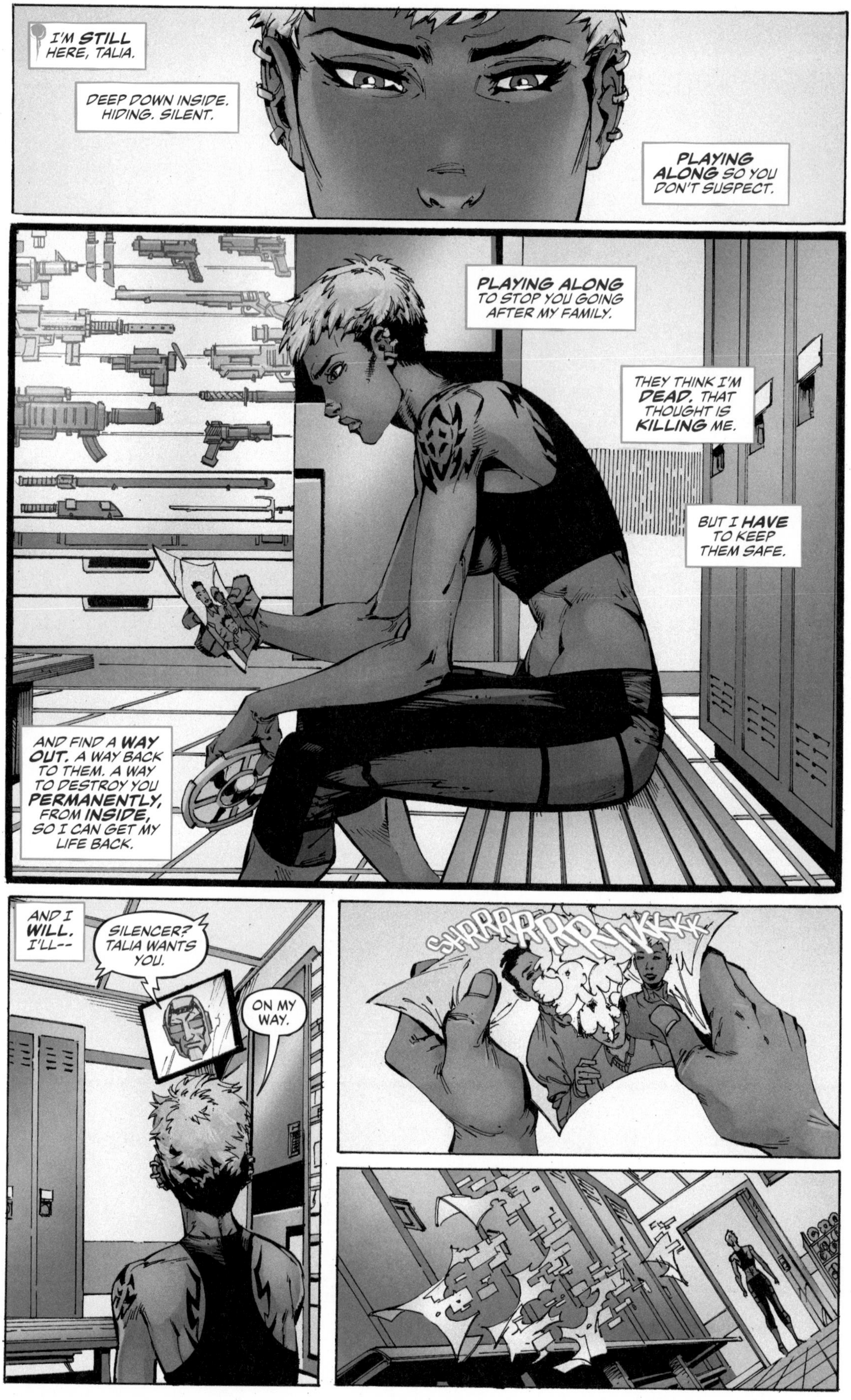

I'M STILL HERE, TALIA.
DEEP DOWN INSIDE. HIDING. SILENT.
PLAYING ALONG SO YOU DON'T SUSPECT.
PLAYING ALONG TO STOP YOU GOING AFTER MY FAMILY.
THEY THINK I'M DEAD. THAT THOUGHT IS KILLING ME.
BUT I HAVE TO KEEP THEM SAFE.
AND FIND A WAY OUT. A WAY BACK TO THEM. A WAY TO DESTROY YOU PERMANENTLY, FROM INSIDE, SO I CAN GET MY LIFE BACK.
AND I WILL. I'LL--
SILENCER? TALIA WANTS YOU.
ON MY WAY.
SHRRRRRRRIIKKKK

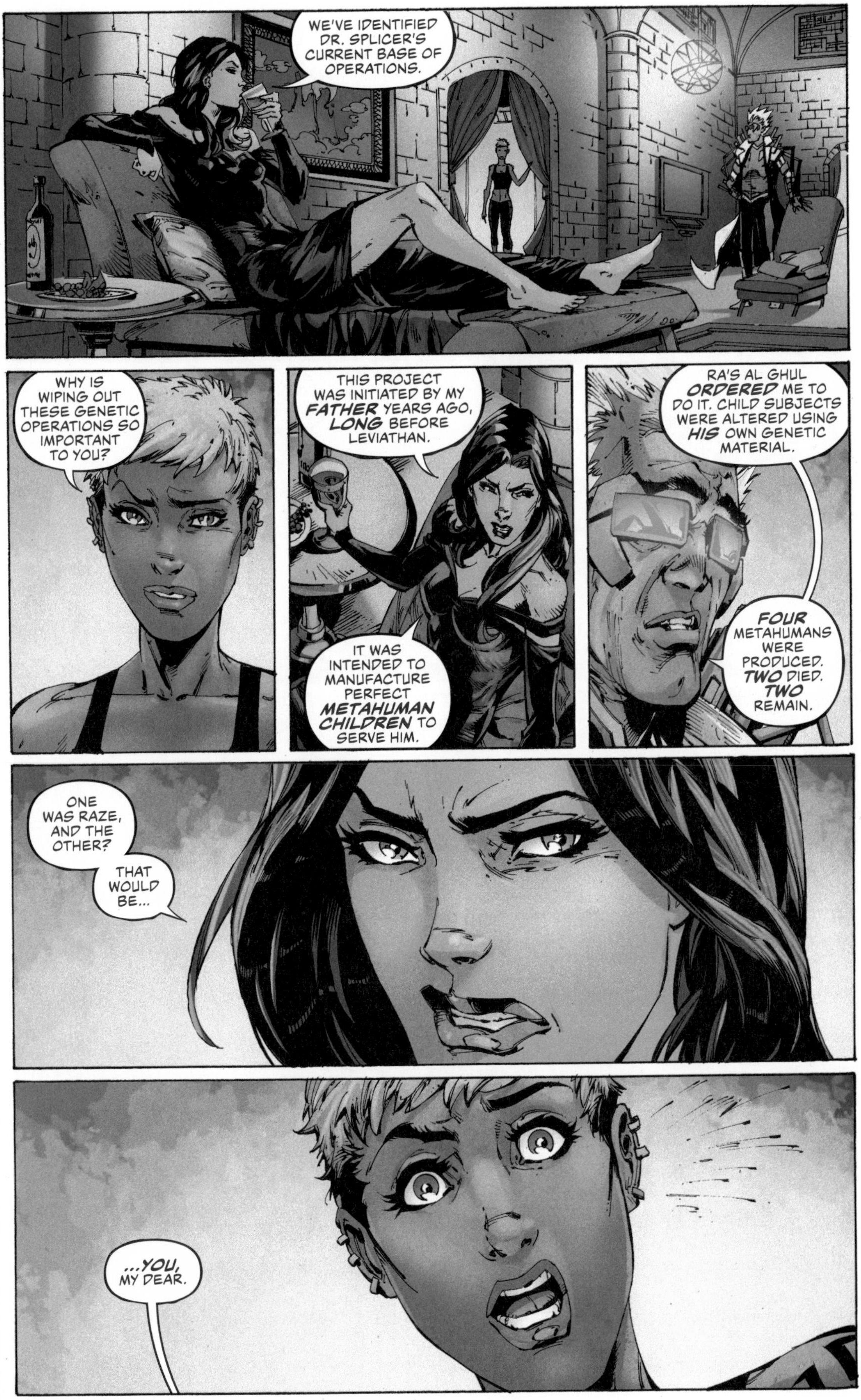

WE'VE IDENTIFIED DR. SPLICER'S CURRENT BASE OF OPERATIONS.
WHY IS WIPING OUT THESE GENETIC OPERATIONS SO IMPORTANT TO YOU?
THIS PROJECT WAS INITIATED BY MY FATHER YEARS AGO, LONG BEFORE LEVIATHAN.
IT WAS INTENDED TO MANUFACTURE PERFECT METAHUMAN CHILDREN TO SERVE HIM.
RA'S AL GHUL ORDERED ME TO DO IT. CHILD SUBJECTS WERE ALTERED USING HIS OWN GENETIC MATERIAL.
FOUR METAHUMANS WERE PRODUCED. TWO DIED. TWO REMAIN.
ONE WAS RAZE, AND THE OTHER?
THAT WOULD BE...
...YOU, MY DEAR.

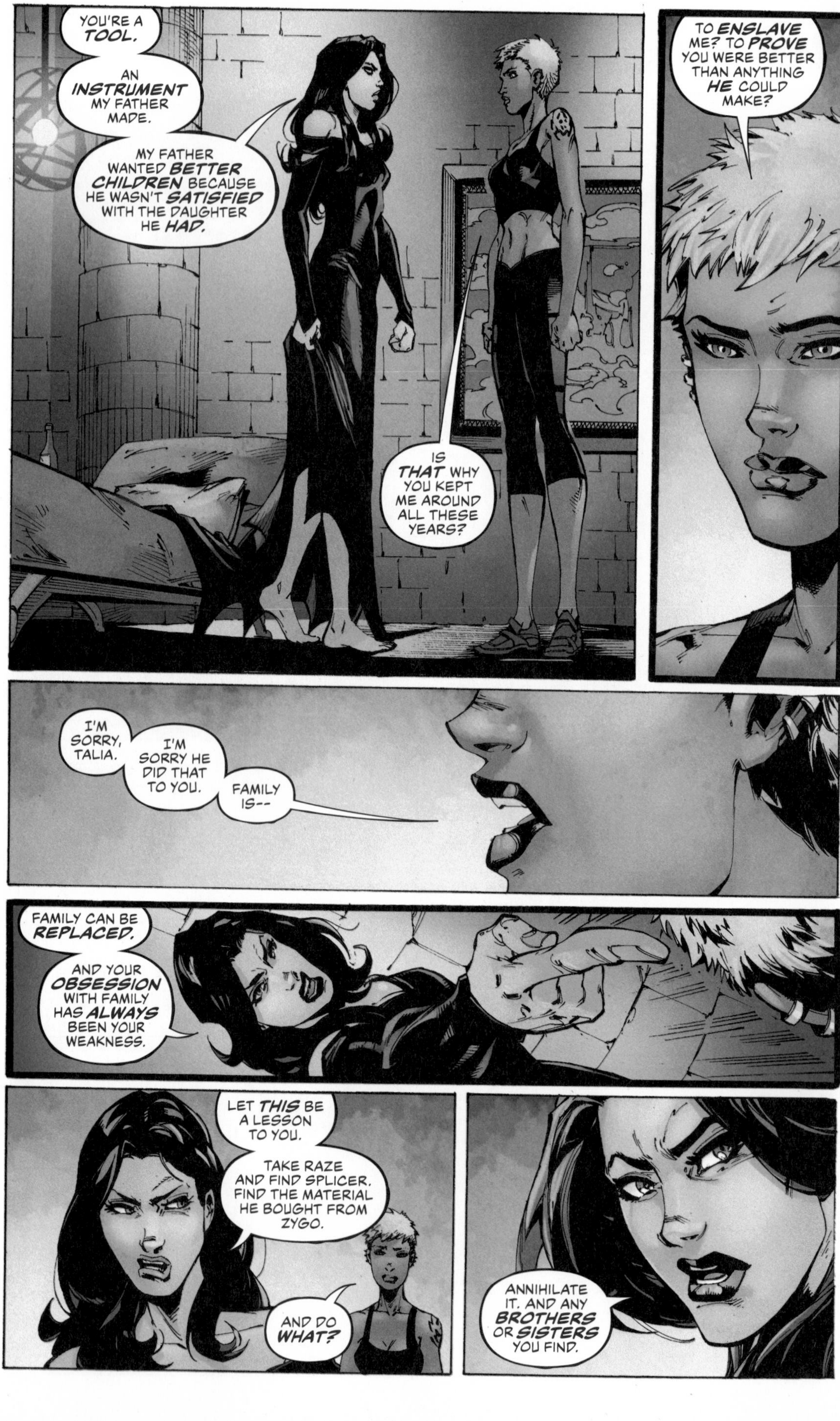
YOU'RE A TOOL.
AN INSTRUMENT MY FATHER MADE.
MY FATHER WANTED BETTER CHILDREN BECAUSE HE WASN'T SATISFIED WITH THE DAUGHTER HE HAD.
IS THAT WHY YOU KEPT ME AROUND ALL THESE YEARS?
TO ENSLAVE ME? TO PROVE YOU WERE BETTER THAN ANYTHING HE COULD MAKE?
I'M SORRY, TALIA.
I'M SORRY HE DID THAT TO YOU.
FAMILY IS--
FAMILY CAN BE REPLACED.
AND YOUR OBSESSION WITH FAMILY HAS ALWAYS BEEN YOUR WEAKNESS.
LET THIS BE A LESSON TO YOU.
TAKE RAZE AND FIND SPLICER. FIND THE MATERIAL HE BOUGHT FROM ZYGO.
AND DO WHAT?
ANNIHILATE IT. AND ANY BROTHERS OR SISTERS YOU FIND.

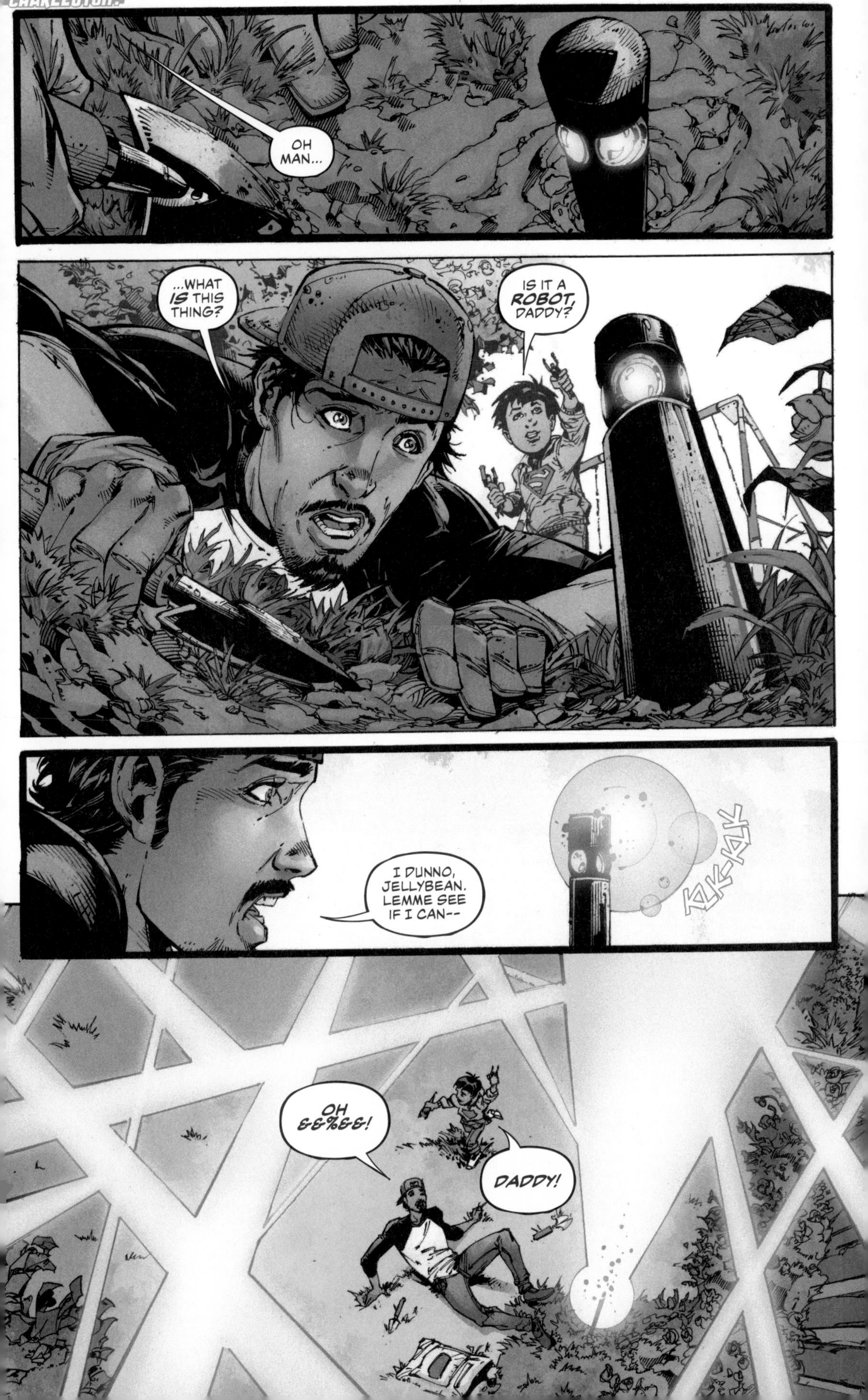
OH MAN...
...WHAT *IS* THIS THING?
IS IT A *ROBOT,* DADDY?
I DUNNO, JELLYBEAN. LEMME SEE IF I CAN--
KLIK-KLIK
OH &&%&&!
DADDY!

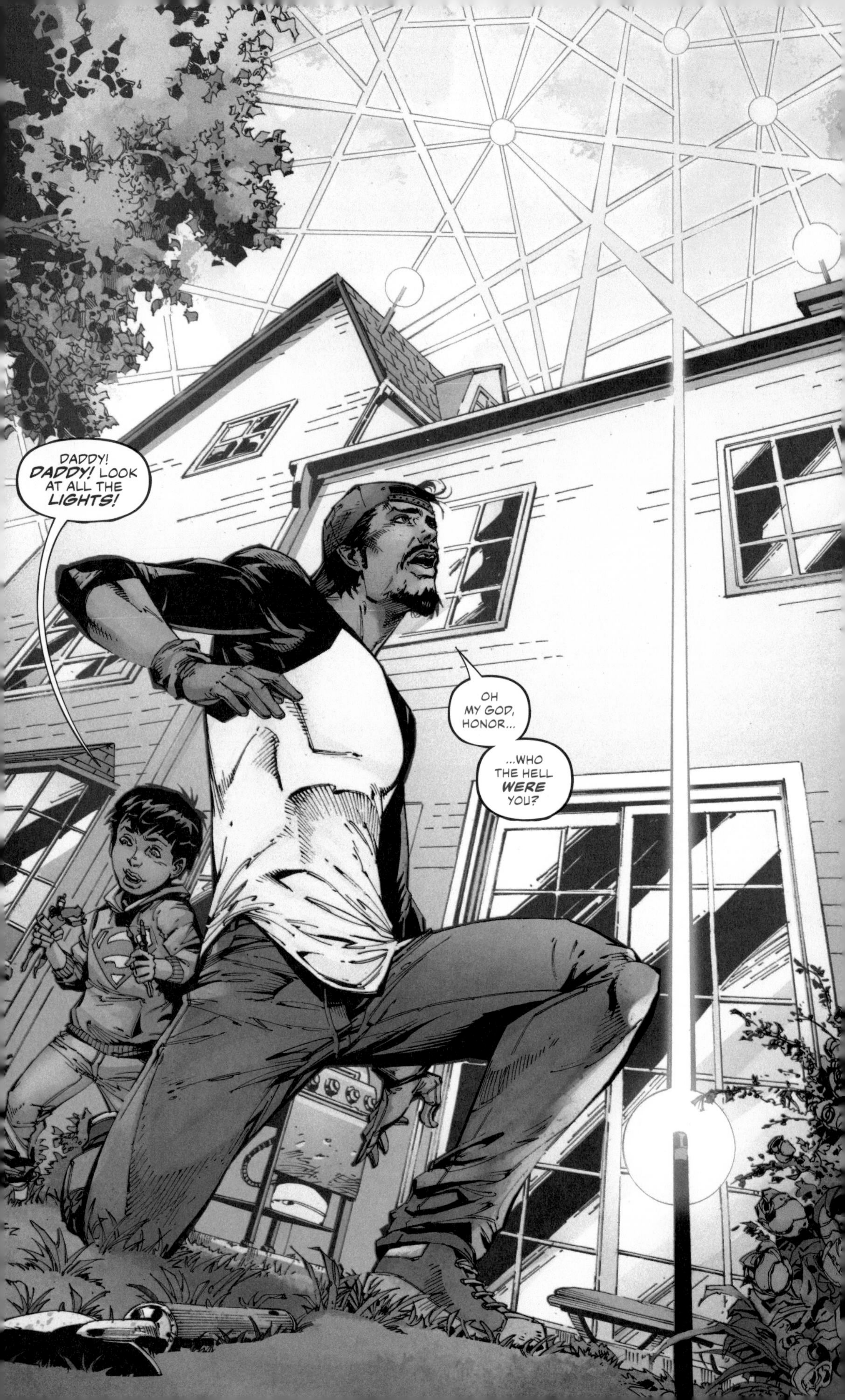
DADDY! DADDY! LOOK AT ALL THE LIGHTS!
OH MY GOD, HONOR...
...WHO THE HELL WERE YOU?

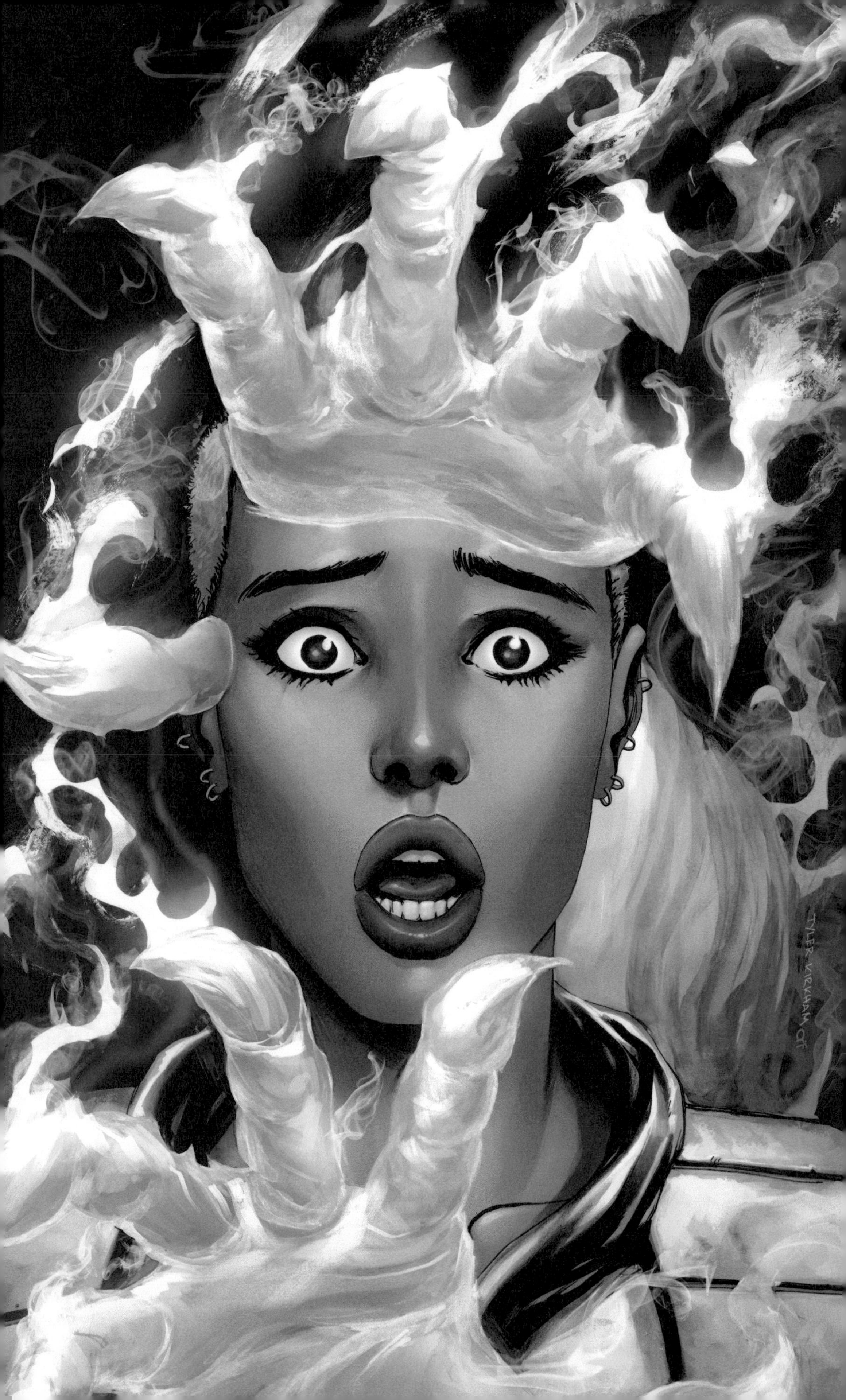
TYLER KIRKHAM

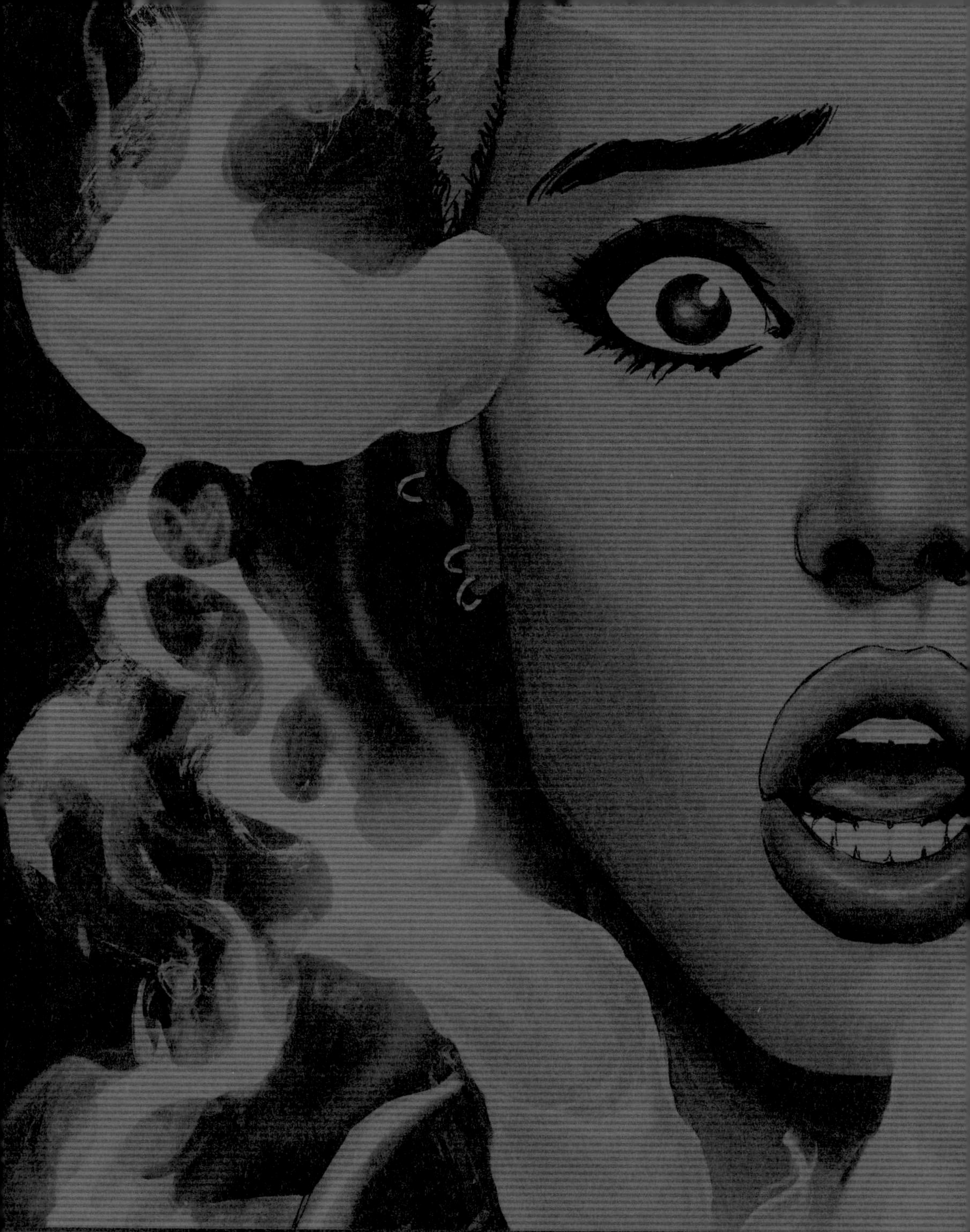

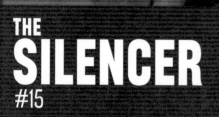

THE SILENCER
#15

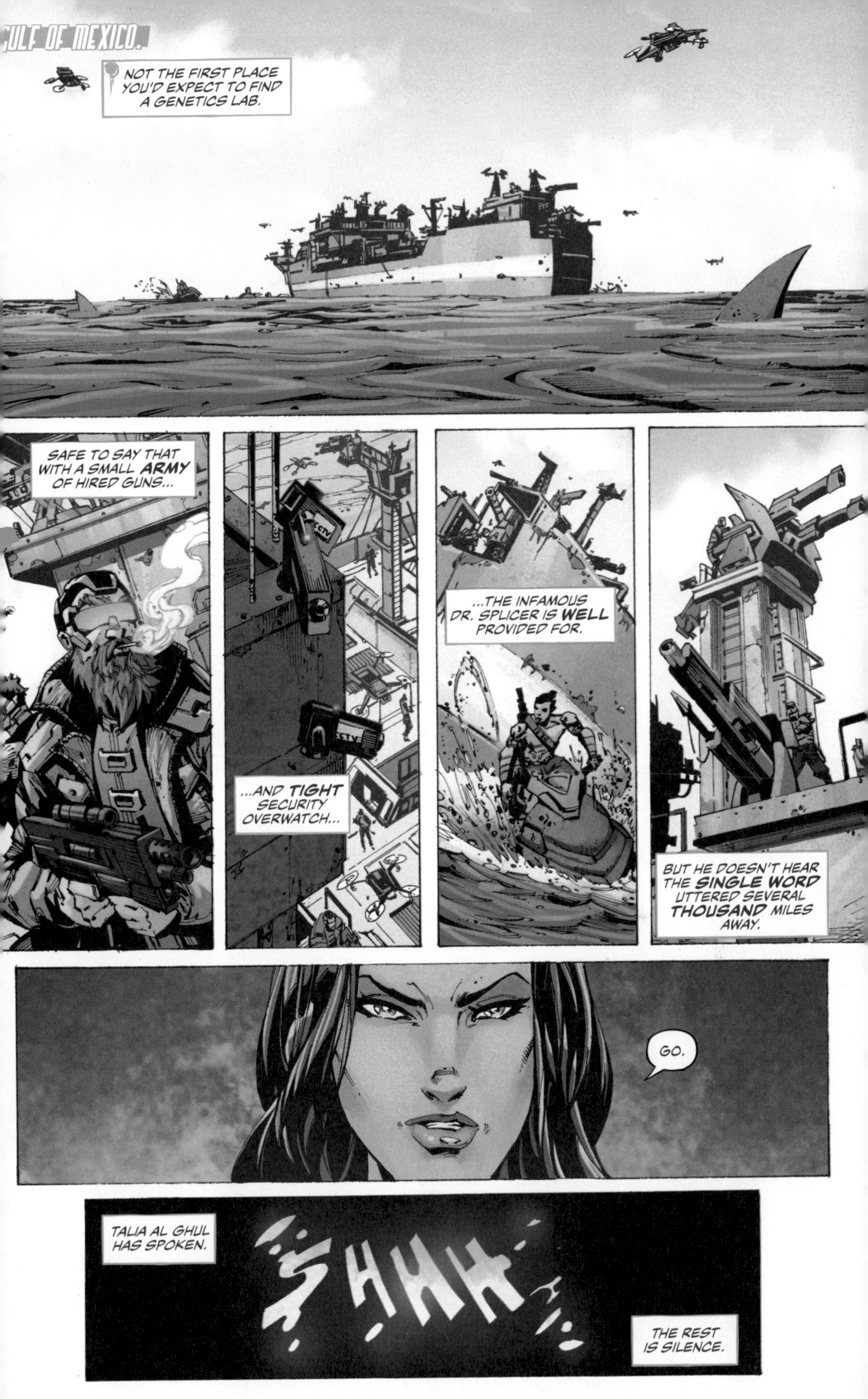

GULF OF MEXICO.
NOT THE FIRST PLACE YOU'D EXPECT TO FIND A GENETICS LAB.
SAFE TO SAY THAT WITH A SMALL ARMY OF HIRED GUNS...
...AND TIGHT SECURITY OVERWATCH...
...THE INFAMOUS DR. SPLICER IS WELL PROVIDED FOR.
BUT HE DOESN'T HEAR THE SINGLE WORD UTTERED SEVERAL THOUSAND MILES AWAY.
GO.
TALIA AL GHUL HAS SPOKEN.
SHHK
THE REST IS SILENCE.

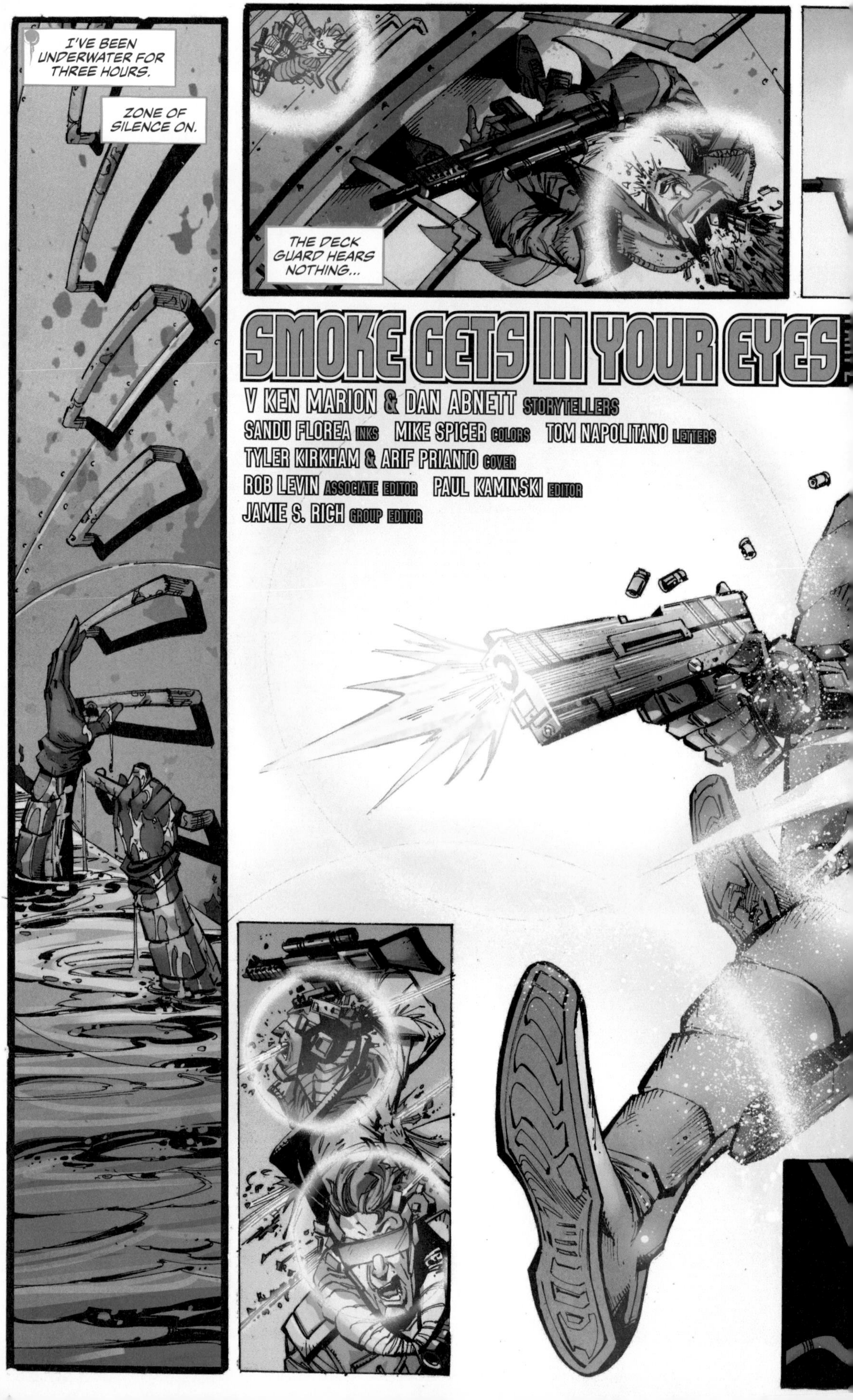

I'VE BEEN UNDERWATER FOR THREE HOURS.
ZONE OF SILENCE ON.
THE DECK GUARD HEARS NOTHING...
SMOKE GETS IN YOUR EYES
V KEN MARION & DAN ABNETT STORYTELLERS
SANDU FLOREA INKS MIKE SPICER COLORS TOM NAPOLITANO LETTERS
TYLER KIRKHAM & ARIF PRIANTO COVER
ROB LEVIN ASSOCIATE EDITOR PAUL KAMINSKI EDITOR
JAMIE S. RICH GROUP EDITOR

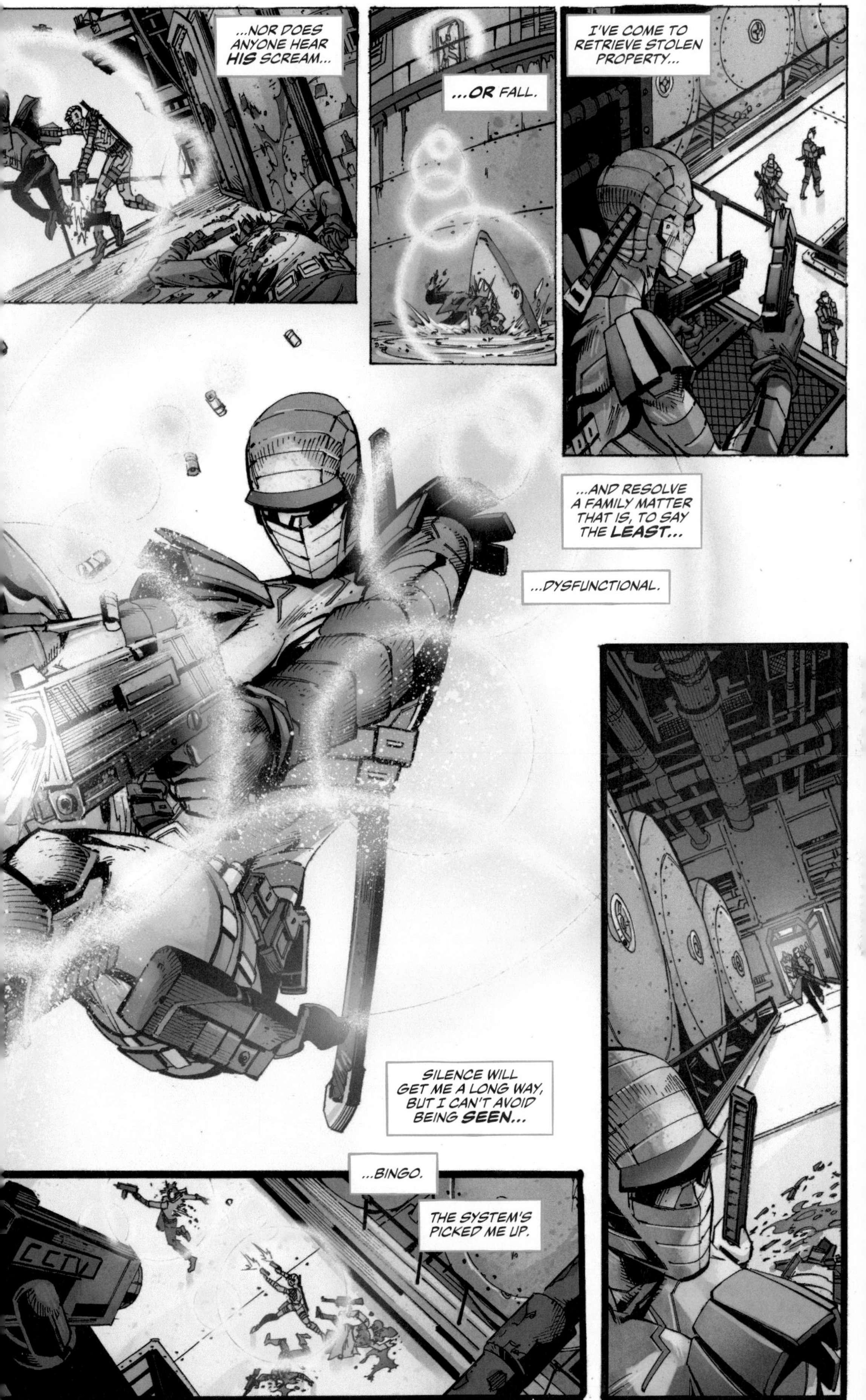

...NOR DOES ANYONE HEAR **HIS** SCREAM...
...**OR** FALL.
I'VE COME TO RETRIEVE STOLEN PROPERTY...
...AND RESOLVE A FAMILY MATTER THAT IS, TO SAY THE **LEAST**...
...DYSFUNCTIONAL.
SILENCE WILL GET ME A LONG WAY, BUT I CAN'T AVOID BEING **SEEN**...
...BINGO.
THE SYSTEM'S PICKED ME UP.
CCTV

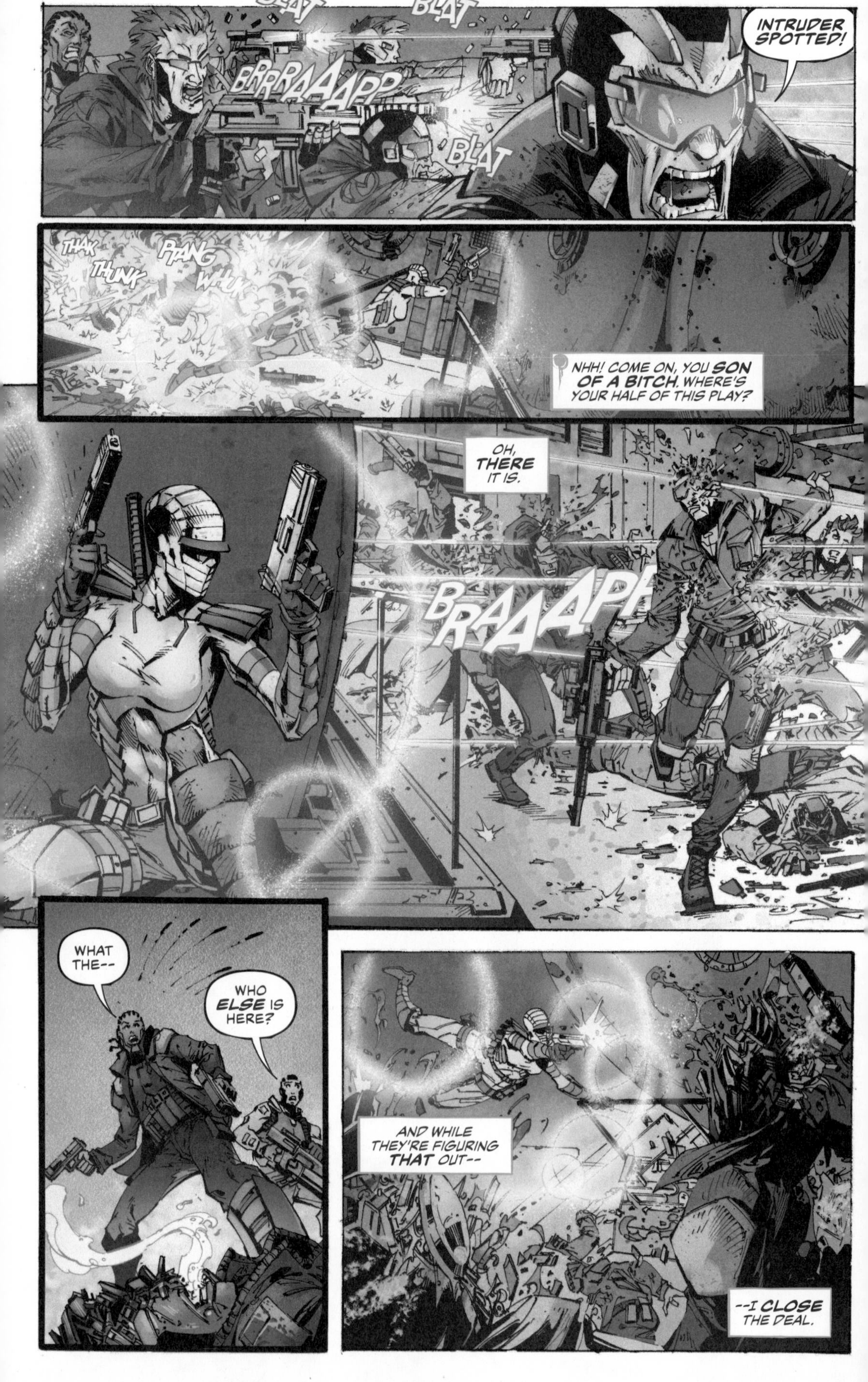
BLAT
BLAT
BRRRAAAPP
BLAT
INTRUDER SPOTTED!
THAK
THUNK
PTANG
WHUK
NHH! COME ON, YOU SON OF A BITCH. WHERE'S YOUR HALF OF THIS PLAY?
OH, THERE IT IS.
BRAAAPP
WHAT THE--
WHO ELSE IS HERE?
AND WHILE THEY'RE FIGURING THAT OUT--
--I CLOSE THE DEAL.

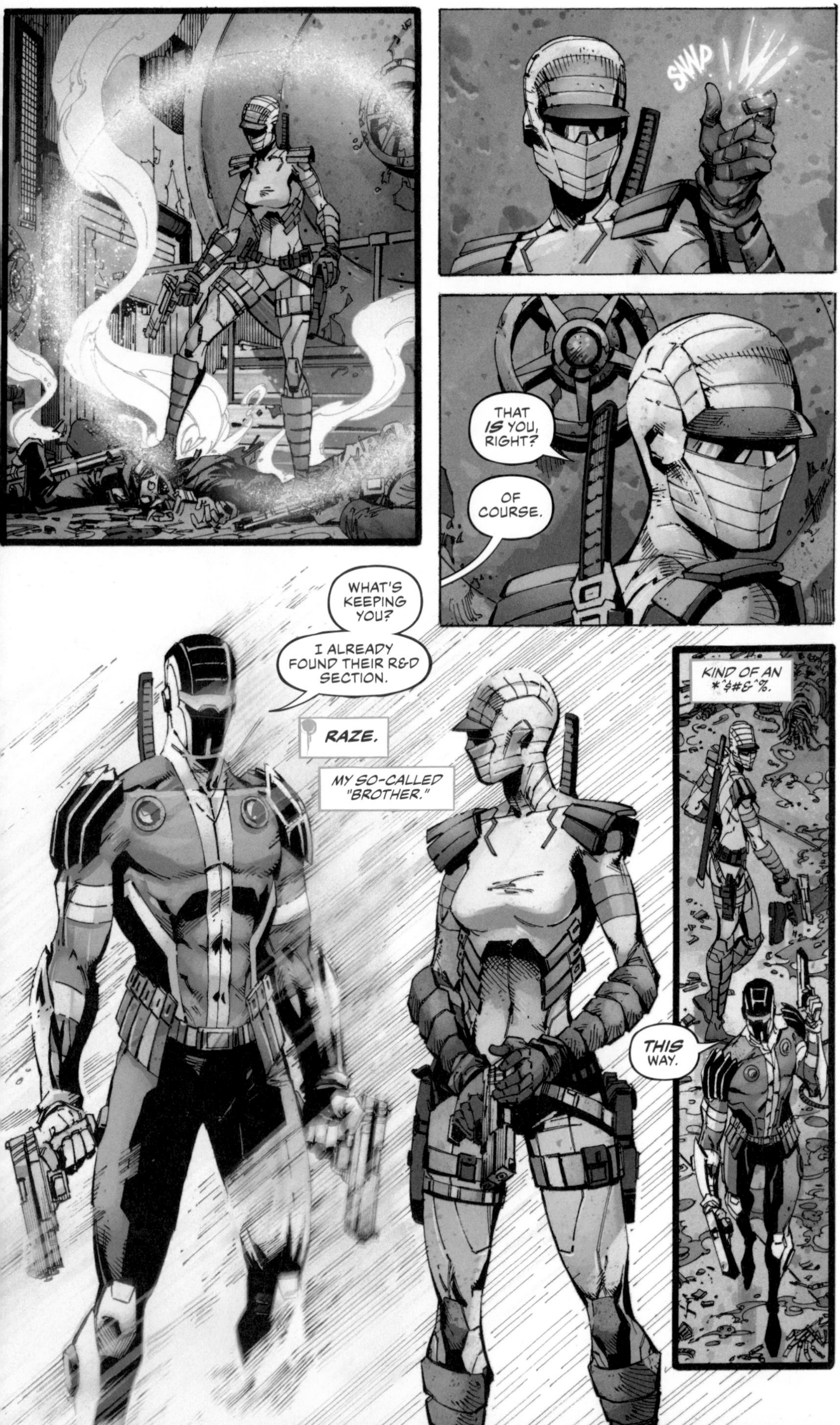

SNAP
THAT IS YOU, RIGHT?
OF COURSE.
WHAT'S KEEPING YOU?
I ALREADY FOUND THEIR R&D SECTION.
RAZE.
MY SO-CALLED "BROTHER."
KIND OF AN *^$#&^%.
THIS WAY.

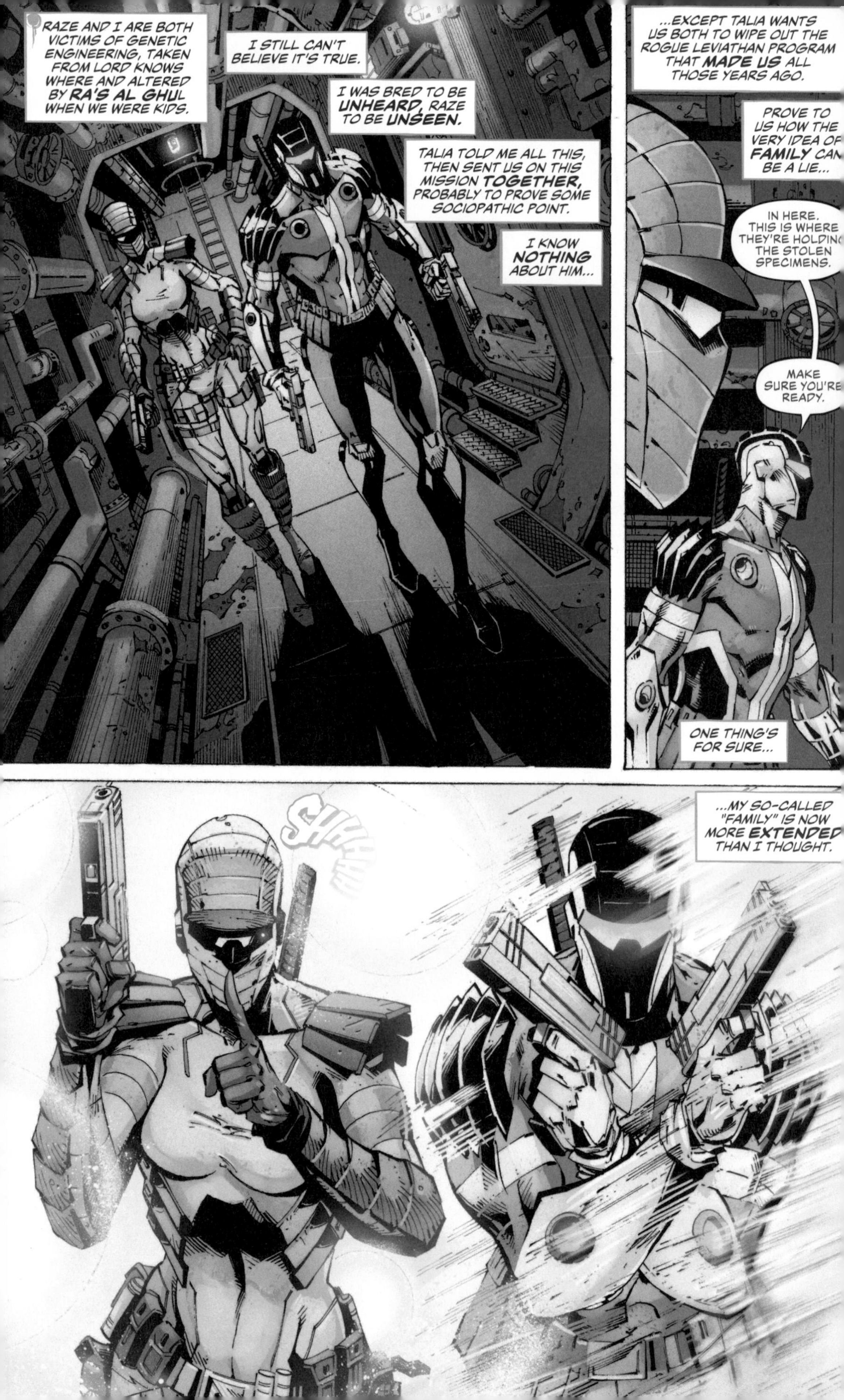
RAZE AND I ARE BOTH VICTIMS OF GENETIC ENGINEERING, TAKEN FROM LORD KNOWS WHERE AND ALTERED BY RA'S AL GHUL WHEN WE WERE KIDS.
I STILL CAN'T BELIEVE IT'S TRUE.
I WAS BRED TO BE UNHEARD, RAZE TO BE UNSEEN.
TALIA TOLD ME ALL THIS, THEN SENT US ON THIS MISSION TOGETHER, PROBABLY TO PROVE SOME SOCIOPATHIC POINT.
I KNOW NOTHING ABOUT HIM...
...EXCEPT TALIA WANTS US BOTH TO WIPE OUT THE ROGUE LEVIATHAN PROGRAM THAT MADE US ALL THOSE YEARS AGO.
PROVE TO US HOW THE VERY IDEA OF FAMILY CAN BE A LIE...
IN HERE. THIS IS WHERE THEY'RE HOLDING THE STOLEN SPECIMENS.
MAKE SURE YOU'RE READY.
ONE THING'S FOR SURE...
...MY SO-CALLED "FAMILY" IS NOW MORE EXTENDED THAN I THOUGHT.

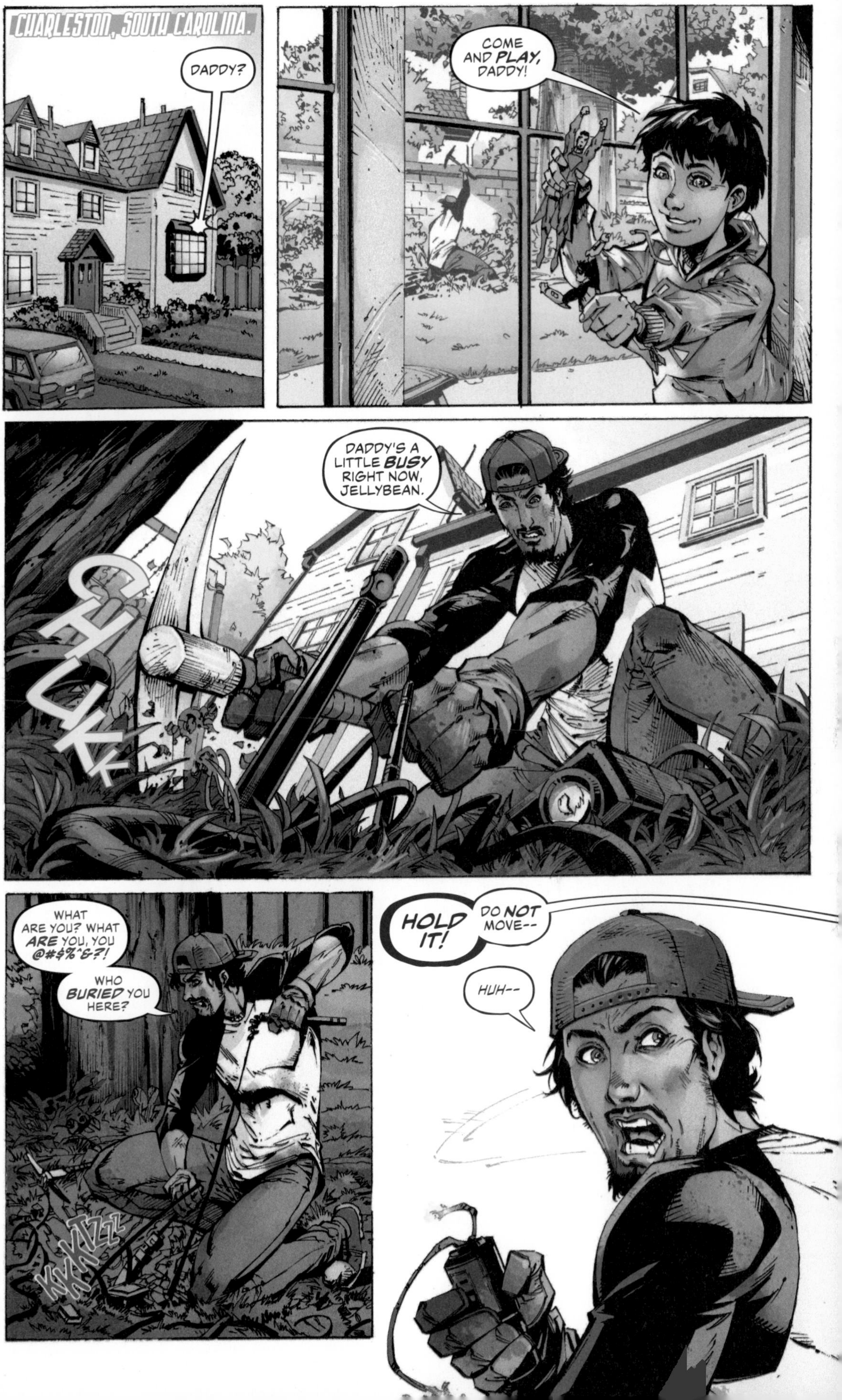
CHARLESTON, SOUTH CAROLINA.
DADDY?
COME AND PLAY, DADDY!
DADDY'S A LITTLE BUSY RIGHT NOW, JELLYBEAN.
CHUKK
WHAT ARE YOU? WHAT ARE YOU, YOU @#$%^&?!
WHO BURIED YOU HERE?
KKKTZZZ
HOLD IT!
DO NOT MOVE--
HUH--

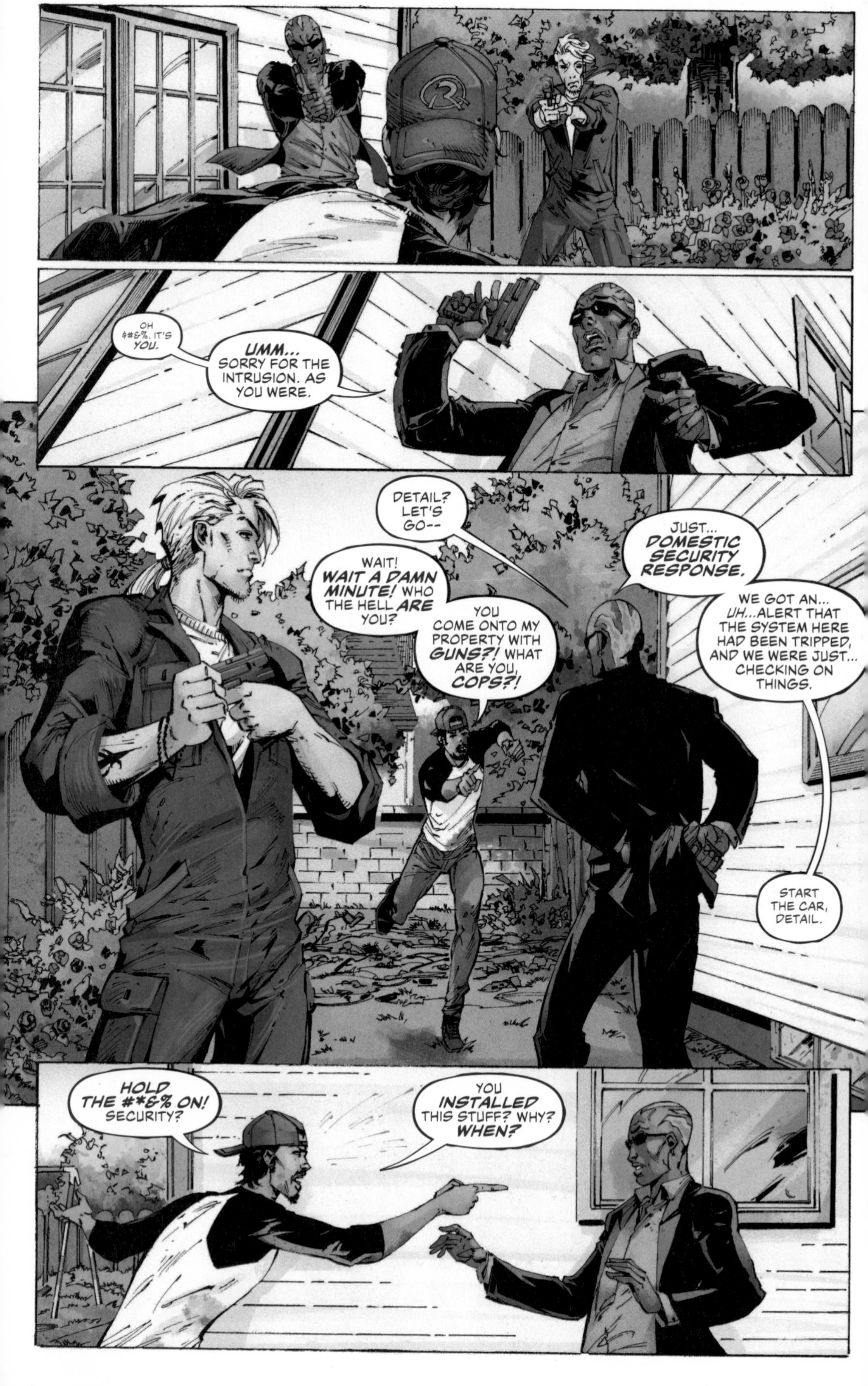

OH $#&%. IT'S YOU.
UMM... SORRY FOR THE INTRUSION. AS YOU WERE.
DETAIL? LET'S GO--
WAIT! WAIT A DAMN MINUTE! WHO THE HELL ARE YOU?
YOU COME ONTO MY PROPERTY WITH GUNS?! WHAT ARE YOU, COPS?!
JUST... DOMESTIC SECURITY RESPONSE.
WE GOT AN... UH...ALERT THAT THE SYSTEM HERE HAD BEEN TRIPPED, AND WE WERE JUST... CHECKING ON THINGS.
START THE CAR, DETAIL.
HOLD THE #*&% ON! SECURITY?
YOU INSTALLED THIS STUFF? WHY? WHEN?

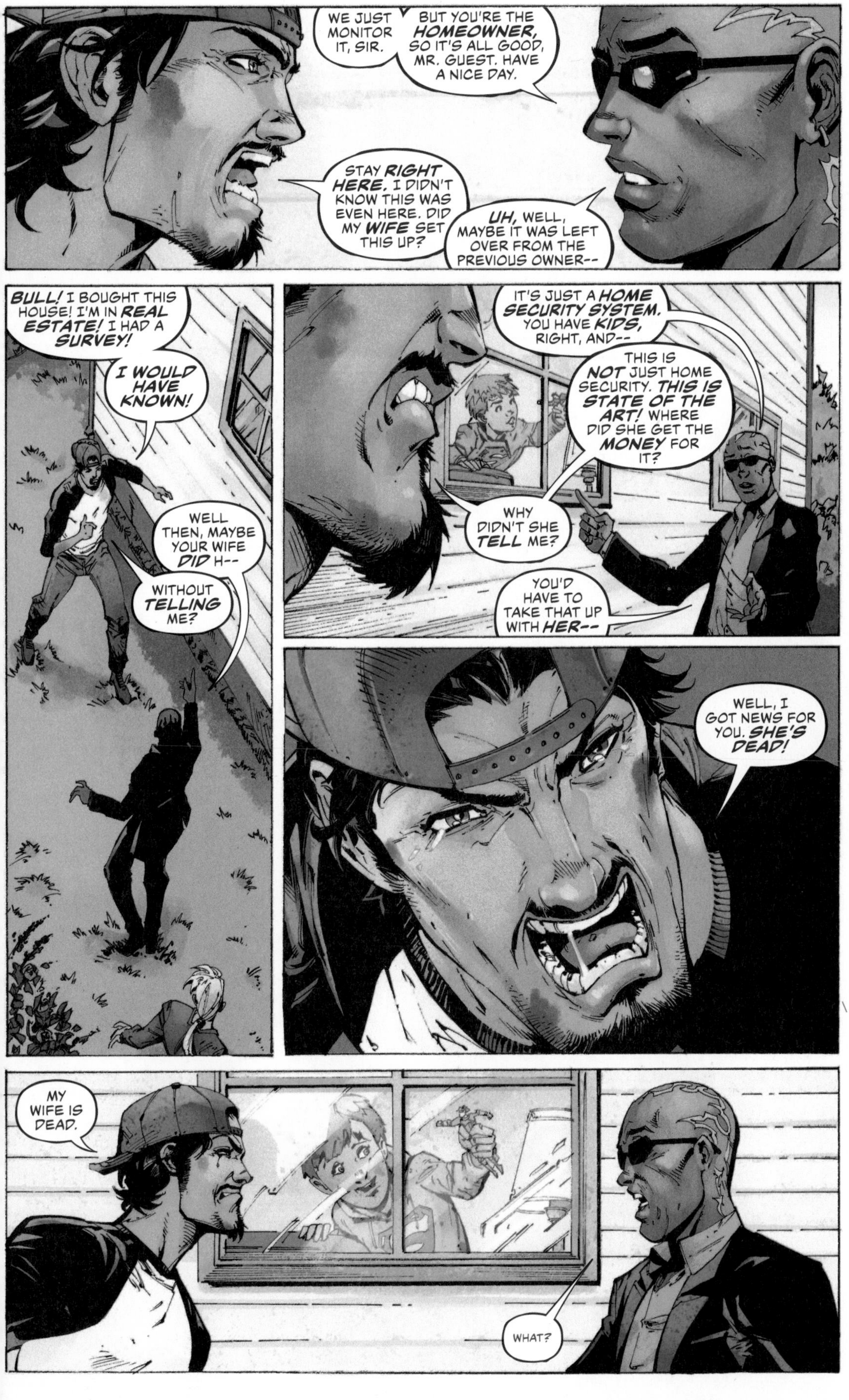

WE JUST MONITOR IT, SIR.
BUT YOU'RE THE HOMEOWNER, SO IT'S ALL GOOD, MR. GUEST. HAVE A NICE DAY.
STAY RIGHT HERE. I DIDN'T KNOW THIS WAS EVEN HERE. DID MY WIFE SET THIS UP?
UH, WELL, MAYBE IT WAS LEFT OVER FROM THE PREVIOUS OWNER--
BULL! I BOUGHT THIS HOUSE! I'M IN REAL ESTATE! I HAD A SURVEY!
I WOULD HAVE KNOWN!
WELL THEN, MAYBE YOUR WIFE DID H--
WITHOUT TELLING ME?
IT'S JUST A HOME SECURITY SYSTEM. YOU HAVE KIDS, RIGHT, AND--
THIS IS NOT JUST HOME SECURITY. THIS IS STATE OF THE ART! WHERE DID SHE GET THE MONEY FOR IT?
WHY DIDN'T SHE TELL ME?
YOU'D HAVE TO TAKE THAT UP WITH HER--
WELL, I GOT NEWS FOR YOU. SHE'S DEAD!
MY WIFE IS DEAD.
WHAT?

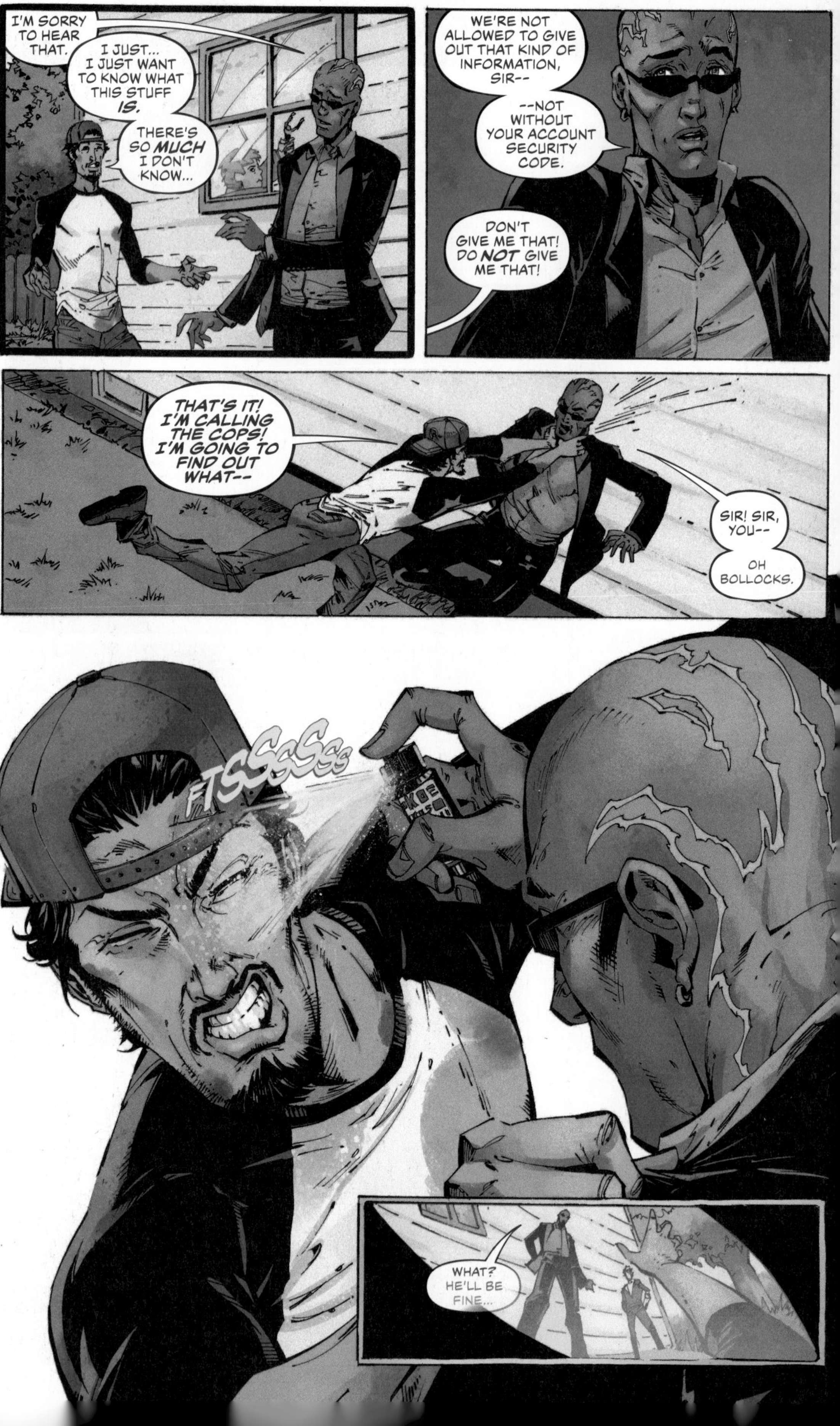
I'M SORRY TO HEAR THAT.
I JUST... I JUST WANT TO KNOW WHAT THIS STUFF IS.
THERE'S SO MUCH I DON'T KNOW...
WE'RE NOT ALLOWED TO GIVE OUT THAT KIND OF INFORMATION, SIR--
--NOT WITHOUT YOUR ACCOUNT SECURITY CODE.
DON'T GIVE ME THAT! DO NOT GIVE ME THAT!
THAT'S IT! I'M CALLING THE COPS! I'M GOING TO FIND OUT WHAT--
SIR! SIR, YOU--
OH BOLLOCKS.
FTSSsSss
WHAT? HE'LL BE FINE...

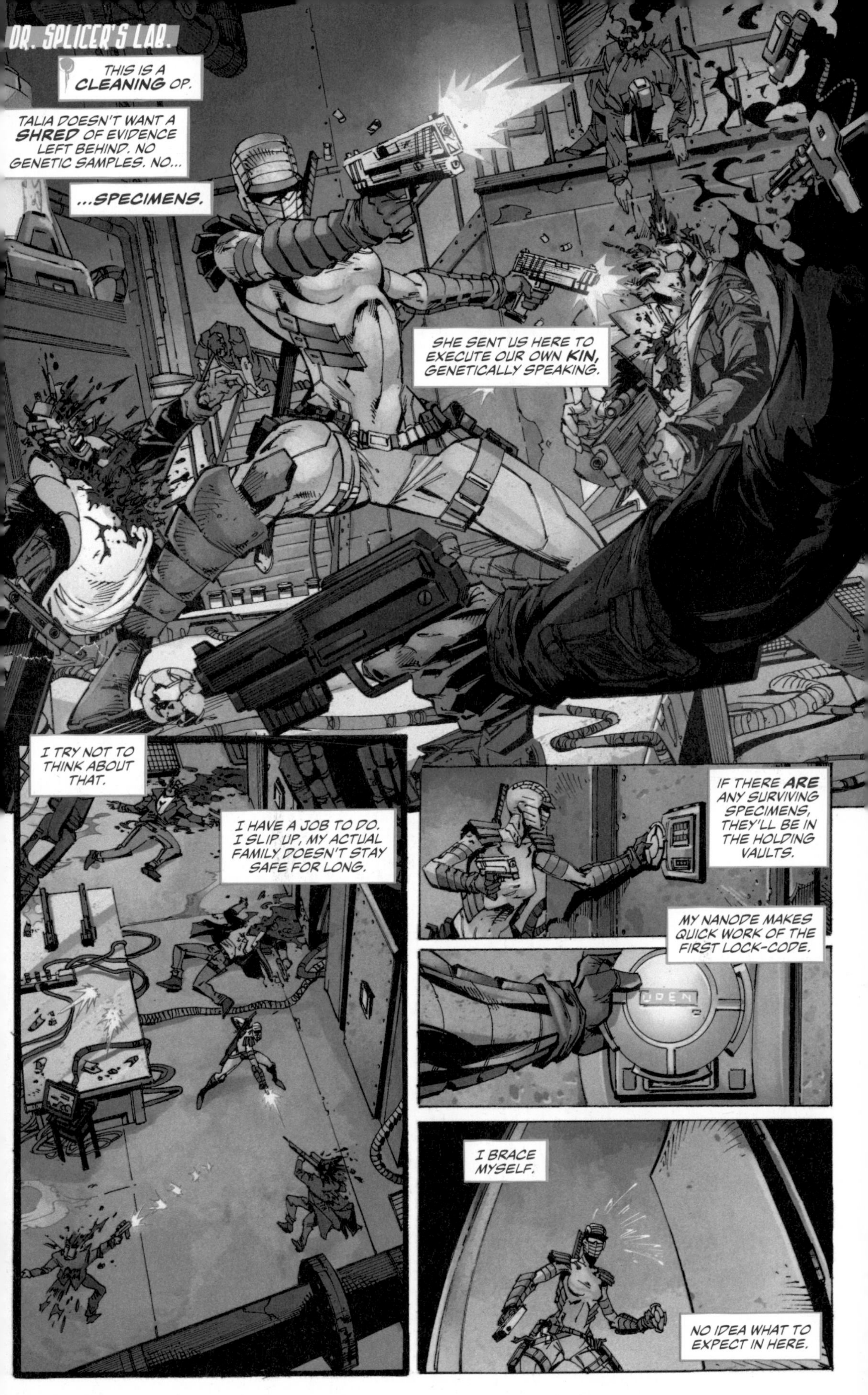
DR. SPLICER'S LAB.
THIS IS A CLEANING OP.
TALIA DOESN'T WANT A SHRED OF EVIDENCE LEFT BEHIND. NO GENETIC SAMPLES. NO...
...SPECIMENS.
SHE SENT US HERE TO EXECUTE OUR OWN KIN, GENETICALLY SPEAKING.
I TRY NOT TO THINK ABOUT THAT.
I HAVE A JOB TO DO. I SLIP UP, MY ACTUAL FAMILY DOESN'T STAY SAFE FOR LONG.
IF THERE ARE ANY SURVIVING SPECIMENS, THEY'LL BE IN THE HOLDING VAULTS.
MY NANODE MAKES QUICK WORK OF THE FIRST LOCK-CODE.
OPEN
I BRACE MYSELF.
NO IDEA WHAT TO EXPECT IN HERE.

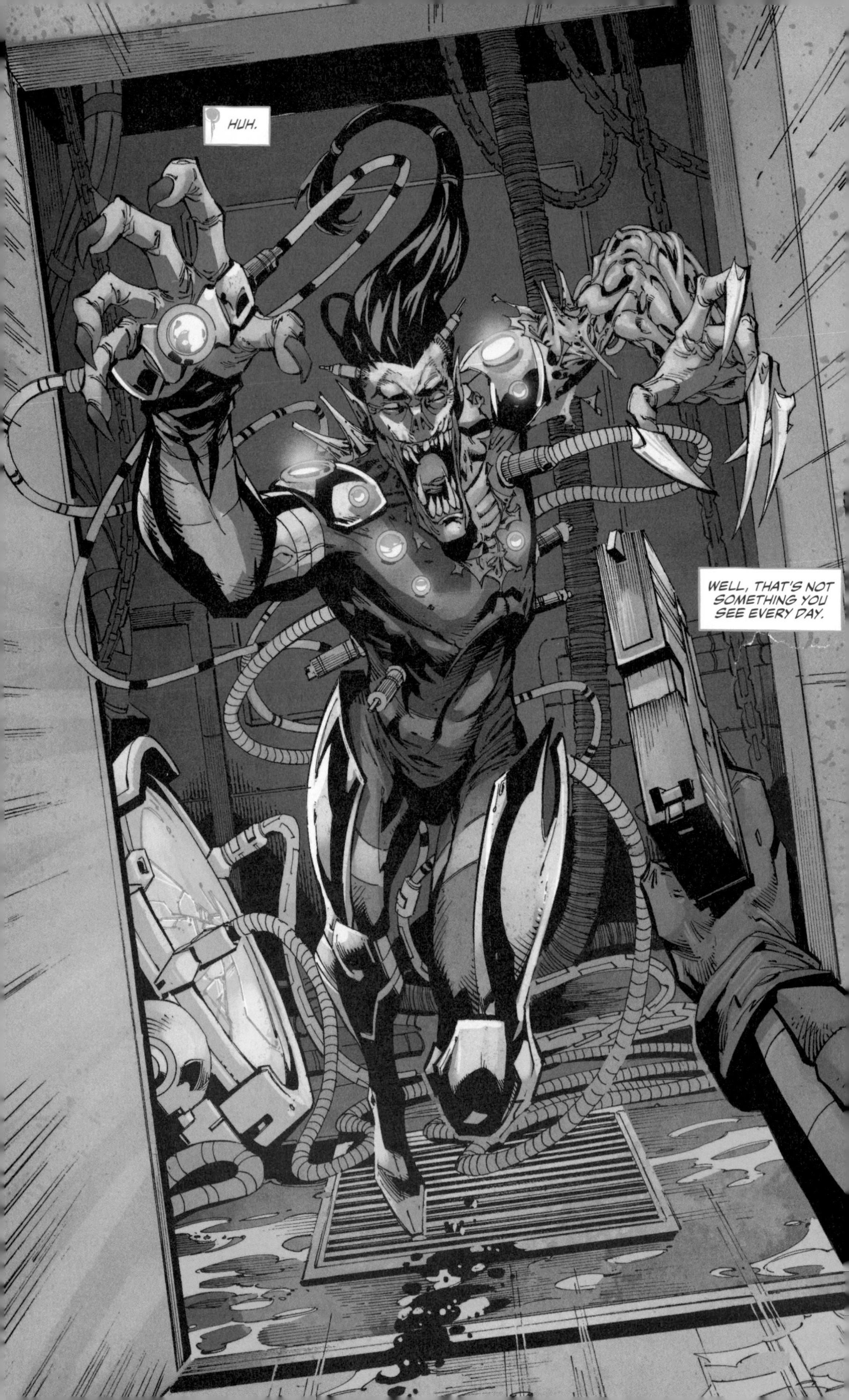
HUH.
WELL, THAT'S NOT SOMETHING YOU SEE EVERY DAY.

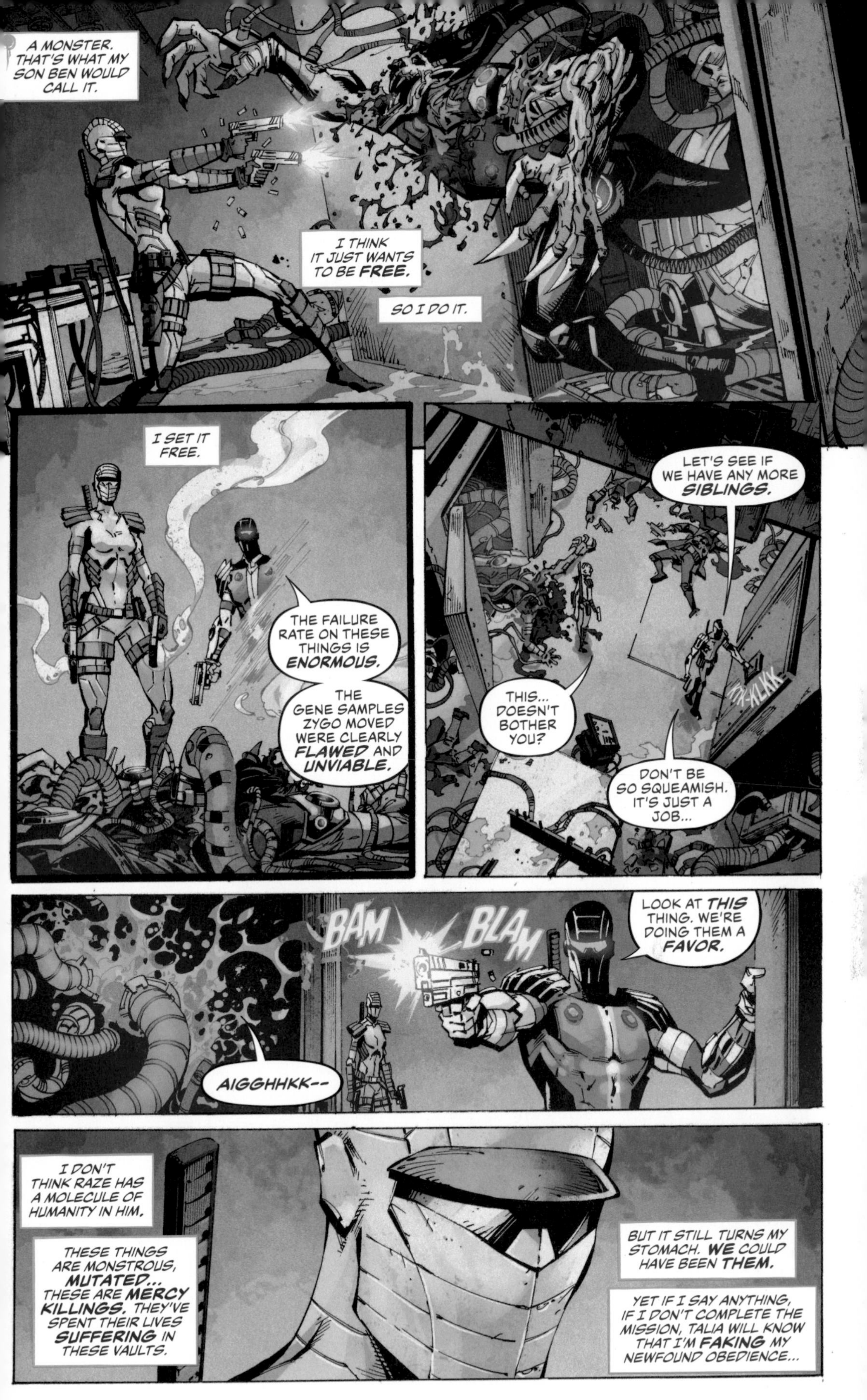

A MONSTER. THAT'S WHAT MY SON BEN WOULD CALL IT.
I THINK IT JUST WANTS TO BE **FREE.**
SO I DO IT.
I SET IT FREE.
THE FAILURE RATE ON THESE THINGS IS **ENORMOUS.**
THE GENE SAMPLES ZYGO MOVED WERE CLEARLY **FLAWED** AND **UNVIABLE.**
LET'S SEE IF WE HAVE ANY MORE **SIBLINGS.**
THIS... DOESN'T BOTHER YOU?
DON'T BE SO SQUEAMISH. IT'S JUST A JOB...
BAM
BLAM
LOOK AT **THIS** THING. WE'RE DOING THEM A **FAVOR.**
AIGGHHKK--
I DON'T THINK RAZE HAS A MOLECULE OF HUMANITY IN HIM.
THESE THINGS ARE MONSTROUS, **MUTATED...** THESE ARE **MERCY KILLINGS.** THEY'VE SPENT THEIR LIVES **SUFFERING** IN THESE VAULTS.
BUT IT STILL TURNS MY STOMACH. **WE** COULD HAVE BEEN **THEM.**
YET IF I SAY ANYTHING, IF I DON'T COMPLETE THE MISSION, TALIA WILL KNOW THAT I'M **FAKING** MY NEWFOUND OBEDIENCE...

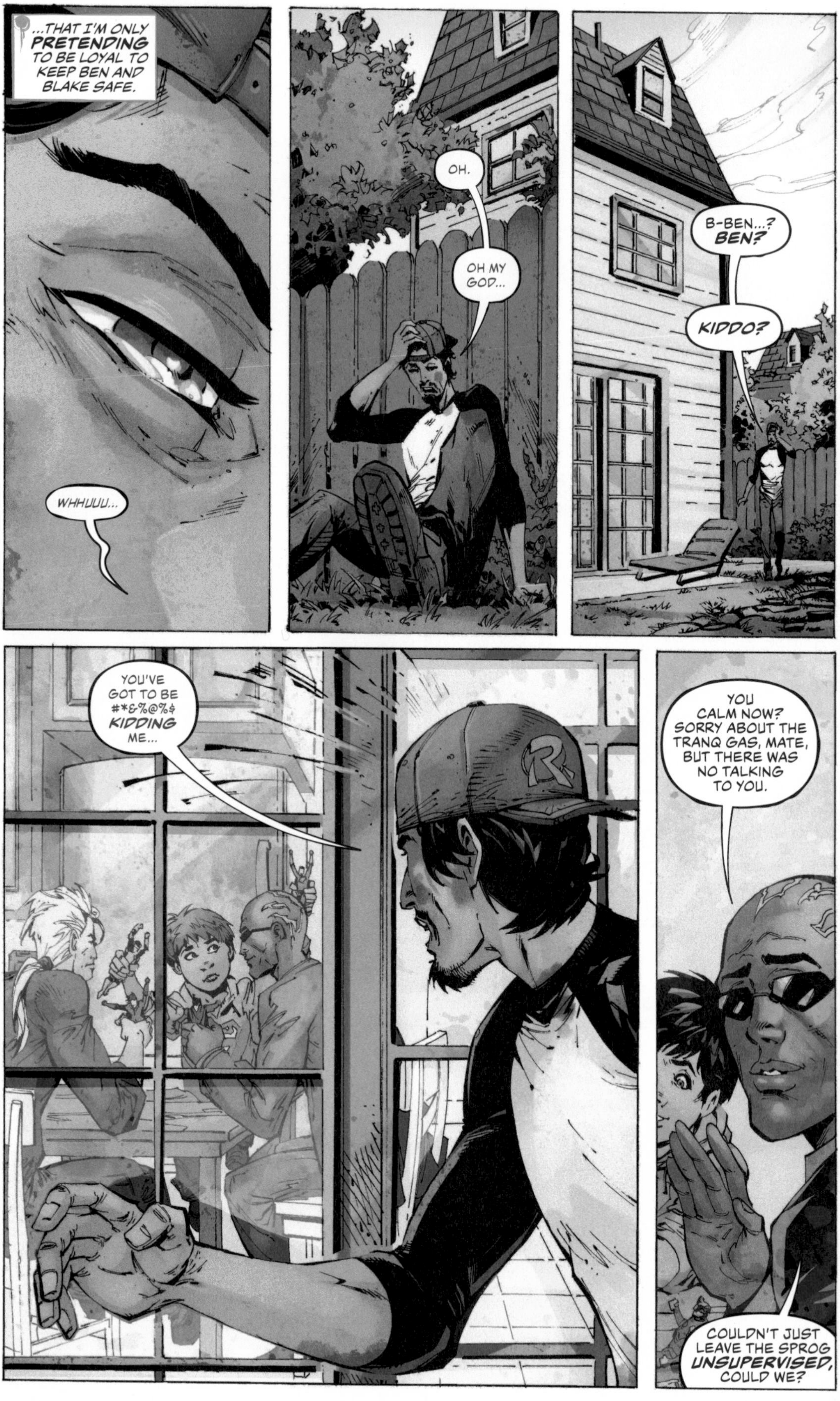
...THAT I'M ONLY PRETENDING TO BE LOYAL TO KEEP BEN AND BLAKE SAFE.
WHHUUU...
OH.
OH MY GOD...
B-BEN...? BEN?
KIDDO?
YOU'VE GOT TO BE #*&%@%$ KIDDING ME...
YOU CALM NOW? SORRY ABOUT THE TRANQ GAS, MATE, BUT THERE WAS NO TALKING TO YOU.
COULDN'T JUST LEAVE THE SPROG UNSUPERVISED, COULD WE?

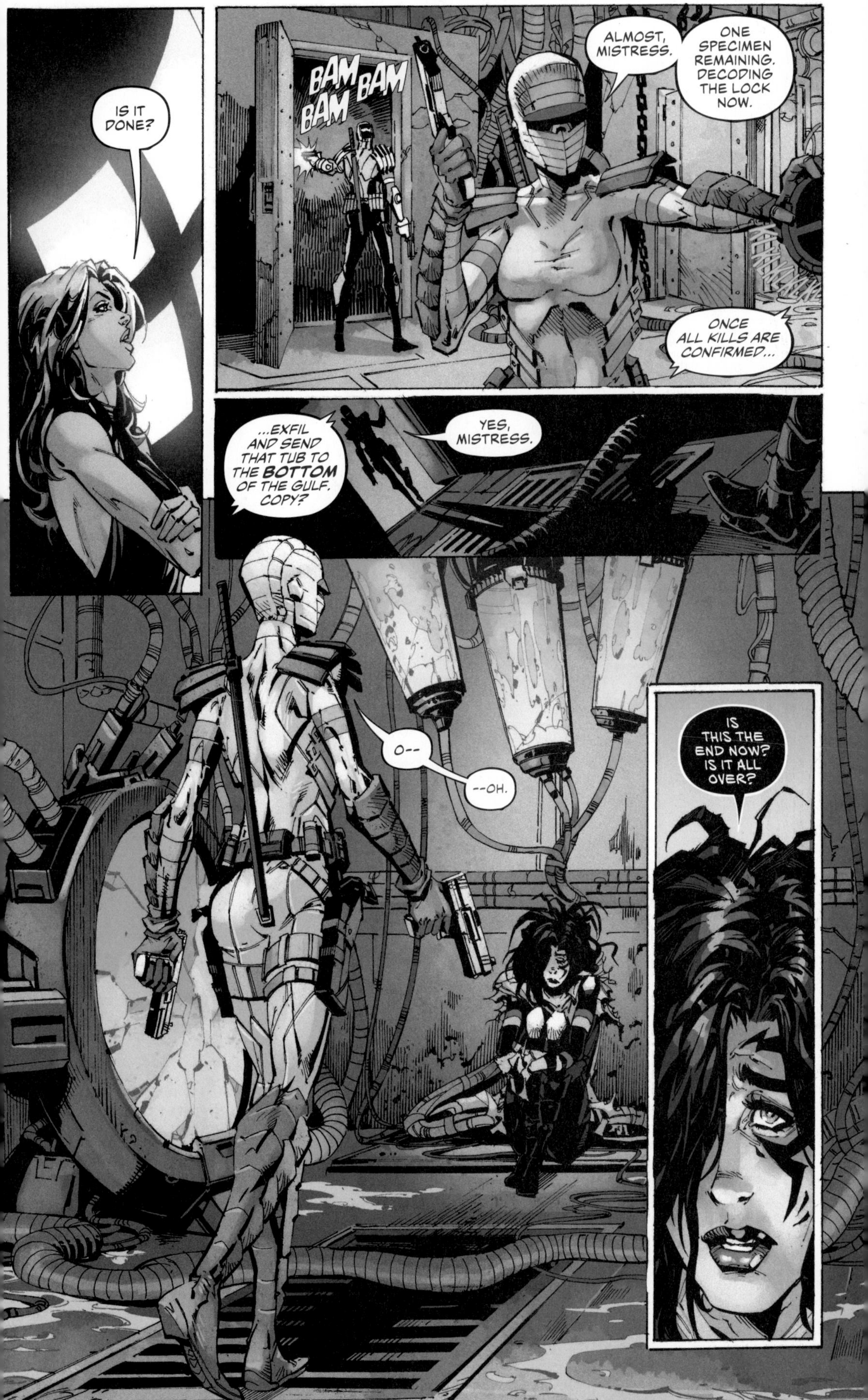
IS IT DONE?
BAM BAM BAM
ALMOST, MISTRESS.
ONE SPECIMEN REMAINING. DECODING THE LOCK NOW.
ONCE ALL KILLS ARE CONFIRMED...
...EXFIL AND SEND THAT TUB TO THE **BOTTOM** OF THE GULF. COPY?
YES, MISTRESS.
O--
--OH.
IS THIS THE END NOW? IS IT ALL OVER?

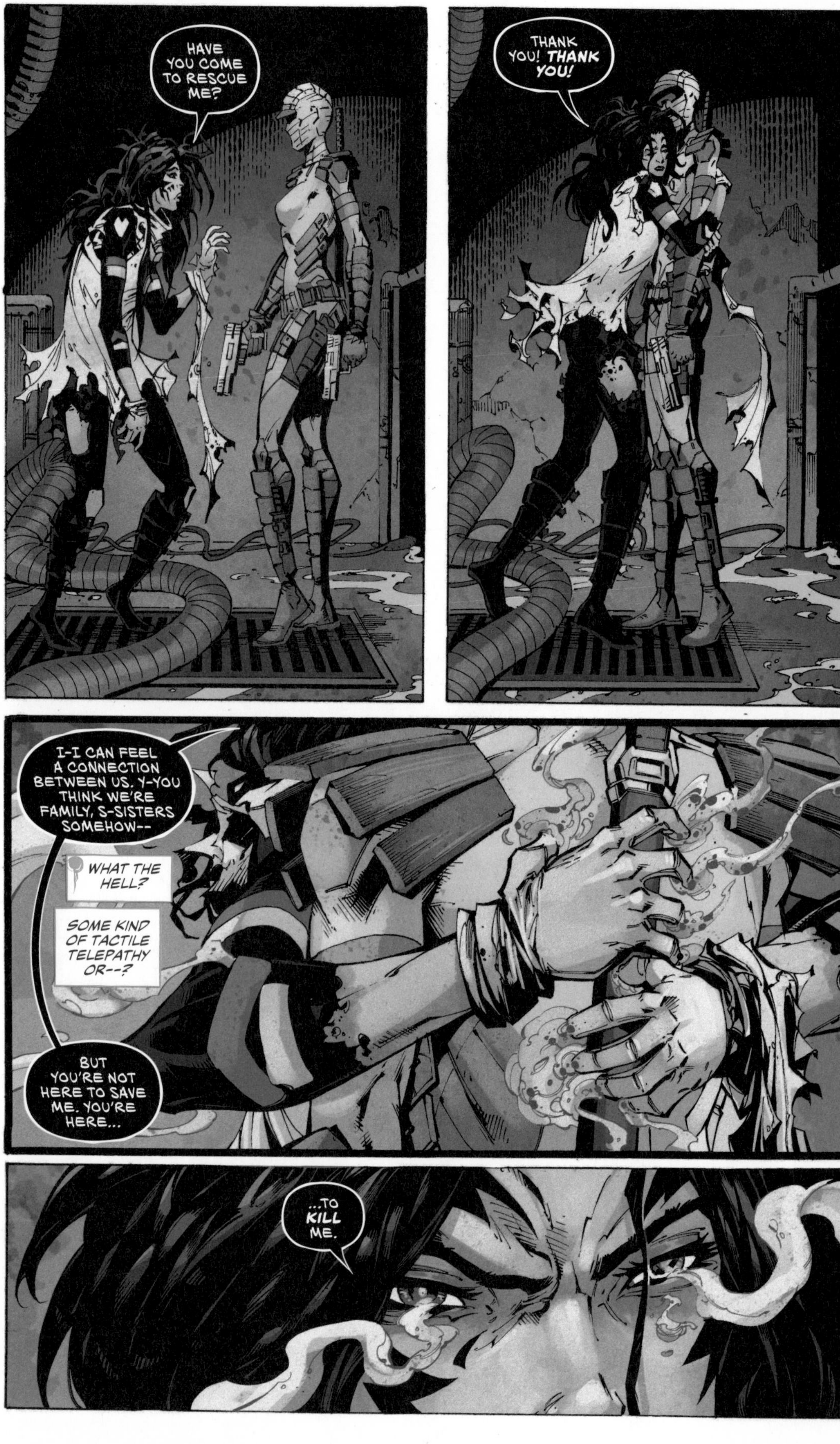
HAVE YOU COME TO RESCUE ME?
THANK YOU! **THANK YOU!**
I-I CAN FEEL A CONNECTION BETWEEN US. Y-YOU THINK WE'RE FAMILY, S-SISTERS SOMEHOW--
WHAT THE HELL?
SOME KIND OF TACTILE TELEPATHY OR--?
BUT YOU'RE NOT HERE TO SAVE ME. YOU'RE HERE...
...TO **KILL** ME.

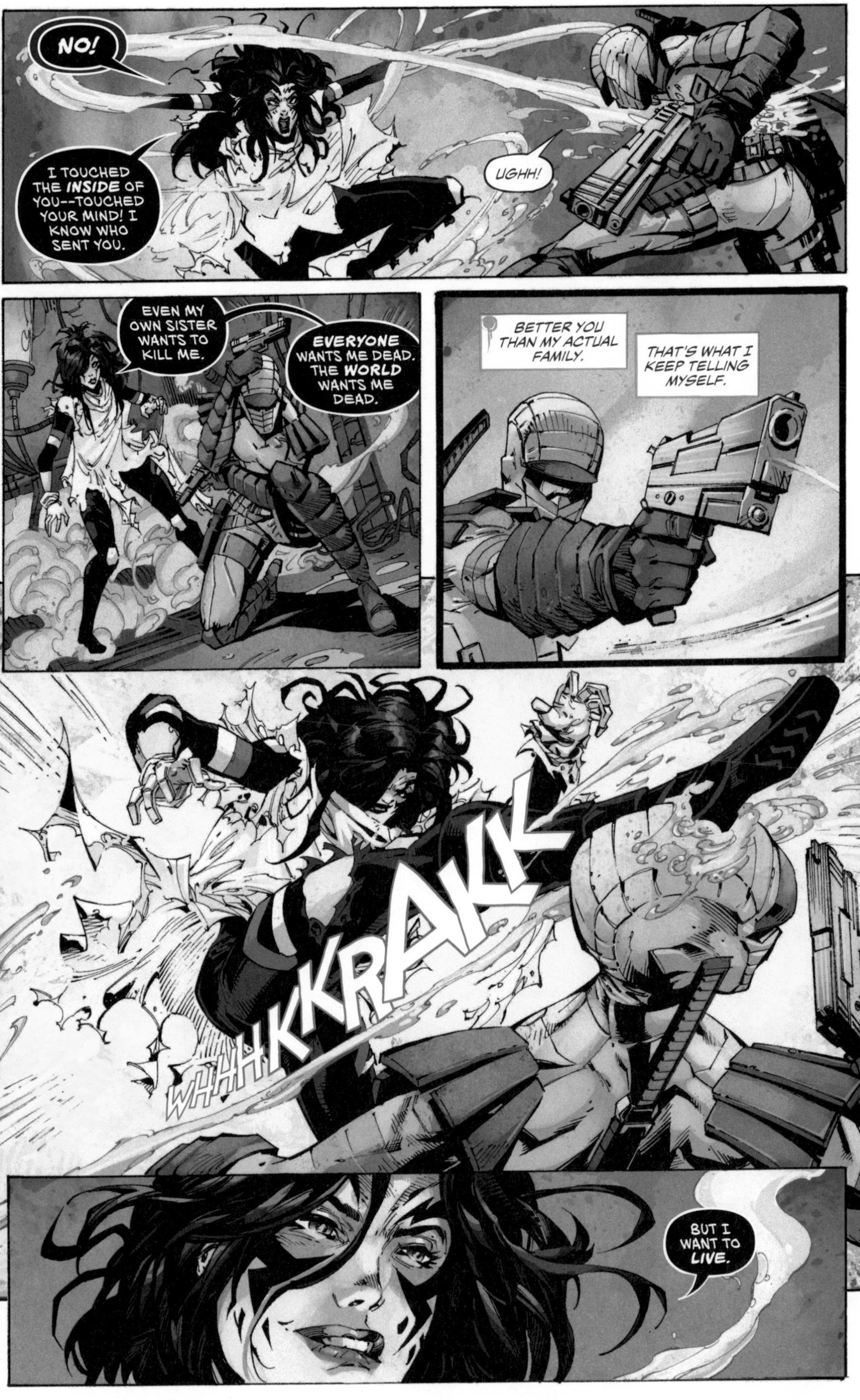
NO!
I TOUCHED THE INSIDE OF YOU--TOUCHED YOUR MIND! I KNOW WHO SENT YOU.
UGHH!
EVEN MY OWN SISTER WANTS TO KILL ME.
EVERYONE WANTS ME DEAD. THE WORLD WANTS ME DEAD.
BETTER YOU THAN MY ACTUAL FAMILY.
THAT'S WHAT I KEEP TELLING MYSELF.
WHHHKKRAKK
BUT I WANT TO LIVE.

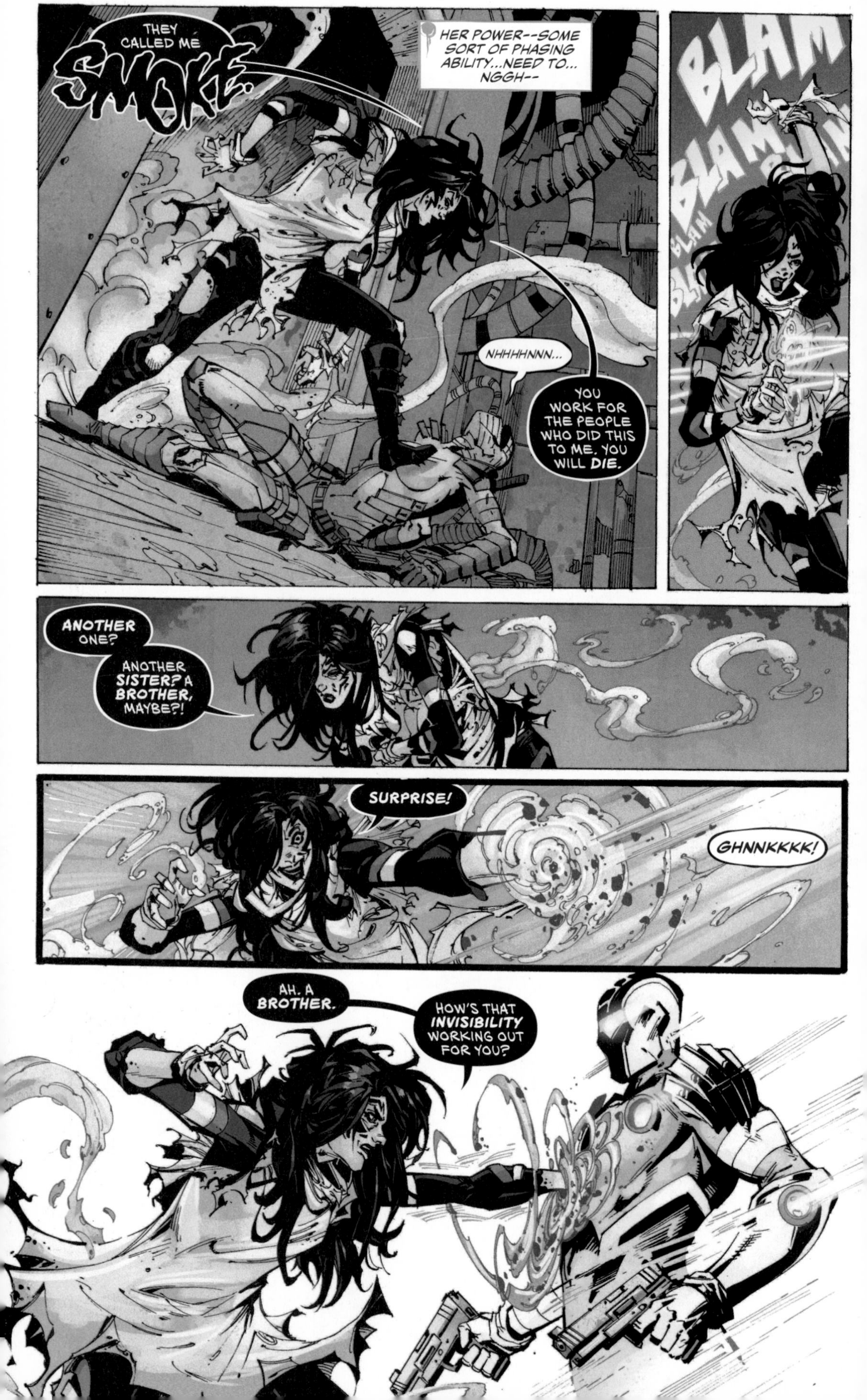
THEY CALLED ME
SMOKE.
HER POWER--SOME SORT OF PHASING ABILITY...NEED TO... NGGH--
NHHHHNNN...
YOU WORK FOR THE PEOPLE WHO DID THIS TO ME. YOU WILL DIE.
BLAM
BLAM
BLAM
BLAM
BLAM
BLAM
ANOTHER ONE?
ANOTHER SISTER? A BROTHER, MAYBE?!
SURPRISE!
GHNNKKKK!
AH. A BROTHER.
HOW'S THAT INVISIBILITY WORKING OUT FOR YOU?

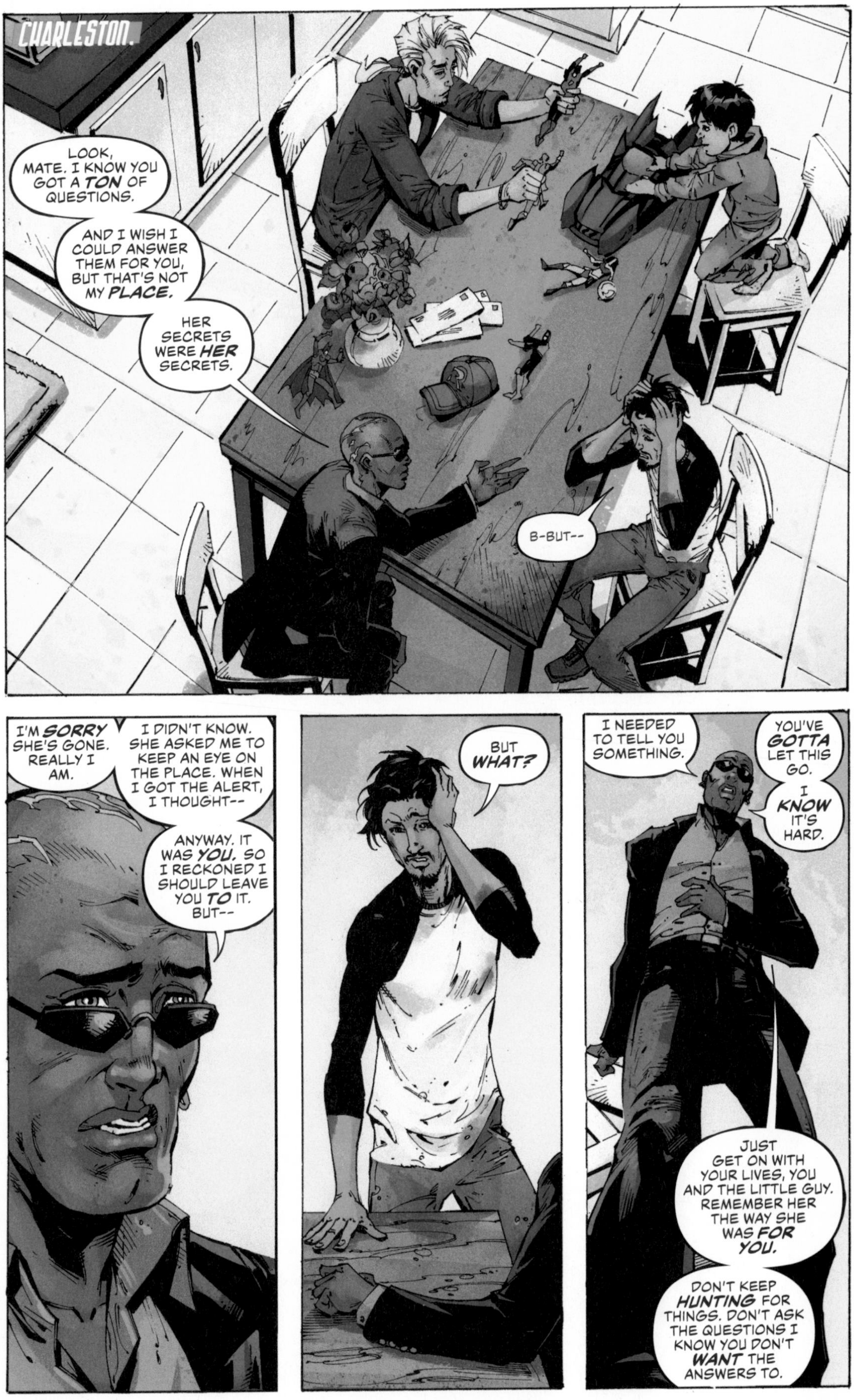
CHARLESTON.
LOOK, MATE. I KNOW YOU GOT A TON OF QUESTIONS.
AND I WISH I COULD ANSWER THEM FOR YOU, BUT THAT'S NOT MY PLACE.
HER SECRETS WERE HER SECRETS.
B-BUT--
I'M SORRY SHE'S GONE. REALLY I AM.
I DIDN'T KNOW. SHE ASKED ME TO KEEP AN EYE ON THE PLACE. WHEN I GOT THE ALERT, I THOUGHT--
ANYWAY. IT WAS YOU. SO I RECKONED I SHOULD LEAVE YOU TO IT. BUT--
BUT WHAT?
I NEEDED TO TELL YOU SOMETHING.
YOU'VE GOTTA LET THIS GO.
I KNOW IT'S HARD.
JUST GET ON WITH YOUR LIVES, YOU AND THE LITTLE GUY. REMEMBER HER THE WAY SHE WAS FOR YOU.
DON'T KEEP HUNTING FOR THINGS. DON'T ASK THE QUESTIONS I KNOW YOU DON'T WANT THE ANSWERS TO.

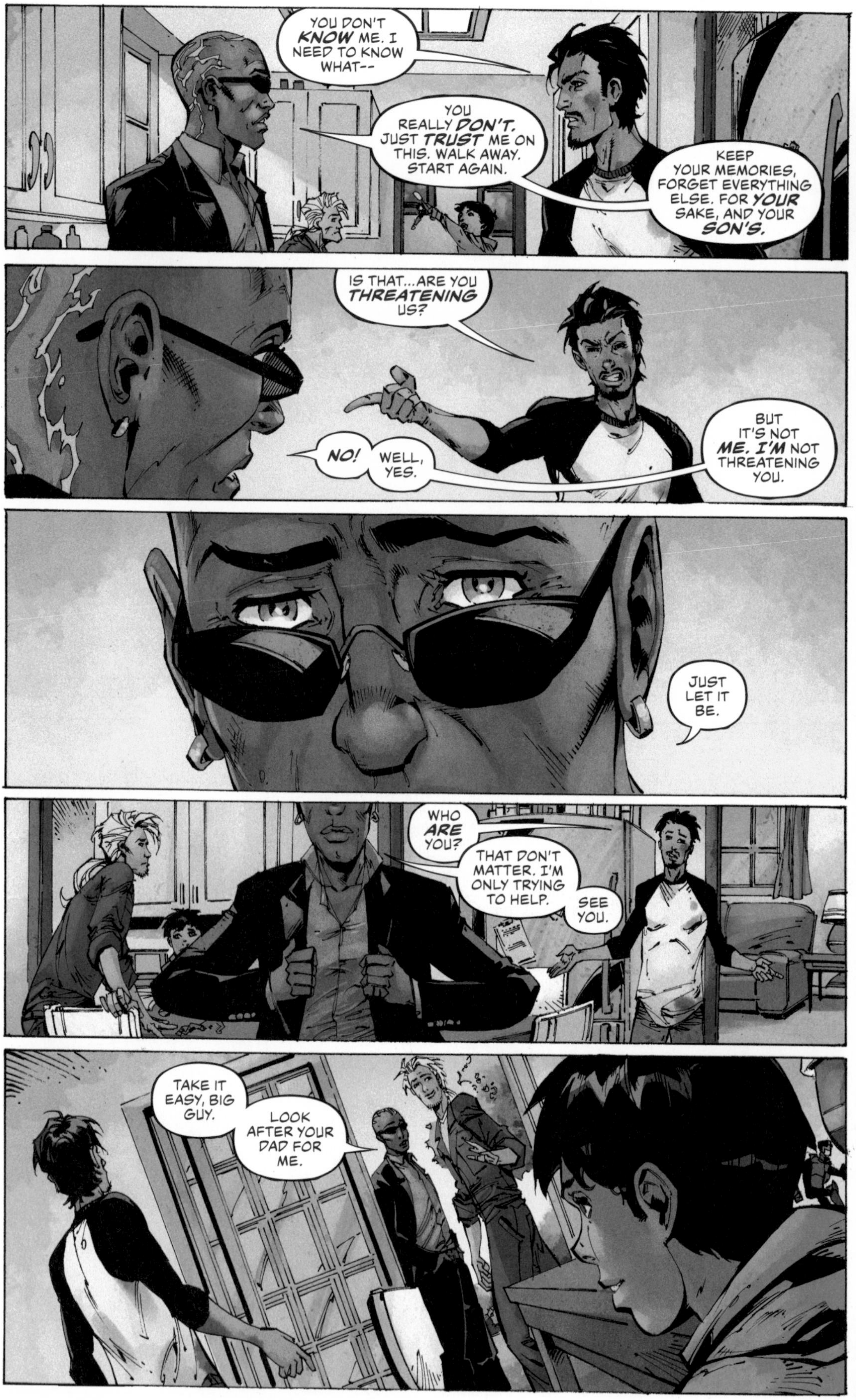
YOU DON'T KNOW ME. I NEED TO KNOW WHAT--
YOU REALLY DON'T. JUST TRUST ME ON THIS. WALK AWAY. START AGAIN.
KEEP YOUR MEMORIES, FORGET EVERYTHING ELSE. FOR YOUR SAKE, AND YOUR SON'S.
IS THAT...ARE YOU THREATENING US?
NO!
WELL, YES.
BUT IT'S NOT ME. I'M NOT THREATENING YOU.
JUST LET IT BE.
WHO ARE YOU?
THAT DON'T MATTER. I'M ONLY TRYING TO HELP.
SEE YOU.
TAKE IT EASY, BIG GUY.
LOOK AFTER YOUR DAD FOR ME.

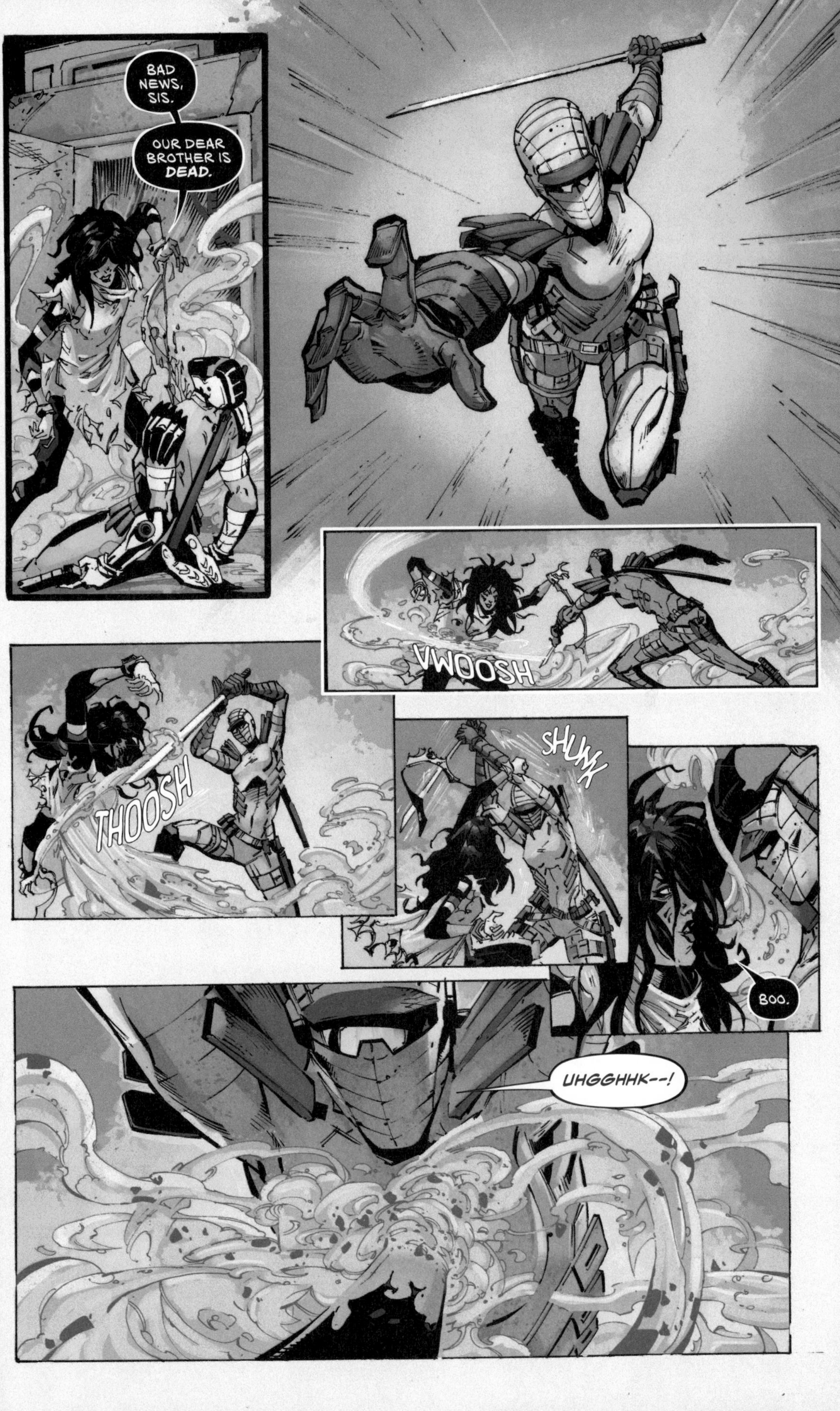
BAD NEWS, SIS.
OUR DEAR BROTHER IS DEAD.
VWOOSH
THOOSH
SHUNK
BOO.
UHGGHHK--!

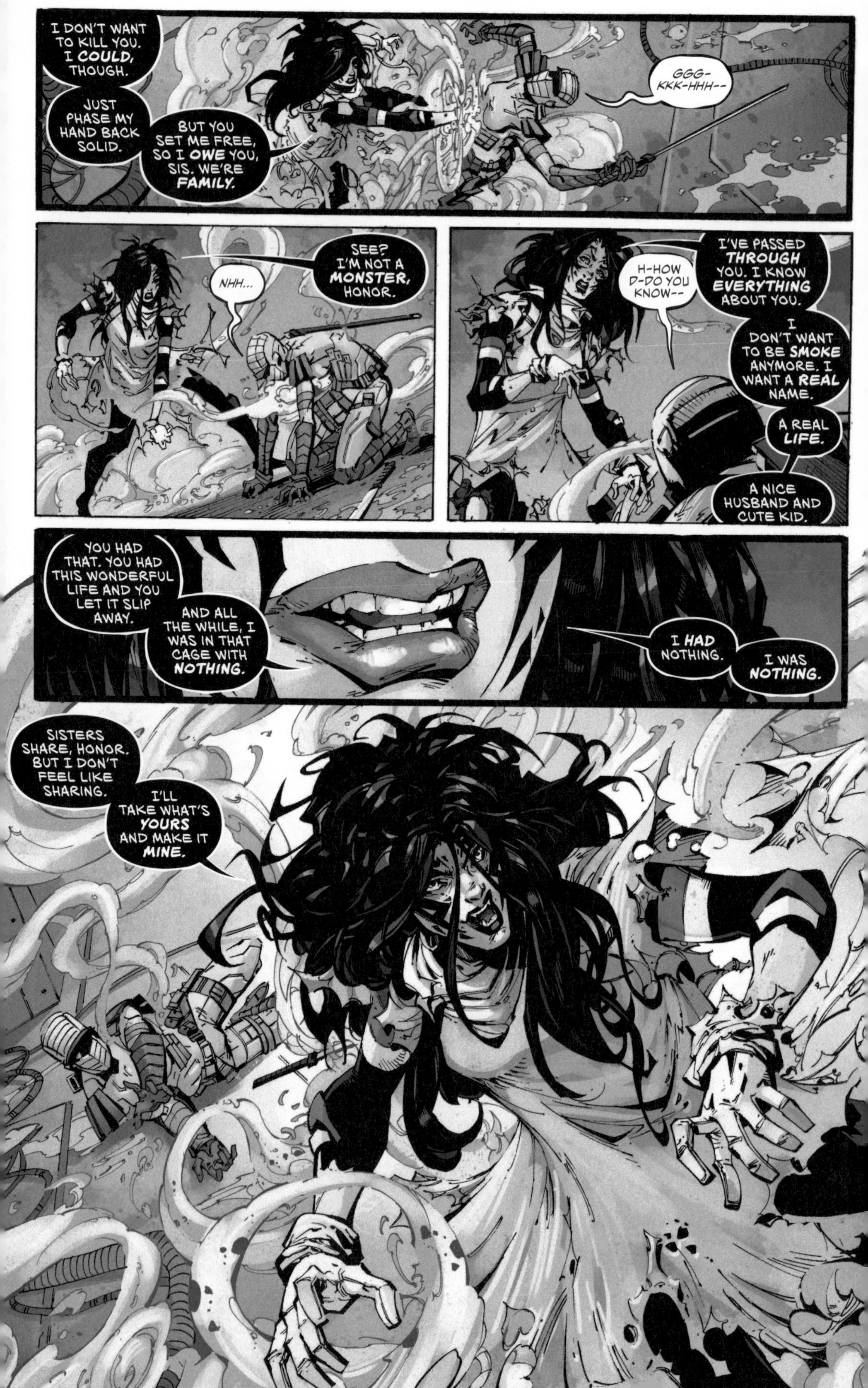
I DON'T WANT TO KILL YOU. I COULD, THOUGH.
JUST PHASE MY HAND BACK SOLID.
BUT YOU SET ME FREE, SO I OWE YOU, SIS. WE'RE FAMILY.
GGG-KKK-HHH--
NHH...
SEE? I'M NOT A MONSTER, HONOR.
H-HOW D-DO YOU KNOW--
I'VE PASSED THROUGH YOU. I KNOW EVERYTHING ABOUT YOU.
I DON'T WANT TO BE SMOKE ANYMORE. I WANT A REAL NAME.
A REAL LIFE.
A NICE HUSBAND AND CUTE KID.
YOU HAD THAT. YOU HAD THIS WONDERFUL LIFE AND YOU LET IT SLIP AWAY.
AND ALL THE WHILE, I WAS IN THAT CAGE WITH NOTHING.
I HAD NOTHING.
I WAS NOTHING.
SISTERS SHARE, HONOR. BUT I DON'T FEEL LIKE SHARING.
I'LL TAKE WHAT'S YOURS AND MAKE IT MINE.

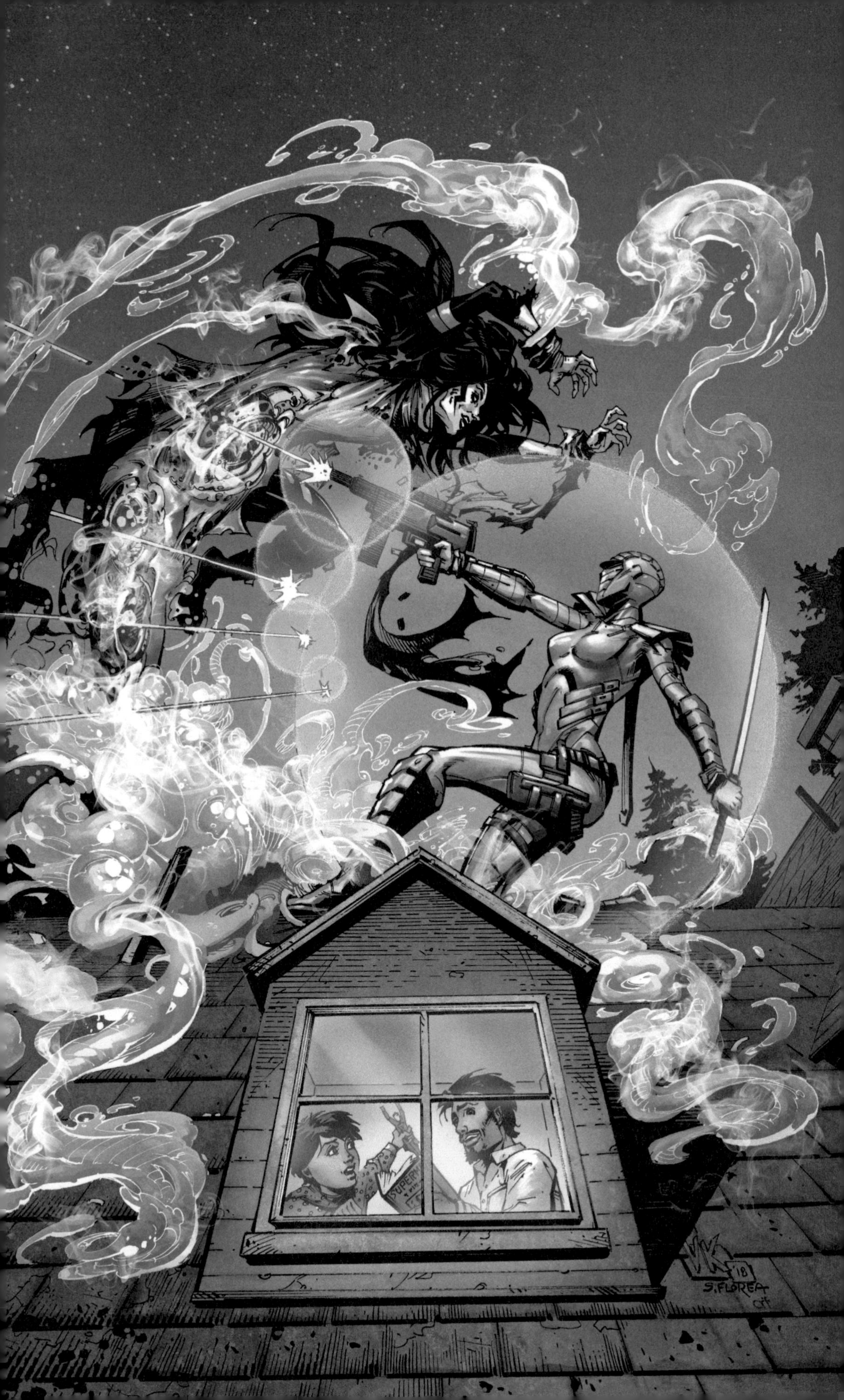
S.FLOREA

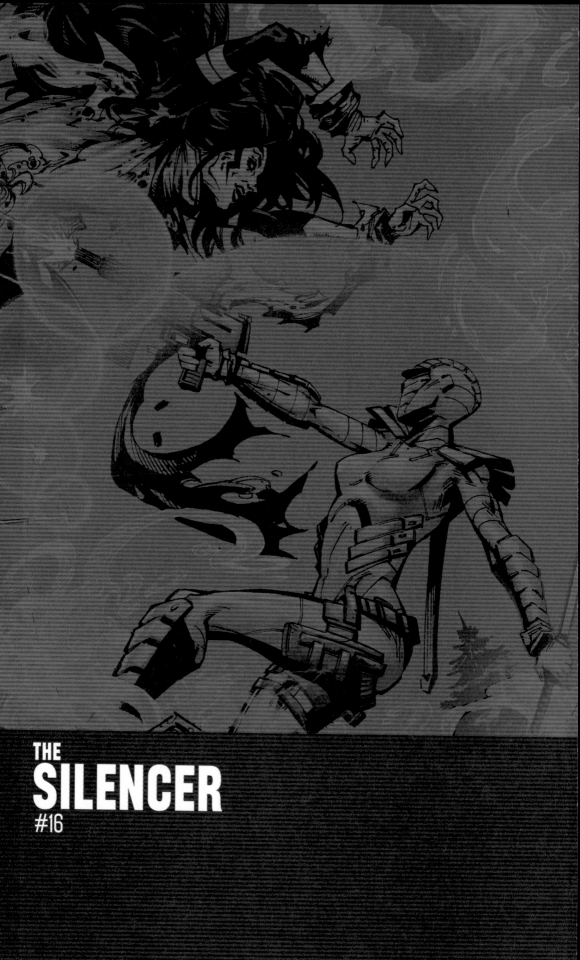

THE **SILENCER**
#16

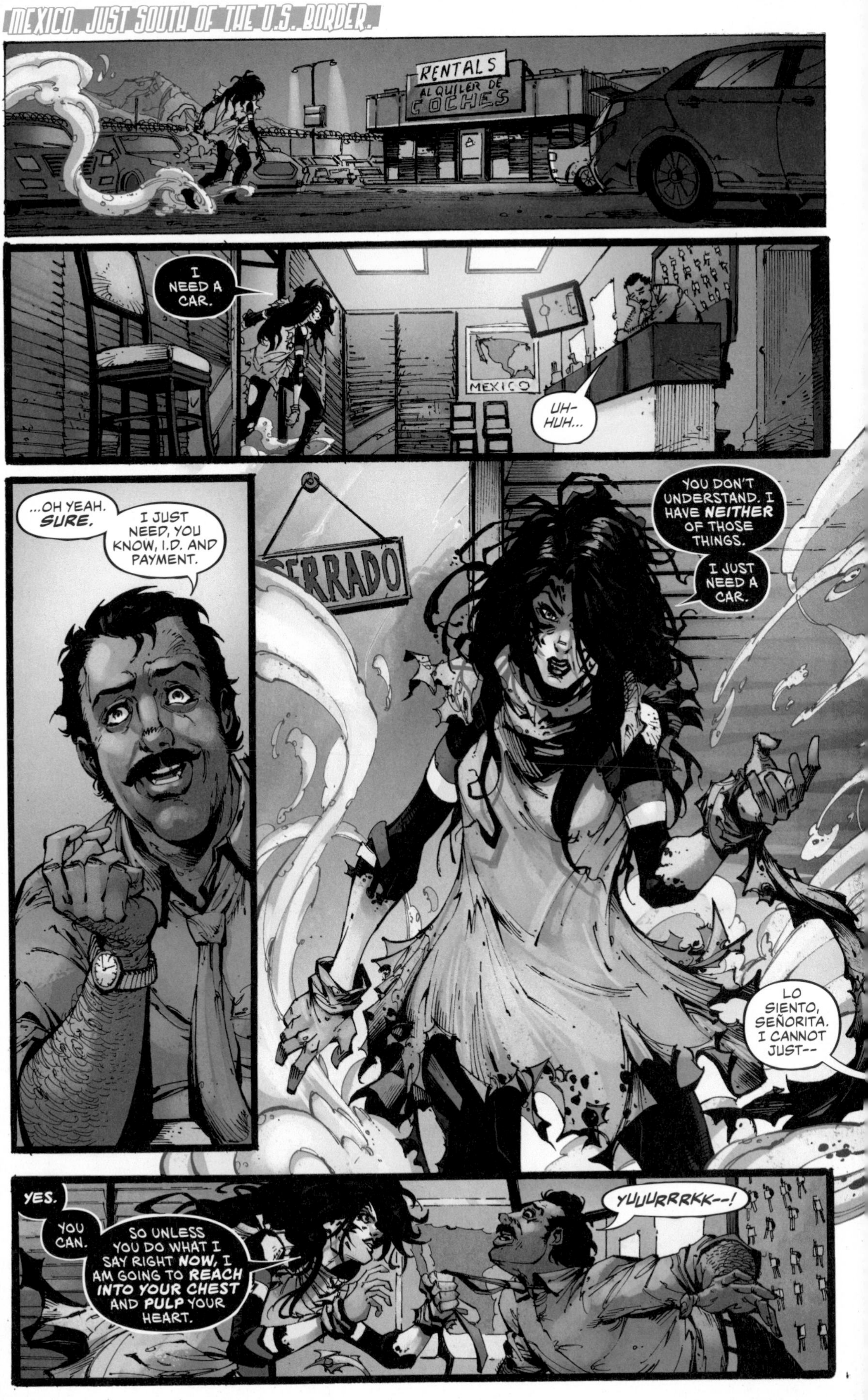
MEXICO. JUST SOUTH OF THE U.S. BORDER.
RENTALS
ALQUILER DE COCHES
I NEED A CAR.
MEXICO
UH-HUH...
...OH YEAH. SURE.
I JUST NEED, YOU KNOW, I.D. AND PAYMENT.
ERRADO
YOU DON'T UNDERSTAND. I HAVE NEITHER OF THOSE THINGS.
I JUST NEED A CAR.
LO SIENTO, SEÑORITA. I CANNOT JUST--
YES.
YOU CAN.
SO UNLESS YOU DO WHAT I SAY RIGHT NOW, I AM GOING TO REACH INTO YOUR CHEST AND PULP YOUR HEART.
YUUURRRKK--!

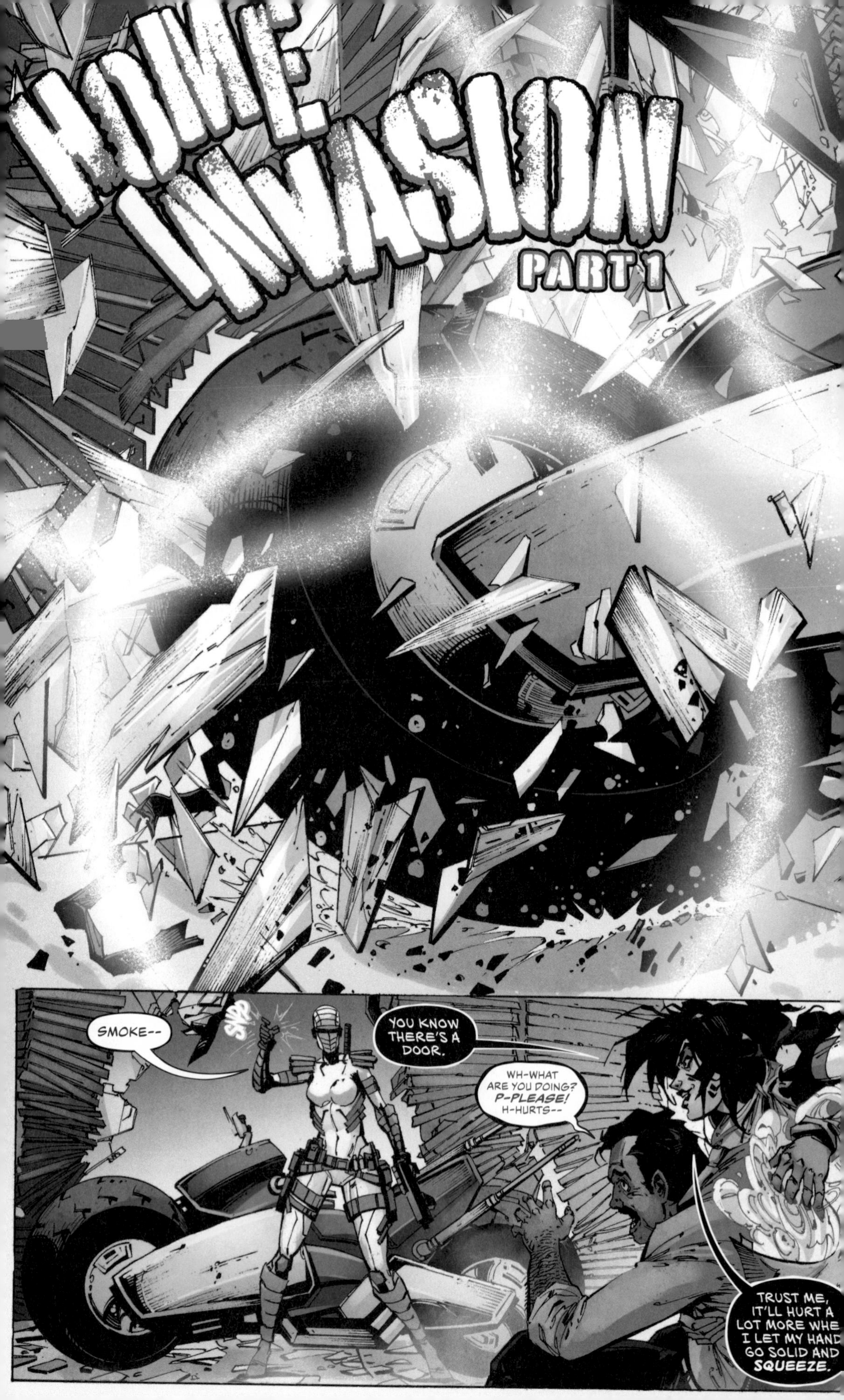
HOME INVASION
PART 1
SMOKE--
SNAP
YOU KNOW THERE'S A DOOR.
WH-WHAT ARE YOU DOING? *P-PLEASE!* H-HURTS--
TRUST ME, IT'LL HURT A LOT MORE WHEN I LET MY HAND GO SOLID AND **SQUEEZE.**

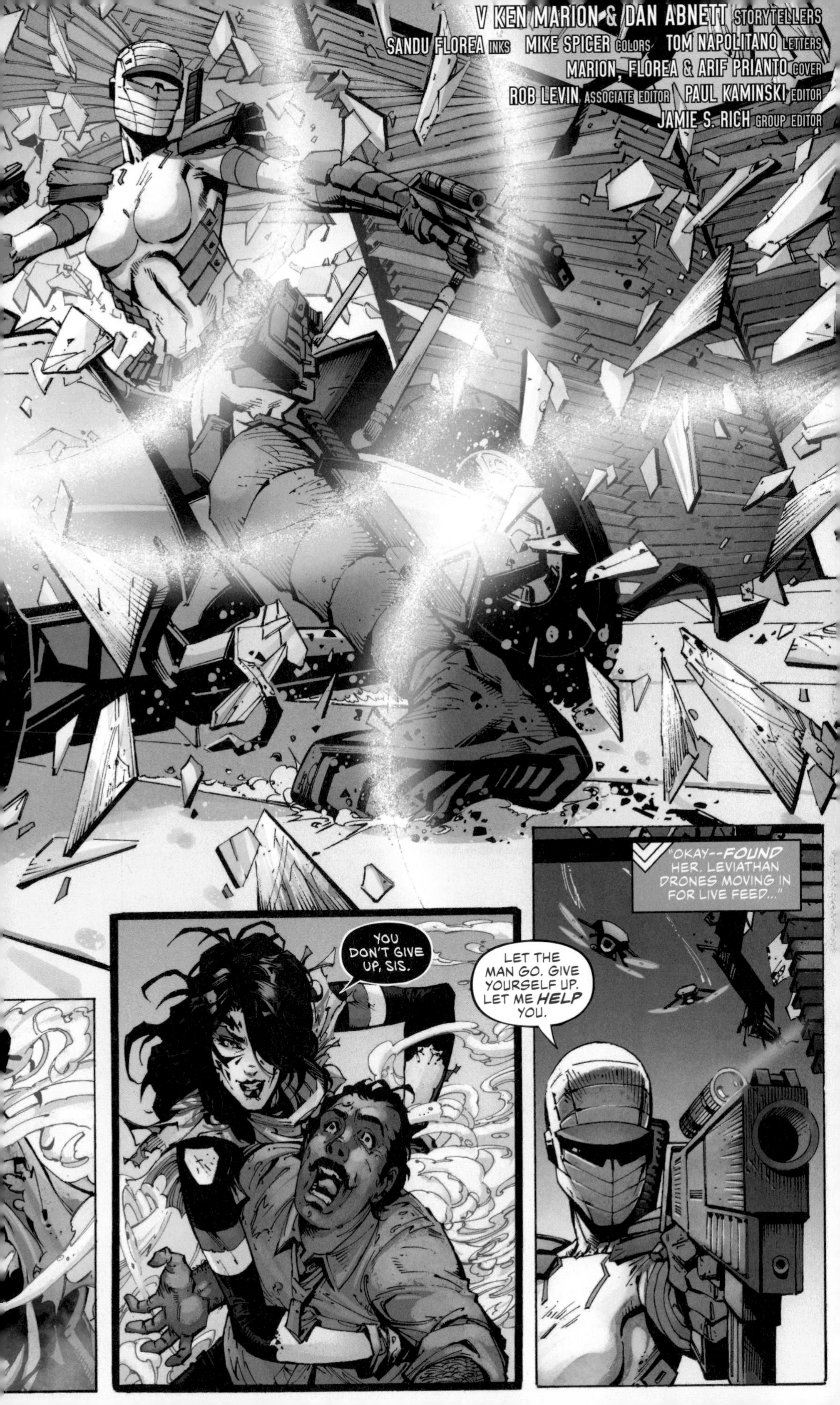

V KEN MARION & DAN ABNETT STORYTELLERS
SANDU FLOREA INKS MIKE SPICER COLORS TOM NAPOLITANO LETTERS
MARION, FLOREA & ARIF PRIANTO COVER
ROB LEVIN ASSOCIATE EDITOR PAUL KAMINSKI EDITOR
JAMIE S. RICH GROUP EDITOR
"OKAY--FOUND HER. LEVIATHAN DRONES MOVING IN FOR LIVE FEED..."
YOU DON'T GIVE UP, SIS.
LET THE MAN GO. GIVE YOURSELF UP. LET ME HELP YOU.

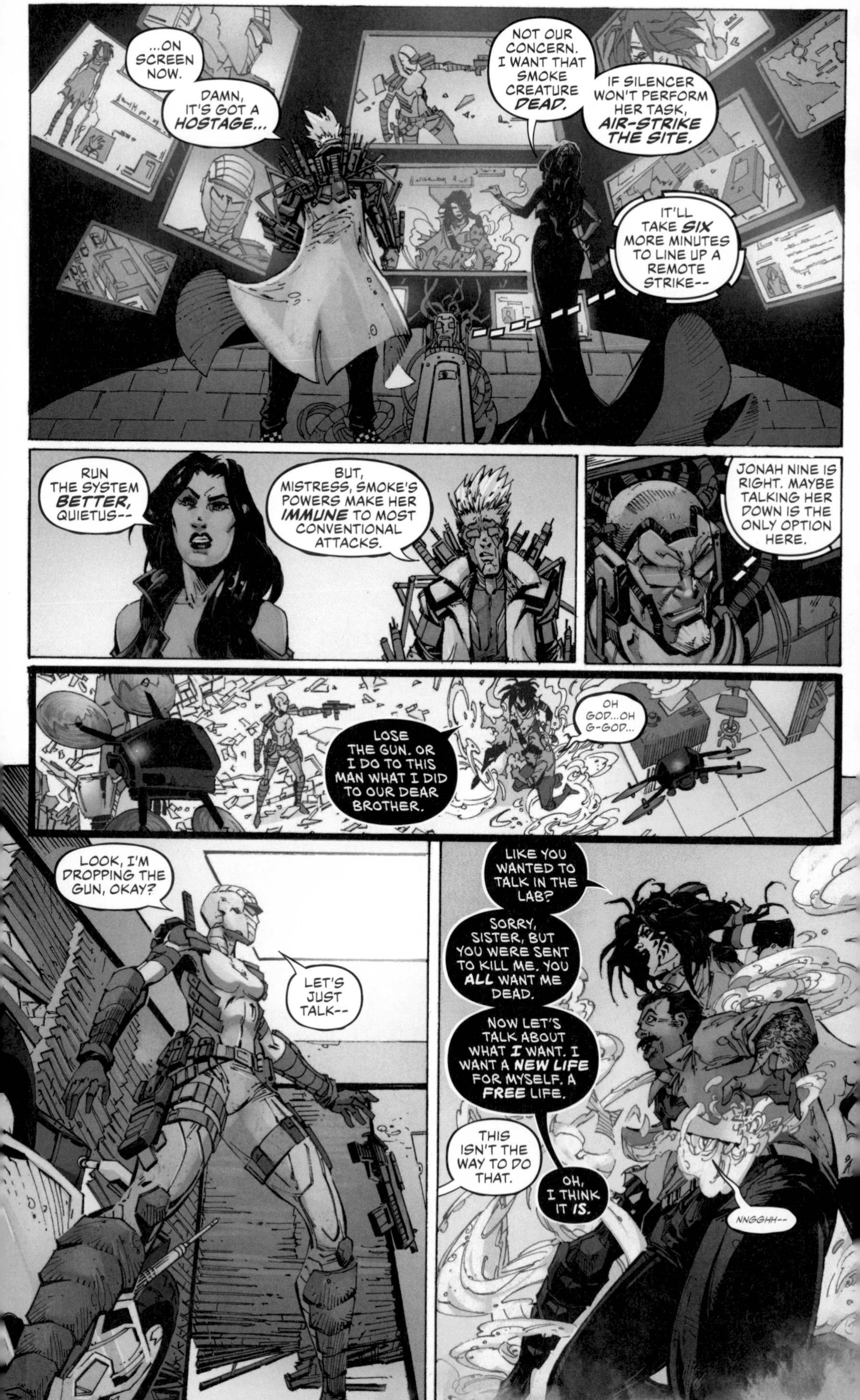

...ON SCREEN NOW.
DAMN, IT'S GOT A HOSTAGE...
NOT OUR CONCERN. I WANT THAT SMOKE CREATURE DEAD.
IF SILENCER WON'T PERFORM HER TASK, AIR-STRIKE THE SITE.
IT'LL TAKE SIX MORE MINUTES TO LINE UP A REMOTE STRIKE--
RUN THE SYSTEM BETTER, QUIETUS--
BUT, MISTRESS, SMOKE'S POWERS MAKE HER IMMUNE TO MOST CONVENTIONAL ATTACKS.
JONAH NINE IS RIGHT. MAYBE TALKING HER DOWN IS THE ONLY OPTION HERE.
LOSE THE GUN. OR I DO TO THIS MAN WHAT I DID TO OUR DEAR BROTHER.
OH GOD...OH G-GOD...
LOOK, I'M DROPPING THE GUN, OKAY?
LET'S JUST TALK--
LIKE YOU WANTED TO TALK IN THE LAB?
SORRY, SISTER, BUT YOU WERE SENT TO KILL ME. YOU ALL WANT ME DEAD.
NOW LET'S TALK ABOUT WHAT I WANT. I WANT A NEW LIFE FOR MYSELF. A FREE LIFE.
THIS ISN'T THE WAY TO DO THAT.
OH, I THINK IT IS.
NNGGHH--

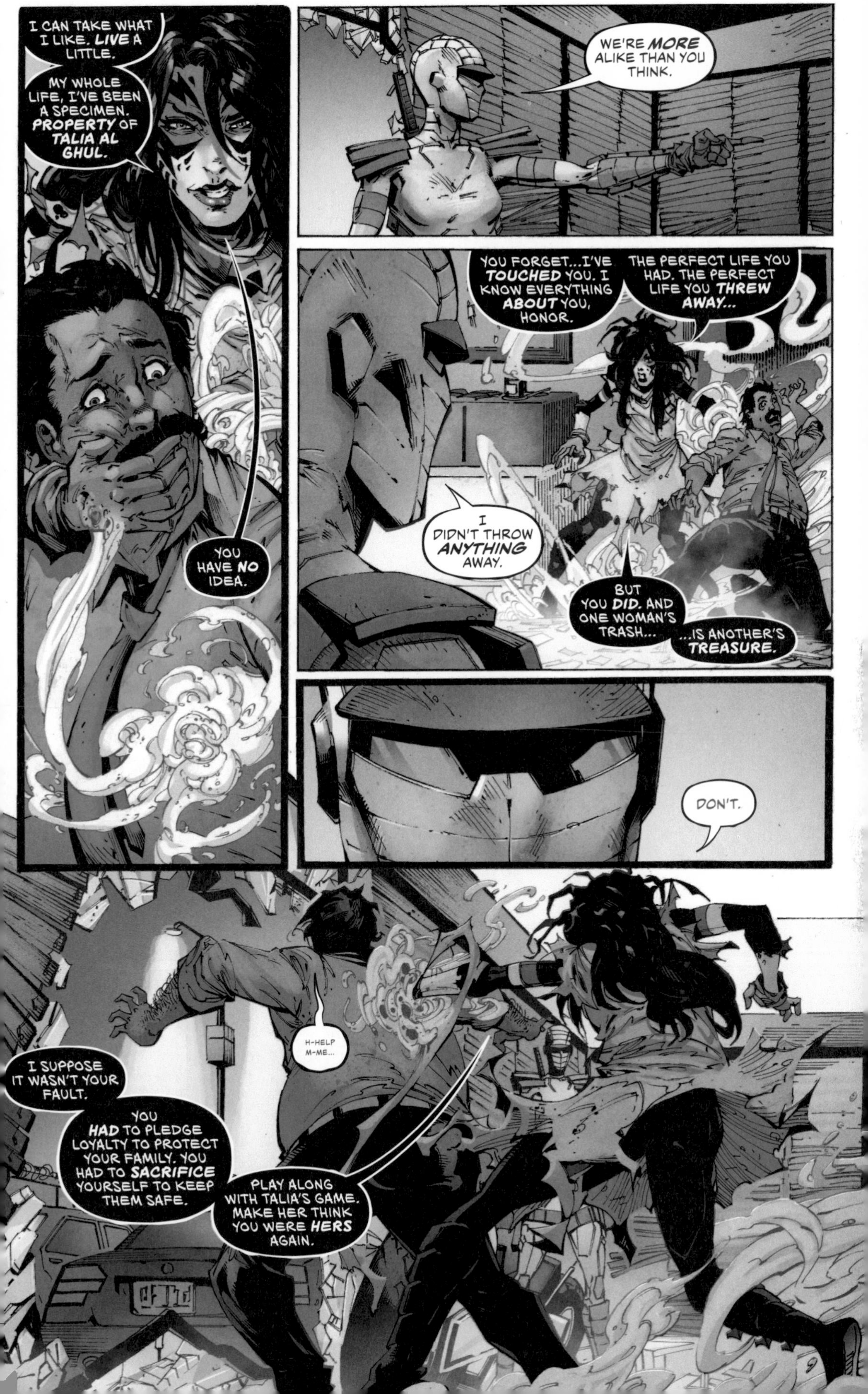

I CAN TAKE WHAT I LIKE. LIVE A LITTLE.
MY WHOLE LIFE, I'VE BEEN A SPECIMEN. PROPERTY OF TALIA AL GHUL.
YOU HAVE NO IDEA.
WE'RE MORE ALIKE THAN YOU THINK.
YOU FORGET...I'VE TOUCHED YOU. I KNOW EVERYTHING ABOUT YOU, HONOR.
THE PERFECT LIFE YOU HAD. THE PERFECT LIFE YOU THREW AWAY...
I DIDN'T THROW ANYTHING AWAY.
BUT YOU DID. AND ONE WOMAN'S TRASH...
...IS ANOTHER'S TREASURE.
DON'T.
H-HELP M-ME...
I SUPPOSE IT WASN'T YOUR FAULT.
YOU HAD TO PLEDGE LOYALTY TO PROTECT YOUR FAMILY. YOU HAD TO SACRIFICE YOURSELF TO KEEP THEM SAFE.
PLAY ALONG WITH TALIA'S GAME. MAKE HER THINK YOU WERE HERS AGAIN.

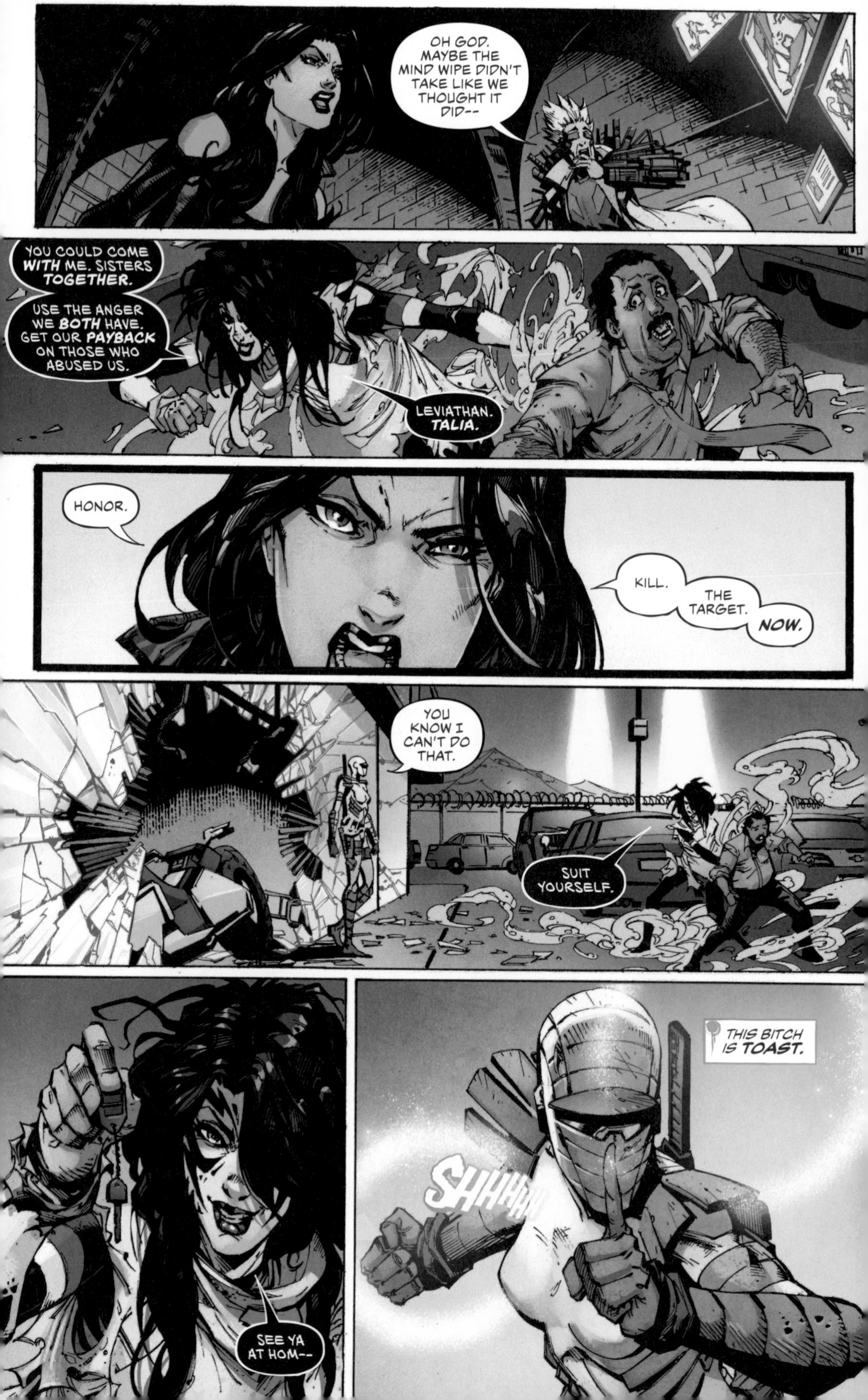
OH GOD. MAYBE THE MIND WIPE DIDN'T TAKE LIKE WE THOUGHT IT DID--
YOU COULD COME WITH ME. SISTERS TOGETHER.
USE THE ANGER WE BOTH HAVE. GET OUR PAYBACK ON THOSE WHO ABUSED US.
LEVIATHAN. TALIA.
HONOR.
KILL.
THE TARGET.
NOW.
YOU KNOW I CAN'T DO THAT.
SUIT YOURSELF.
SEE YA AT HOM--
THIS BITCH IS TOAST.
SHHHHH

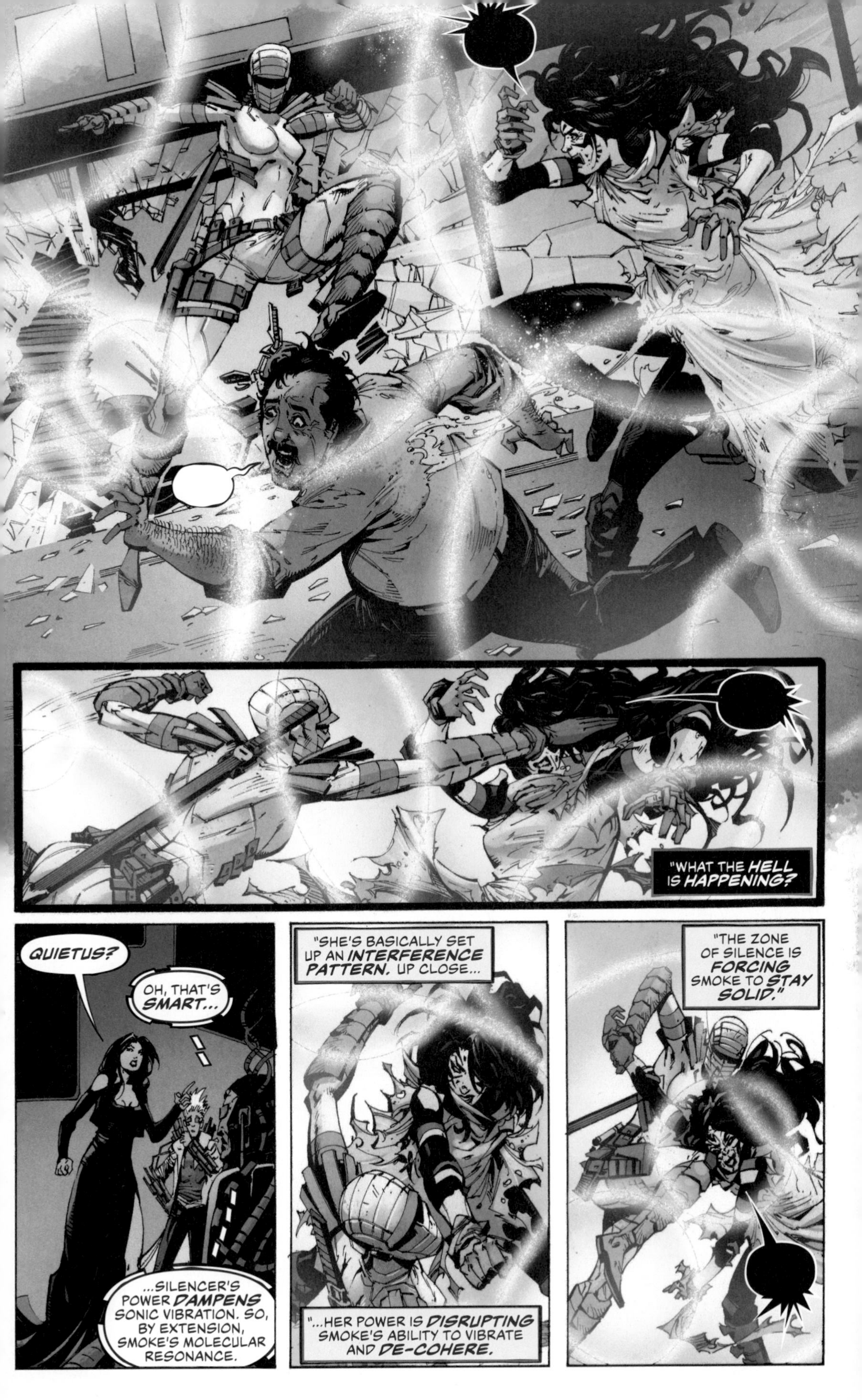
"WHAT THE HELL IS HAPPENING?
QUIETUS?
OH, THAT'S SMART...
...SILENCER'S POWER DAMPENS SONIC VIBRATION. SO, BY EXTENSION, SMOKE'S MOLECULAR RESONANCE.
"SHE'S BASICALLY SET UP AN INTERFERENCE PATTERN. UP CLOSE...
"...HER POWER IS DISRUPTING SMOKE'S ABILITY TO VIBRATE AND DE-COHERE.
"THE ZONE OF SILENCE IS FORCING SMOKE TO STAY SOLID."

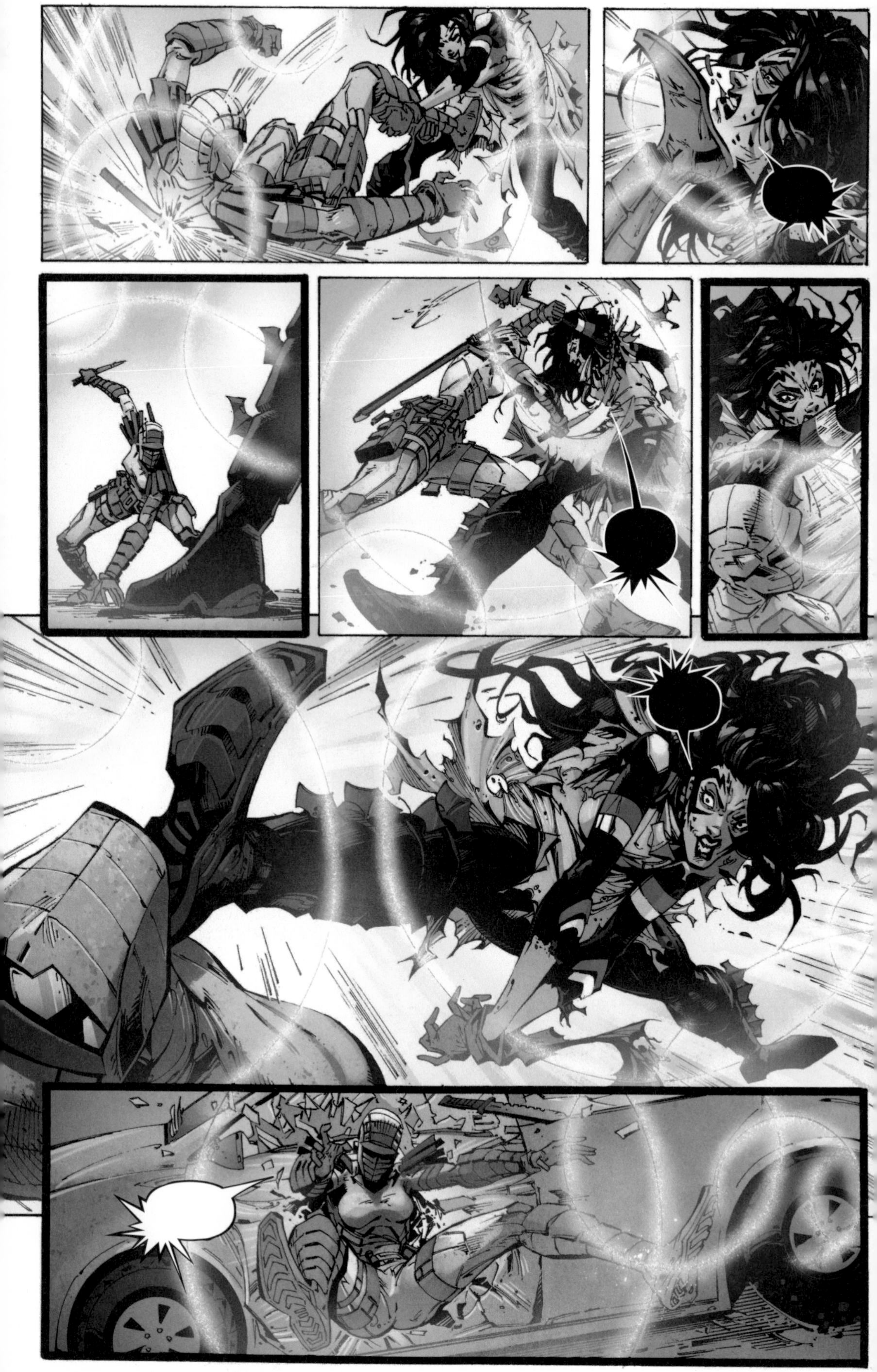

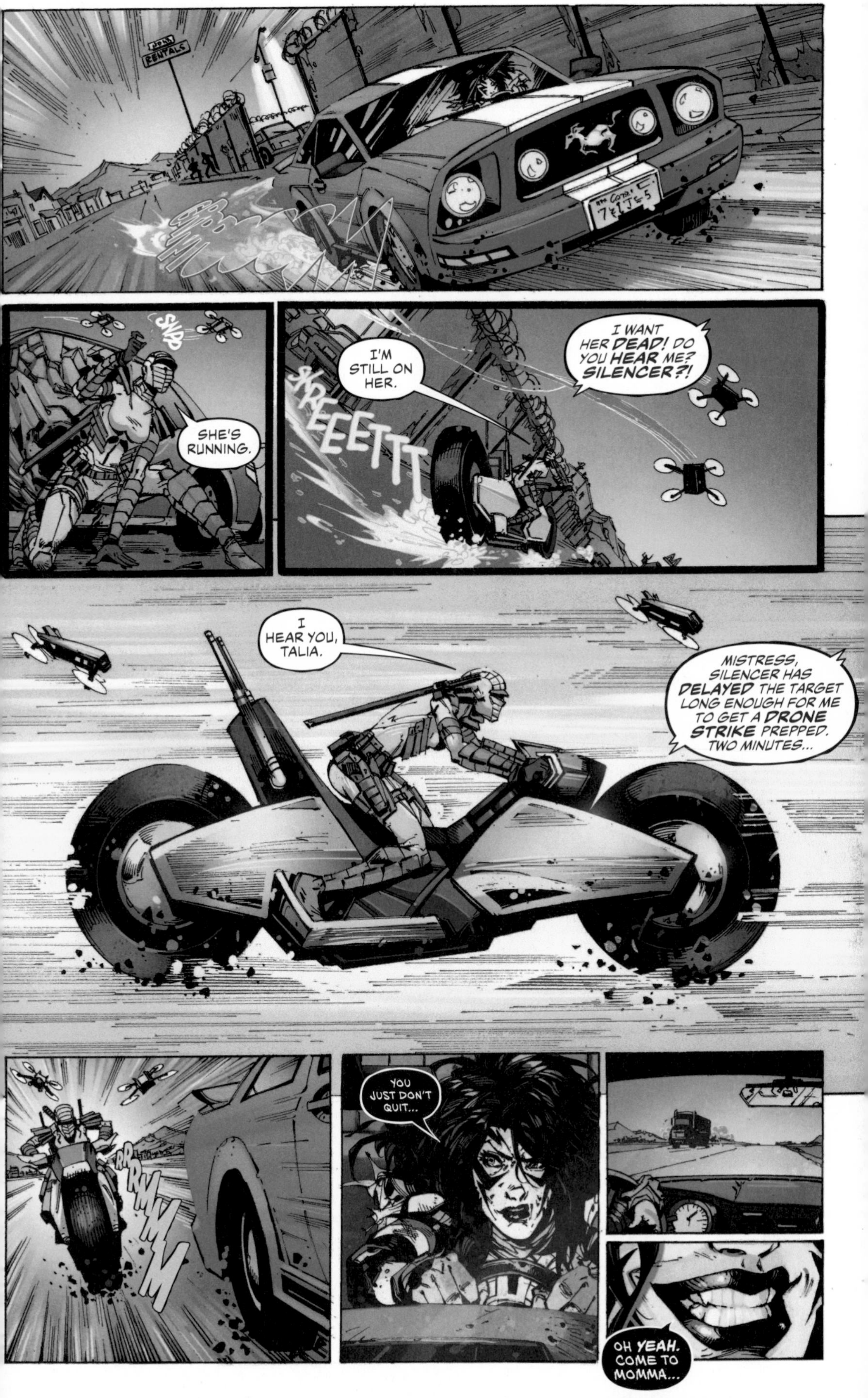
RENTALS
SNIP
SHE'S RUNNING.
SKREEETTT
I'M STILL ON HER.
I WANT HER DEAD! DO YOU HEAR ME? SILENCER?!
I HEAR YOU, TALIA.
MISTRESS, SILENCER HAS DELAYED THE TARGET LONG ENOUGH FOR ME TO GET A DRONE STRIKE PREPPED. TWO MINUTES...
RRRMMMM
YOU JUST DON'T QUIT...
OH YEAH. COME TO MOMMA...

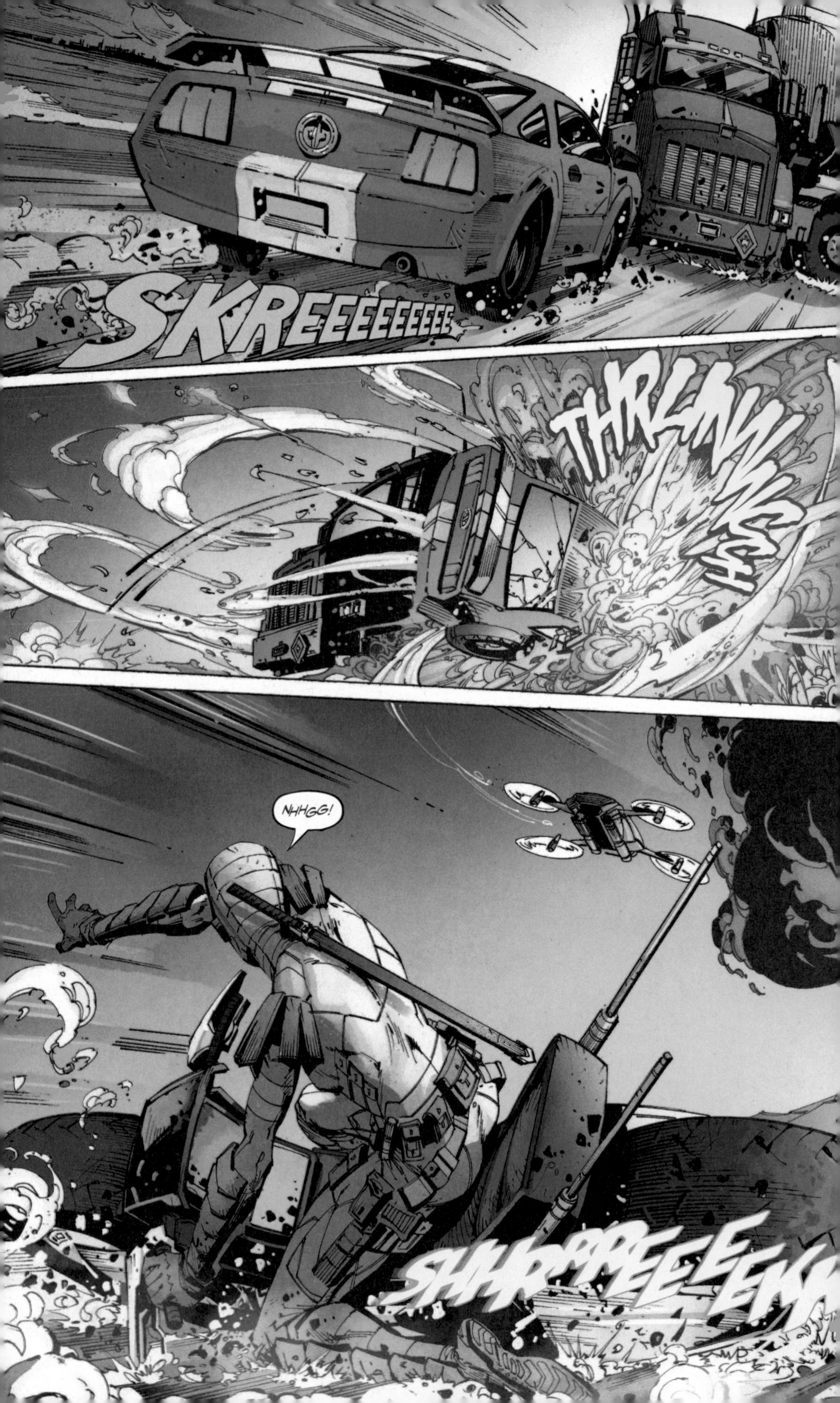
SKREEEEEEEEE
THRUNNKSH
NHHGG!
SHHRRREEEEEK

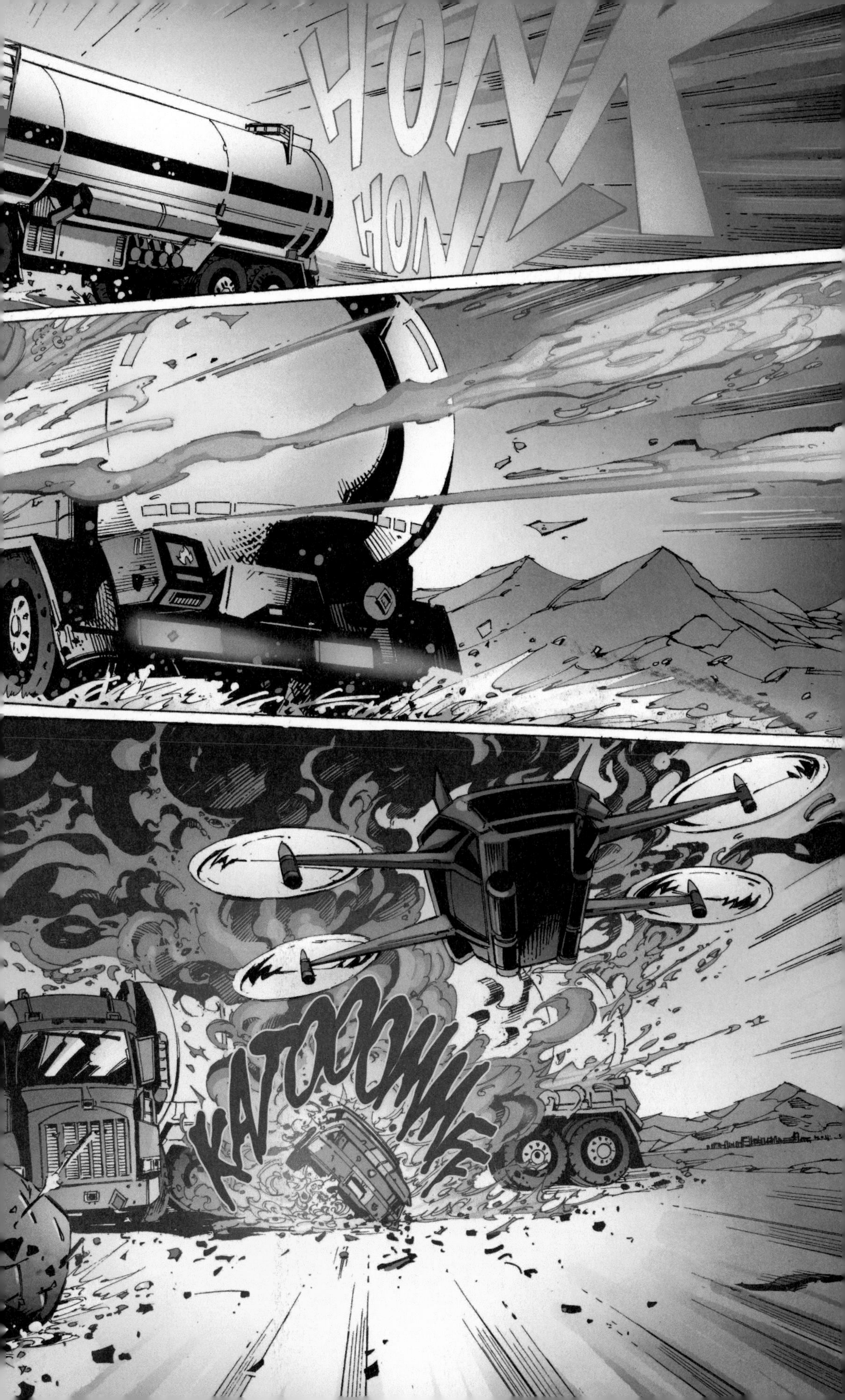
HONK
HONK
KATOOOMM

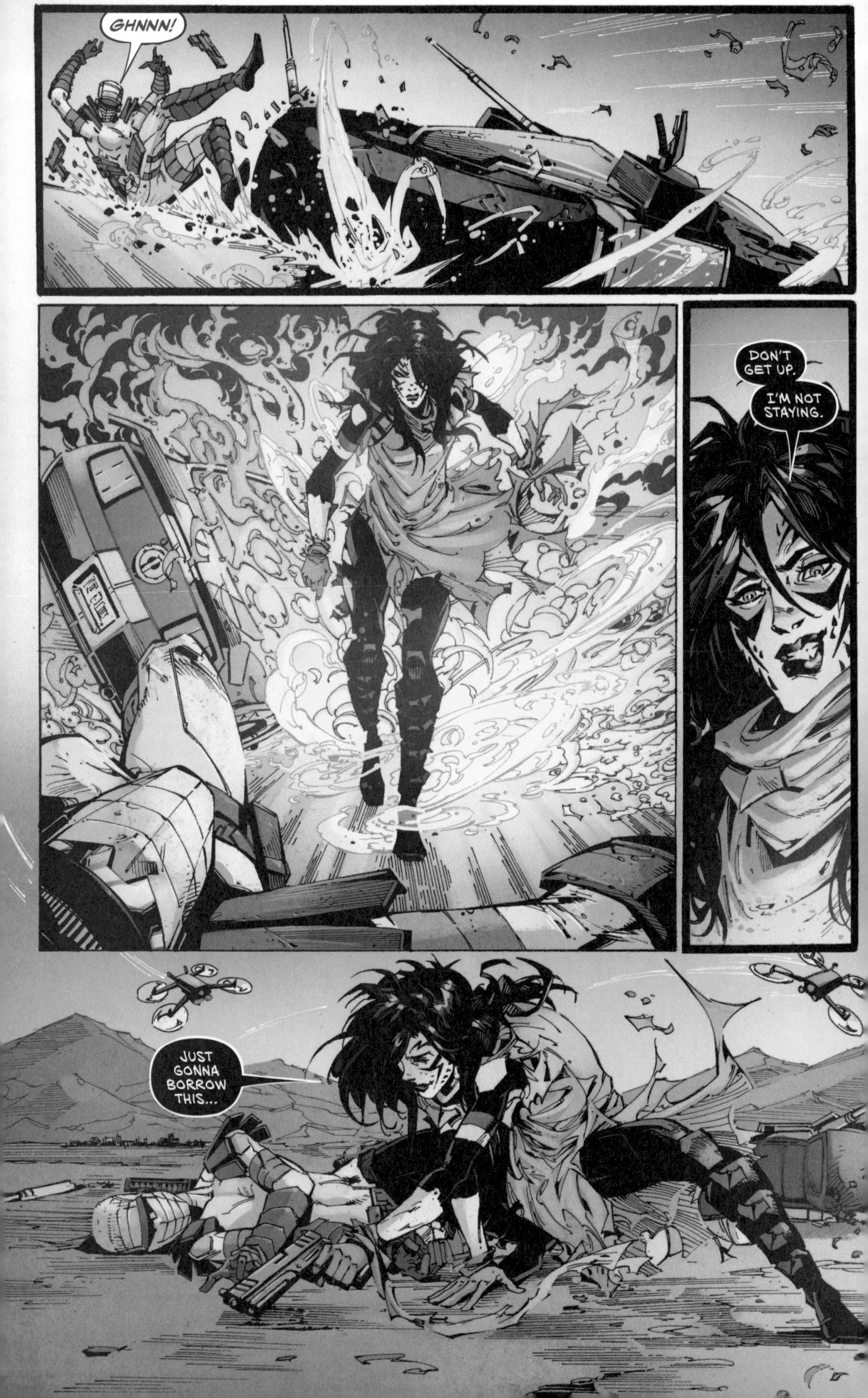
GHNNN!
DON'T GET UP.
I'M NOT STAYING.
JUST GONNA BORROW THIS...

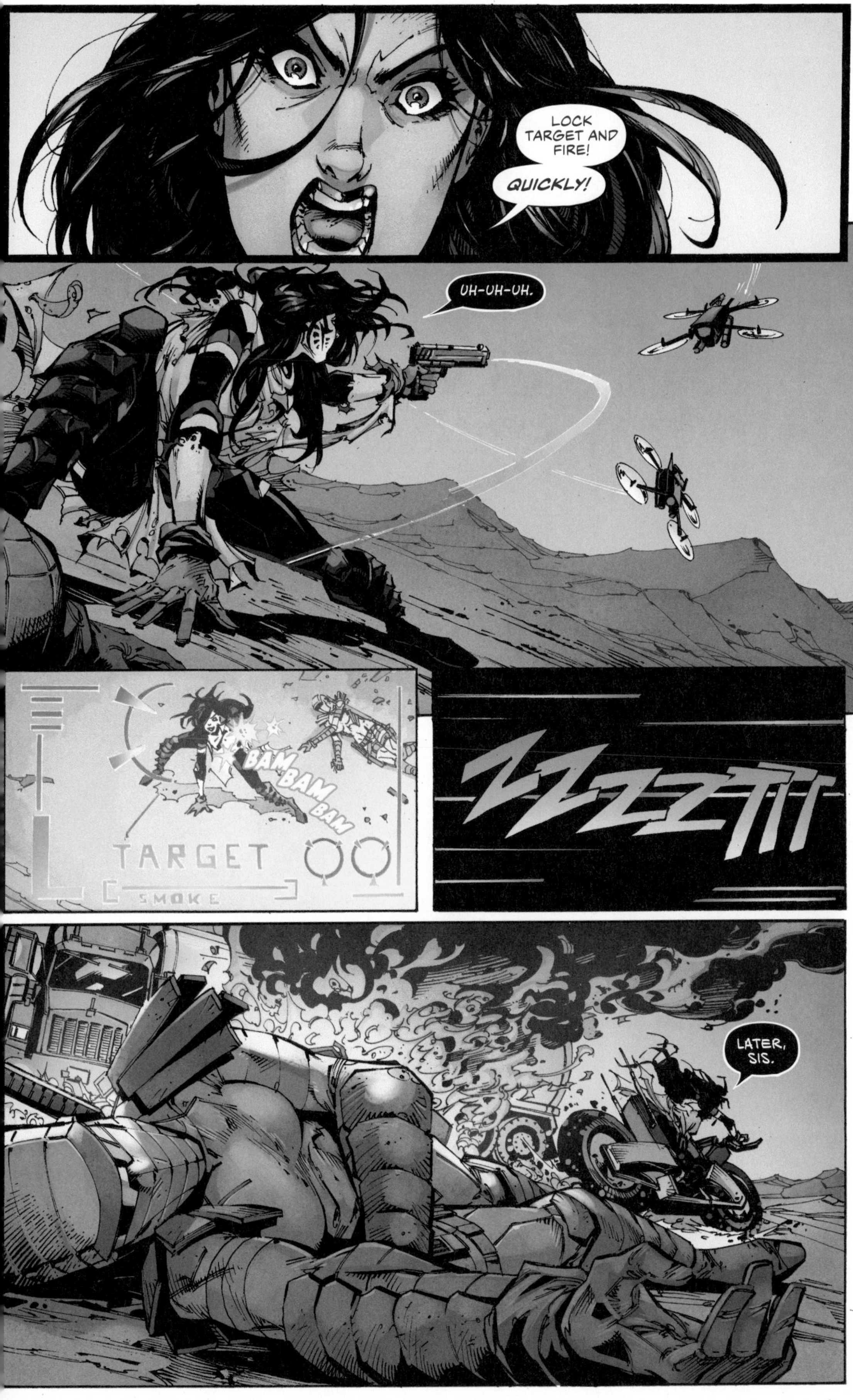
LOCK TARGET AND FIRE!
QUICKLY!
UH-UH-UH.
BAM BAM BAM
TARGET
SMOKE
ZZZZTTT
LATER, SIS.

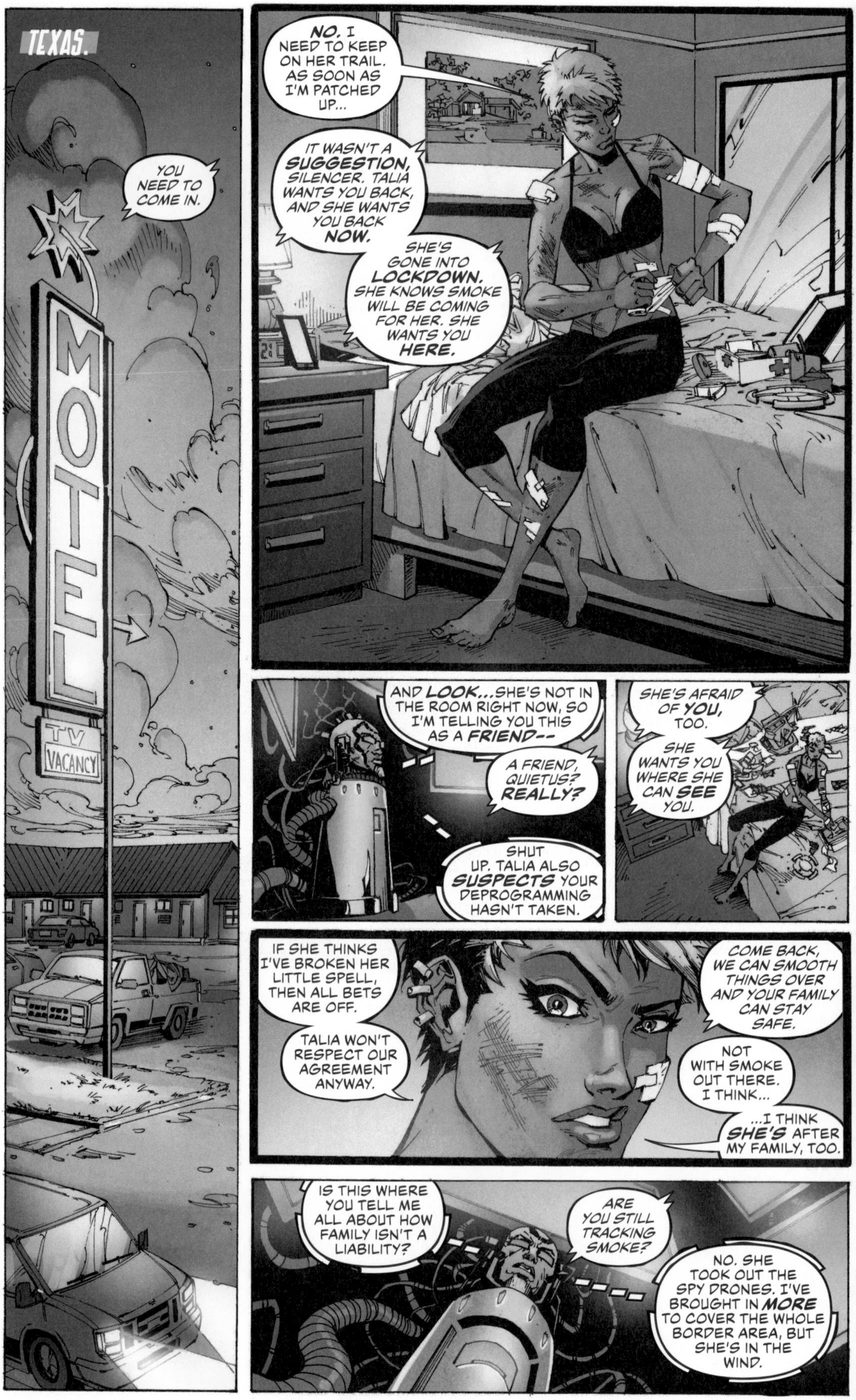
TEXAS.
NO. I NEED TO KEEP ON HER TRAIL. AS SOON AS I'M PATCHED UP...
YOU NEED TO COME IN.
IT WASN'T A SUGGESTION, SILENCER. TALIA WANTS YOU BACK, AND SHE WANTS YOU BACK NOW.
SHE'S GONE INTO LOCKDOWN. SHE KNOWS SMOKE WILL BE COMING FOR HER. SHE WANTS YOU HERE.
MOTEL
TV
VACANCY
AND LOOK...SHE'S NOT IN THE ROOM RIGHT NOW, SO I'M TELLING YOU THIS AS A FRIEND--
A FRIEND, QUIETUS? REALLY?
SHUT UP. TALIA ALSO SUSPECTS YOUR DEPROGRAMMING HASN'T TAKEN.
SHE'S AFRAID OF YOU, TOO.
SHE WANTS YOU WHERE SHE CAN SEE YOU.
IF SHE THINKS I'VE BROKEN HER LITTLE SPELL, THEN ALL BETS ARE OFF.
TALIA WON'T RESPECT OUR AGREEMENT ANYWAY.
COME BACK, WE CAN SMOOTH THINGS OVER AND YOUR FAMILY CAN STAY SAFE.
NOT WITH SMOKE OUT THERE. I THINK...
...I THINK SHE'S AFTER MY FAMILY, TOO.
IS THIS WHERE YOU TELL ME ALL ABOUT HOW FAMILY ISN'T A LIABILITY?
ARE YOU STILL TRACKING SMOKE?
NO. SHE TOOK OUT THE SPY DRONES. I'VE BROUGHT IN MORE TO COVER THE WHOLE BORDER AREA, BUT SHE'S IN THE WIND.

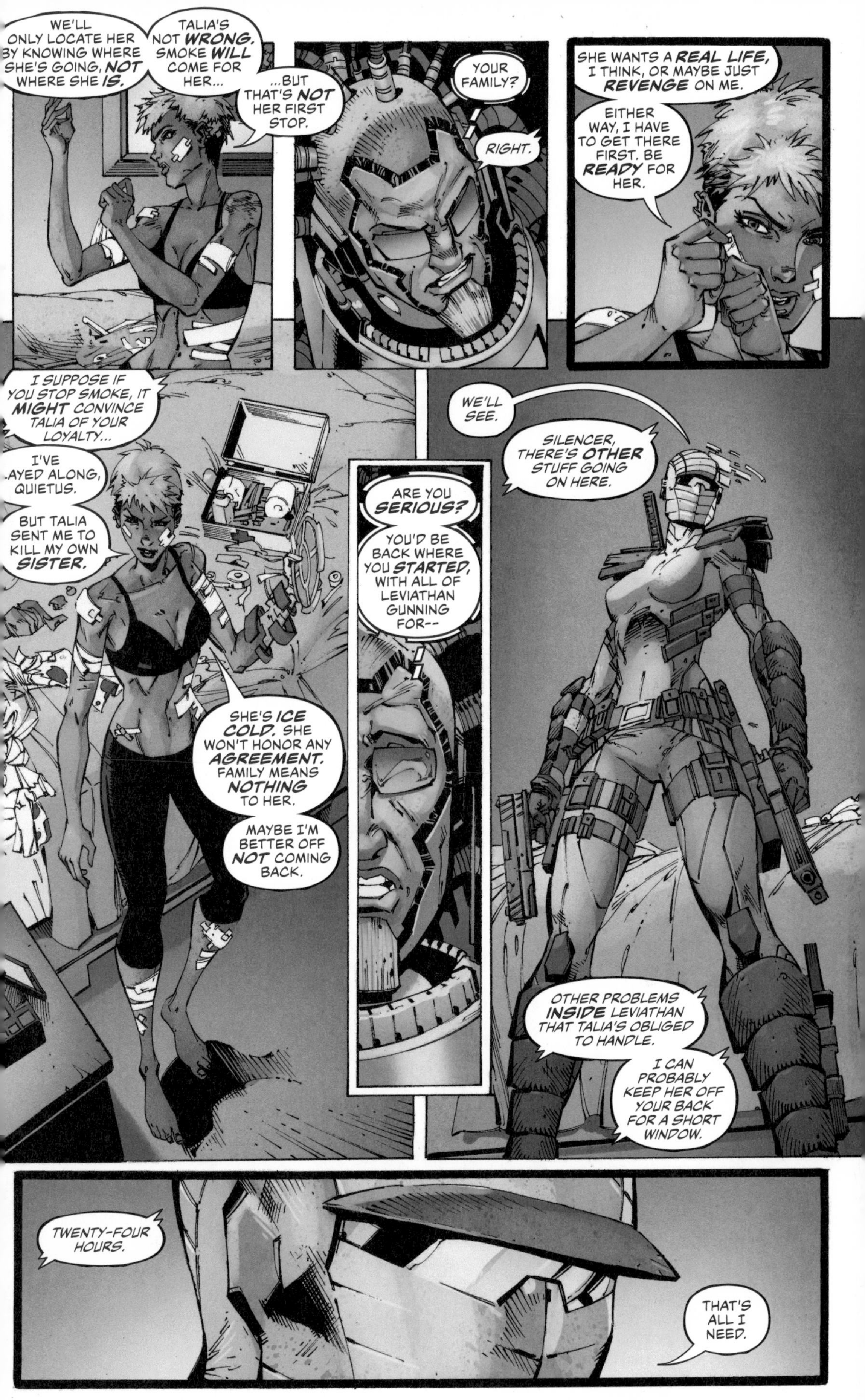
WE'LL ONLY LOCATE HER BY KNOWING WHERE SHE'S GOING, NOT WHERE SHE IS.
TALIA'S NOT WRONG. SMOKE WILL COME FOR HER...
...BUT THAT'S NOT HER FIRST STOP.
YOUR FAMILY?
RIGHT.
SHE WANTS A REAL LIFE, I THINK, OR MAYBE JUST REVENGE ON ME.
EITHER WAY, I HAVE TO GET THERE FIRST. BE READY FOR HER.
I SUPPOSE IF YOU STOP SMOKE, IT MIGHT CONVINCE TALIA OF YOUR LOYALTY...
I'VE PLAYED ALONG, QUIETUS.
BUT TALIA SENT ME TO KILL MY OWN SISTER.
SHE'S ICE COLD. SHE WON'T HONOR ANY AGREEMENT. FAMILY MEANS NOTHING TO HER.
MAYBE I'M BETTER OFF NOT COMING BACK.
ARE YOU SERIOUS?
YOU'D BE BACK WHERE YOU STARTED, WITH ALL OF LEVIATHAN GUNNING FOR--
WE'LL SEE.
SILENCER, THERE'S OTHER STUFF GOING ON HERE.
OTHER PROBLEMS INSIDE LEVIATHAN THAT TALIA'S OBLIGED TO HANDLE.
I CAN PROBABLY KEEP HER OFF YOUR BACK FOR A SHORT WINDOW.
TWENTY-FOUR HOURS.
THAT'S ALL I NEED.

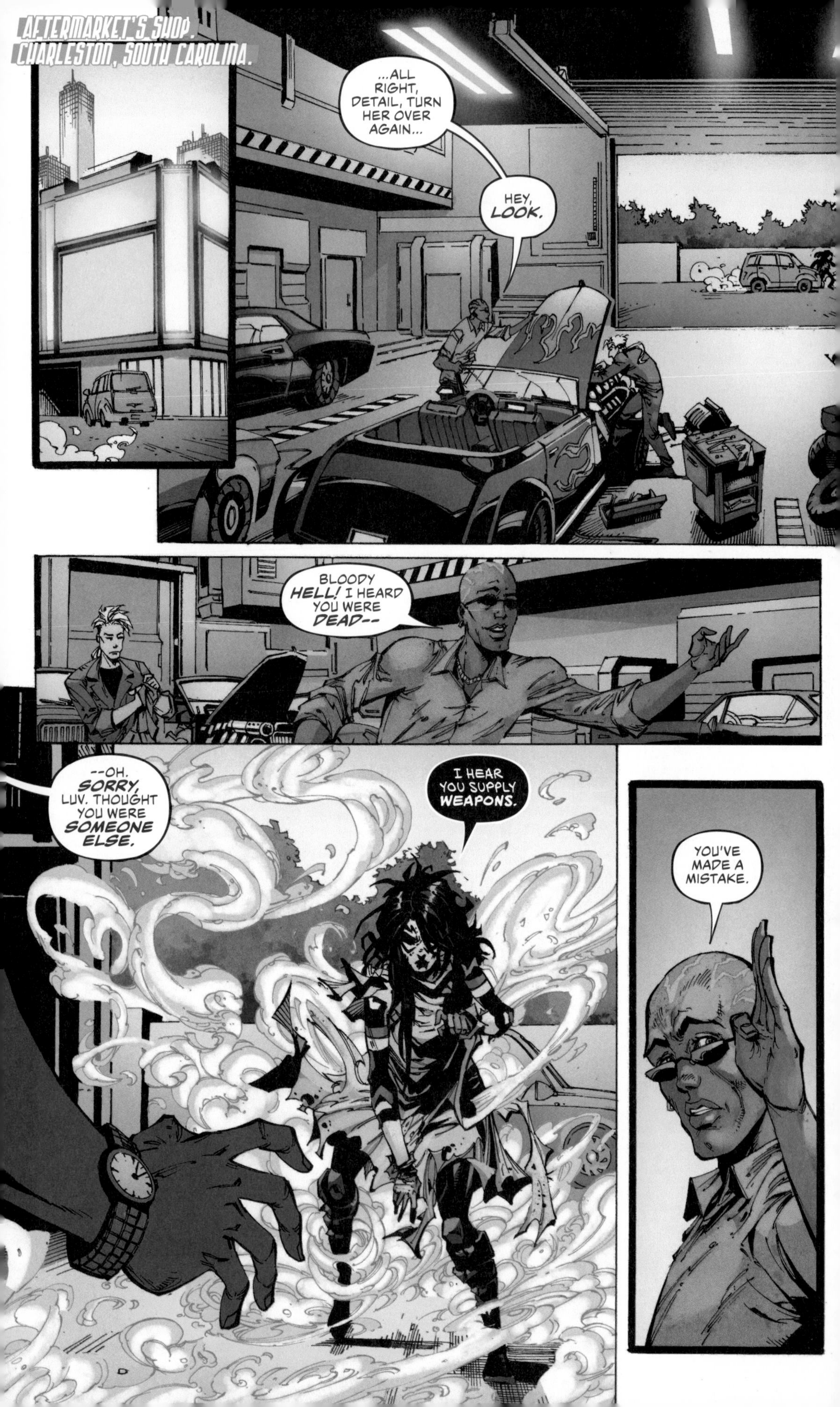
AFTERMARKET'S SHOP. CHARLESTON, SOUTH CAROLINA.
...ALL RIGHT, DETAIL, TURN HER OVER AGAIN...
HEY, LOOK.
BLOODY HELL! I HEARD YOU WERE DEAD--
--OH. SORRY, LUV. THOUGHT YOU WERE SOMEONE ELSE.
I HEAR YOU SUPPLY WEAPONS.
YOU'VE MADE A MISTAKE.

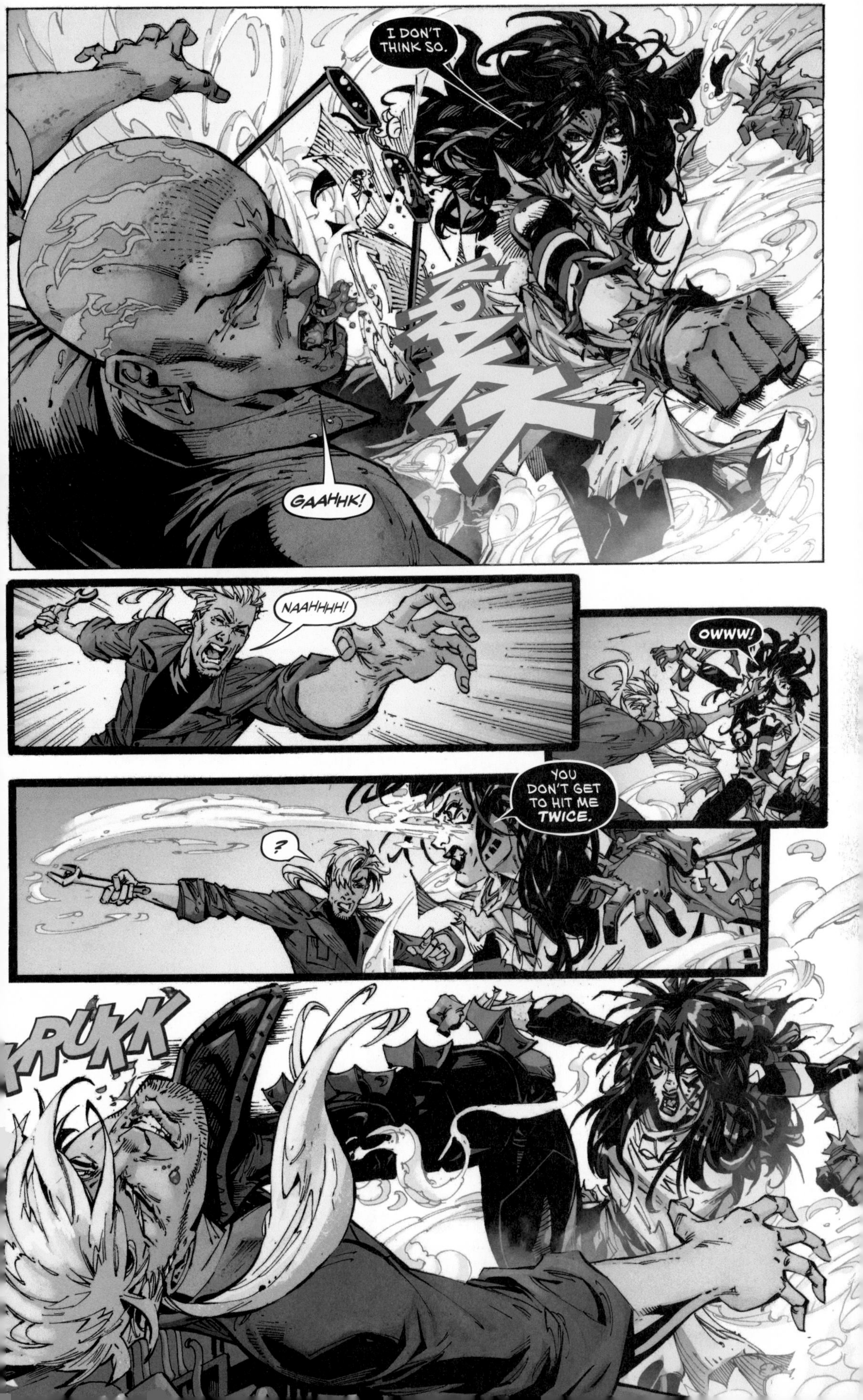
I DON'T THINK SO.
KRAKK
GAAHHK!
NAAHHHH!
OWWW!
YOU DON'T GET TO HIT ME TWICE.
?
KRUKK

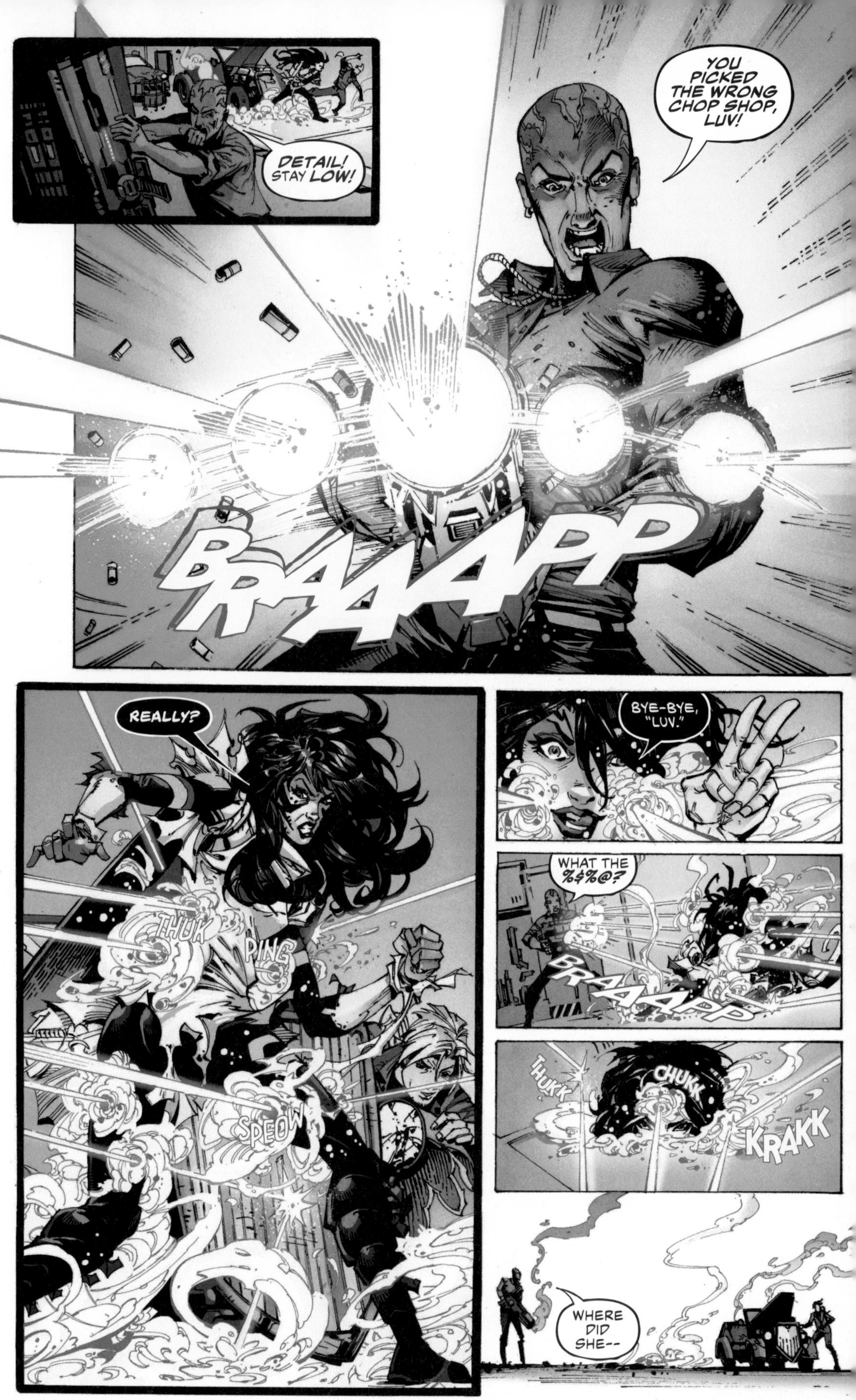
DETAIL! STAY LOW!
YOU PICKED THE WRONG CHOP SHOP, LUV!
BRAAAPP
REALLY?
THUK
PING
SPEOW
BYE-BYE, "LUV."
WHAT THE %$%@?
BRAAAPP
THUKK
CHUKK
KRAKK
WHERE DID SHE--

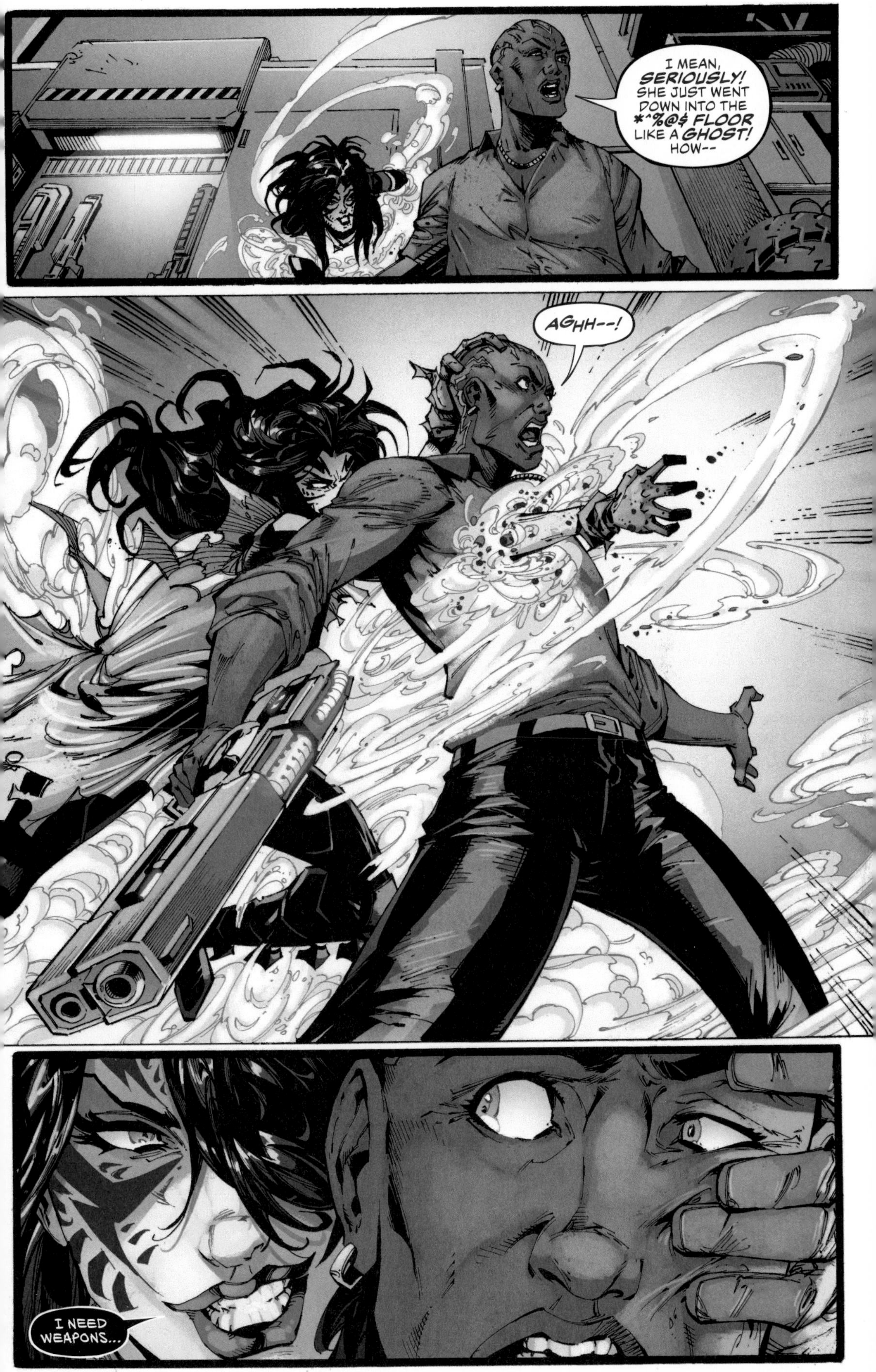
I MEAN, SERIOUSLY! SHE JUST WENT DOWN INTO THE *^%@$ FLOOR LIKE A GHOST! HOW--
AGHH--!
I NEED WEAPONS...

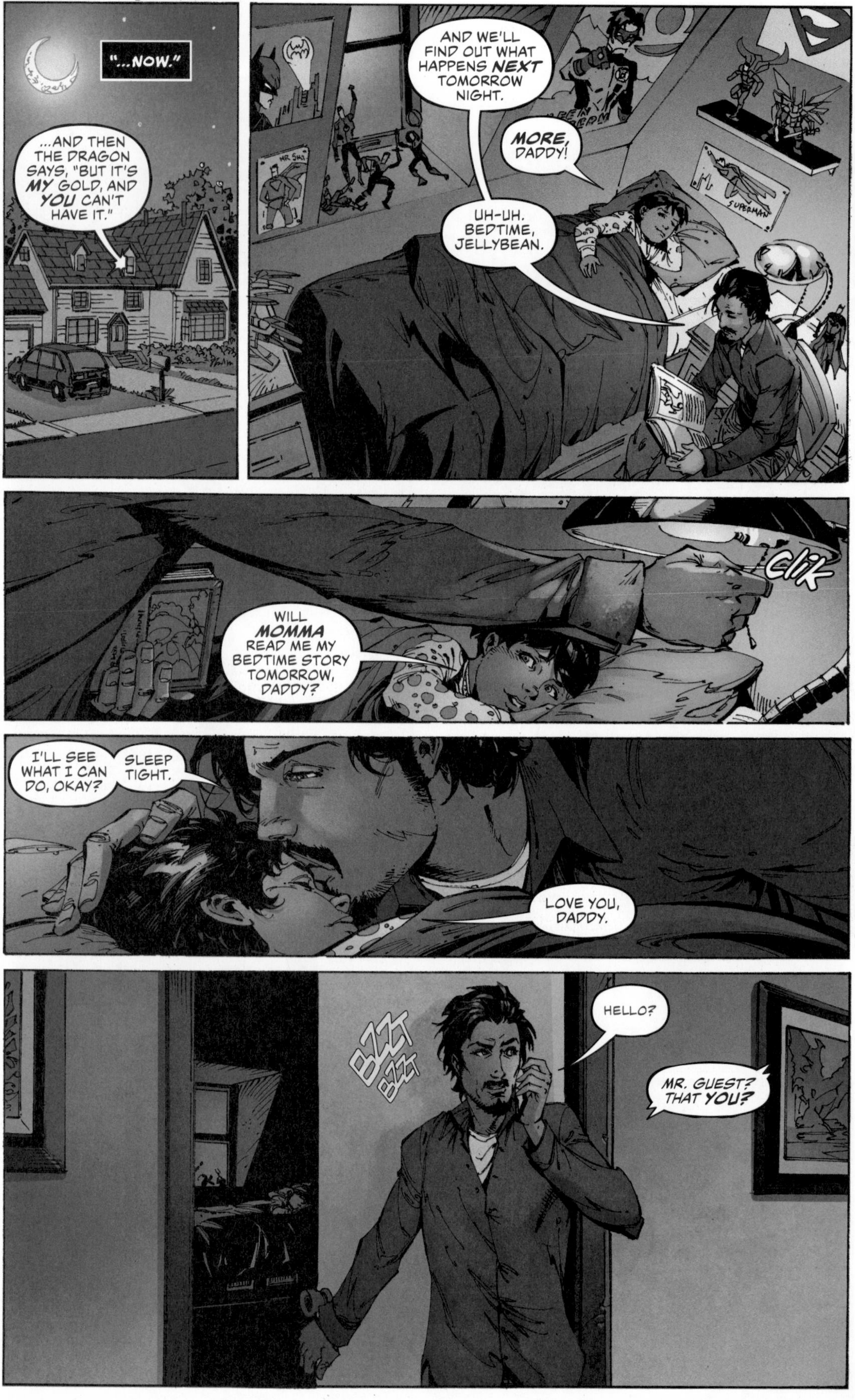
GUEST FAMILY HOME, CHARLESTON.
"...NOW."
...AND THEN THE DRAGON SAYS, "BUT IT'S MY GOLD, AND YOU CAN'T HAVE IT."
AND WE'LL FIND OUT WHAT HAPPENS NEXT TOMORROW NIGHT.
MORE, DADDY!
UH-UH. BEDTIME, JELLYBEAN.
SUPERMAN
CLIK
WILL MOMMA READ ME MY BEDTIME STORY TOMORROW, DADDY?
I'LL SEE WHAT I CAN DO, OKAY?
SLEEP TIGHT.
LOVE YOU, DADDY.
BZZT BZZT
HELLO?
MR. GUEST? THAT YOU?

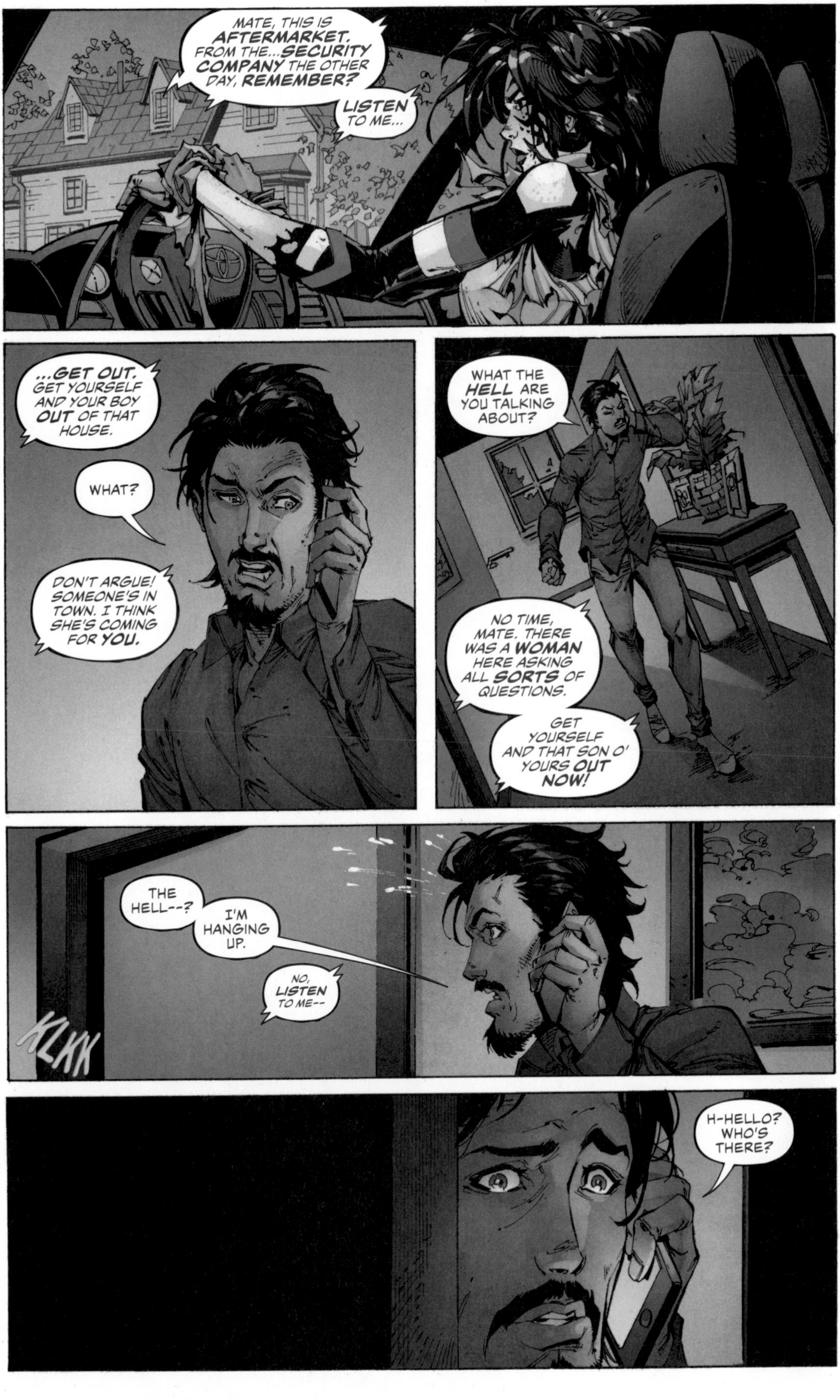
MATE, THIS IS AFTERMARKET. FROM THE...SECURITY COMPANY THE OTHER DAY, REMEMBER?
LISTEN TO ME...
...GET OUT. GET YOURSELF AND YOUR BOY OUT OF THAT HOUSE.
WHAT?
DON'T ARGUE! SOMEONE'S IN TOWN. I THINK SHE'S COMING FOR YOU.
WHAT THE HELL ARE YOU TALKING ABOUT?
NO TIME, MATE. THERE WAS A WOMAN HERE ASKING ALL SORTS OF QUESTIONS.
GET YOURSELF AND THAT SON O' YOURS OUT NOW!
THE HELL--?
I'M HANGING UP.
NO, LISTEN TO ME--
KLKK
H-HELLO? WHO'S THERE?

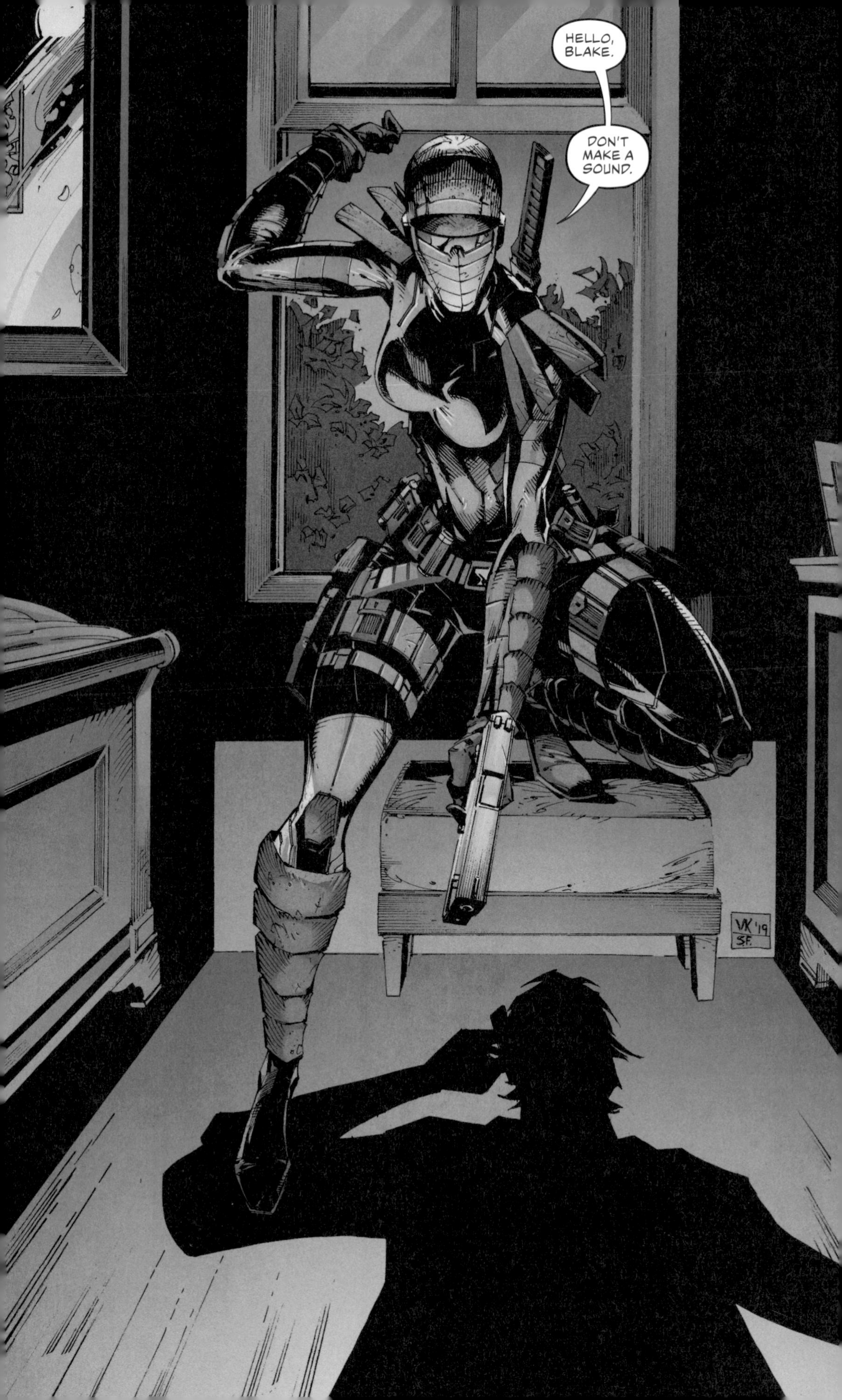
HELLO, BLAKE.
DON'T MAKE A SOUND.
VK '19 S.F.

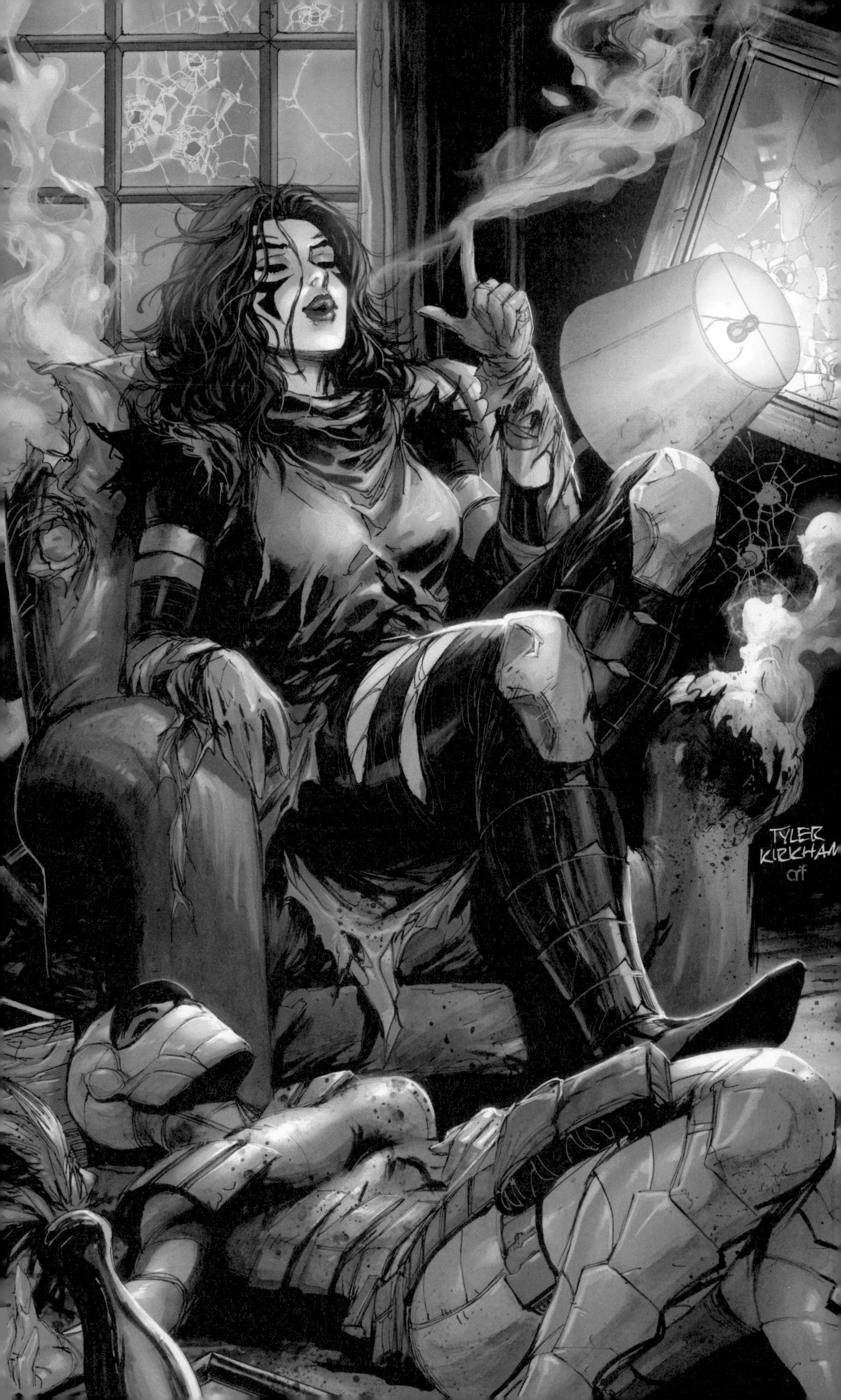
TYLER KIRKHAM art

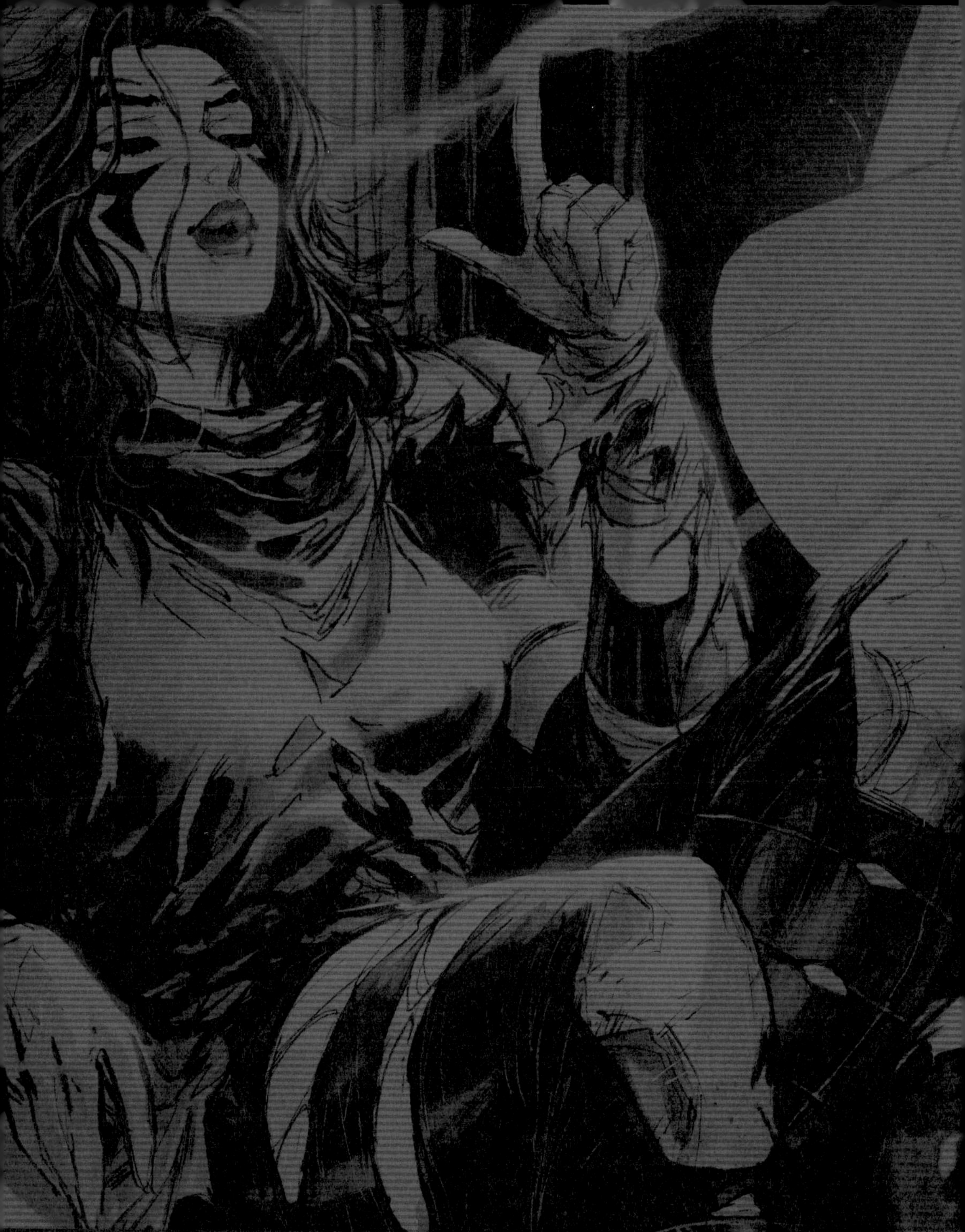

THE SILENCER

#17

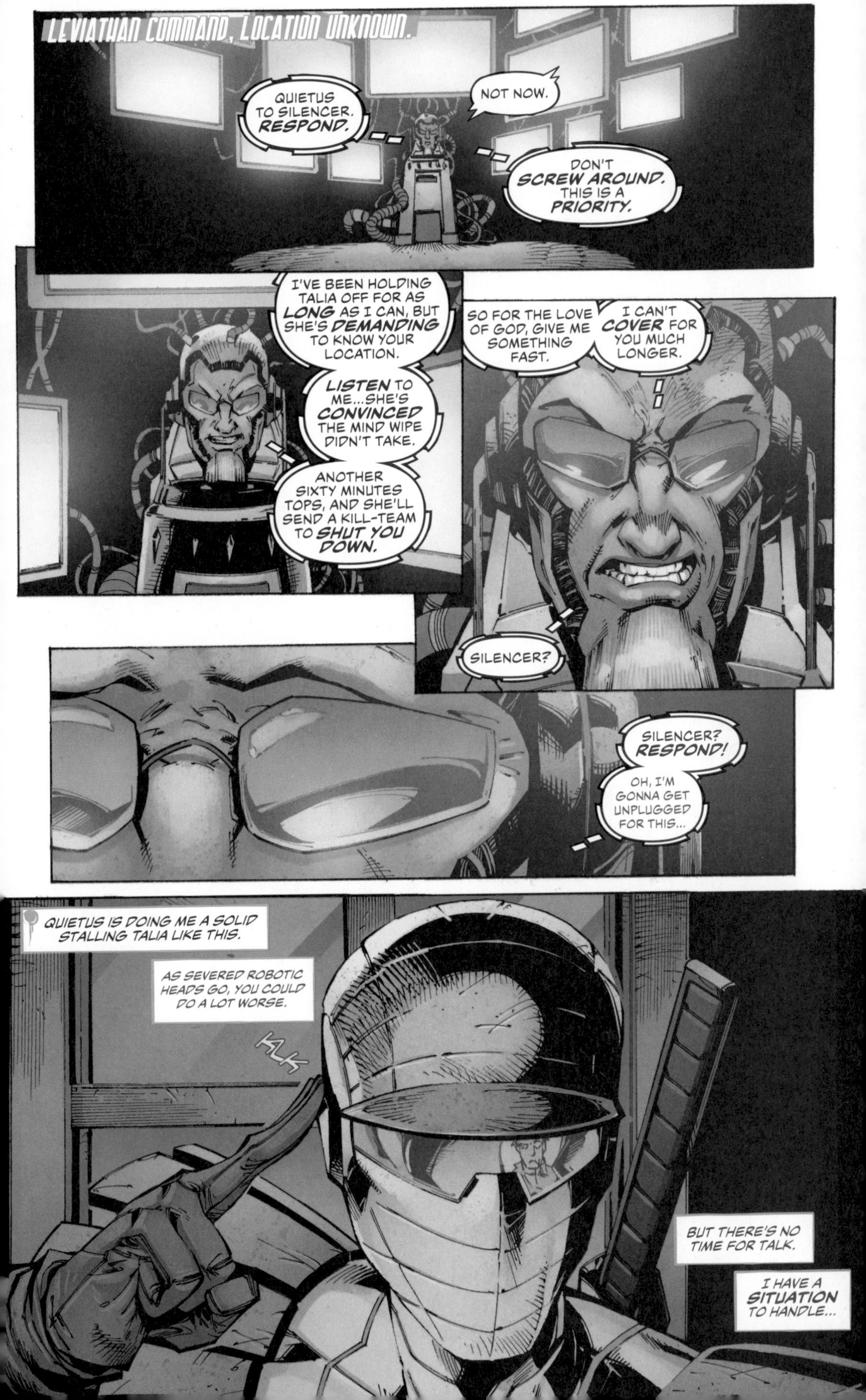
LEVIATHAN COMMAND, LOCATION UNKNOWN.
QUIETUS TO SILENCER. RESPOND.
NOT NOW.
DON'T SCREW AROUND. THIS IS A PRIORITY.
I'VE BEEN HOLDING TALIA OFF FOR AS LONG AS I CAN, BUT SHE'S DEMANDING TO KNOW YOUR LOCATION.
LISTEN TO ME...SHE'S CONVINCED THE MIND WIPE DIDN'T TAKE.
ANOTHER SIXTY MINUTES TOPS, AND SHE'LL SEND A KILL-TEAM TO SHUT YOU DOWN.
SO FOR THE LOVE OF GOD, GIVE ME SOMETHING FAST.
I CAN'T COVER FOR YOU MUCH LONGER.
SILENCER?
SILENCER? RESPOND!
OH, I'M GONNA GET UNPLUGGED FOR THIS...
QUIETUS IS DOING ME A SOLID STALLING TALIA LIKE THIS.
AS SEVERED ROBOTIC HEADS GO, YOU COULD DO A LOT WORSE.
KLIK
BUT THERE'S NO TIME FOR TALK.
I HAVE A SITUATION TO HANDLE...

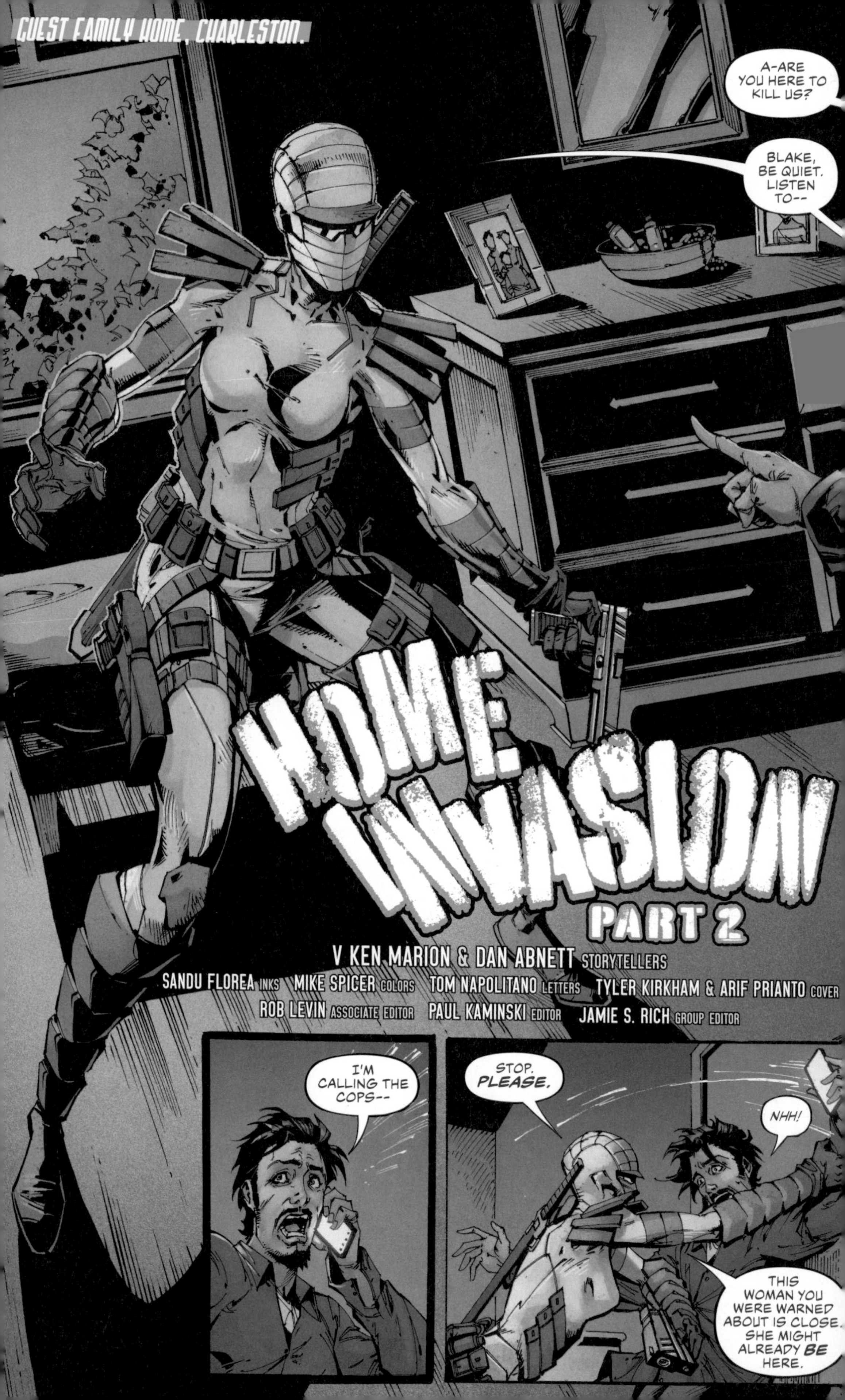
GUEST FAMILY HOME, CHARLESTON.
A-ARE YOU HERE TO KILL US?
BLAKE, BE QUIET. LISTEN TO--
HOME: INVASION
PART 2
V KEN MARION & DAN ABNETT STORYTELLERS
SANDU FLOREA INKS MIKE SPICER COLORS TOM NAPOLITANO LETTERS TYLER KIRKHAM & ARIF PRIANTO COVER
ROB LEVIN ASSOCIATE EDITOR PAUL KAMINSKI EDITOR JAMIE S. RICH GROUP EDITOR
I'M CALLING THE COPS--
STOP. PLEASE.
NHH!
THIS WOMAN YOU WERE WARNED ABOUT IS CLOSE. SHE MIGHT ALREADY BE HERE.

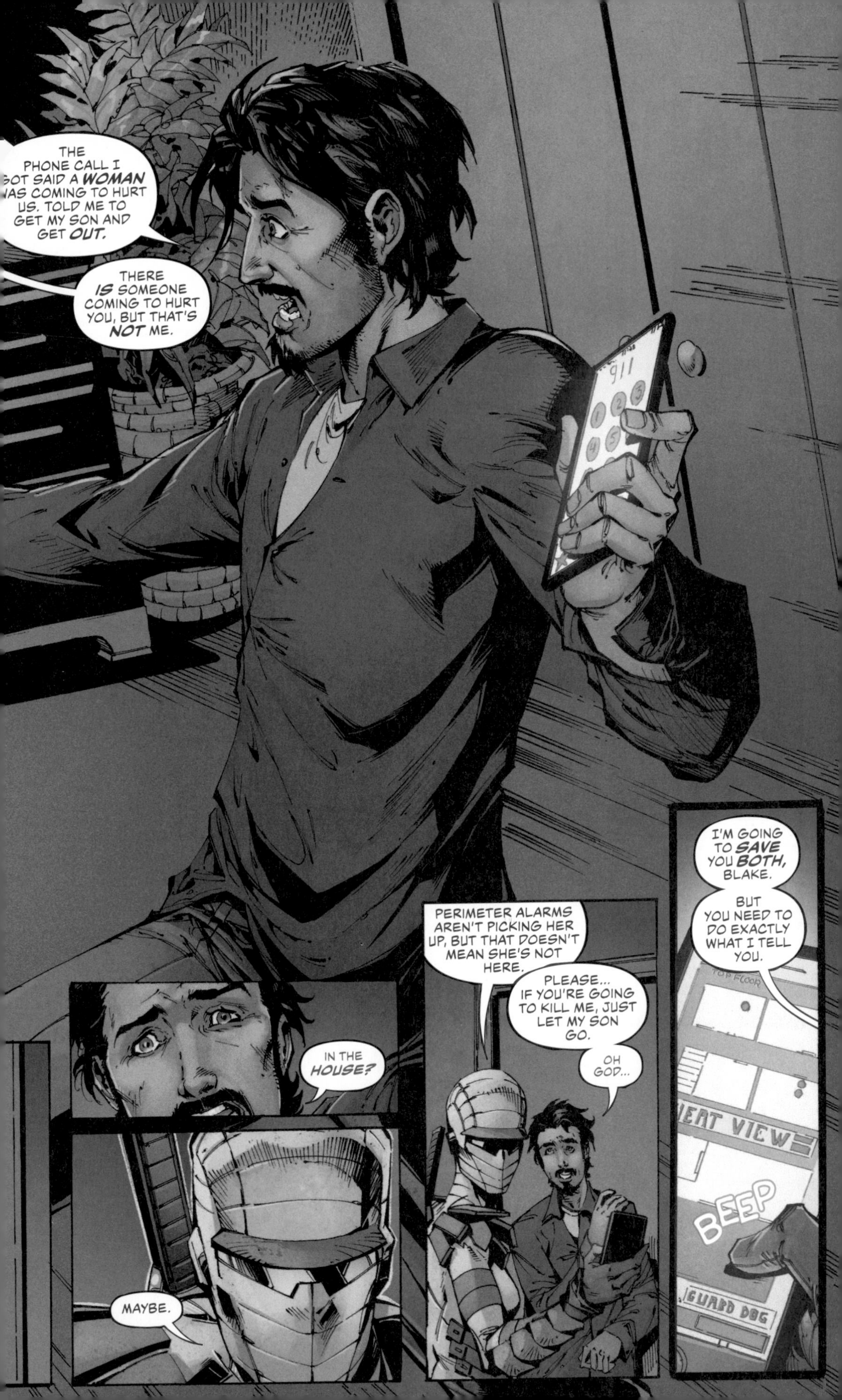

THE PHONE CALL I GOT SAID A WOMAN WAS COMING TO HURT US. TOLD ME TO GET MY SON AND GET OUT.
THERE IS SOMEONE COMING TO HURT YOU, BUT THAT'S NOT ME.
911
IN THE HOUSE?
MAYBE.
PERIMETER ALARMS AREN'T PICKING HER UP, BUT THAT DOESN'T MEAN SHE'S NOT HERE.
PLEASE... IF YOU'RE GOING TO KILL ME, JUST LET MY SON GO.
OH GOD...
I'M GOING TO SAVE YOU BOTH, BLAKE.
BUT YOU NEED TO DO EXACTLY WHAT I TELL YOU.
TOP FLOOR
BEEP
GUARD DOG

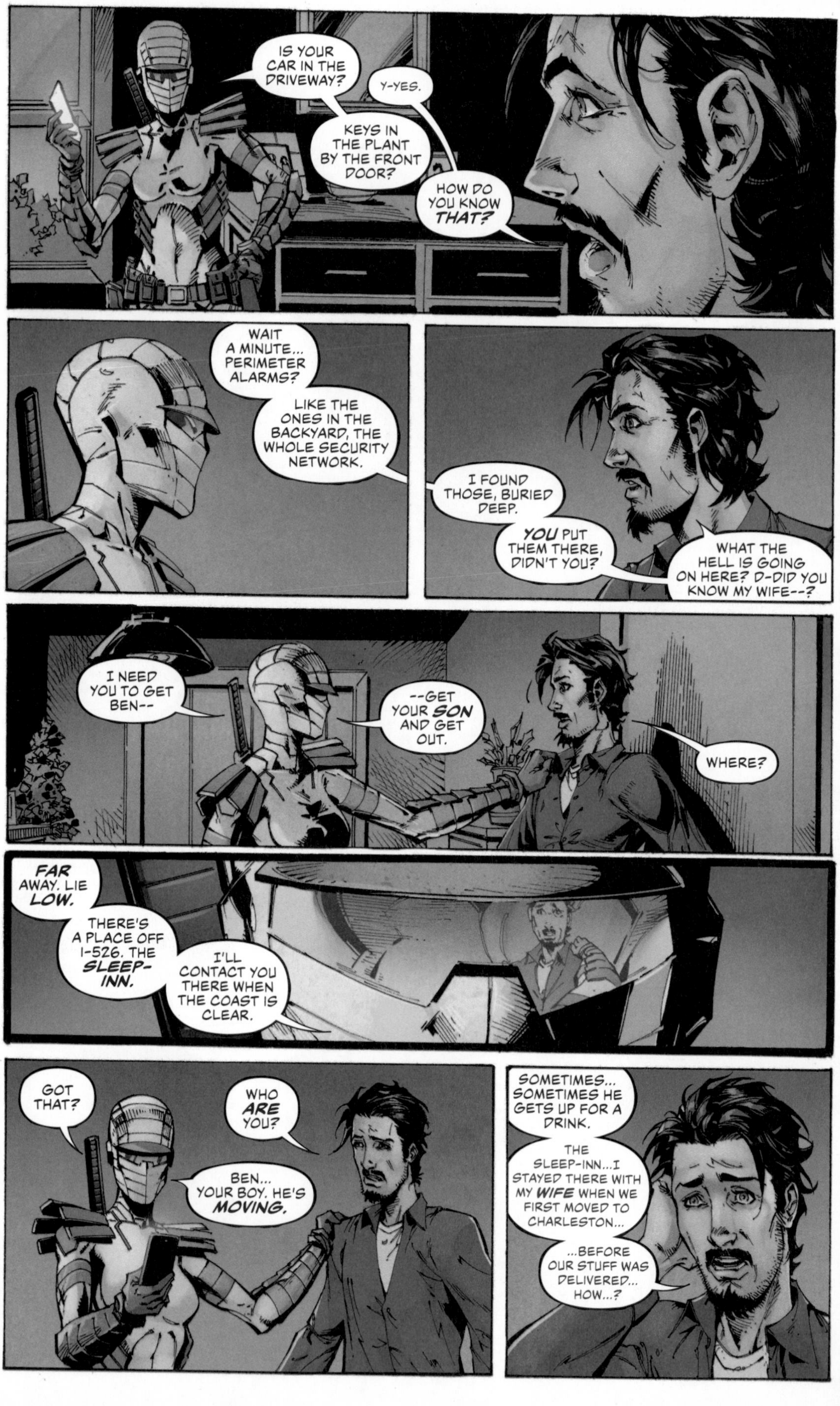
IS YOUR CAR IN THE DRIVEWAY?
Y-YES.
KEYS IN THE PLANT BY THE FRONT DOOR?
HOW DO YOU KNOW THAT?
WAIT A MINUTE... PERIMETER ALARMS?
LIKE THE ONES IN THE BACKYARD, THE WHOLE SECURITY NETWORK.
I FOUND THOSE, BURIED DEEP.
YOU PUT THEM THERE, DIDN'T YOU?
WHAT THE HELL IS GOING ON HERE? D-DID YOU KNOW MY WIFE--?
I NEED YOU TO GET BEN--
--GET YOUR SON AND GET OUT.
WHERE?
FAR AWAY. LIE LOW.
THERE'S A PLACE OFF I-526. THE SLEEP-INN.
I'LL CONTACT YOU THERE WHEN THE COAST IS CLEAR.
GOT THAT?
WHO ARE YOU?
BEN... YOUR BOY. HE'S MOVING.
SOMETIMES... SOMETIMES HE GETS UP FOR A DRINK.
THE SLEEP-INN...I STAYED THERE WITH MY WIFE WHEN WE FIRST MOVED TO CHARLESTON...
...BEFORE OUR STUFF WAS DELIVERED... HOW...?

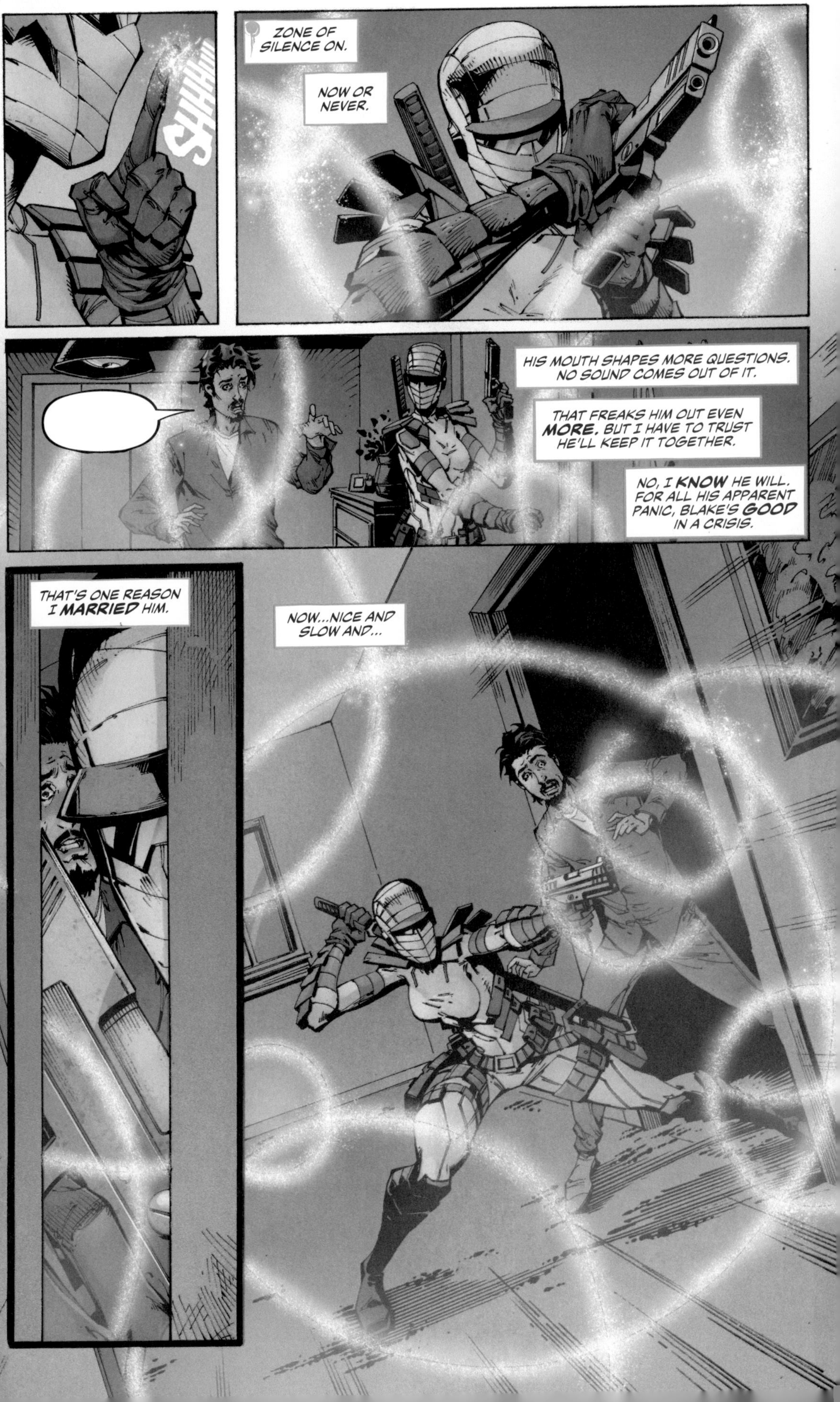
SHHH
ZONE OF SILENCE ON.
NOW OR NEVER.
HIS MOUTH SHAPES MORE QUESTIONS. NO SOUND COMES OUT OF IT.
THAT FREAKS HIM OUT EVEN MORE. BUT I HAVE TO TRUST HE'LL KEEP IT TOGETHER.
NO, I KNOW HE WILL. FOR ALL HIS APPARENT PANIC, BLAKE'S GOOD IN A CRISIS.
THAT'S ONE REASON I MARRIED HIM.
NOW...NICE AND SLOW AND...

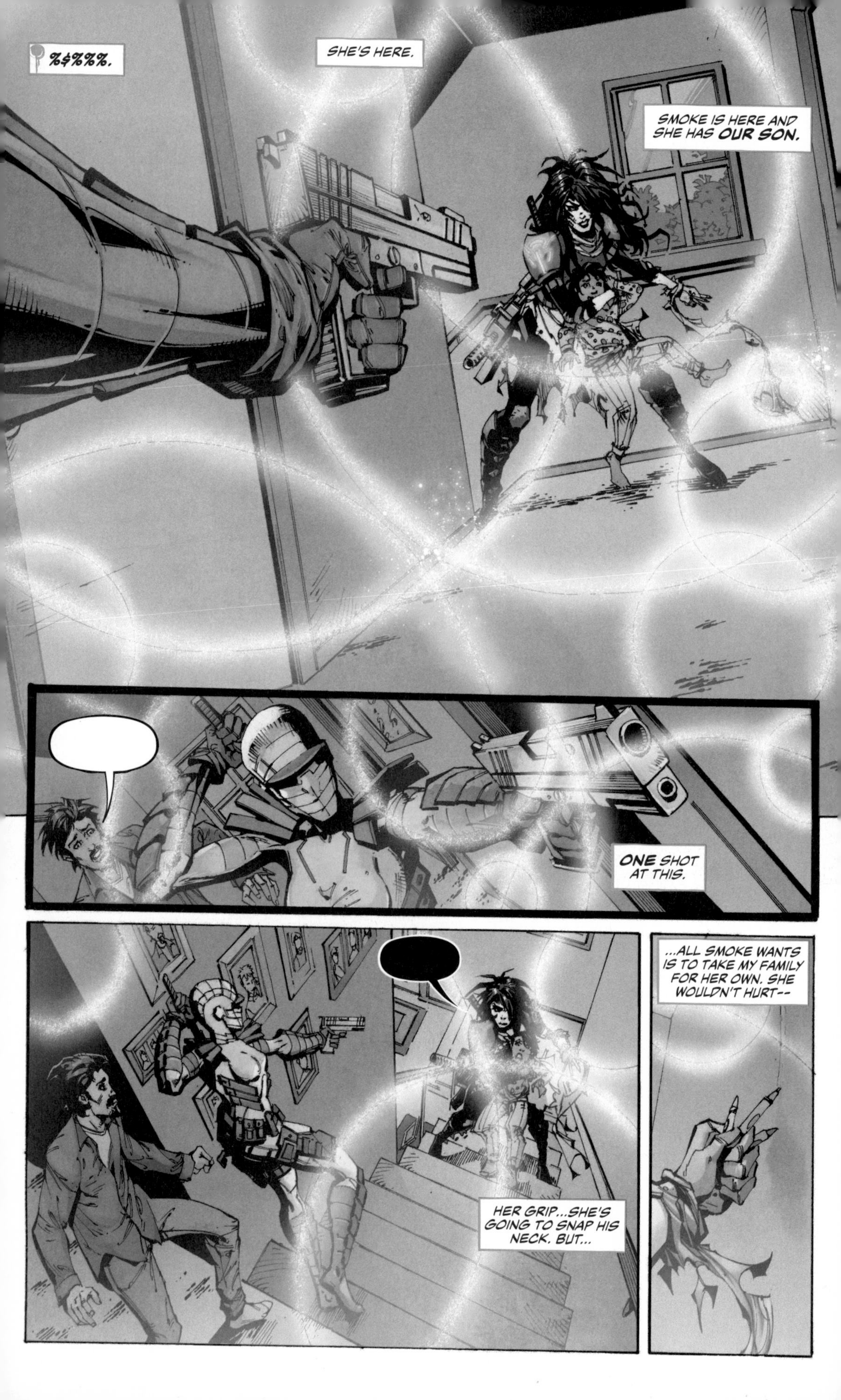
%$%%%.
SHE'S HERE.
SMOKE IS HERE AND SHE HAS OUR SON.
ONE SHOT AT THIS.
...ALL SMOKE WANTS IS TO TAKE MY FAMILY FOR HER OWN. SHE WOULDN'T HURT--
HER GRIP...SHE'S GOING TO SNAP HIS NECK. BUT...

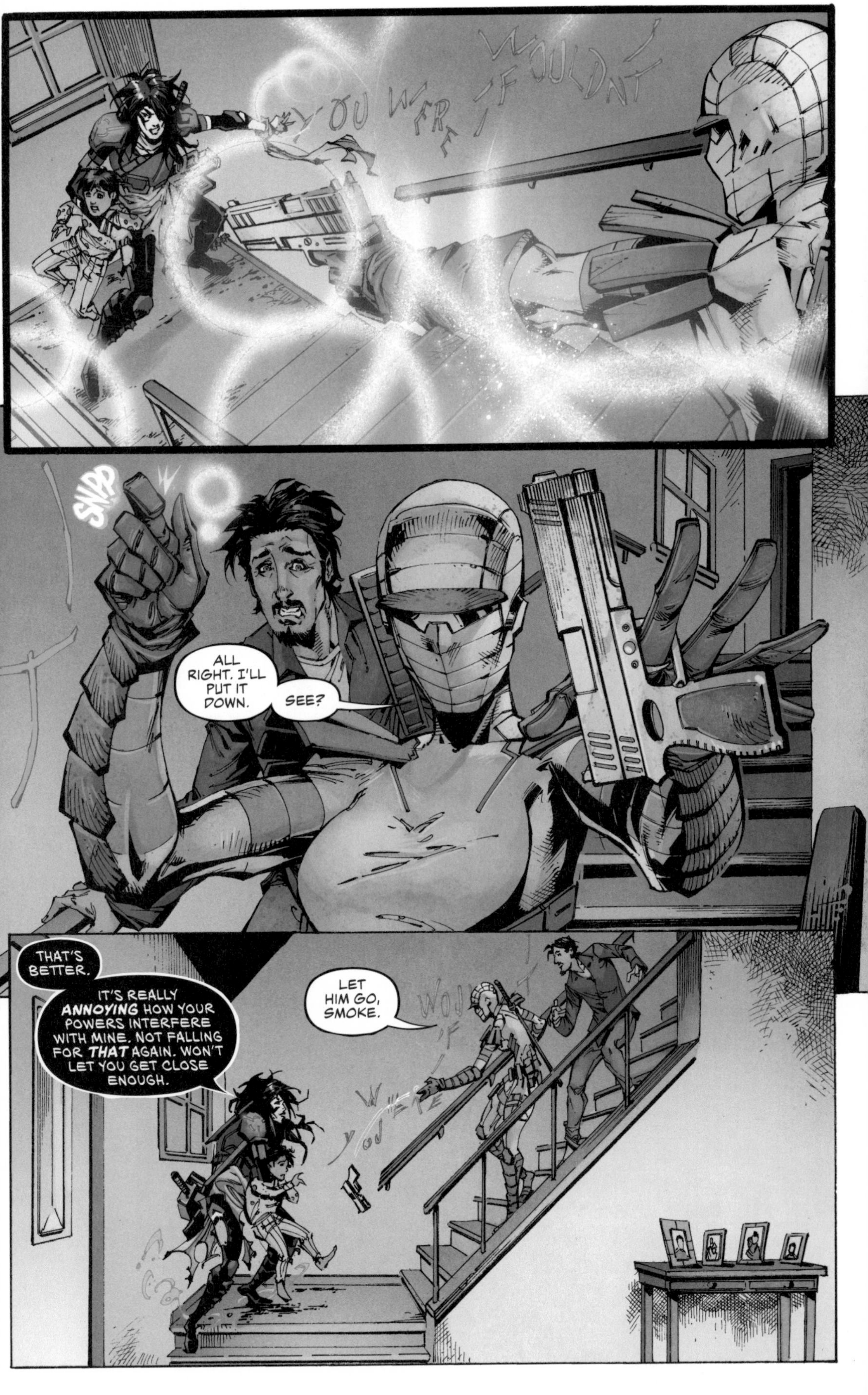
SNPP
ALL RIGHT. I'LL PUT IT DOWN.
SEE?
THAT'S BETTER.
IT'S REALLY ANNOYING HOW YOUR POWERS INTERFERE WITH MINE. NOT FALLING FOR THAT AGAIN. WON'T LET YOU GET CLOSE ENOUGH.
LET HIM GO, SMOKE.

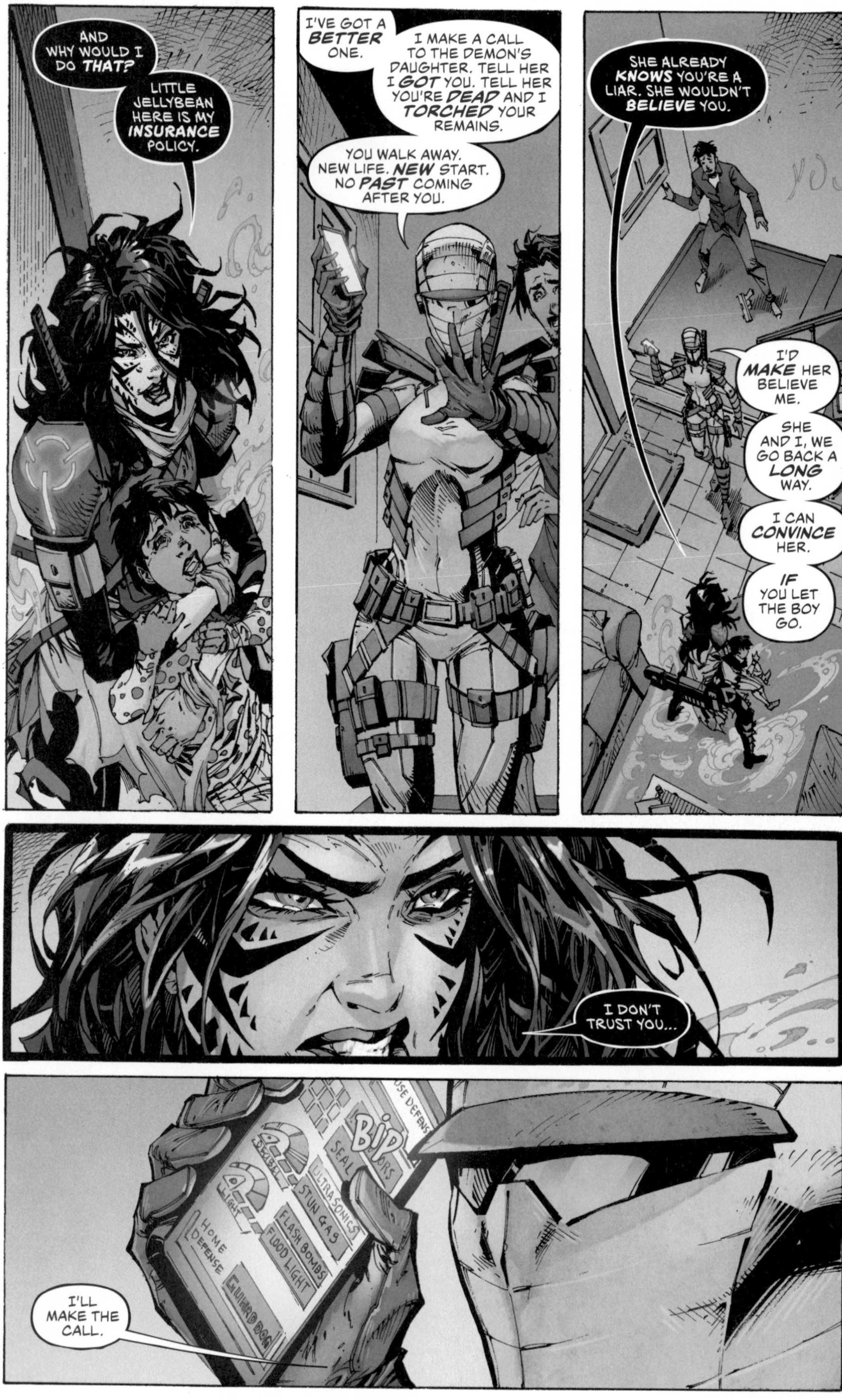
AND WHY WOULD I DO THAT?
LITTLE JELLYBEAN HERE IS MY INSURANCE POLICY.
I'VE GOT A BETTER ONE.
I MAKE A CALL TO THE DEMON'S DAUGHTER. TELL HER I GOT YOU. TELL HER YOU'RE DEAD AND I TORCHED YOUR REMAINS.
YOU WALK AWAY. NEW LIFE. NEW START. NO PAST COMING AFTER YOU.
SHE ALREADY KNOWS YOU'RE A LIAR. SHE WOULDN'T BELIEVE YOU.
I'D MAKE HER BELIEVE ME.
SHE AND I, WE GO BACK A LONG WAY.
I CAN CONVINCE HER.
IF YOU LET THE BOY GO.
I DON'T TRUST YOU...
BIP
SEAL
ULTRASONICS
STUN GAG
FLASH BOMBS
FLOOD LIGHT
HOME DEFENSE
GUARD DOG
I'LL MAKE THE CALL.

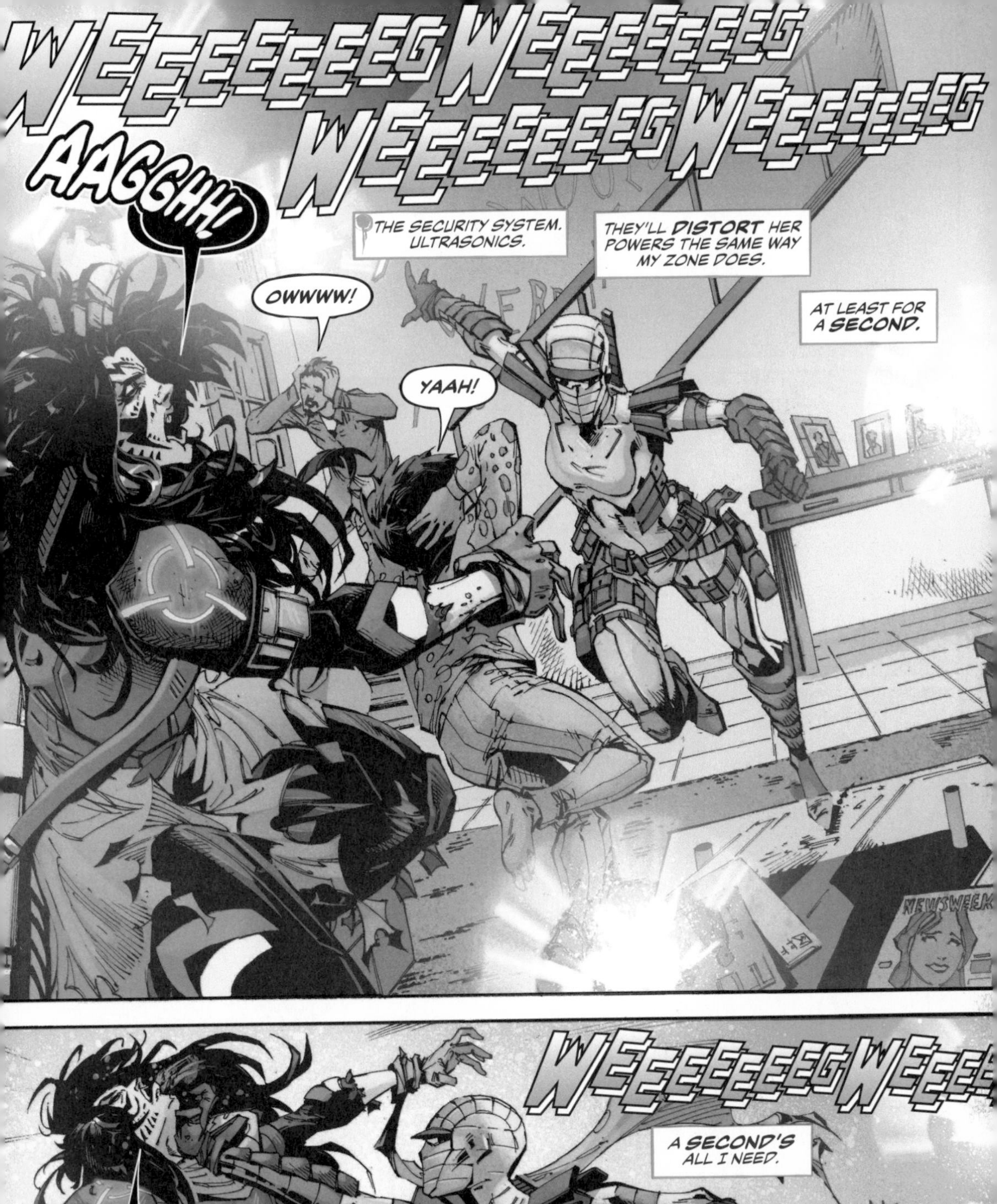
WEEEEEEEEG WEEEEEEEEG
WEEEEEEEEG WEEEEEEEEG
AAGGHH!
THE SECURITY SYSTEM. ULTRASONICS.
THEY'LL **DISTORT** HER POWERS THE SAME WAY MY ZONE DOES.
OWWWW!
AT LEAST FOR A **SECOND**.
YAAH!
NEWSWEEK

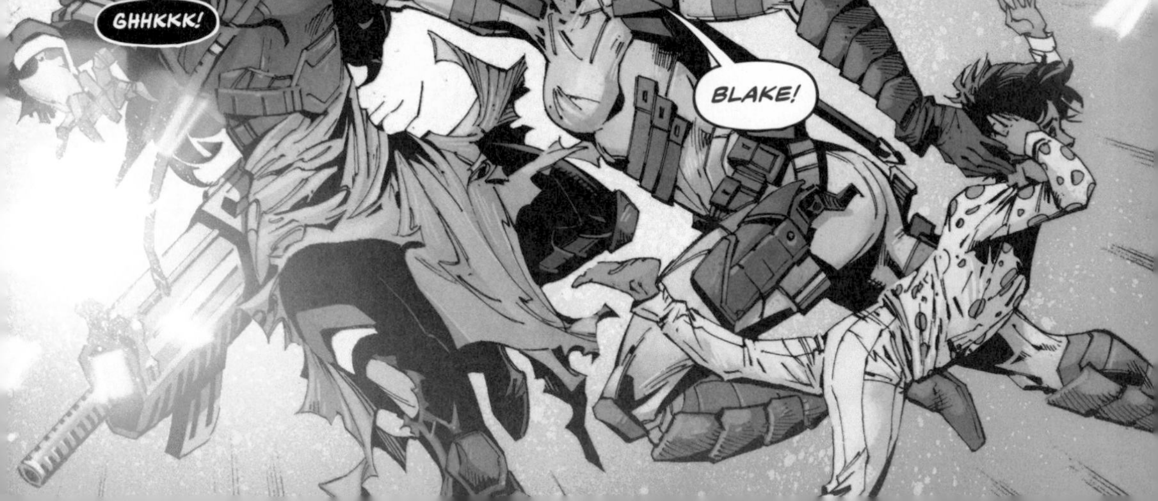
WEEEEEEEEG
A **SECOND'S** ALL I NEED.
GHHKKK!
BLAKE!

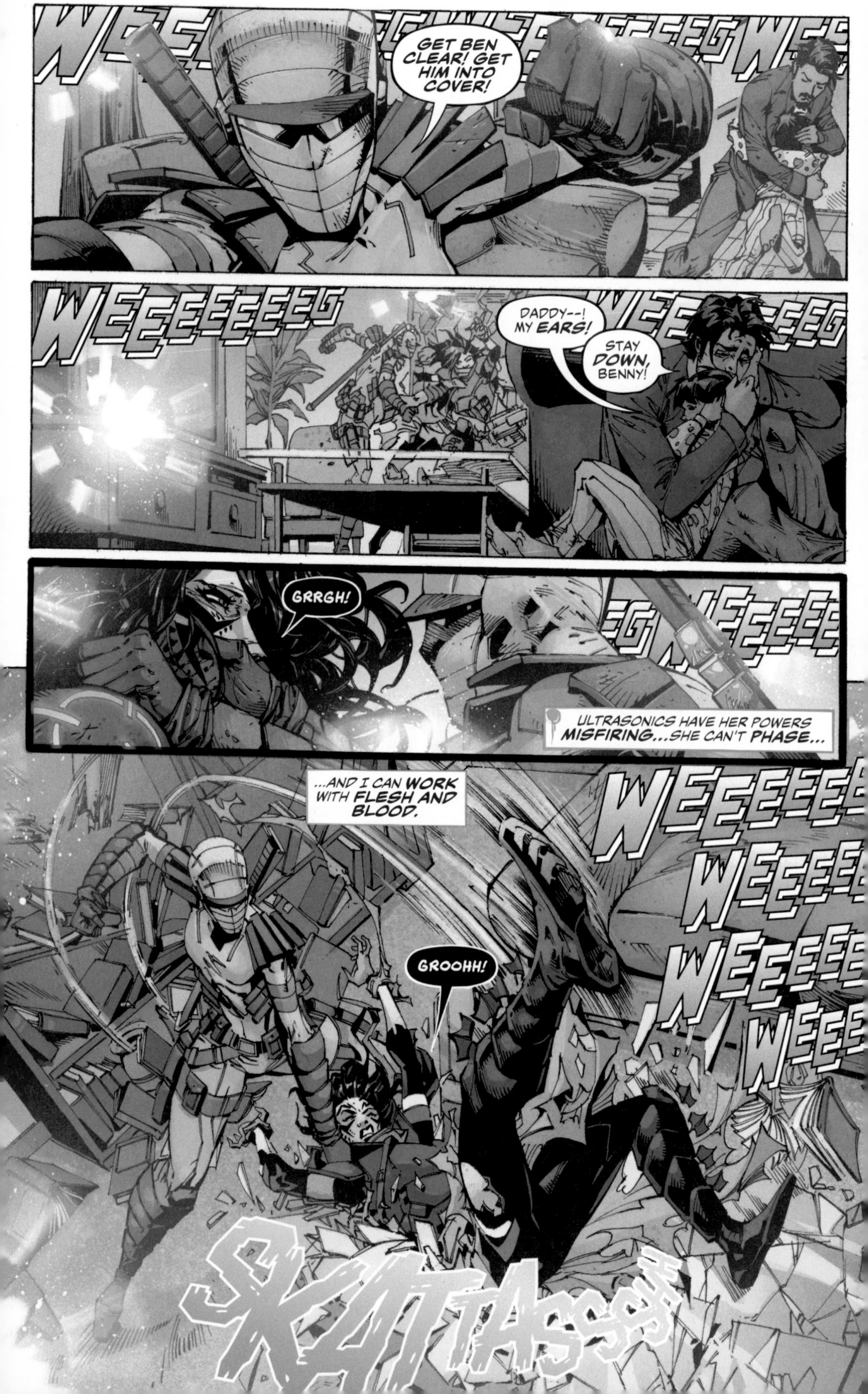

GET BEN CLEAR! GET HIM INTO COVER!
DADDY--! MY EARS!
STAY DOWN, BENNY!
GRRGH!
ULTRASONICS HAVE HER POWERS MISFIRING...SHE CAN'T PHASE...
...AND I CAN WORK WITH FLESH AND BLOOD.
GROOHH!

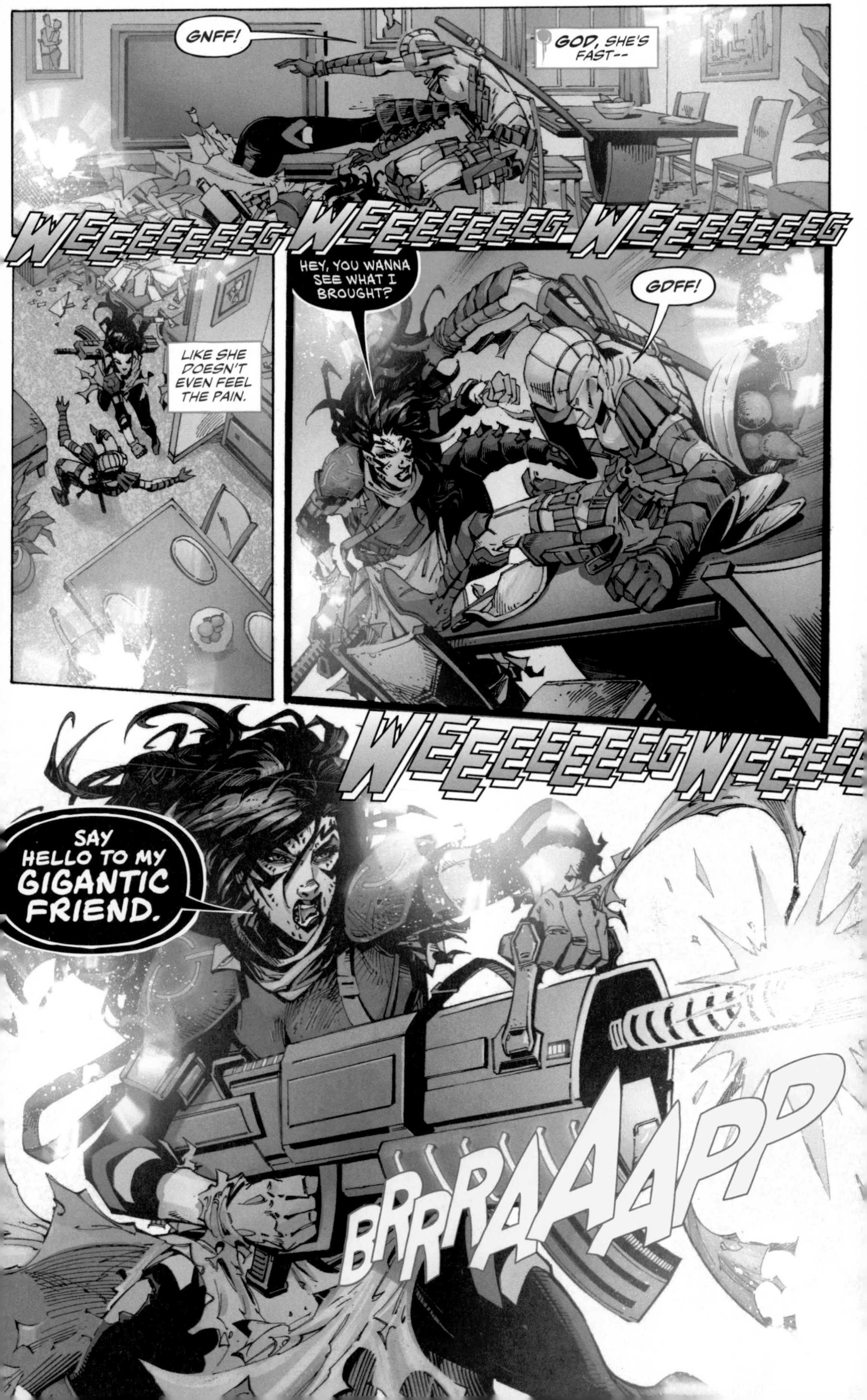
GNFF!
GOD, SHE'S FAST--
WEEEEEEEG WEEEEEEEG WEEEEEEEG
LIKE SHE DOESN'T EVEN FEEL THE PAIN.
HEY, YOU WANNA SEE WHAT I BROUGHT?
GDFF!
WEEEEEEEGWEEEEE
SAY HELLO TO MY GIGANTIC FRIEND.
BRRRAAAPP

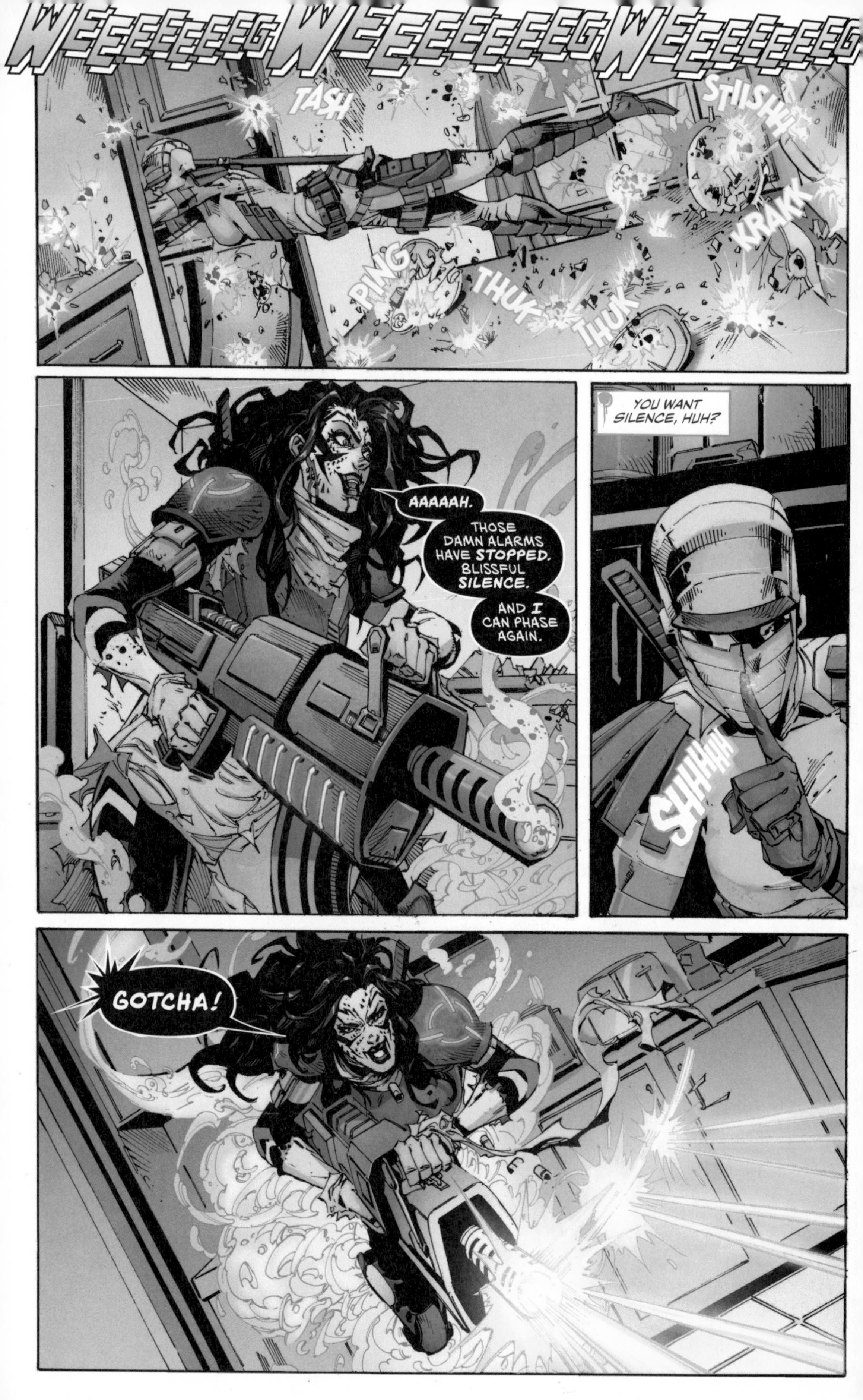
WEEEEEEEG WEEEEEEEEG WEEEEEEEG
TASH
STIISHH
KRAKK
PING
THUK
THUK
AAAAAH.
THOSE DAMN ALARMS HAVE STOPPED. BLISSFUL SILENCE.
AND I CAN PHASE AGAIN.
YOU WANT SILENCE, HUH?
SHHHH
GOTCHA!

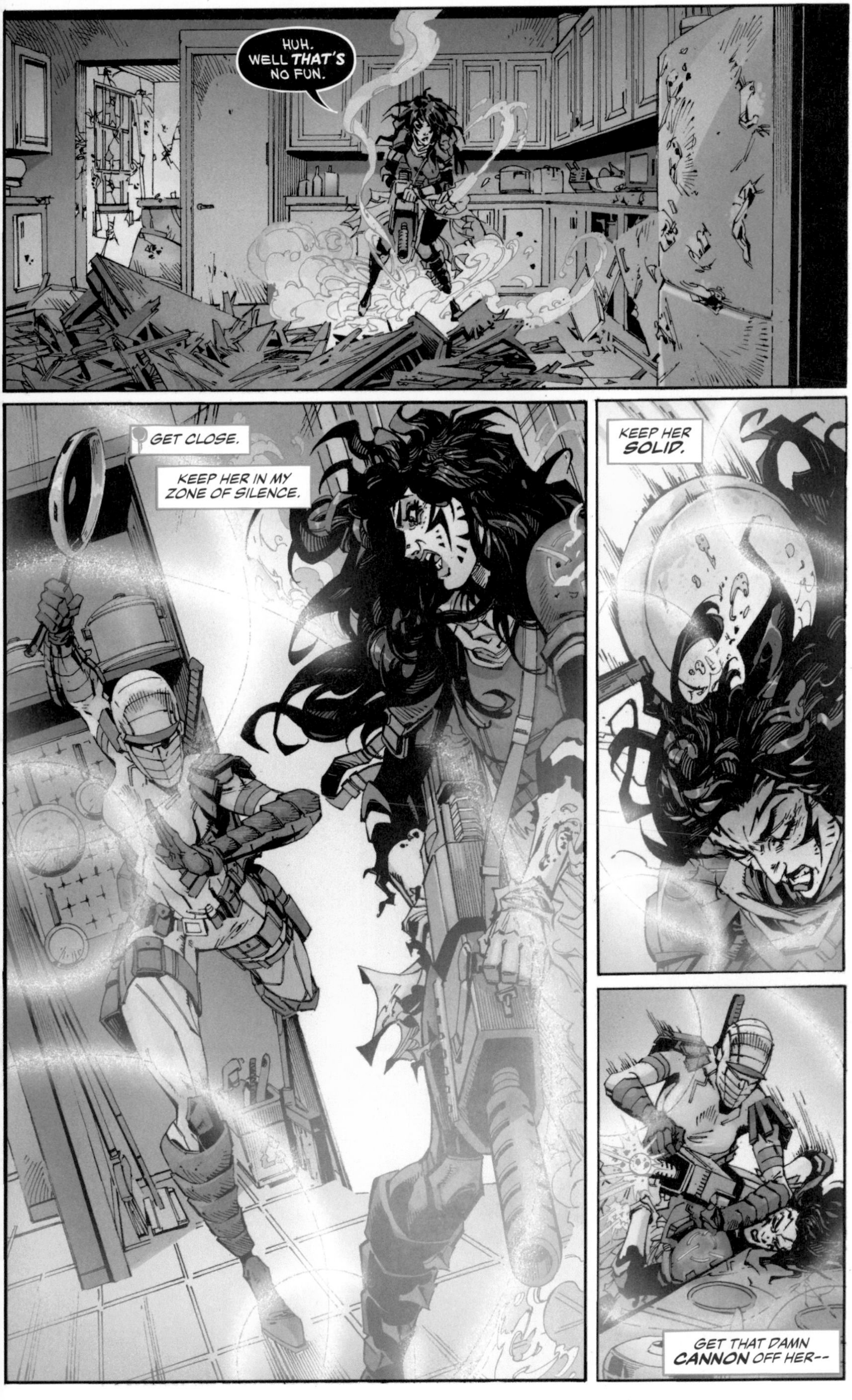
HUH. WELL THAT'S NO FUN.
GET CLOSE.
KEEP HER IN MY ZONE OF SILENCE.
KEEP HER SOLID.
GET THAT DAMN CANNON OFF HER--

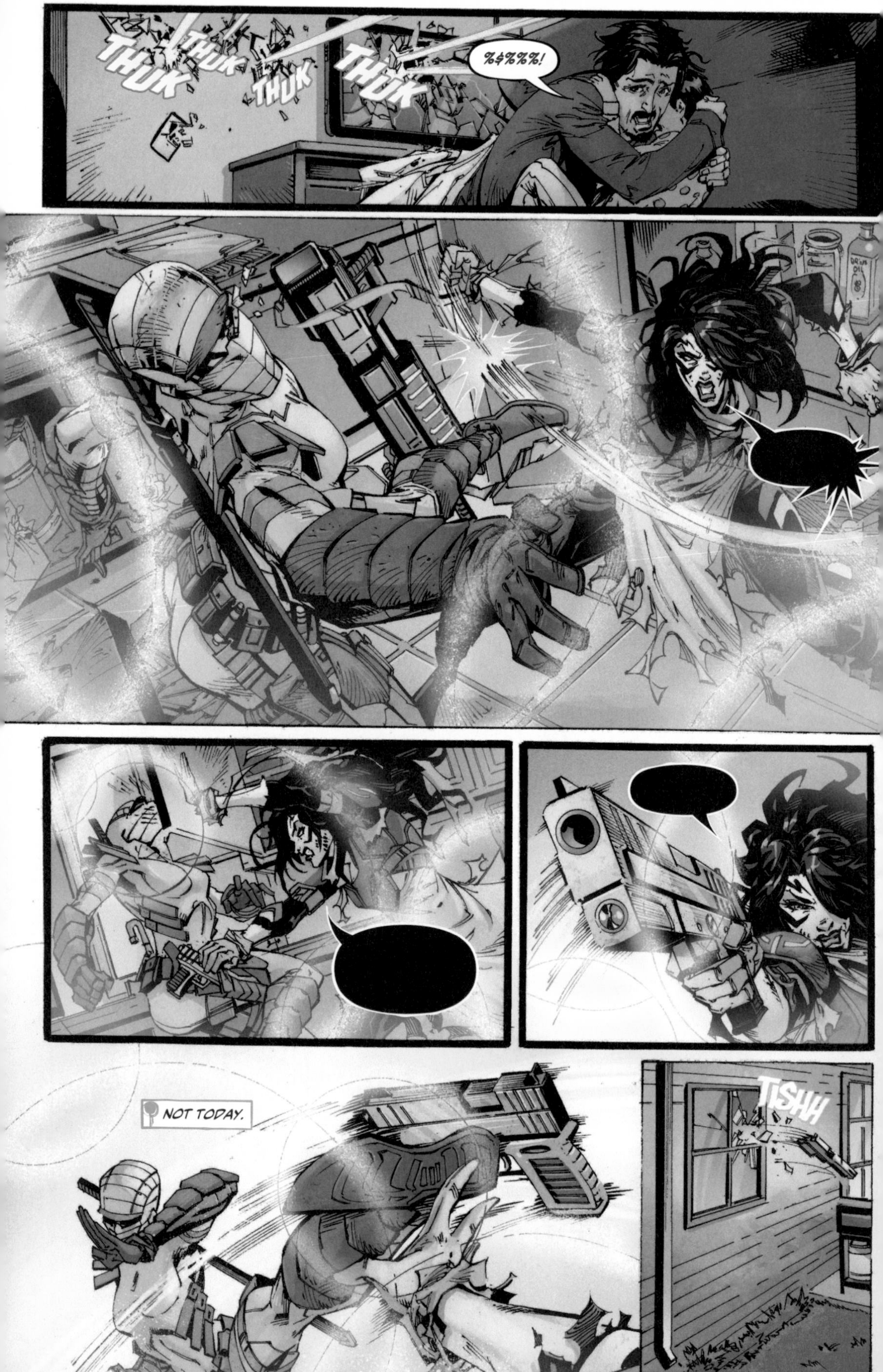
THUK
THUK
THUK
THUK
THUK
%$%%%!
NOT TODAY.
TISHH

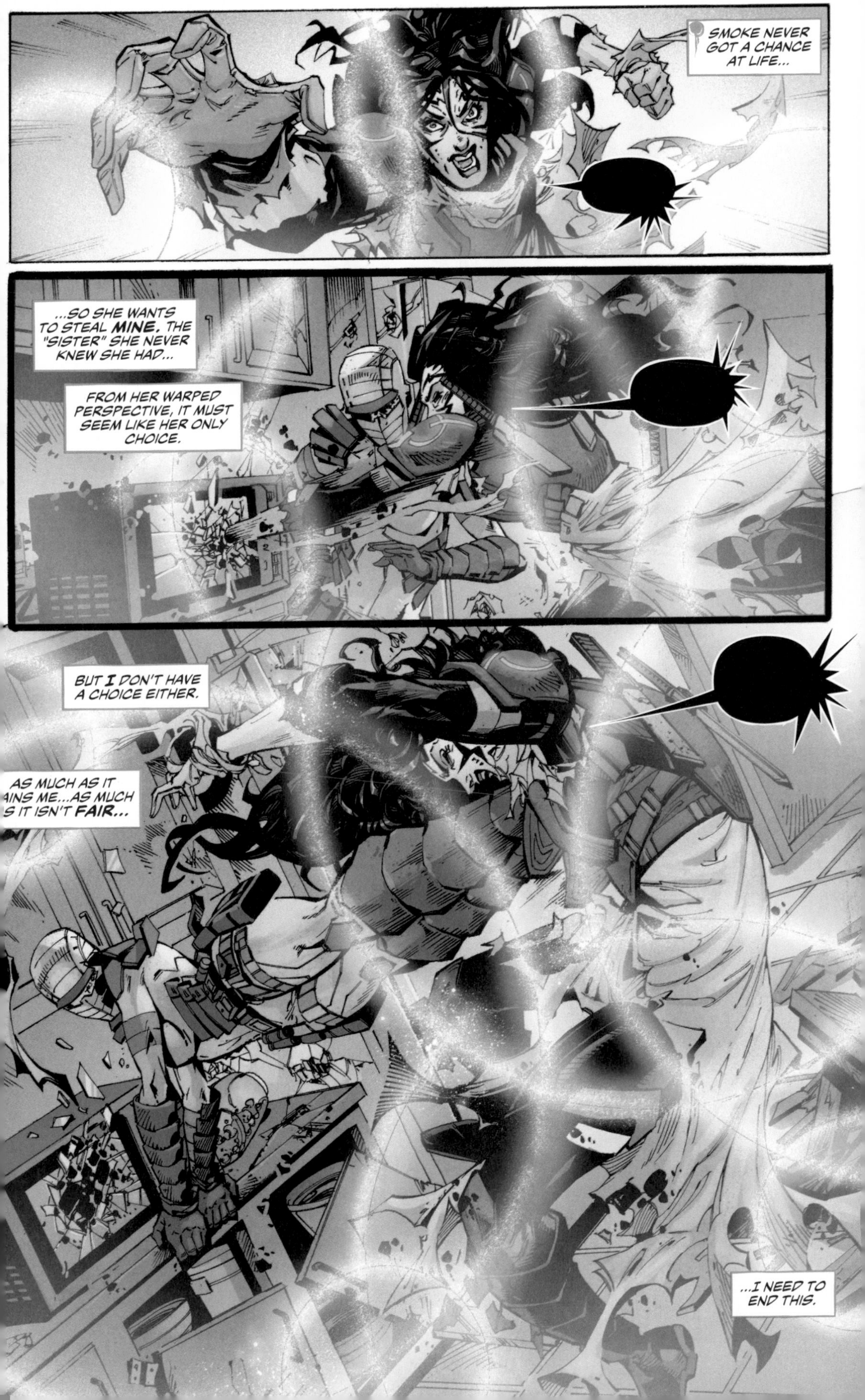
SMOKE NEVER GOT A CHANCE AT LIFE...
...SO SHE WANTS TO STEAL MINE. THE "SISTER" SHE NEVER KNEW SHE HAD...
FROM HER WARPED PERSPECTIVE, IT MUST SEEM LIKE HER ONLY CHOICE.
BUT I DON'T HAVE A CHOICE EITHER.
AS MUCH AS IT AINS ME...AS MUCH S IT ISN'T FAIR...
...I NEED TO END THIS.

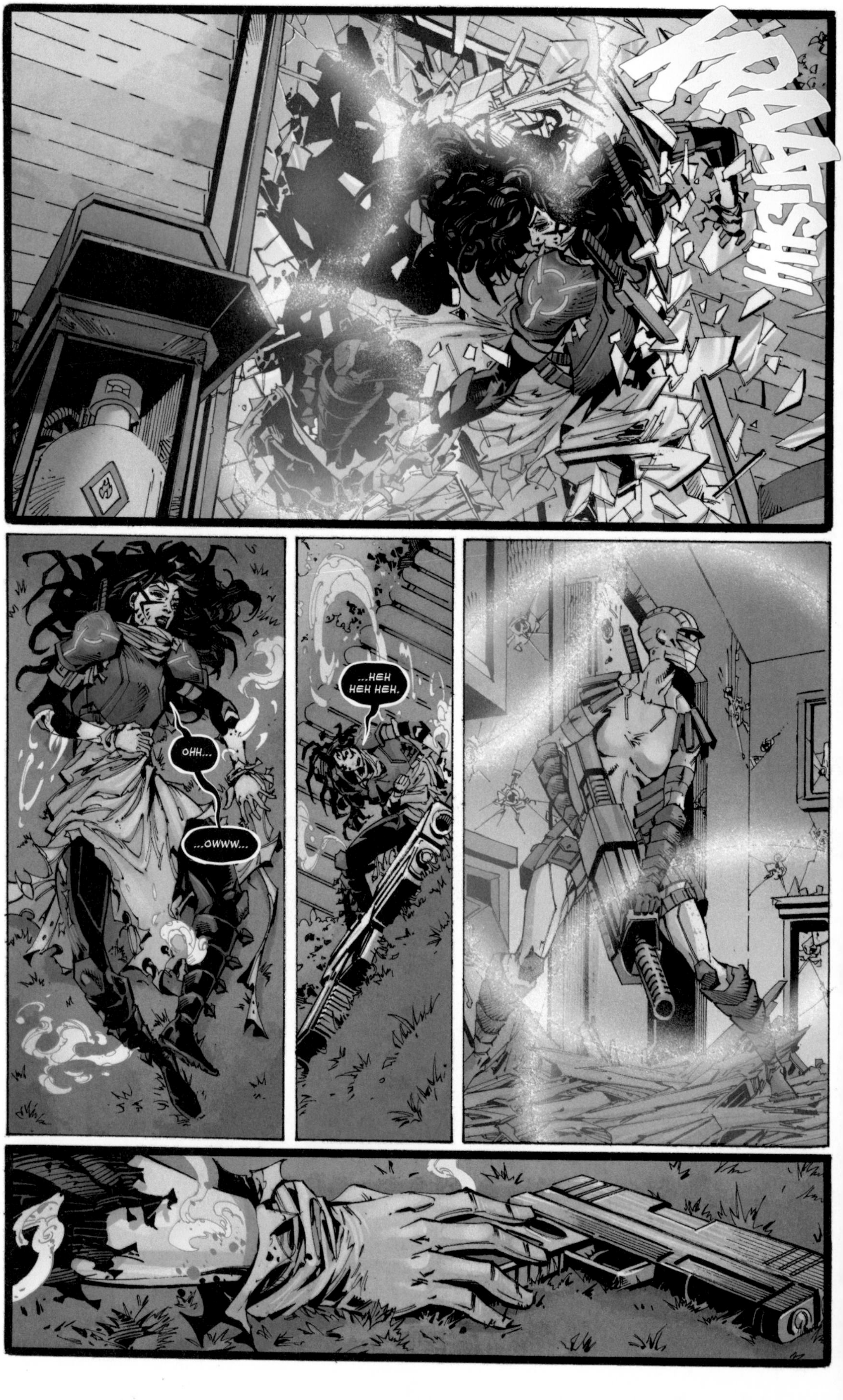
KRAATSH
OHH...
...OWWW...
...HEH HEH HEH.

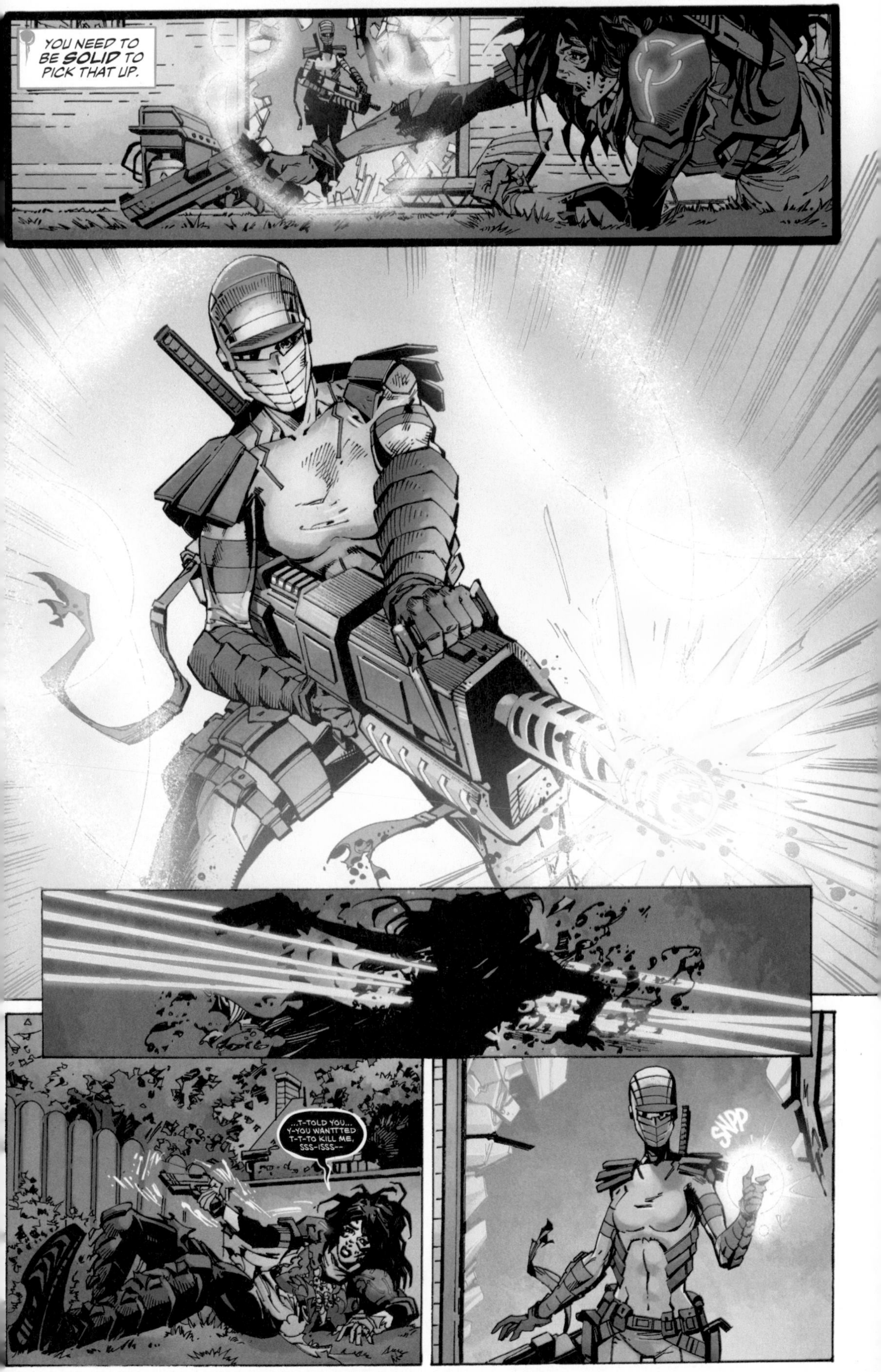
YOU NEED TO BE SOLID TO PICK THAT UP.
...T-TOLD YOU... Y-YOU WANTTTED T-T-TO KILL ME, SSS-ISSS--
SNPP

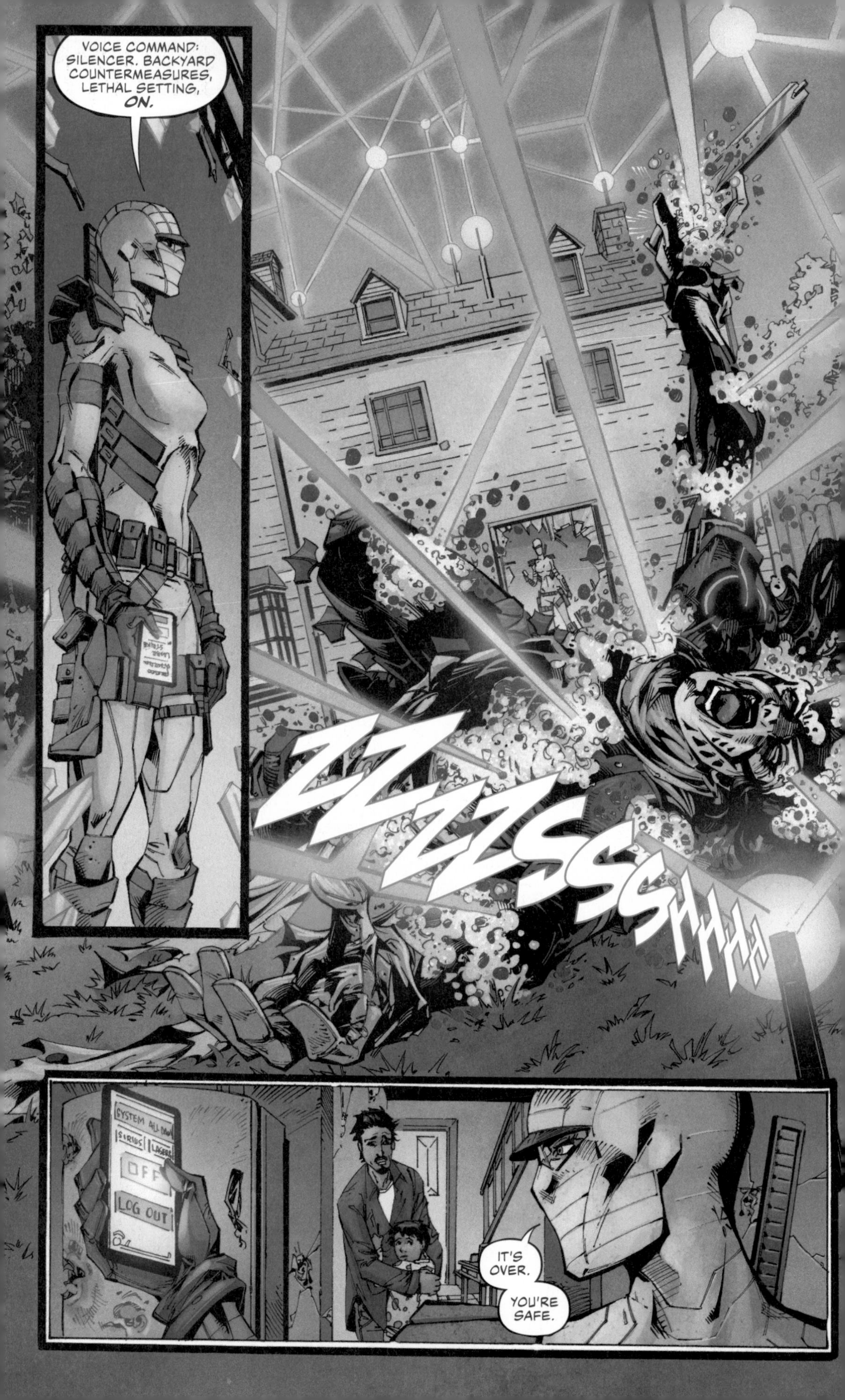
VOICE COMMAND: SILENCER. BACKYARD COUNTERMEASURES, LETHAL SETTING, ON.
ZZZZSSSHHHH
OFF
LOG OUT
IT'S OVER.
YOU'RE SAFE.

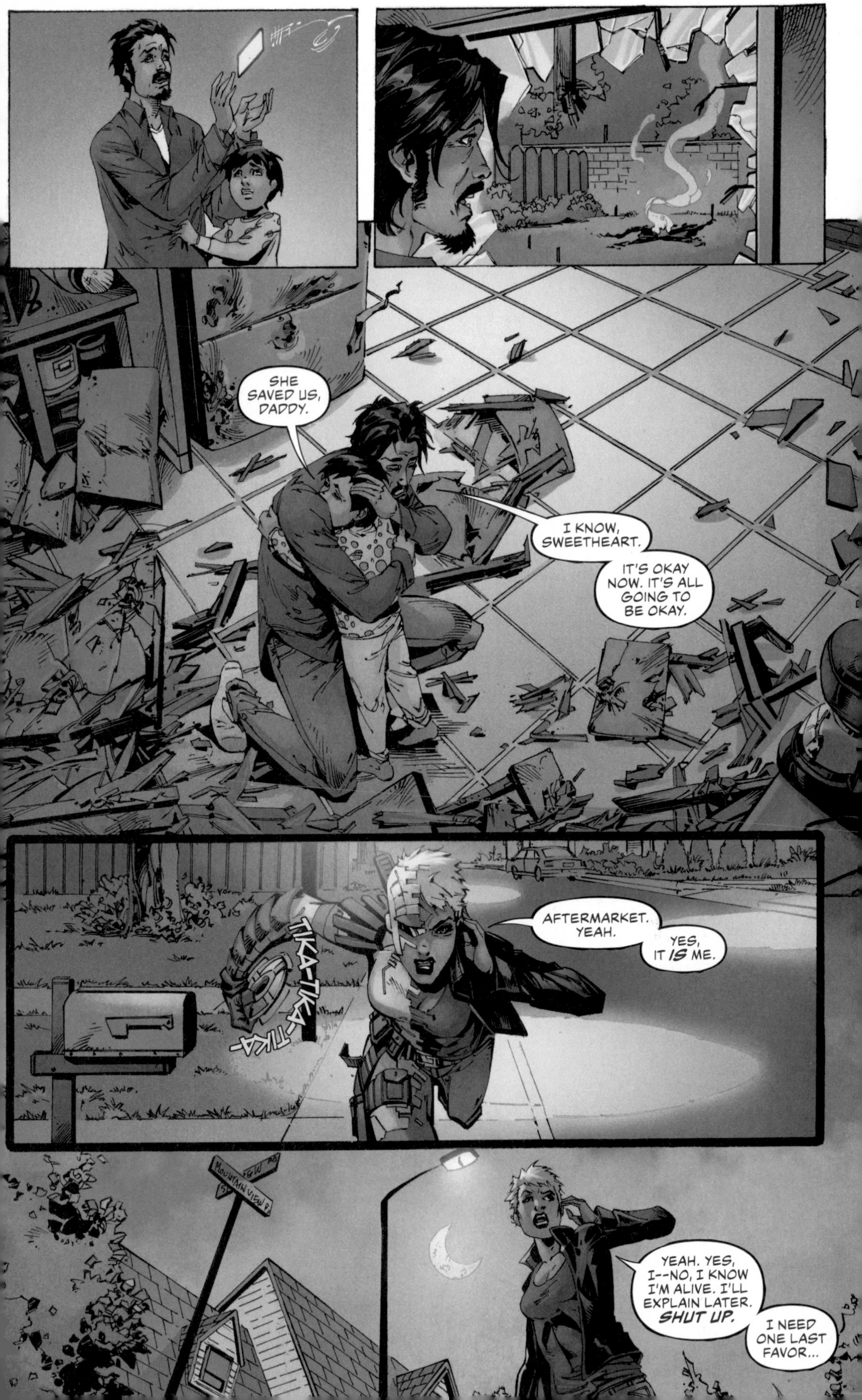
SHE SAVED US, DADDY.
I KNOW, SWEETHEART.
IT'S OKAY NOW. IT'S ALL GOING TO BE OKAY.
TIKA-TIKA-TIKA-
AFTERMARKET. YEAH.
YES, IT *IS* ME.
MOUNTAIN VIEW D.
YEAH. YES, I--NO, I KNOW I'M ALIVE. I'LL EXPLAIN LATER. ***SHUT UP.***
I NEED ONE LAST FAVOR...

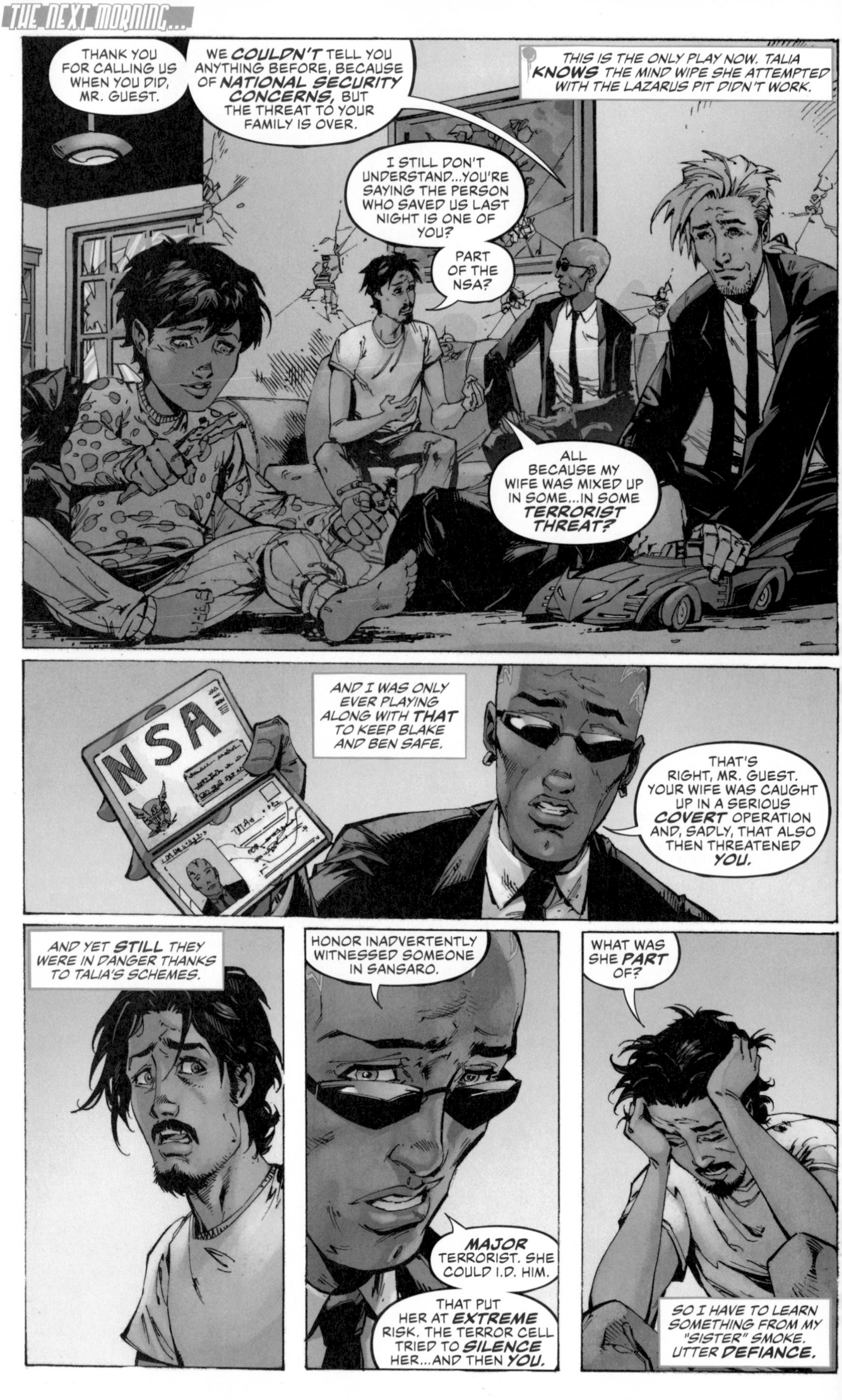
THE NEXT MORNING...
THANK YOU FOR CALLING US WHEN YOU DID, MR. GUEST.
WE COULDN'T TELL YOU ANYTHING BEFORE, BECAUSE OF NATIONAL SECURITY CONCERNS, BUT THE THREAT TO YOUR FAMILY IS OVER.
THIS IS THE ONLY PLAY NOW. TALIA KNOWS THE MIND WIPE SHE ATTEMPTED WITH THE LAZARUS PIT DIDN'T WORK.
I STILL DON'T UNDERSTAND...YOU'RE SAYING THE PERSON WHO SAVED US LAST NIGHT IS ONE OF YOU?
PART OF THE NSA?
ALL BECAUSE MY WIFE WAS MIXED UP IN SOME...IN SOME TERRORIST THREAT?
NSA
AND I WAS ONLY EVER PLAYING ALONG WITH THAT TO KEEP BLAKE AND BEN SAFE.
THAT'S RIGHT, MR. GUEST. YOUR WIFE WAS CAUGHT UP IN A SERIOUS COVERT OPERATION AND, SADLY, THAT ALSO THEN THREATENED YOU.
AND YET STILL THEY WERE IN DANGER THANKS TO TALIA'S SCHEMES.
HONOR INADVERTENTLY WITNESSED SOMEONE IN SANSARO.
MAJOR TERRORIST. SHE COULD I.D. HIM.
THAT PUT HER AT EXTREME RISK. THE TERROR CELL TRIED TO SILENCE HER...AND THEN YOU.
WHAT WAS SHE PART OF?
SO I HAVE TO LEARN SOMETHING FROM MY "SISTER" SMOKE. UTTER DEFIANCE.

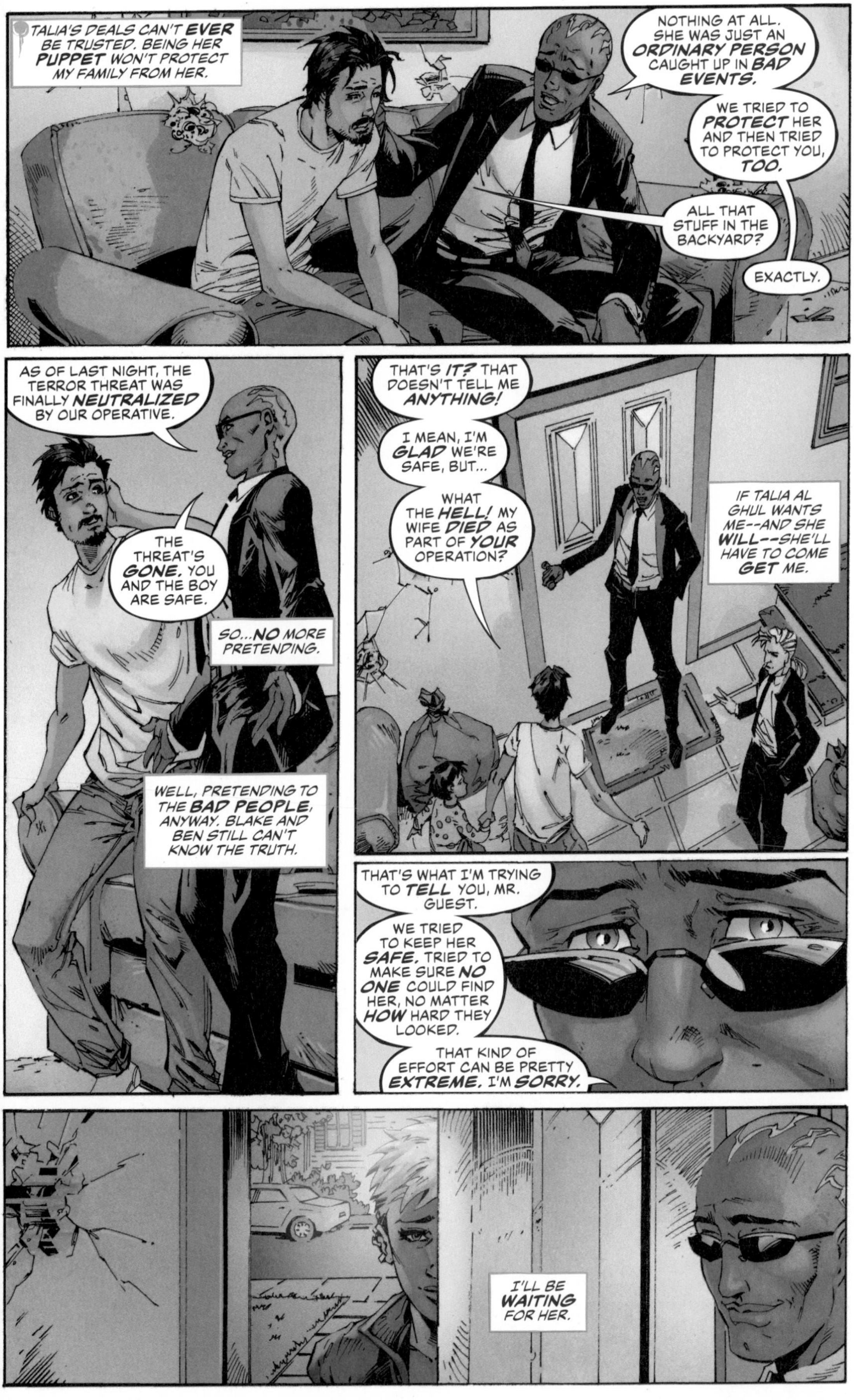
TALIA'S DEALS CAN'T EVER BE TRUSTED. BEING HER PUPPET WON'T PROTECT MY FAMILY FROM HER.
NOTHING AT ALL. SHE WAS JUST AN ORDINARY PERSON CAUGHT UP IN BAD EVENTS.
WE TRIED TO PROTECT HER AND THEN TRIED TO PROTECT YOU, TOO.
ALL THAT STUFF IN THE BACKYARD?
EXACTLY.
AS OF LAST NIGHT, THE TERROR THREAT WAS FINALLY NEUTRALIZED BY OUR OPERATIVE.
THE THREAT'S GONE. YOU AND THE BOY ARE SAFE.
SO...NO MORE PRETENDING.
WELL, PRETENDING TO THE BAD PEOPLE, ANYWAY. BLAKE AND BEN STILL CAN'T KNOW THE TRUTH.
THAT'S IT? THAT DOESN'T TELL ME ANYTHING!
I MEAN, I'M GLAD WE'RE SAFE, BUT...
WHAT THE HELL! MY WIFE DIED AS PART OF YOUR OPERATION?
IF TALIA AL GHUL WANTS ME--AND SHE WILL--SHE'LL HAVE TO COME GET ME.
THAT'S WHAT I'M TRYING TO TELL YOU, MR. GUEST.
WE TRIED TO KEEP HER SAFE. TRIED TO MAKE SURE NO ONE COULD FIND HER, NO MATTER HOW HARD THEY LOOKED.
THAT KIND OF EFFORT CAN BE PRETTY EXTREME. I'M SORRY.
I'LL BE WAITING FOR HER.

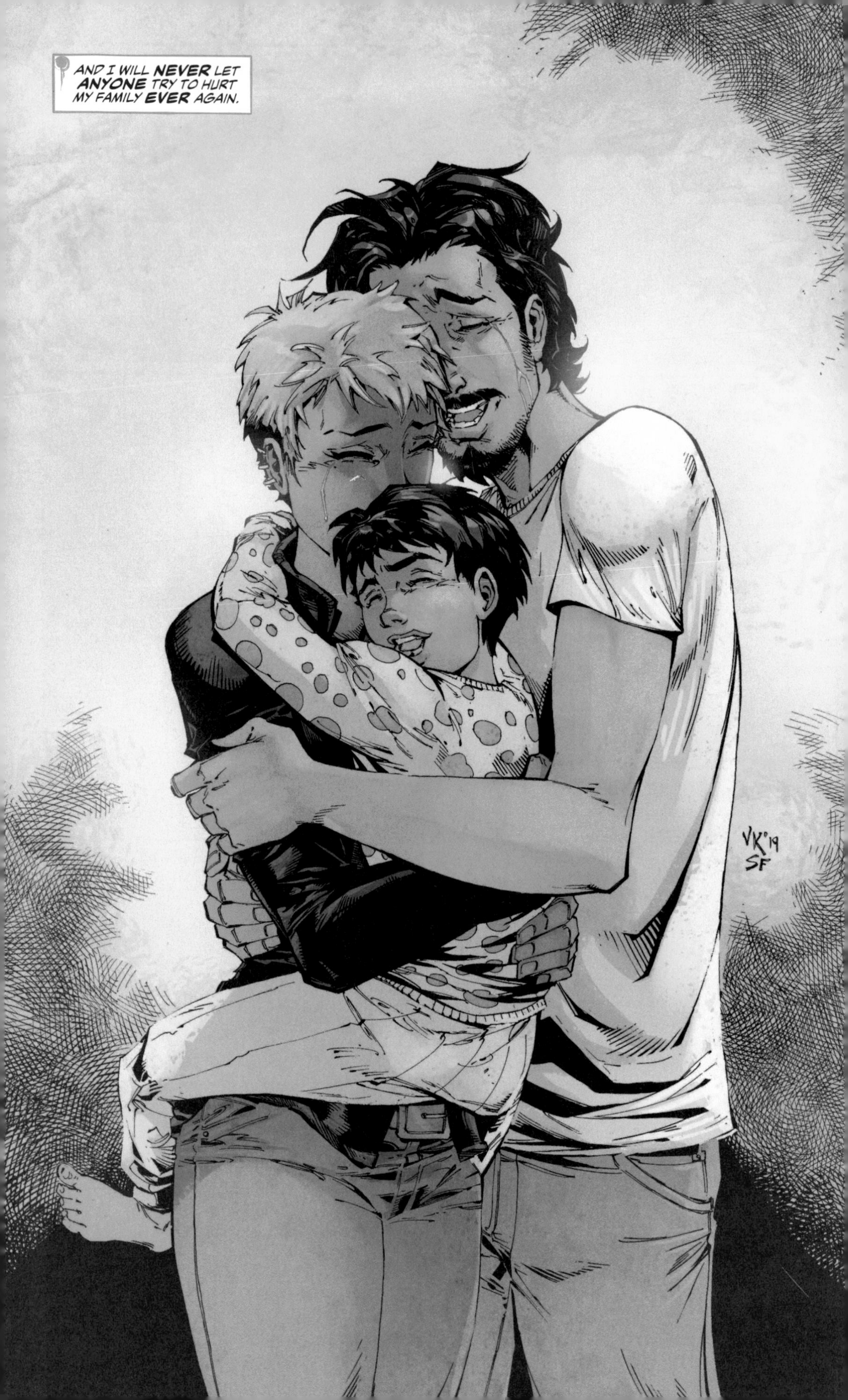
AND I WILL NEVER LET ANYONE TRY TO HURT MY FAMILY EVER AGAIN.

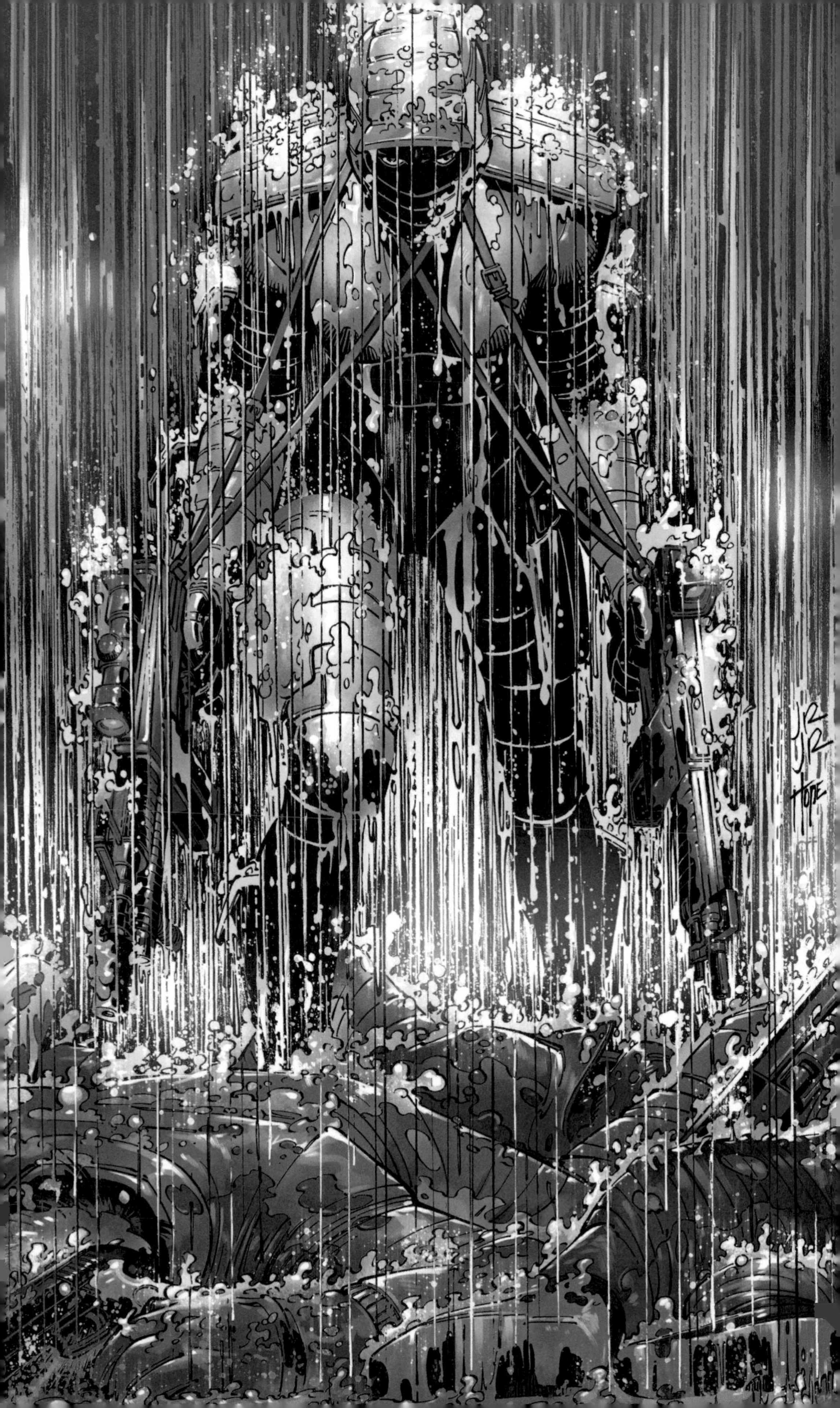

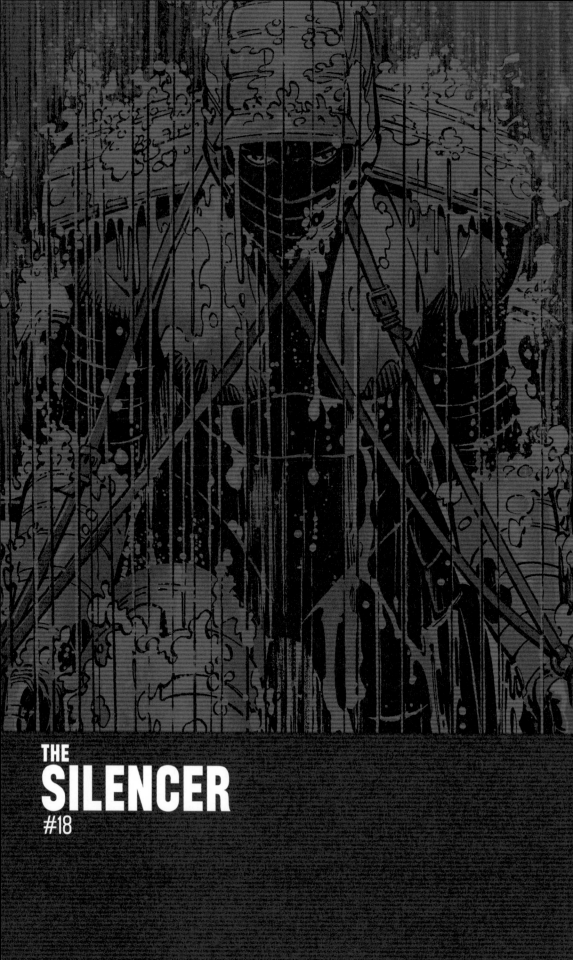

THE
SILENCER
#18

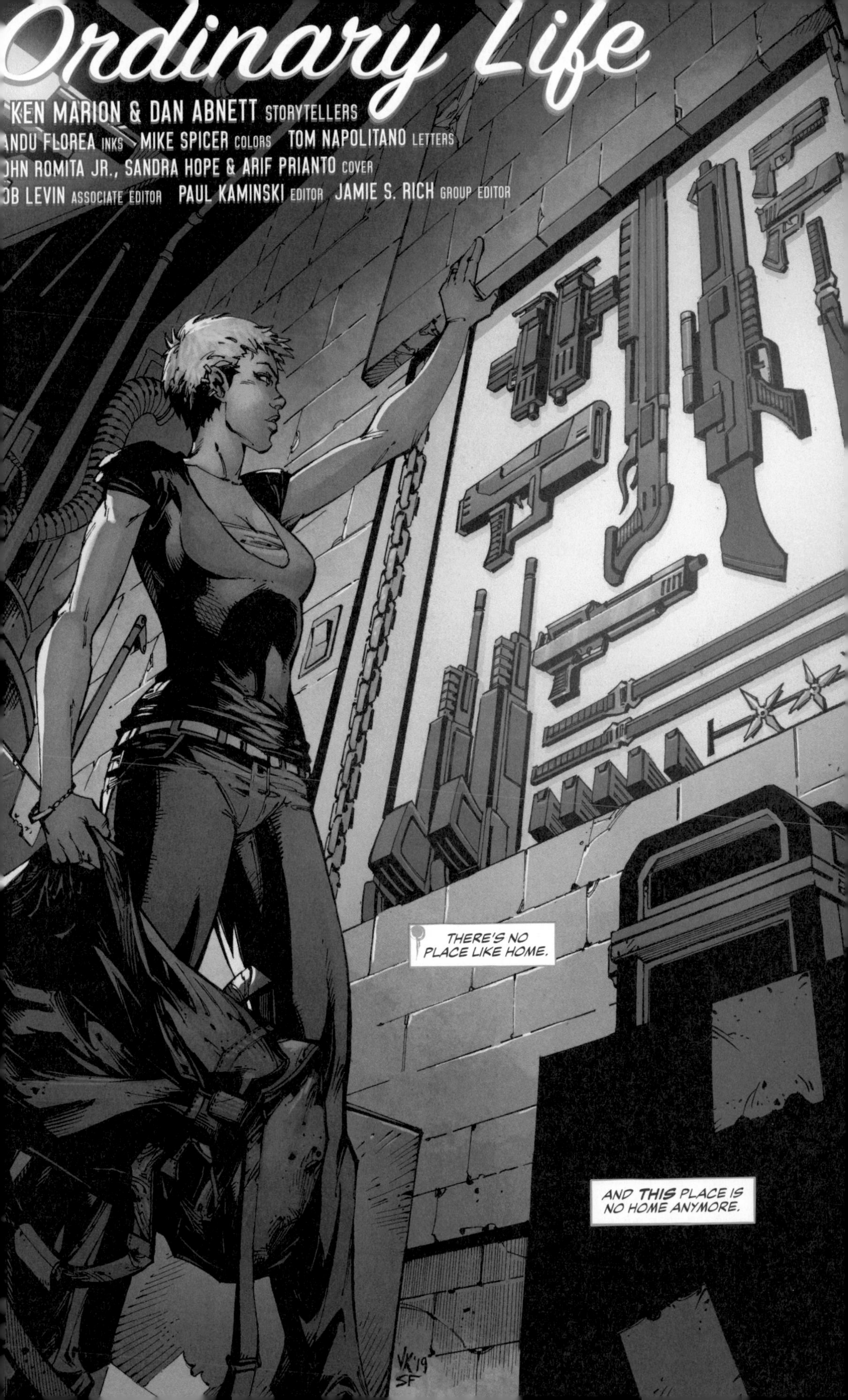

Ordinary Life
KEN MARION & DAN ABNETT STORYTELLERS
ANDU FLOREA INKS MIKE SPICER COLORS TOM NAPOLITANO LETTERS
OHN ROMITA JR., SANDRA HOPE & ARIF PRIANTO COVER
OB LEVIN ASSOCIATE EDITOR PAUL KAMINSKI EDITOR JAMIE S. RICH GROUP EDITOR
THERE'S NO PLACE LIKE HOME.
AND THIS PLACE IS NO HOME ANYMORE.

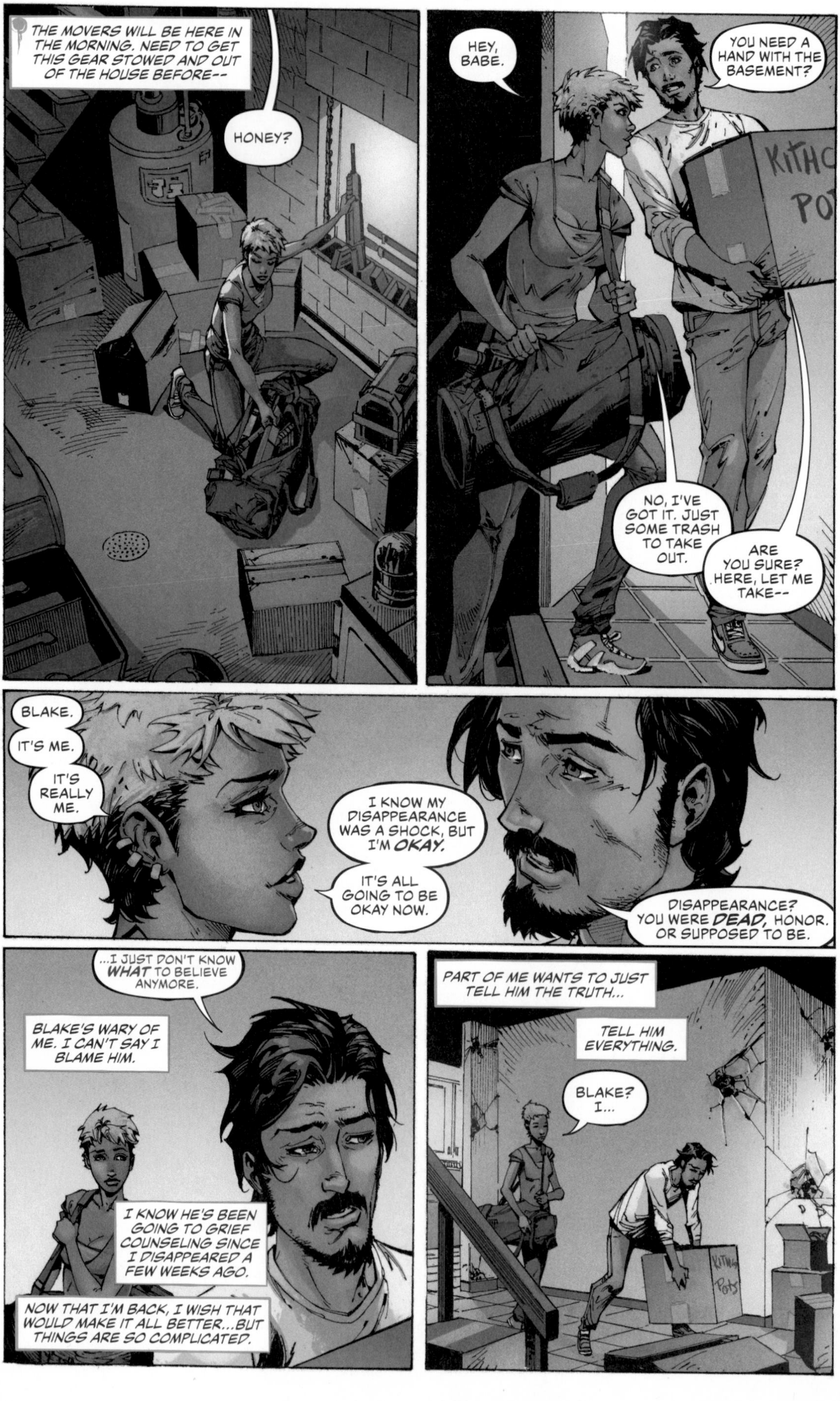
THE MOVERS WILL BE HERE IN THE MORNING. NEED TO GET THIS GEAR STOWED AND OUT OF THE HOUSE BEFORE--
HONEY?
HEY, BABE.
YOU NEED A HAND WITH THE BASEMENT?
KITCH
POTS
NO, I'VE GOT IT. JUST SOME TRASH TO TAKE OUT.
ARE YOU SURE? HERE, LET ME TAKE--
BLAKE.
IT'S ME.
IT'S REALLY ME.
I KNOW MY DISAPPEARANCE WAS A SHOCK, BUT I'M OKAY.
IT'S ALL GOING TO BE OKAY NOW.
DISAPPEARANCE? YOU WERE DEAD, HONOR. OR SUPPOSED TO BE.
...I JUST DON'T KNOW WHAT TO BELIEVE ANYMORE.
BLAKE'S WARY OF ME. I CAN'T SAY I BLAME HIM.
I KNOW HE'S BEEN GOING TO GRIEF COUNSELING SINCE I DISAPPEARED A FEW WEEKS AGO.
NOW THAT I'M BACK, I WISH THAT WOULD MAKE IT ALL BETTER...BUT THINGS ARE SO COMPLICATED.
PART OF ME WANTS TO JUST TELL HIM THE TRUTH...
TELL HIM EVERYTHING.
BLAKE? I...

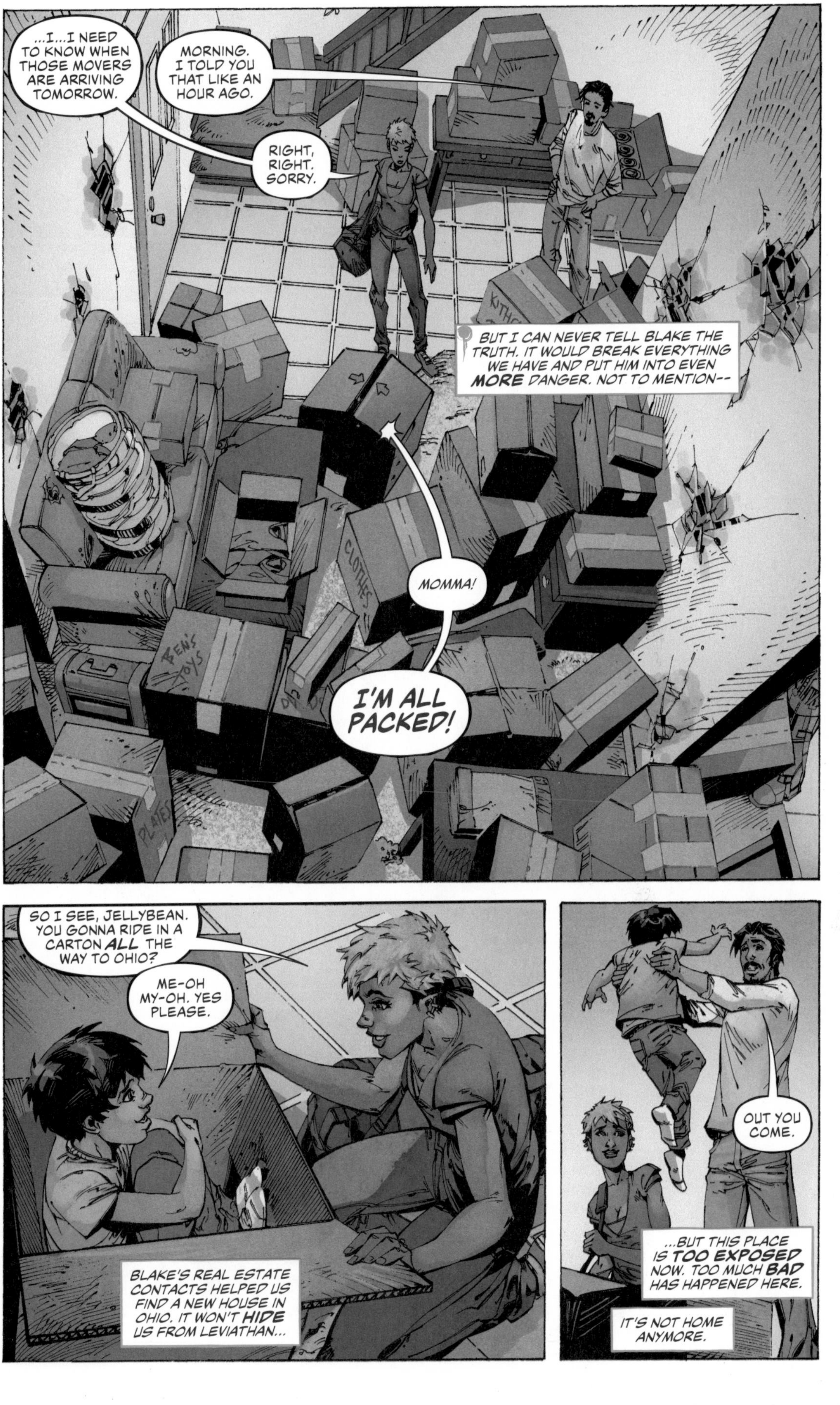
...I...I NEED TO KNOW WHEN THOSE MOVERS ARE ARRIVING TOMORROW.
MORNING. I TOLD YOU THAT LIKE AN HOUR AGO.
RIGHT, RIGHT. SORRY.
BUT I CAN NEVER TELL BLAKE THE TRUTH. IT WOULD BREAK EVERYTHING WE HAVE AND PUT HIM INTO EVEN MORE DANGER. NOT TO MENTION--
MOMMA!
I'M ALL PACKED!
SO I SEE, JELLYBEAN. YOU GONNA RIDE IN A CARTON ALL THE WAY TO OHIO?
ME-OH MY-OH. YES PLEASE.
BLAKE'S REAL ESTATE CONTACTS HELPED US FIND A NEW HOUSE IN OHIO. IT WON'T HIDE US FROM LEVIATHAN...
OUT YOU COME.
...BUT THIS PLACE IS TOO EXPOSED NOW. TOO MUCH BAD HAS HAPPENED HERE.
IT'S NOT HOME ANYMORE.

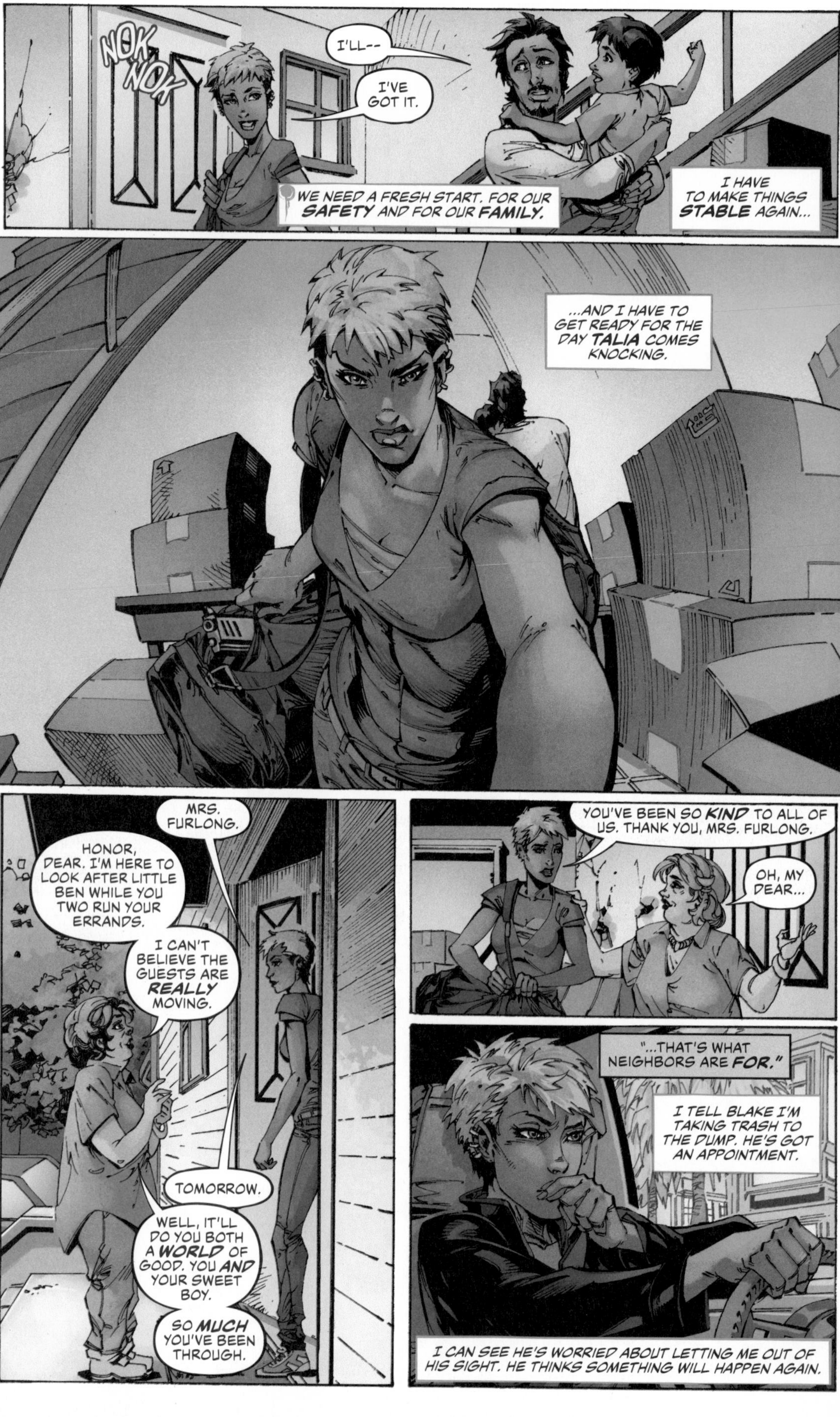
NOK NOK
I'LL--
I'VE GOT IT.
WE NEED A FRESH START. FOR OUR SAFETY AND FOR OUR FAMILY.
I HAVE TO MAKE THINGS STABLE AGAIN...
...AND I HAVE TO GET READY FOR THE DAY TALIA COMES KNOCKING.
MRS. FURLONG.
HONOR, DEAR. I'M HERE TO LOOK AFTER LITTLE BEN WHILE YOU TWO RUN YOUR ERRANDS.
I CAN'T BELIEVE THE GUESTS ARE REALLY MOVING.
TOMORROW.
WELL, IT'LL DO YOU BOTH A WORLD OF GOOD. YOU AND YOUR SWEET BOY.
SO MUCH YOU'VE BEEN THROUGH.
YOU'VE BEEN SO KIND TO ALL OF US. THANK YOU, MRS. FURLONG.
OH, MY DEAR...
"...THAT'S WHAT NEIGHBORS ARE FOR."
I TELL BLAKE I'M TAKING TRASH TO THE DUMP. HE'S GOT AN APPOINTMENT.
I CAN SEE HE'S WORRIED ABOUT LETTING ME OUT OF HIS SIGHT. HE THINKS SOMETHING WILL HAPPEN AGAIN.

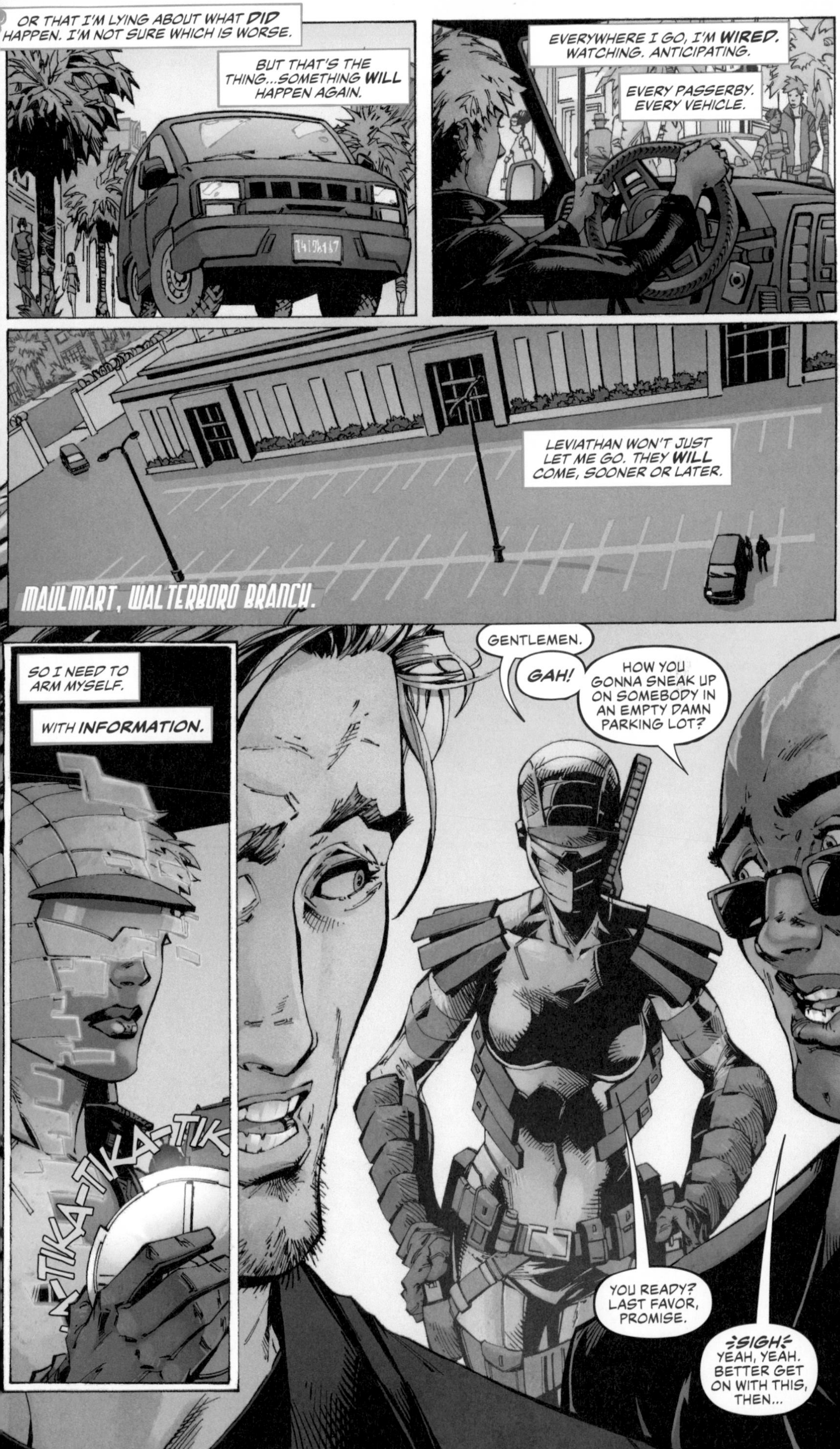
OR THAT I'M LYING ABOUT WHAT DID HAPPEN. I'M NOT SURE WHICH IS WORSE.
BUT THAT'S THE THING...SOMETHING WILL HAPPEN AGAIN.
EVERYWHERE I GO, I'M WIRED. WATCHING. ANTICIPATING.
EVERY PASSERBY. EVERY VEHICLE.
LEVIATHAN WON'T JUST LET ME GO. THEY WILL COME, SOONER OR LATER.
MAULMART, WALTERBORO BRANCH.
SO I NEED TO ARM MYSELF.
WITH INFORMATION.
GENTLEMEN.
GAH!
HOW YOU GONNA SNEAK UP ON SOMEBODY IN AN EMPTY DAMN PARKING LOT?
TIKA-TIKA-TIK
YOU READY? LAST FAVOR, PROMISE.
SIGH YEAH, YEAH. BETTER GET ON WITH THIS, THEN...

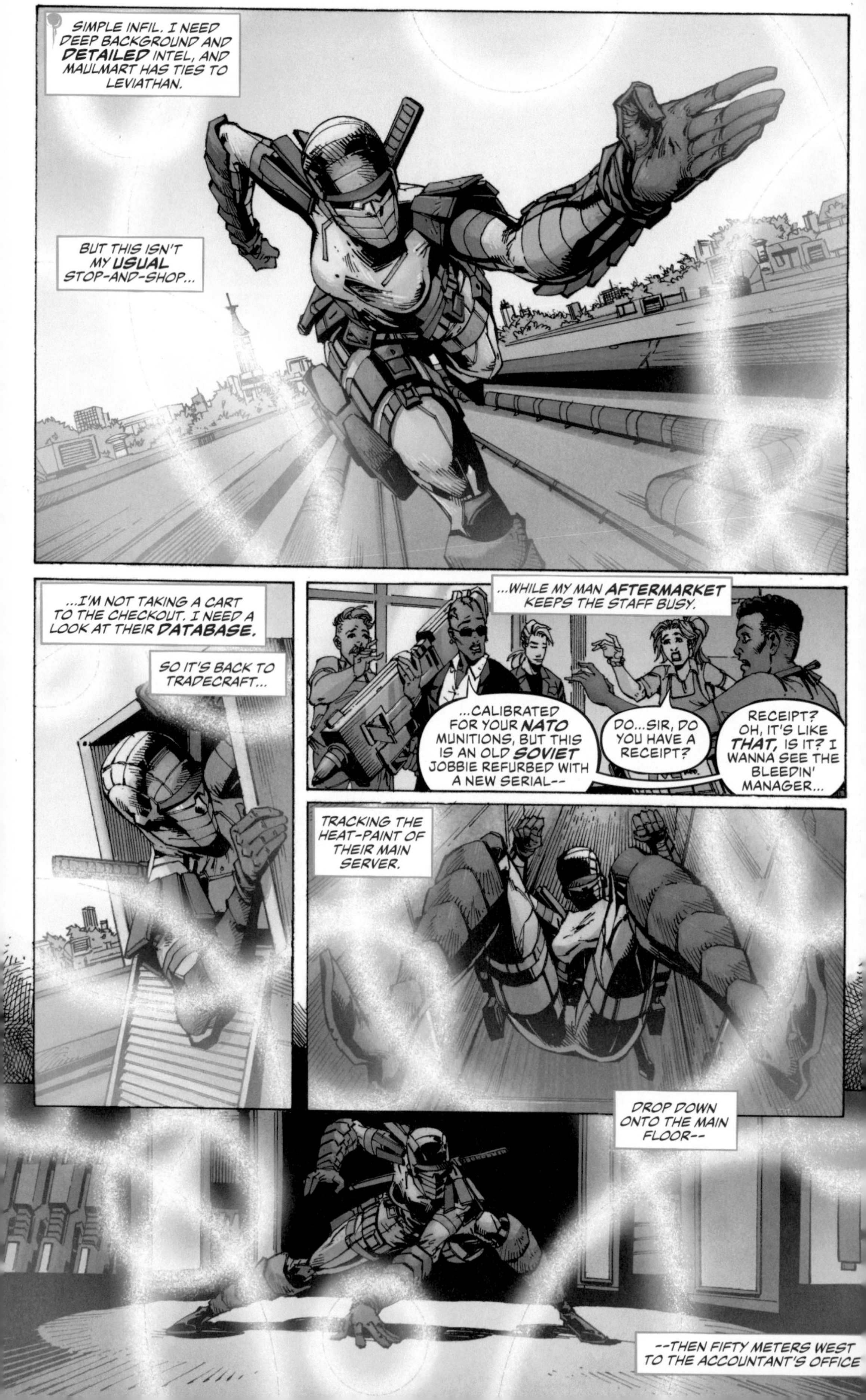
SIMPLE INFIL. I NEED DEEP BACKGROUND AND DETAILED INTEL, AND MAULMART HAS TIES TO LEVIATHAN.
BUT THIS ISN'T MY USUAL STOP-AND-SHOP...
...I'M NOT TAKING A CART TO THE CHECKOUT. I NEED A LOOK AT THEIR DATABASE.
SO IT'S BACK TO TRADECRAFT...
...WHILE MY MAN AFTERMARKET KEEPS THE STAFF BUSY.
...CALIBRATED FOR YOUR NATO MUNITIONS, BUT THIS IS AN OLD SOVIET JOBBIE REFURBED WITH A NEW SERIAL--
DO...SIR, DO YOU HAVE A RECEIPT?
RECEIPT? OH, IT'S LIKE THAT, IS IT? I WANNA SEE THE BLEEDIN' MANAGER...
TRACKING THE HEAT-PAINT OF THEIR MAIN SERVER.
DROP DOWN ONTO THE MAIN FLOOR--
--THEN FIFTY METERS WEST TO THE ACCOUNTANT'S OFFICE

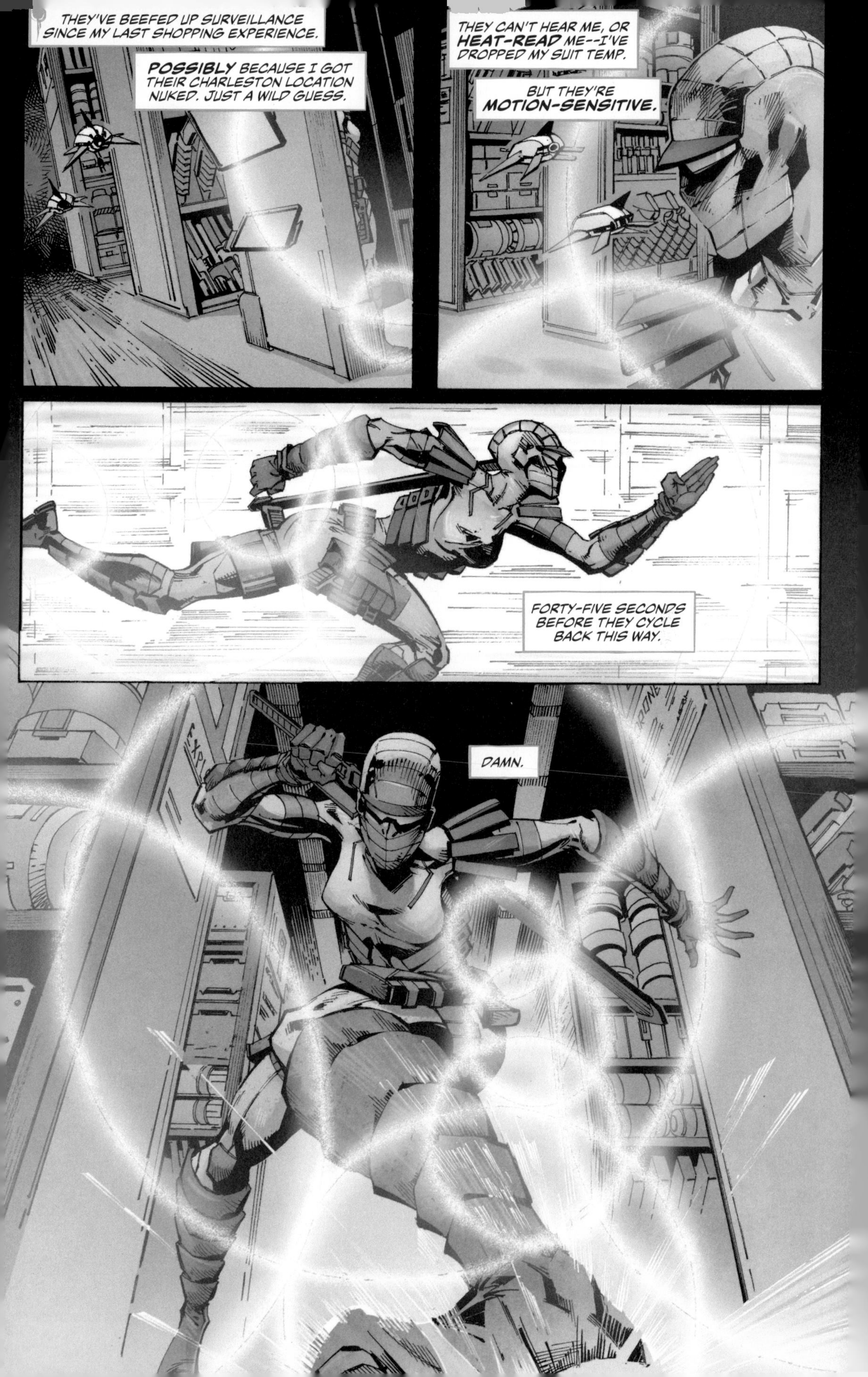
THEY'VE BEEFED UP SURVEILLANCE SINCE MY LAST SHOPPING EXPERIENCE.
POSSIBLY BECAUSE I GOT THEIR CHARLESTON LOCATION NUKED. JUST A WILD GUESS.
THEY CAN'T HEAR ME, OR HEAT-READ ME--I'VE DROPPED MY SUIT TEMP.
BUT THEY'RE MOTION-SENSITIVE.
FORTY-FIVE SECONDS BEFORE THEY CYCLE BACK THIS WAY.
DAMN.

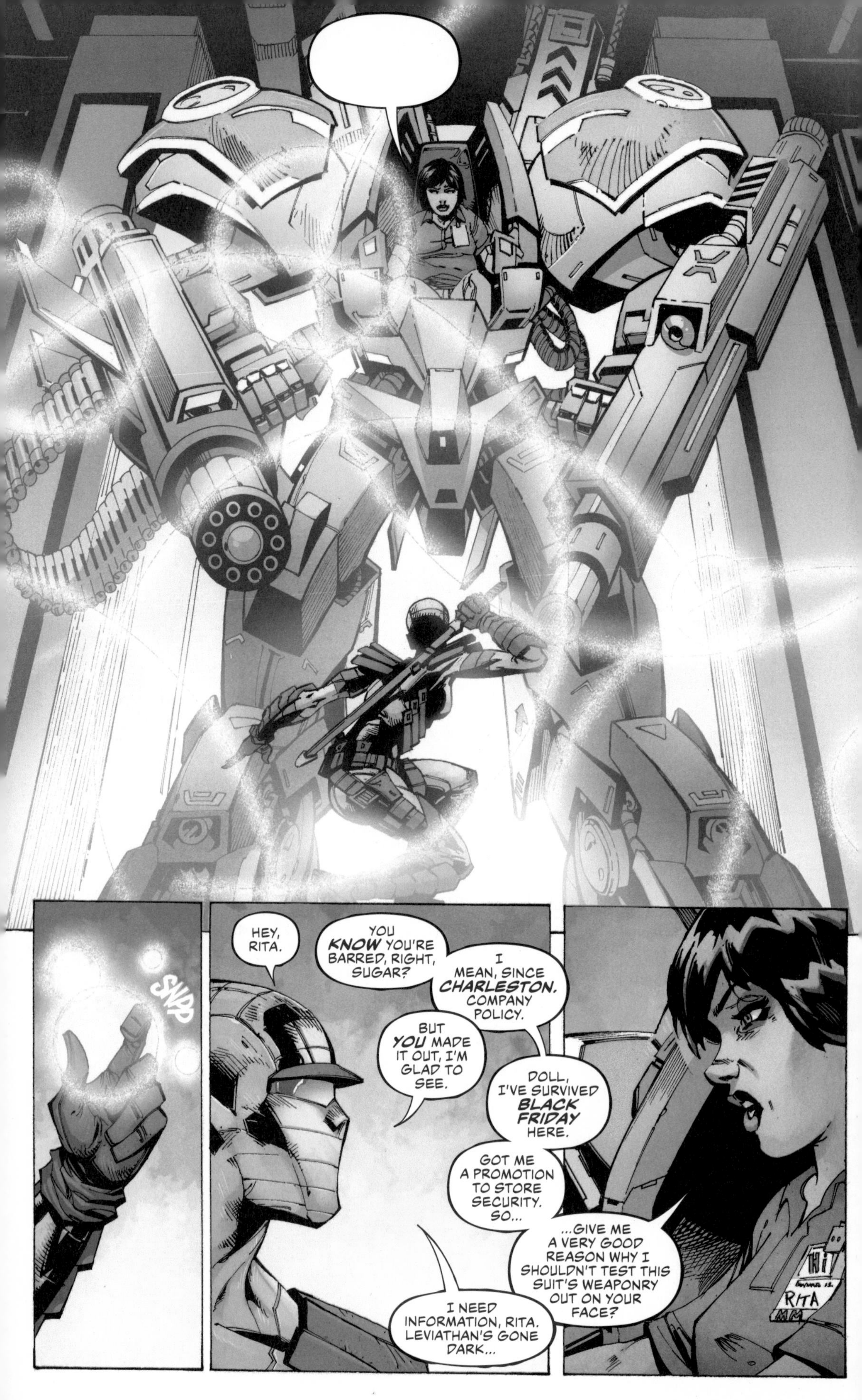
SNPP
HEY, RITA.
YOU KNOW YOU'RE BARRED, RIGHT, SUGAR?
I MEAN, SINCE CHARLESTON. COMPANY POLICY.
BUT YOU MADE IT OUT, I'M GLAD TO SEE.
DOLL, I'VE SURVIVED BLACK FRIDAY HERE.
GOT ME A PROMOTION TO STORE SECURITY. SO...
...GIVE ME A VERY GOOD REASON WHY I SHOULDN'T TEST THIS SUIT'S WEAPONRY OUT ON YOUR FACE?
I NEED INFORMATION, RITA. LEVIATHAN'S GONE DARK...
RITA

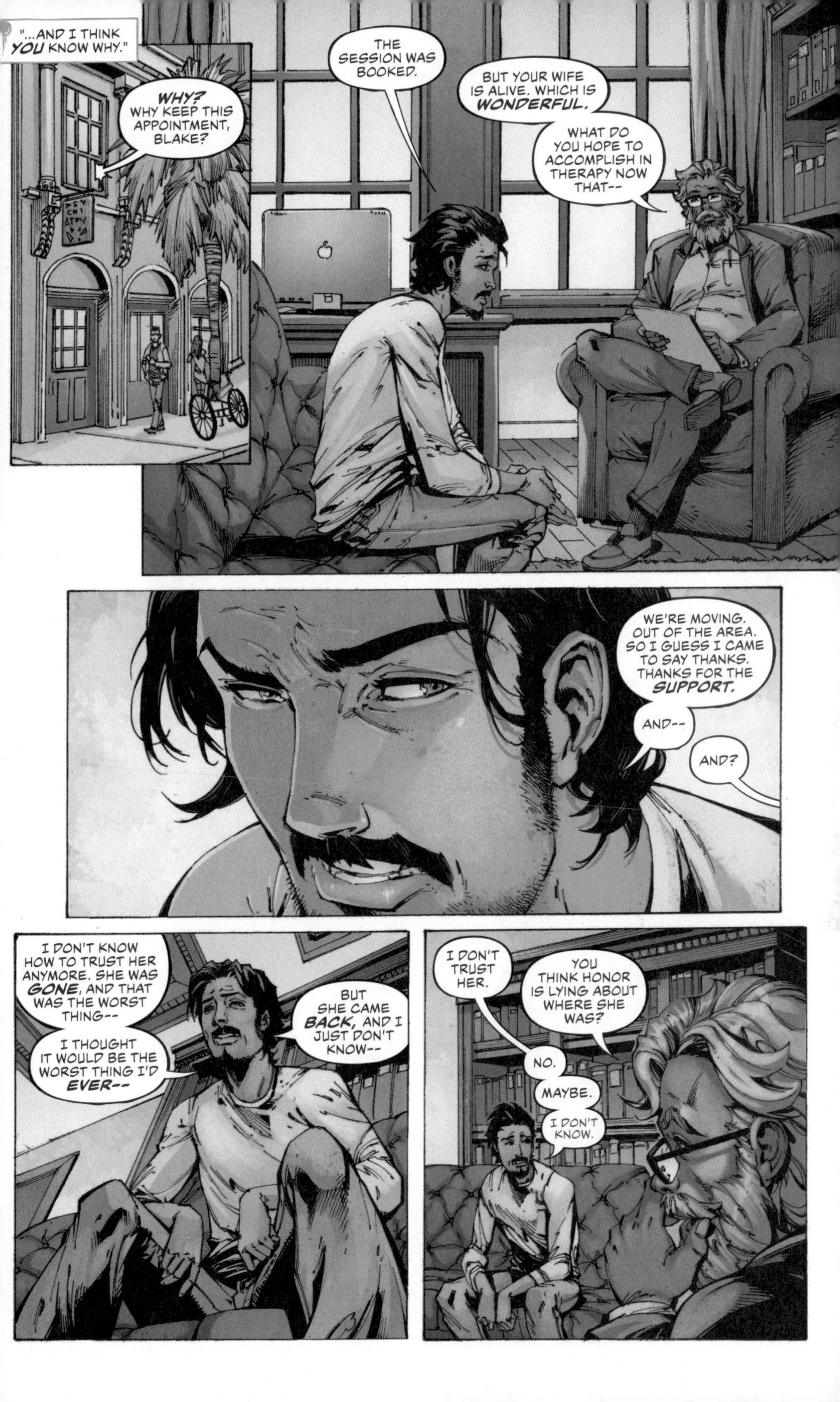
"...AND I THINK *YOU* KNOW WHY."
WHY? WHY KEEP THIS APPOINTMENT, BLAKE?
THE SESSION WAS BOOKED.
BUT YOUR WIFE IS ALIVE. WHICH IS *WONDERFUL.*
WHAT DO YOU HOPE TO ACCOMPLISH IN THERAPY NOW THAT--
WE'RE MOVING. OUT OF THE AREA. SO I GUESS I CAME TO SAY THANKS. THANKS FOR THE *SUPPORT.*
AND--
AND?
I DON'T KNOW HOW TO TRUST HER ANYMORE. SHE WAS *GONE*, AND THAT WAS THE WORST THING--
I THOUGHT IT WOULD BE THE WORST THING I'D *EVER--*
BUT SHE CAME *BACK*, AND I JUST DON'T KNOW--
I DON'T TRUST HER.
YOU THINK HONOR IS LYING ABOUT WHERE SHE WAS?
NO.
MAYBE.
I DON'T KNOW.

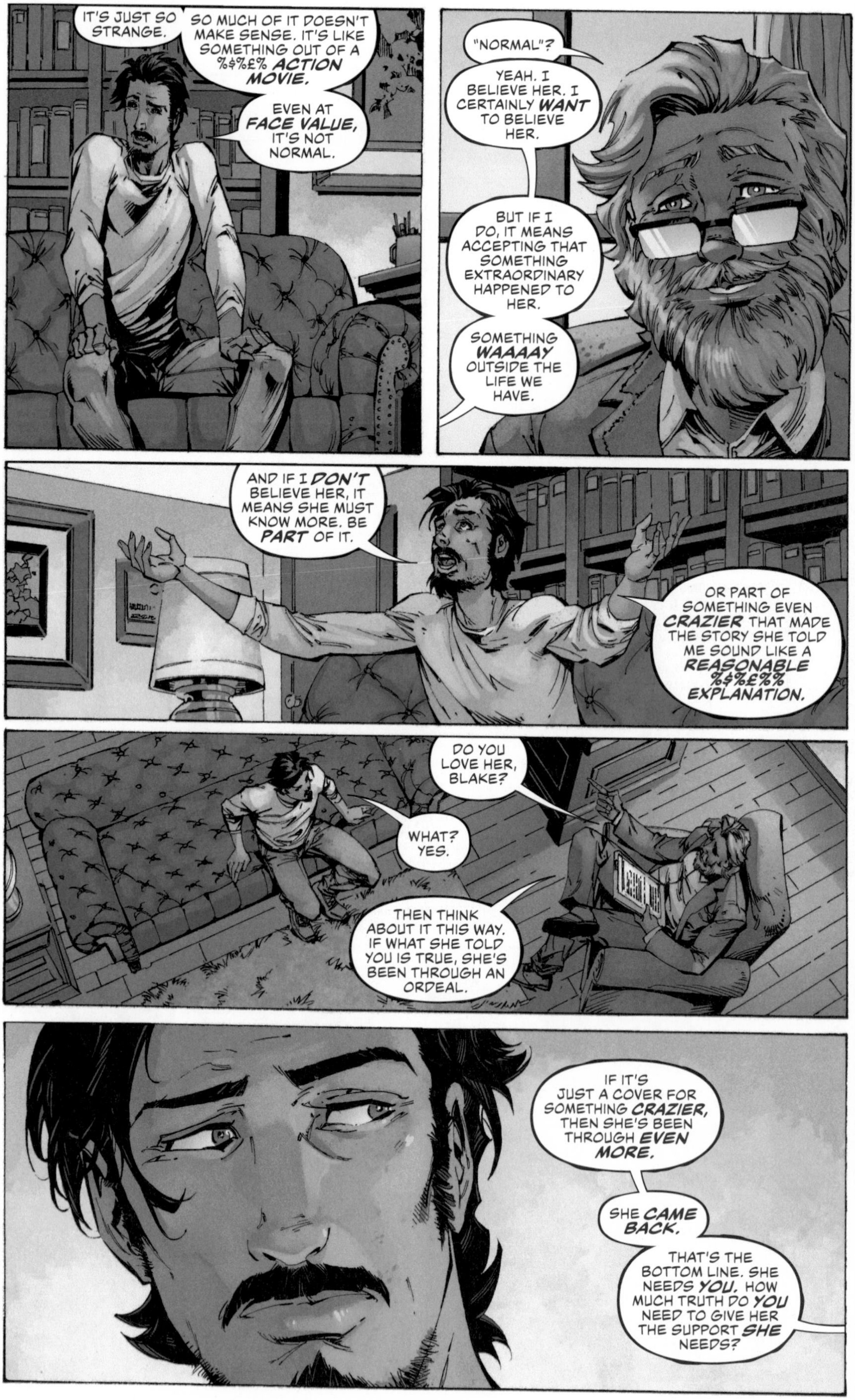
IT'S JUST SO STRANGE.
SO MUCH OF IT DOESN'T MAKE SENSE. IT'S LIKE SOMETHING OUT OF A %$%£% ACTION MOVIE.
EVEN AT FACE VALUE, IT'S NOT NORMAL.
"NORMAL"?
YEAH. I BELIEVE HER. I CERTAINLY WANT TO BELIEVE HER.
BUT IF I DO, IT MEANS ACCEPTING THAT SOMETHING EXTRAORDINARY HAPPENED TO HER.
SOMETHING WAAAAY OUTSIDE THE LIFE WE HAVE.
AND IF I DON'T BELIEVE HER, IT MEANS SHE MUST KNOW MORE. BE PART OF IT.
OR PART OF SOMETHING EVEN CRAZIER THAT MADE THE STORY SHE TOLD ME SOUND LIKE A REASONABLE %$%£% EXPLANATION.
DO YOU LOVE HER, BLAKE?
WHAT? YES.
THEN THINK ABOUT IT THIS WAY. IF WHAT SHE TOLD YOU IS TRUE, SHE'S BEEN THROUGH AN ORDEAL.
IF IT'S JUST A COVER FOR SOMETHING CRAZIER, THEN SHE'S BEEN THROUGH EVEN MORE.
SHE CAME BACK.
THAT'S THE BOTTOM LINE. SHE NEEDS YOU. HOW MUCH TRUTH DO YOU NEED TO GIVE HER THE SUPPORT SHE NEEDS?

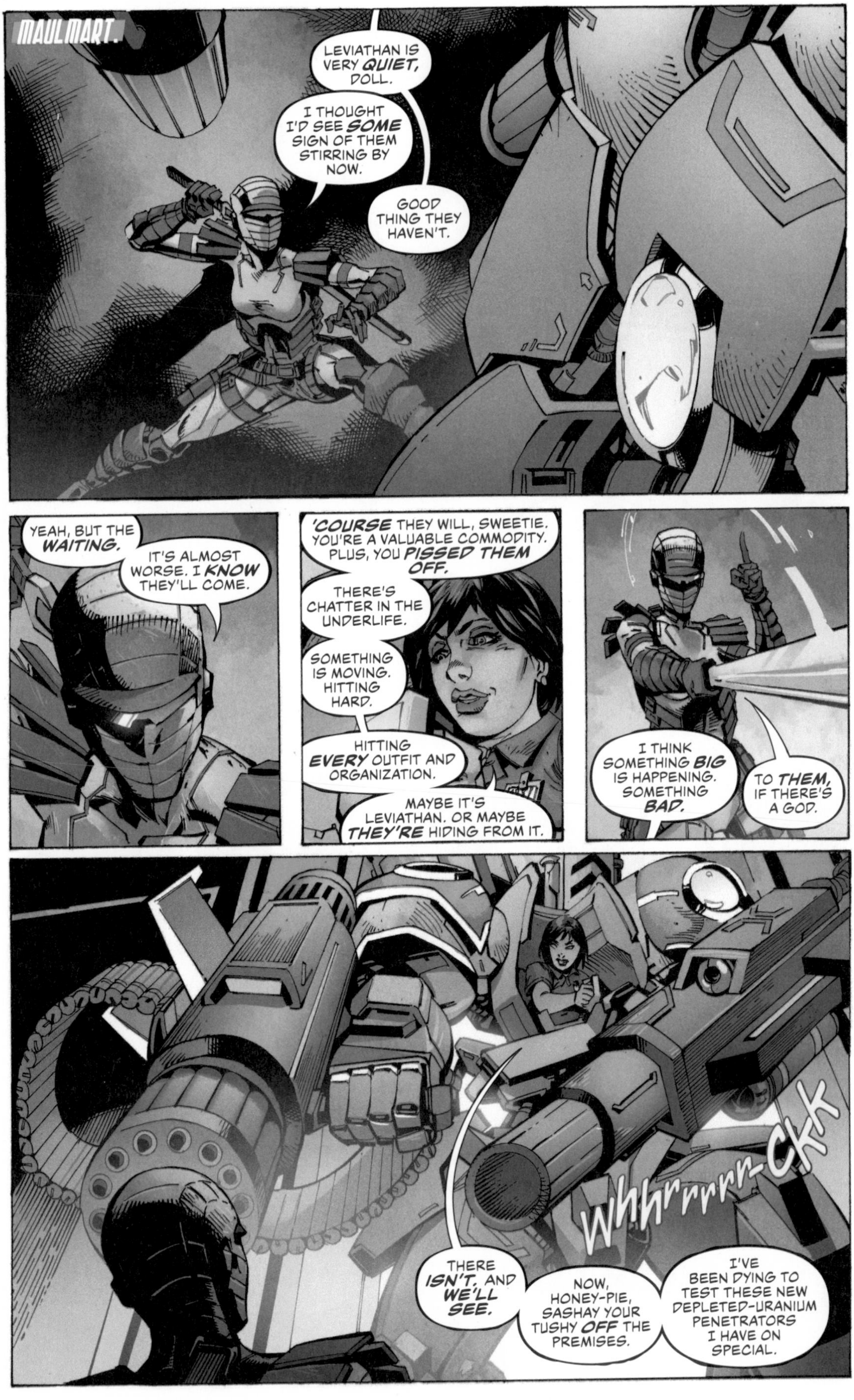
MAULMART.
LEVIATHAN IS VERY QUIET, DOLL.
I THOUGHT I'D SEE SOME SIGN OF THEM STIRRING BY NOW.
GOOD THING THEY HAVEN'T.
YEAH, BUT THE WAITING.
IT'S ALMOST WORSE. I KNOW THEY'LL COME.
'COURSE THEY WILL, SWEETIE. YOU'RE A VALUABLE COMMODITY. PLUS, YOU PISSED THEM OFF.
THERE'S CHATTER IN THE UNDERLIFE.
SOMETHING IS MOVING. HITTING HARD.
HITTING EVERY OUTFIT AND ORGANIZATION.
MAYBE IT'S LEVIATHAN. OR MAYBE THEY'RE HIDING FROM IT.
I THINK SOMETHING BIG IS HAPPENING. SOMETHING BAD.
TO THEM, IF THERE'S A GOD.
WHHRRRRR-CKK
THERE ISN'T. AND WE'LL SEE.
NOW, HONEY-PIE, SASHAY YOUR TUSHY OFF THE PREMISES.
I'VE BEEN DYING TO TEST THESE NEW DEPLETED-URANIUM PENETRATORS I HAVE ON SPECIAL.

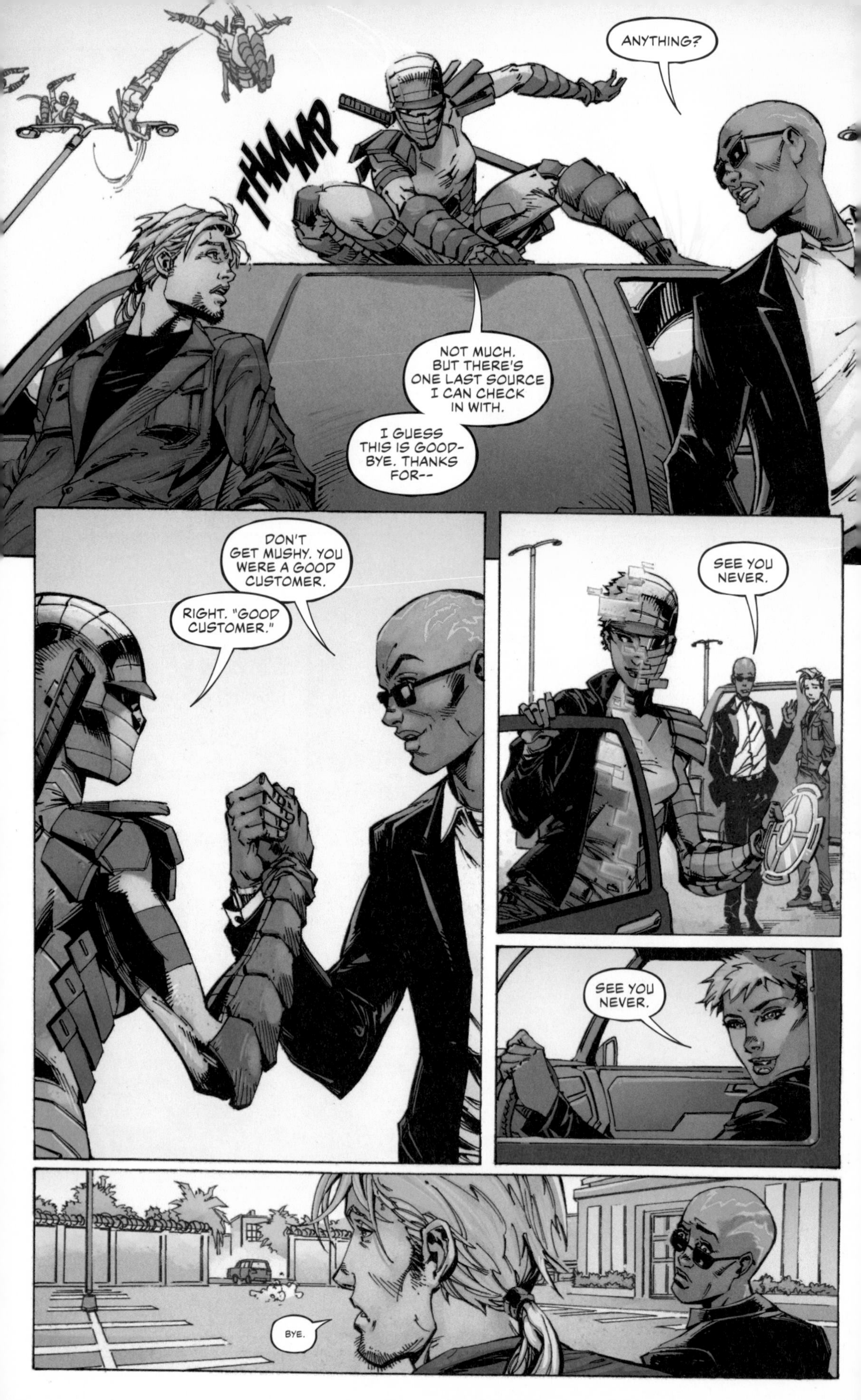
ANYTHING?
THWMP
NOT MUCH. BUT THERE'S ONE LAST SOURCE I CAN CHECK IN WITH.
I GUESS THIS IS GOOD-BYE. THANKS FOR--
DON'T GET MUSHY. YOU WERE A GOOD CUSTOMER.
RIGHT. "GOOD CUSTOMER."
SEE YOU NEVER.
SEE YOU NEVER.
BYE.

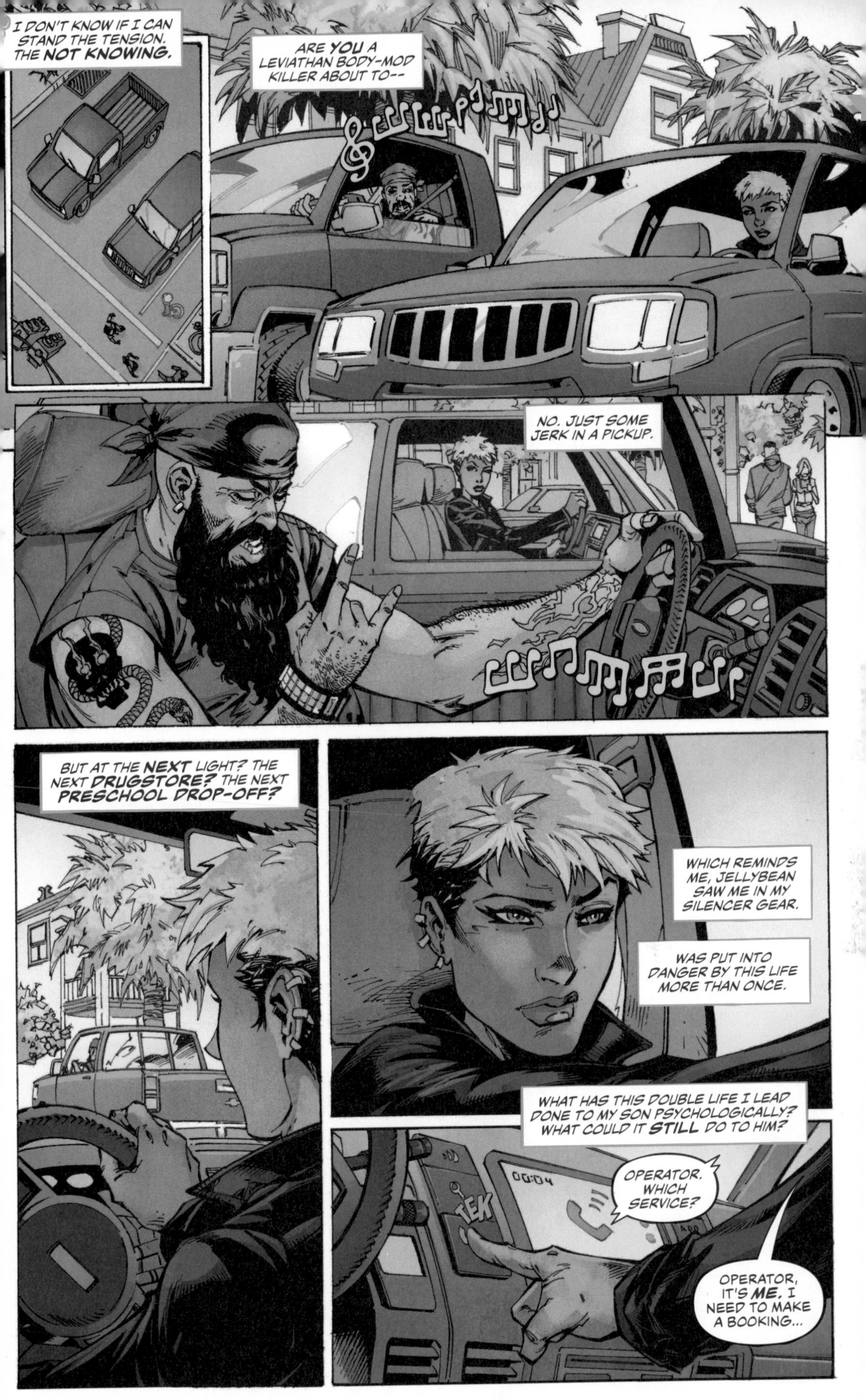
I DON'T KNOW IF I CAN STAND THE TENSION. THE NOT KNOWING.
ARE YOU A LEVIATHAN BODY-MOD KILLER ABOUT TO--
NO. JUST SOME JERK IN A PICKUP.
BUT AT THE NEXT LIGHT? THE NEXT DRUGSTORE? THE NEXT PRESCHOOL DROP-OFF?
WHICH REMINDS ME, JELLYBEAN SAW ME IN MY SILENCER GEAR.
WAS PUT INTO DANGER BY THIS LIFE MORE THAN ONCE.
WHAT HAS THIS DOUBLE LIFE I LEAD DONE TO MY SON PSYCHOLOGICALLY? WHAT COULD IT STILL DO TO HIM?
OPERATOR. WHICH SERVICE?
OPERATOR, IT'S ME. I NEED TO MAKE A BOOKING...

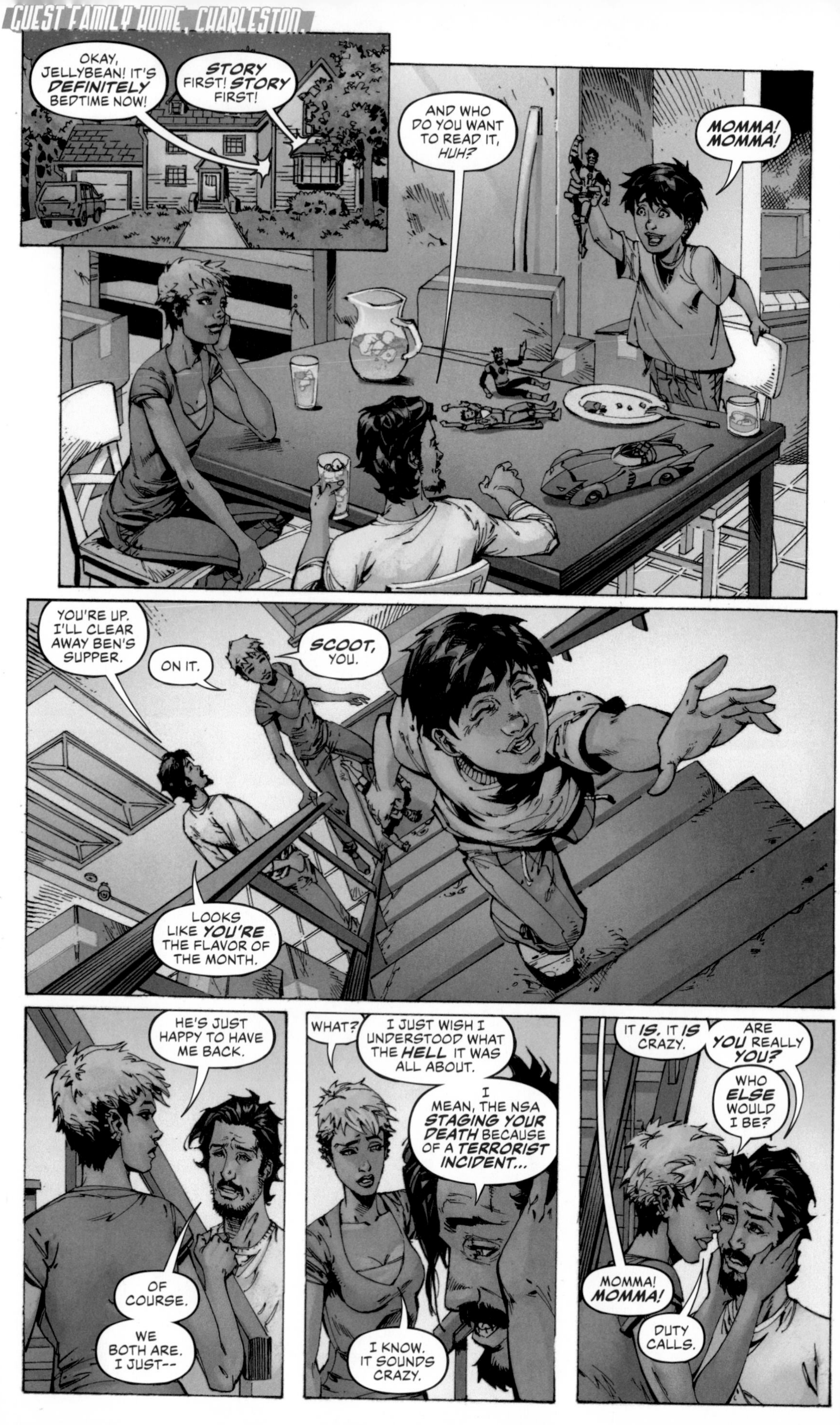
GUEST FAMILY HOME, CHARLESTON.
OKAY, JELLYBEAN! IT'S DEFINITELY BEDTIME NOW!
STORY FIRST! STORY FIRST!
AND WHO DO YOU WANT TO READ IT, HUH?
MOMMA! MOMMA!
YOU'RE UP. I'LL CLEAR AWAY BEN'S SUPPER.
ON IT.
SCOOT, YOU.
LOOKS LIKE YOU'RE THE FLAVOR OF THE MONTH.
HE'S JUST HAPPY TO HAVE ME BACK.
OF COURSE.
WE BOTH ARE. I JUST--
WHAT?
I JUST WISH I UNDERSTOOD WHAT THE HELL IT WAS ALL ABOUT.
I MEAN, THE NSA STAGING YOUR DEATH BECAUSE OF A TERRORIST INCIDENT...
I KNOW. IT SOUNDS CRAZY.
IT IS, IT IS CRAZY.
ARE YOU REALLY YOU?
WHO ELSE WOULD I BE?
MOMMA! MOMMA!
DUTY CALLS.

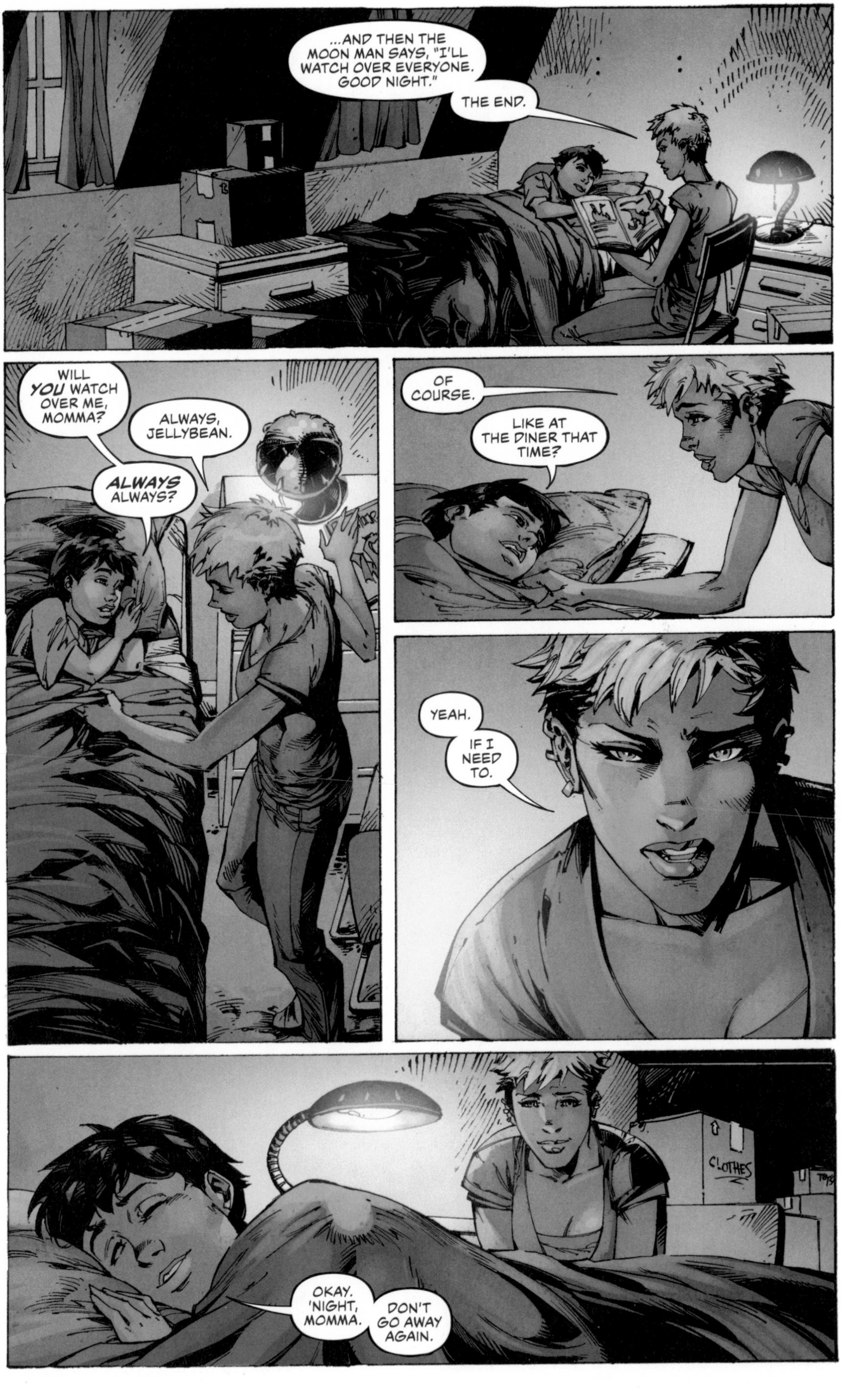
...AND THEN THE MOON MAN SAYS, "I'LL WATCH OVER EVERYONE. GOOD NIGHT."
THE END.
WILL YOU WATCH OVER ME, MOMMA?
ALWAYS, JELLYBEAN.
ALWAYS ALWAYS?
OF COURSE.
LIKE AT THE DINER THAT TIME?
YEAH.
IF I NEED TO.
CLOTHES
OKAY. 'NIGHT, MOMMA.
DON'T GO AWAY AGAIN.

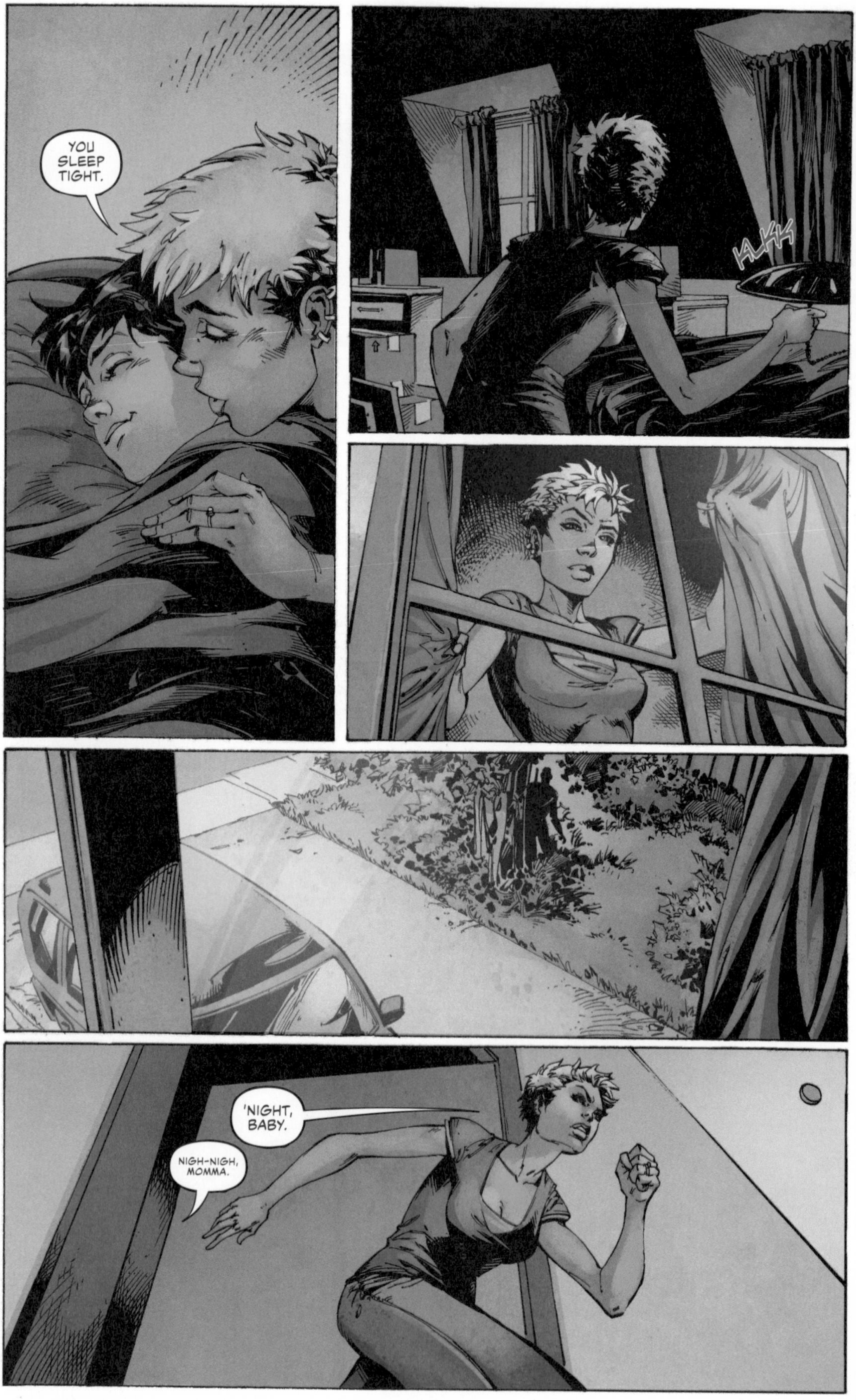
YOU SLEEP TIGHT.
KLIKK
'NIGHT, BABY.
NIGH-NIGH, MOMMA.

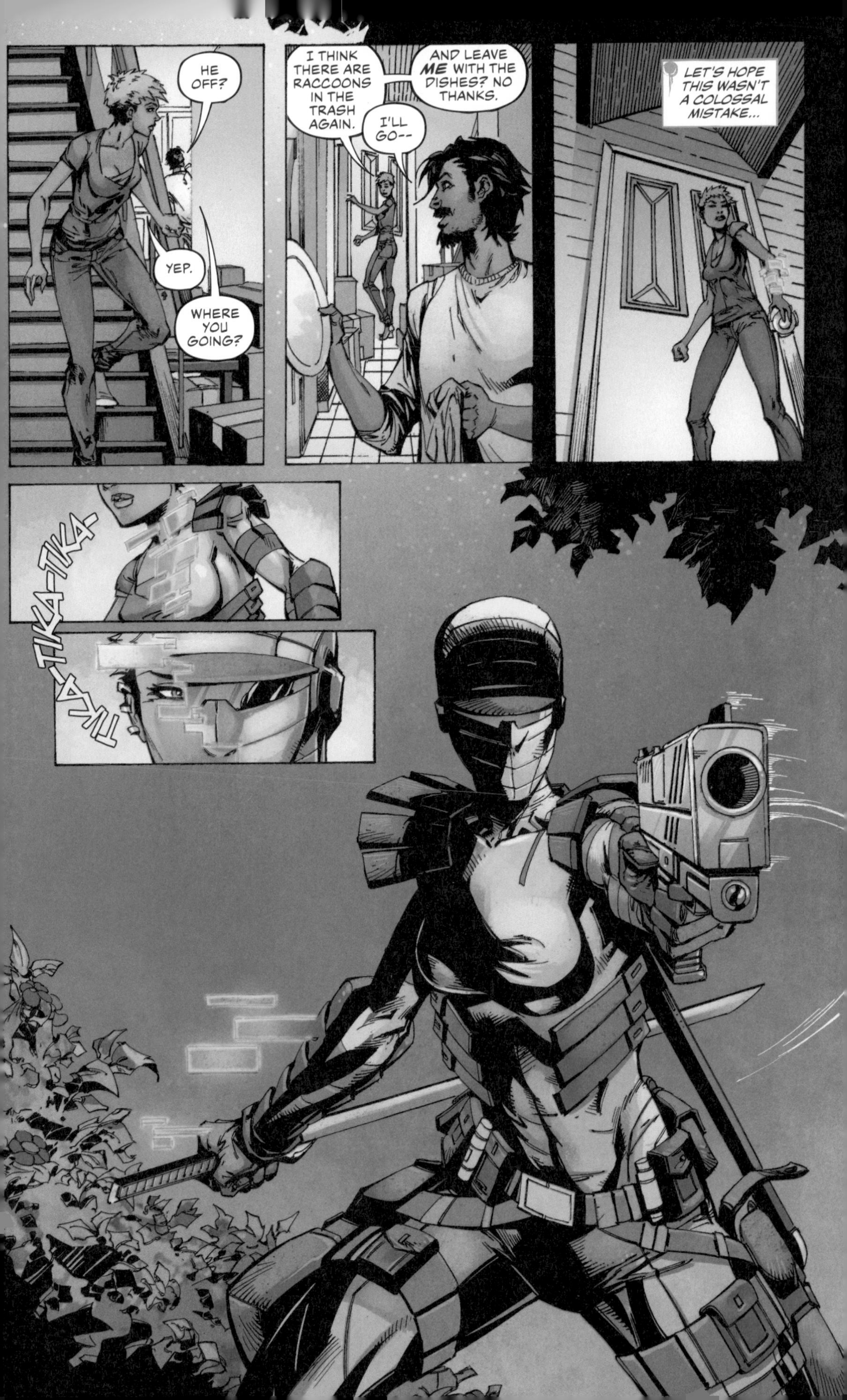
HE OFF?
YEP.
WHERE YOU GOING?
I THINK THERE ARE RACCOONS IN THE TRASH AGAIN.
I'LL GO--
AND LEAVE ME WITH THE DISHES? NO THANKS.
LET'S HOPE THIS WASN'T A COLOSSAL MISTAKE...
TIKA-TIKA-
TIKA-TIKA-

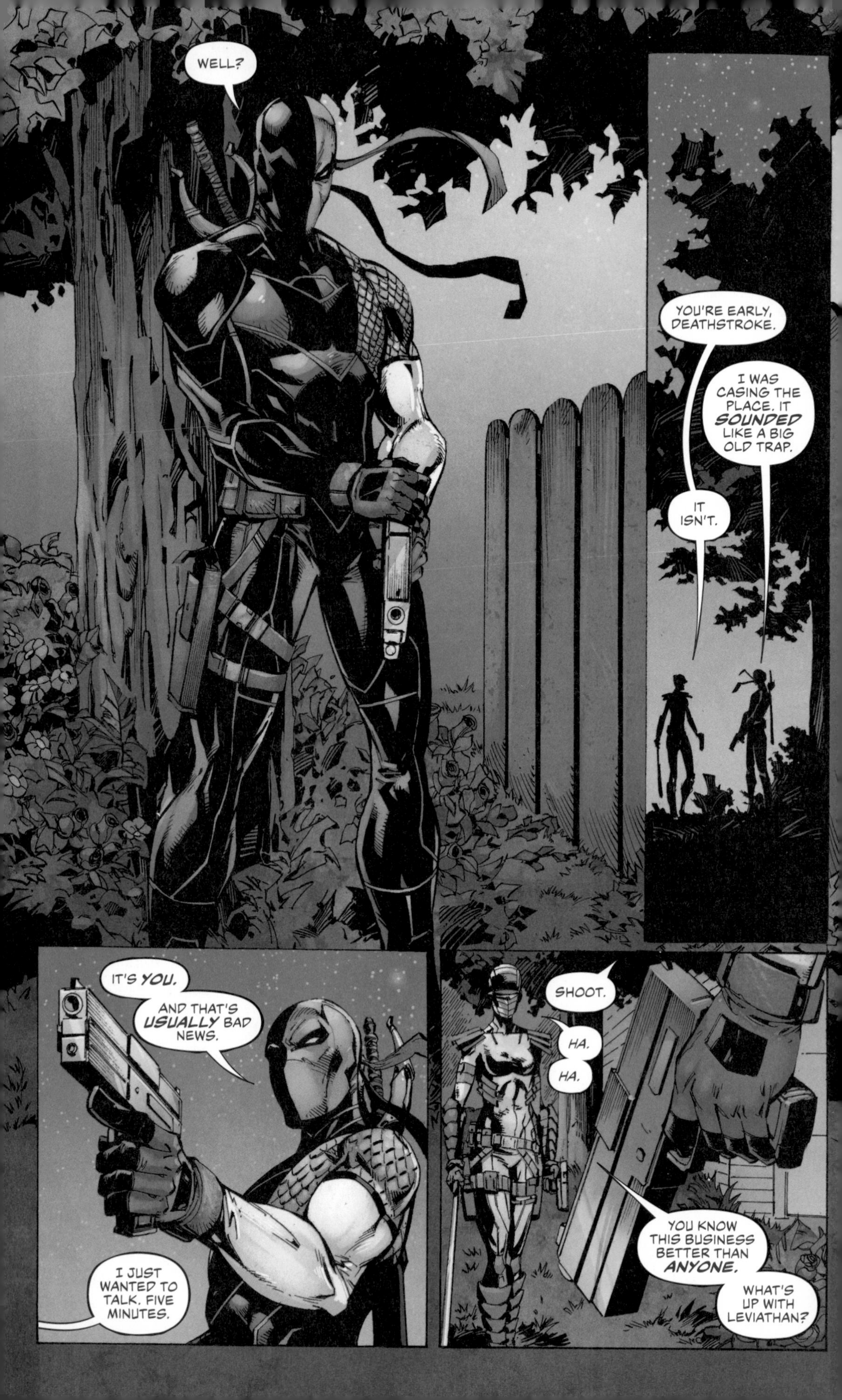
WELL?
YOU'RE EARLY, DEATHSTROKE.
I WAS CASING THE PLACE. IT SOUNDED LIKE A BIG OLD TRAP.
IT ISN'T.
IT'S YOU.
AND THAT'S USUALLY BAD NEWS.
I JUST WANTED TO TALK. FIVE MINUTES.
SHOOT.
HA.
HA.
YOU KNOW THIS BUSINESS BETTER THAN ANYONE.
WHAT'S UP WITH LEVIATHAN?

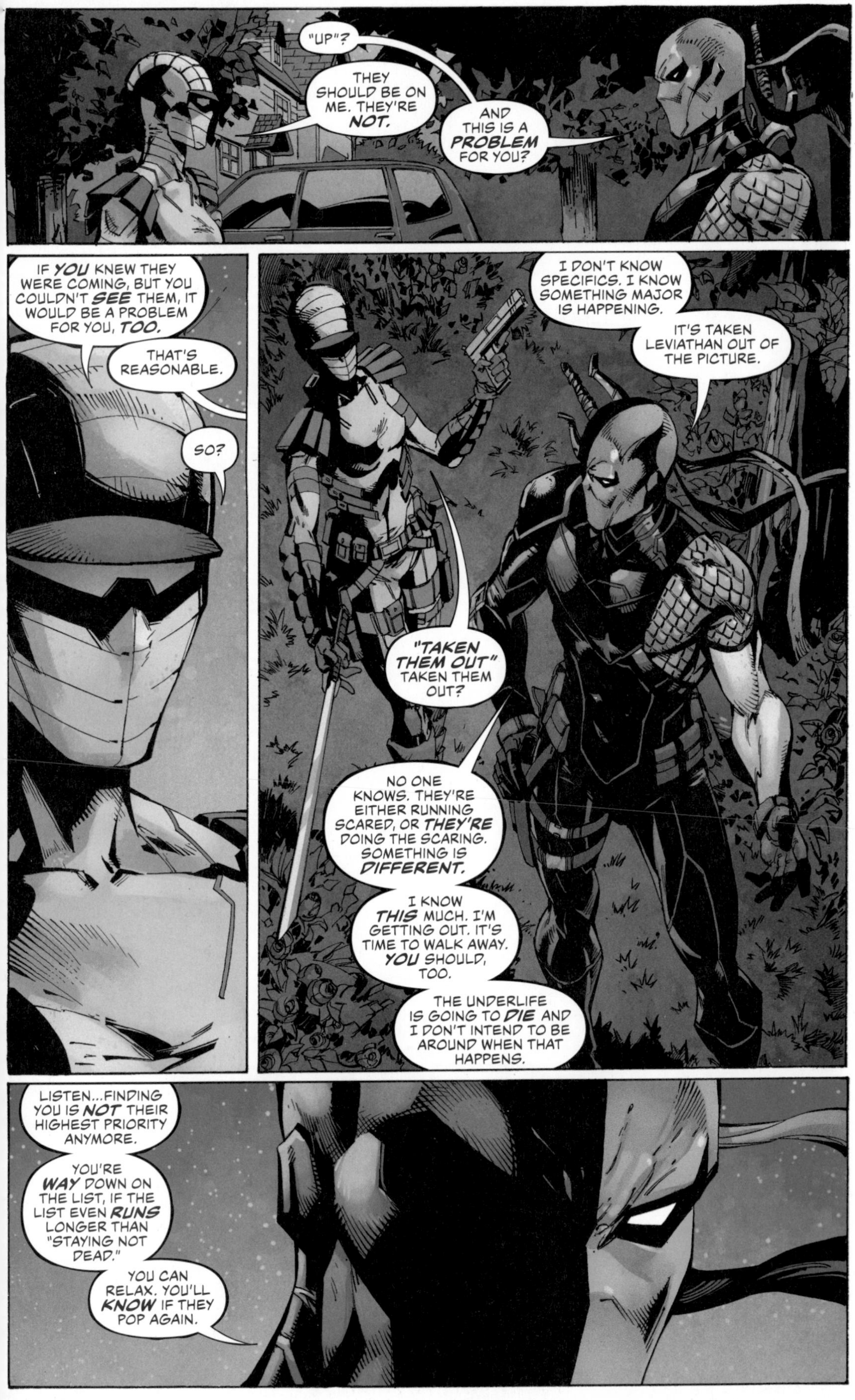

"UP"?
THEY SHOULD BE ON ME. THEY'RE **NOT.**
AND THIS IS A **PROBLEM** FOR YOU?
IF **YOU** KNEW THEY WERE COMING, BUT YOU COULDN'T **SEE** THEM, IT WOULD BE A PROBLEM FOR YOU, **TOO.**
THAT'S REASONABLE.
SO?
I DON'T KNOW SPECIFICS. I KNOW SOMETHING MAJOR IS HAPPENING.
IT'S TAKEN LEVIATHAN OUT OF THE PICTURE.
"TAKEN THEM OUT" TAKEN THEM OUT?
NO ONE KNOWS. THEY'RE EITHER RUNNING SCARED, OR **THEY'RE** DOING THE SCARING. SOMETHING IS **DIFFERENT.**
I KNOW **THIS** MUCH. I'M GETTING OUT. IT'S TIME TO WALK AWAY. **YOU** SHOULD, TOO.
THE UNDERLIFE IS GOING TO **DIE** AND I DON'T INTEND TO BE AROUND WHEN THAT HAPPENS.
LISTEN...FINDING YOU IS **NOT** THEIR HIGHEST PRIORITY ANYMORE.
YOU'RE **WAY** DOWN ON THE LIST, IF THE LIST EVEN **RUNS** LONGER THAN "STAYING NOT DEAD."
YOU CAN RELAX. YOU'LL **KNOW** IF THEY POP AGAIN.

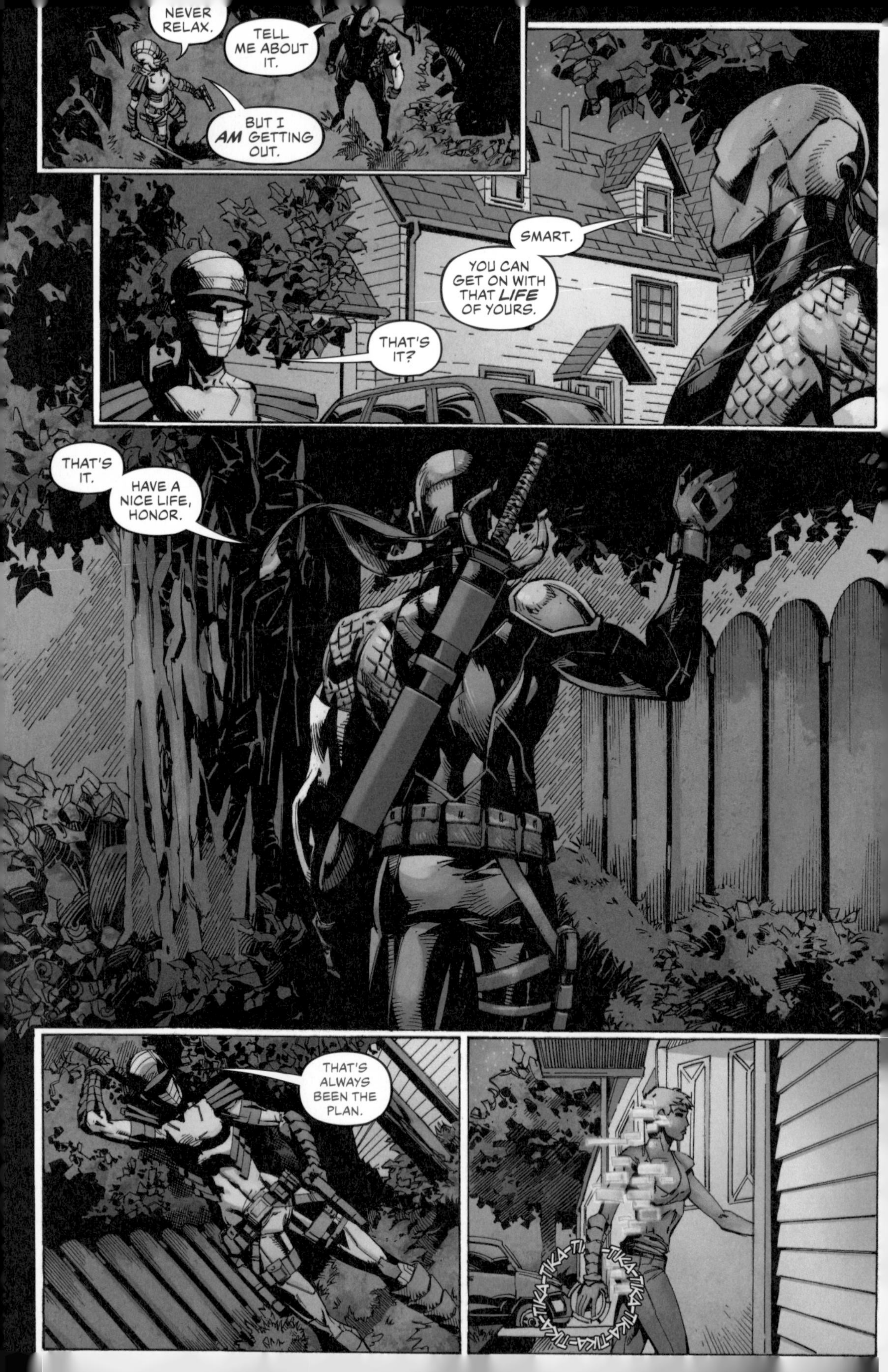
NEVER RELAX.
TELL ME ABOUT IT.
BUT I *AM* GETTING OUT.
SMART.
YOU CAN GET ON WITH THAT *LIFE* OF YOURS.
THAT'S IT?
THAT'S IT.
HAVE A NICE LIFE, HONOR.
THAT'S ALWAYS BEEN THE PLAN.
TIKA-TIKA-TIKA-TIKA-TIKA-TIKA-TIKA-TI

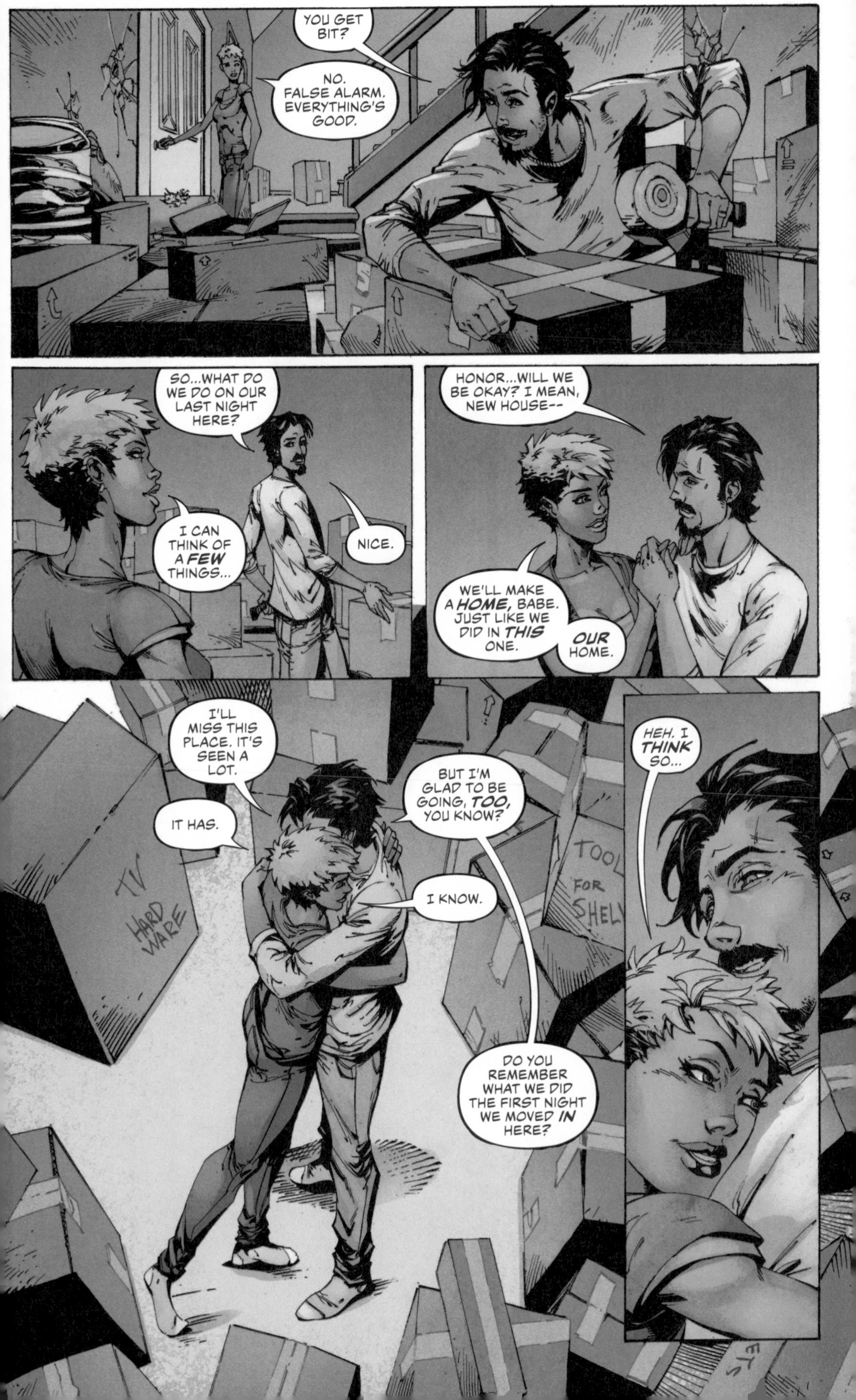
YOU GET BIT?
NO. FALSE ALARM. EVERYTHING'S GOOD.
SO...WHAT DO WE DO ON OUR LAST NIGHT HERE?
I CAN THINK OF A *FEW* THINGS...
NICE.
HONOR...WILL WE BE OKAY? I MEAN, NEW HOUSE--
WE'LL MAKE A *HOME*, BABE. JUST LIKE WE DID IN *THIS* ONE.
OUR HOME.
I'LL MISS THIS PLACE. IT'S SEEN A LOT.
IT HAS.
BUT I'M GLAD TO BE GOING, *TOO*, YOU KNOW?
I KNOW.
DO YOU REMEMBER WHAT WE DID THE FIRST NIGHT WE MOVED *IN* HERE?
HEH. I *THINK* SO...
TV HARD WARE
TOOL FOR SHELY

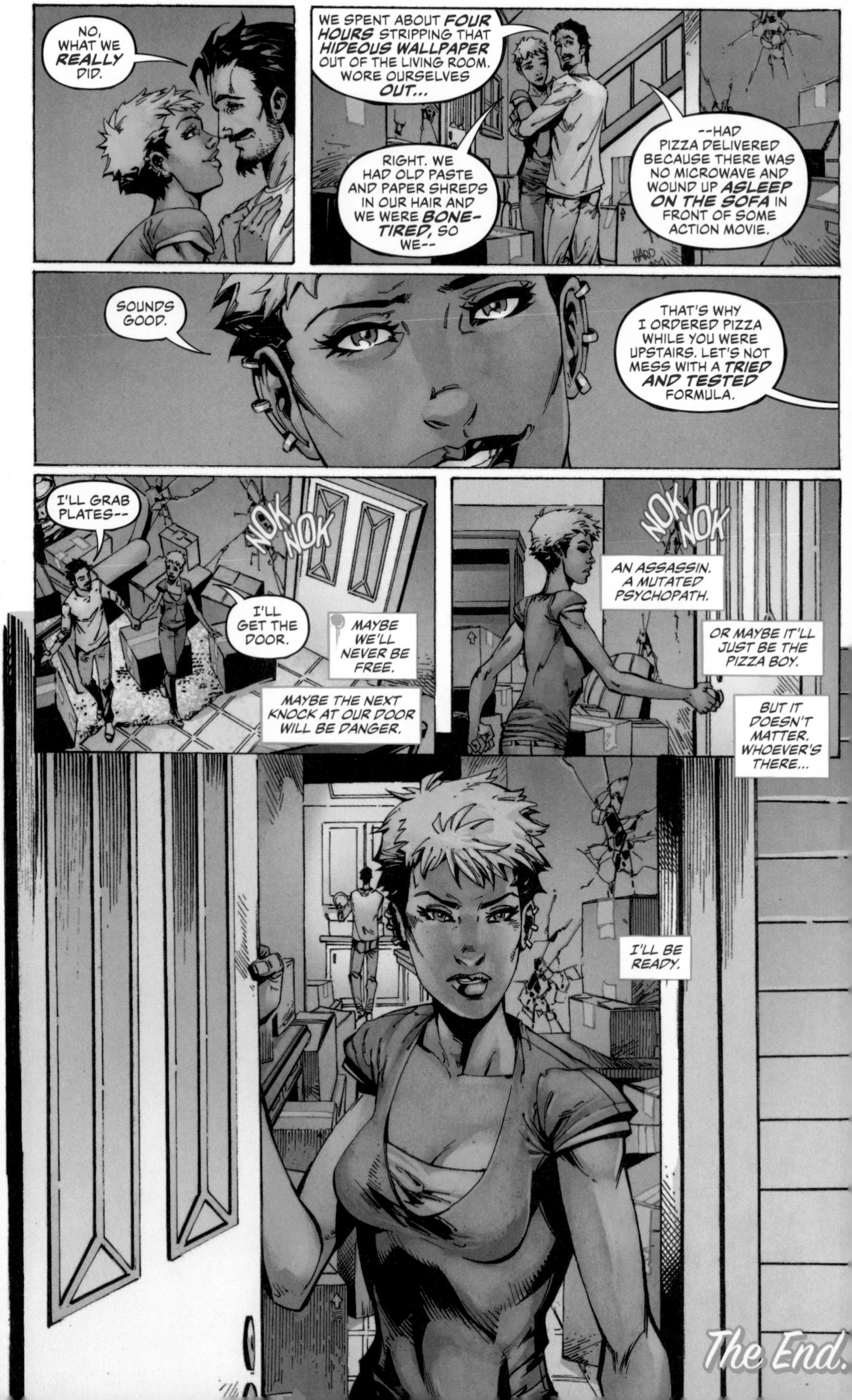
NO, WHAT WE REALLY DID.
WE SPENT ABOUT FOUR HOURS STRIPPING THAT HIDEOUS WALLPAPER OUT OF THE LIVING ROOM. WORE OURSELVES OUT...
RIGHT. WE HAD OLD PASTE AND PAPER SHREDS IN OUR HAIR AND WE WERE BONE-TIRED, SO WE--
--HAD PIZZA DELIVERED BECAUSE THERE WAS NO MICROWAVE AND WOUND UP ASLEEP ON THE SOFA IN FRONT OF SOME ACTION MOVIE.
SOUNDS GOOD.
THAT'S WHY I ORDERED PIZZA WHILE YOU WERE UPSTAIRS. LET'S NOT MESS WITH A TRIED AND TESTED FORMULA.
I'LL GRAB PLATES--
NOK NOK
I'LL GET THE DOOR.
MAYBE WE'LL NEVER BE FREE.
MAYBE THE NEXT KNOCK AT OUR DOOR WILL BE DANGER.
NOK NOK
AN ASSASSIN. A MUTATED PSYCHOPATH.
OR MAYBE IT'LL JUST BE THE PIZZA BOY.
BUT IT DOESN'T MATTER. WHOEVER'S THERE...
I'LL BE READY.
The End.

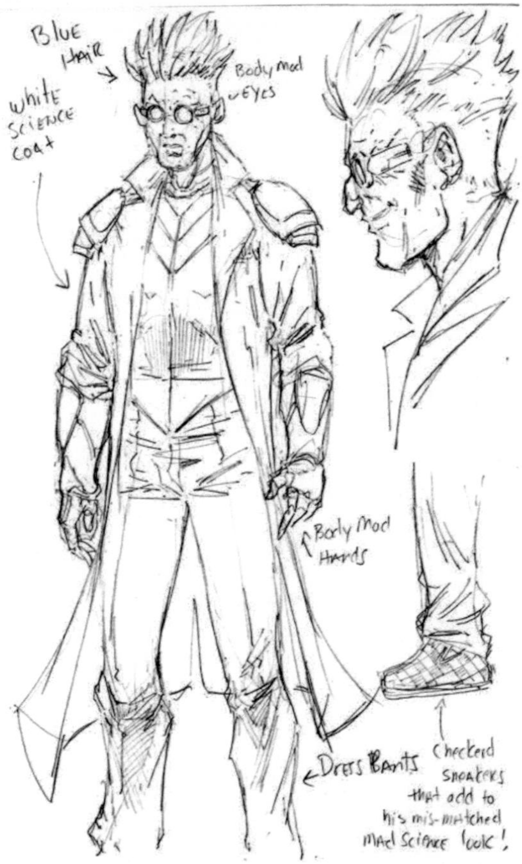
Blue Hair
White Science Coat
Body mod eyes
Body Mod Hands
Dress Pants
Checkerd sneakers that add to his mis-matched mad science look!

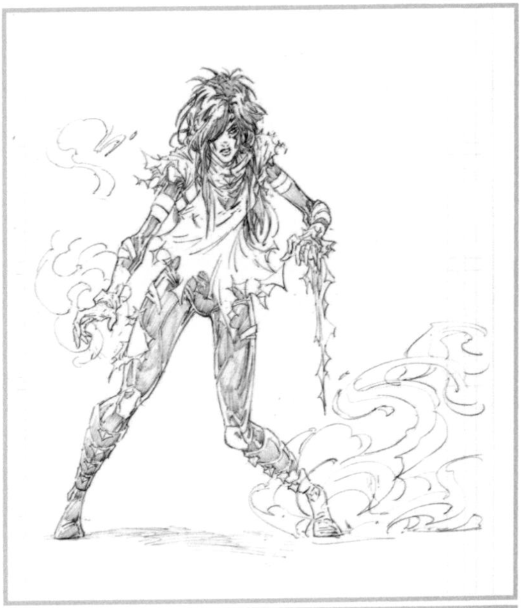

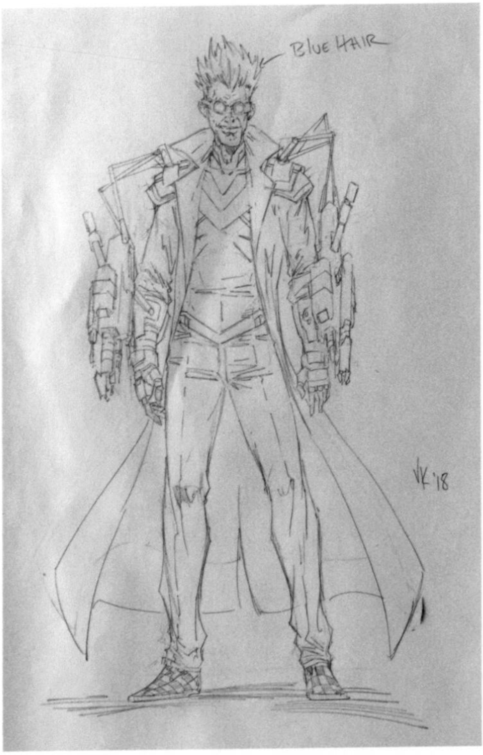
Blue Hair
VK '18

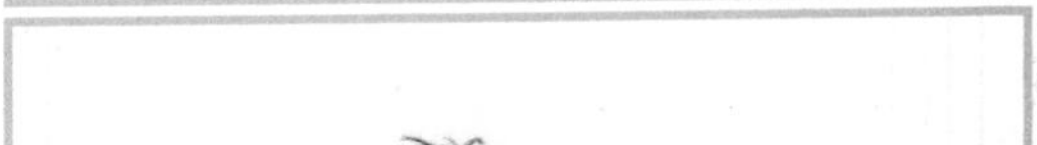

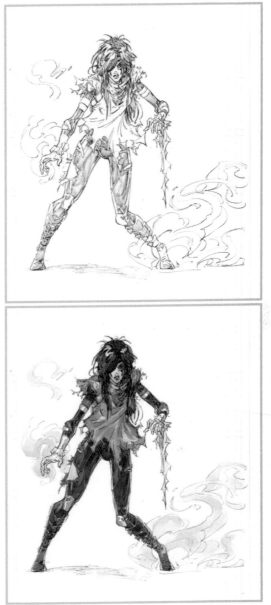

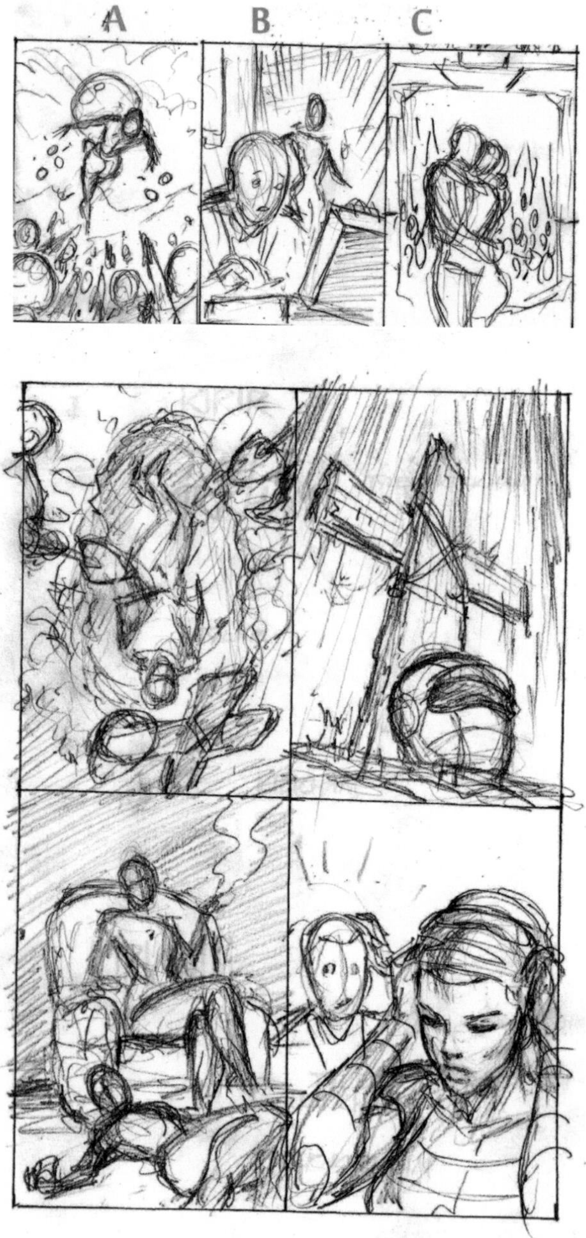
A
B
C

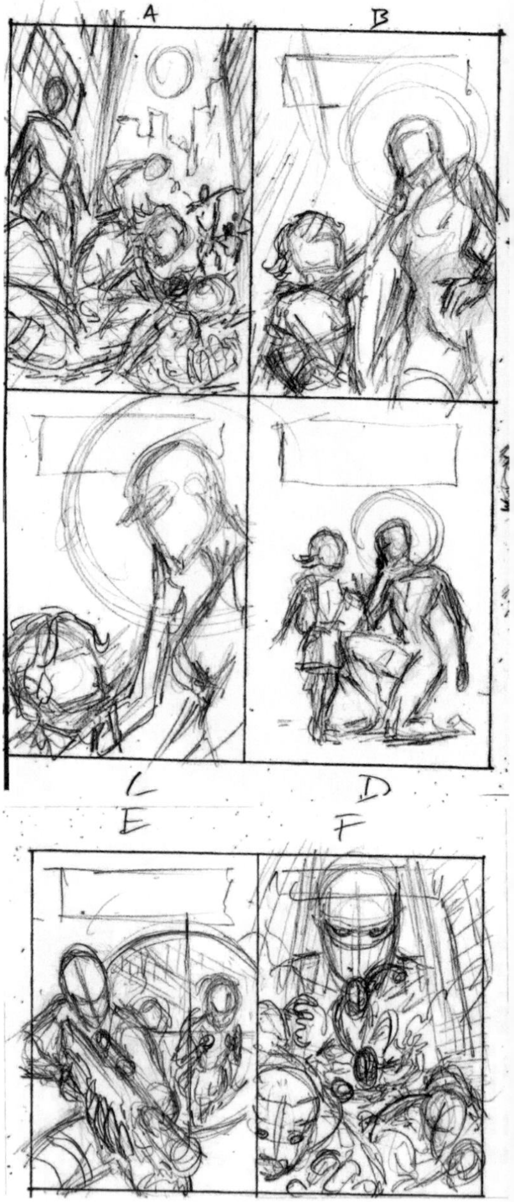
A
B
C
D
E
F

COVER SKETCHES FOR *THE SILENCER* #13-14 AND #17 BY V KEN MARION

PENCILLER V KEN MARION INKER PAGE# COVER

TITLE SILENCER ISSUE # 16 MONTH INTERIORS

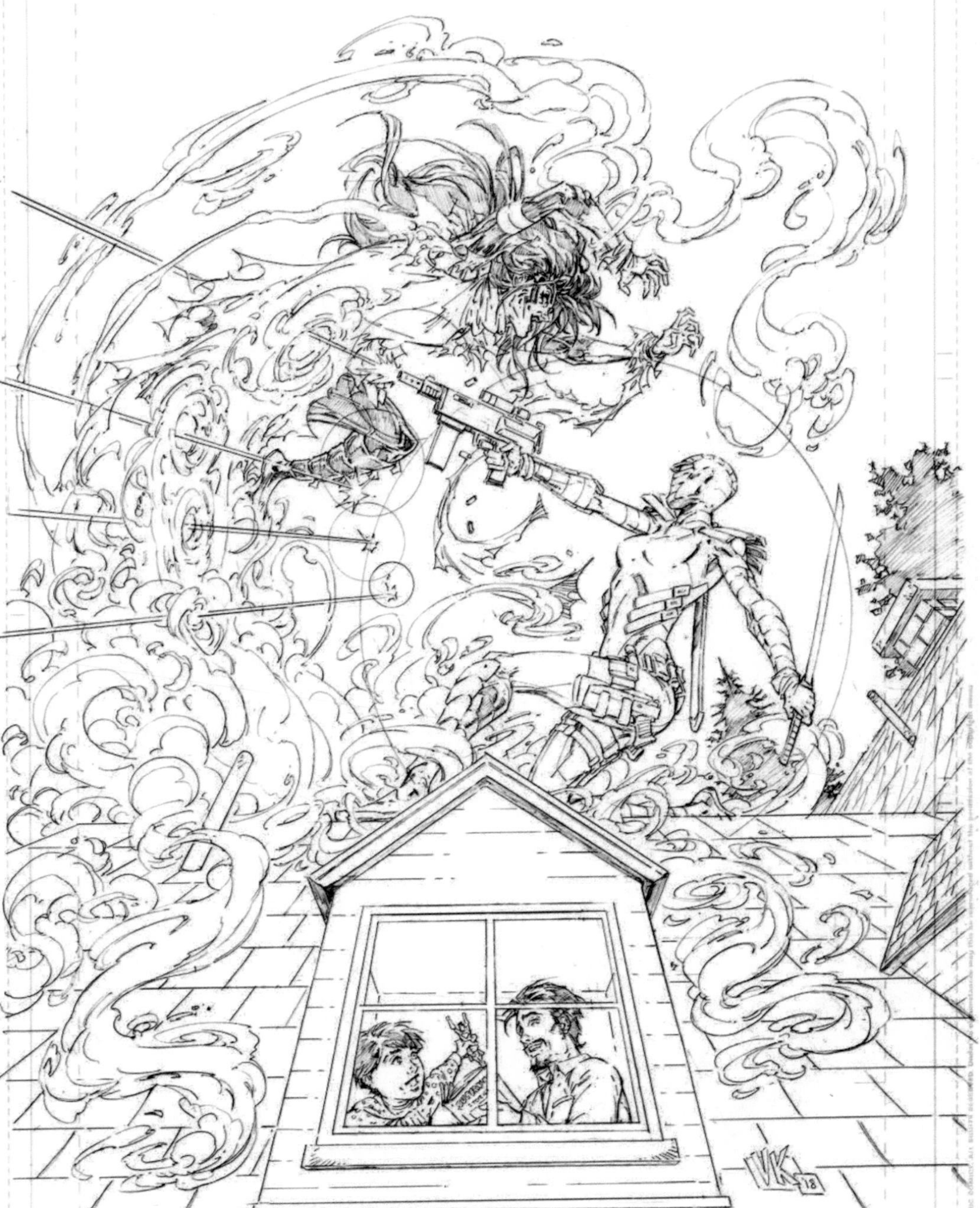

DOUBLE PAGE SPREAD: CUT AS SHOWN, ABUT PAGE EDGES, TAPE ON BACK, DO NOT OVERLAP

CUT RIGHT-HAND PAGE AT THIS LINE CUT LEFT HAND PAGE AT THIS LINE

PENCILLER JK INKER PAGE# COVER -
TITLE SILENCER ISSUE # MONTH

INTERIORS

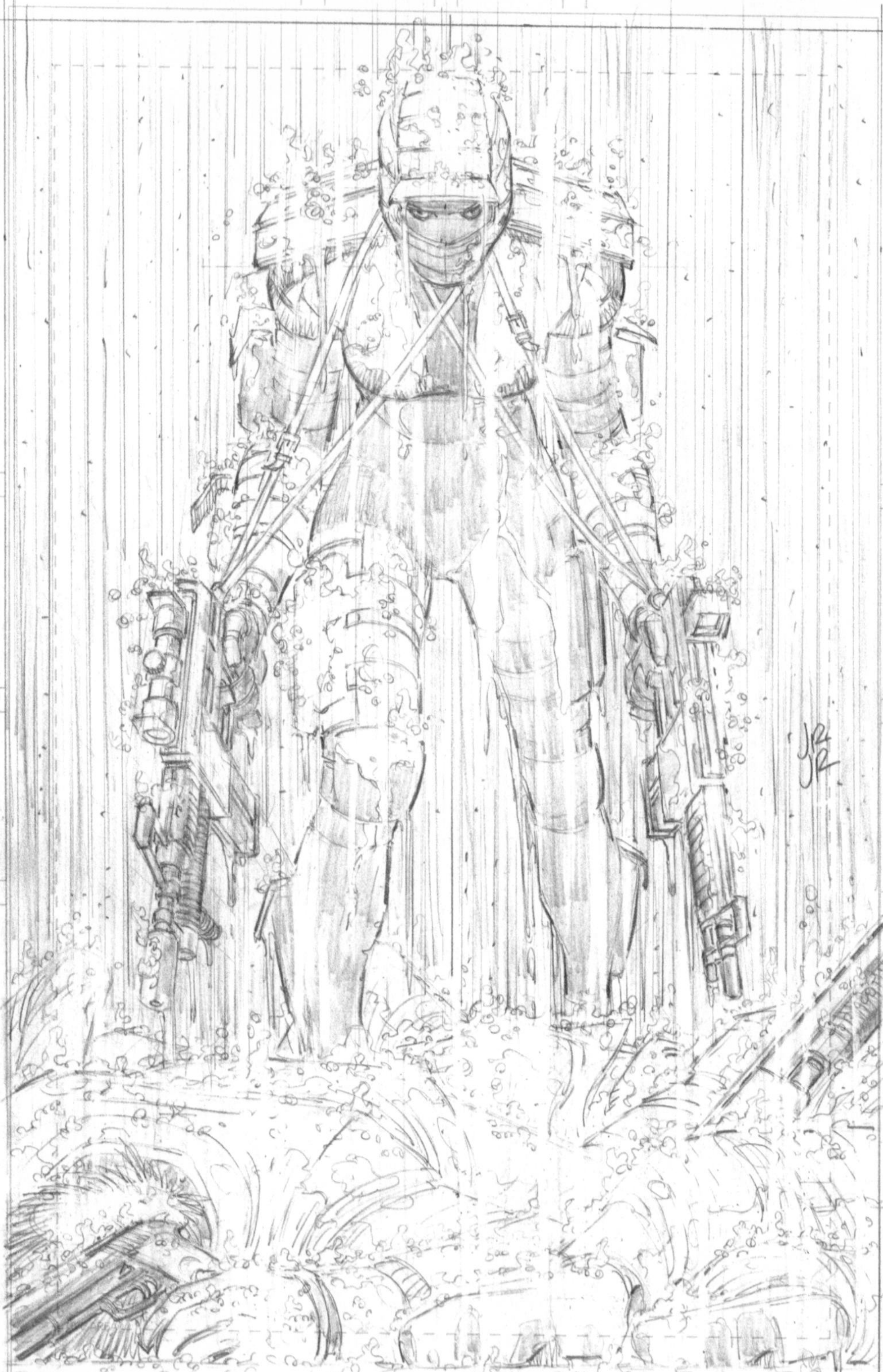
JR JR

CROP

BLEED

MINIMUM BLEED 1/4" ALL AROUND

← CUT RIGHT-HAND PAGE AT THIS LINE DOUBLE PAGE SPREAD: CUT AS SHOWN, ABUT PAGE EDGES, TAPE ON BACK, DO NOT OVERLAP CUT LEFT HAND PAGE AT THIS LINE →